T0306174

ROUTLEDGE LIBRARY EDITIONS:
EDUCATION 1800–1926

Volume 4

HIS TRUTH IS MARCHING ON

HIS TRUTH IS MARCHING ON

African Americans Who Taught the Freedmen
for the American Missionary Association
1861–1877

CLARA MERRITT DEBOER

Routledge
Taylor & Francis Group

LONDON AND NEW YORK

First published in 1995 by Garland Publishing, Inc.

This edition first published in 2017
by Routledge
2 Park Square, Milton Park, Abingdon, Oxon OX14 4RN

and by Routledge
711 Third Avenue, New York, NY 10017

Routledge is an imprint of the Taylor & Francis Group, an informa business

British Library Cataloguing in Publication Data
A catalogue record for this book is available from the British Library

ISBN: 978-1-138-22412-4 (Set)
ISBN: 978-1-315-40302-1 (Set) (ebk)
ISBN: 978-1-138-22220-5 (Volume 4) (hbk)
ISBN: 978-1-138-22221-2 (Volume 4) (pbk)
ISBN: 978-1-315-40834-7 (Volume 4) (ebk)

Publisher's Note
The publisher has gone to great lengths to ensure the quality of this reprint but points out that some imperfections in the original copies may be apparent.

Disclaimer
The publisher has made every effort to trace copyright holders and would welcome correspondence from those they have been unable to trace.

HIS TRUTH IS MARCHING ON

AFRICAN AMERICANS WHO TAUGHT THE
FREEDMEN FOR THE AMERICAN MISSIONARY
ASSOCIATION 1861–1877

CLARA MERRITT DeBOER

GARLAND PUBLISHING, INC.
NEW YORK & LONDON / 1995

Library of Congress Cataloging-in-Publication Data

DeBoer, Clara Merritt, 1925–
 His truth is marching on : African Americans who taught the freedmen for the American Missionary Association, 1861–1877 / Clara
Merritt DeBoer.
  p.   cm. — (Studies in African American history and culture)
 Includes bibliographical references and index.
 ISBN 0-8153-1788-3 (alk. paper)
 1. American Missionary Association. 2. Afro-Americans—Missions. 3. United States—History—Civil War, 1861–1865—Religious
aspects. 4. Freedmen—Education. 5. Freedmen—Religion. 6. Afro-
Americans—Education—History. I. Title. II. Series.
BV2360.A8D43   1995
266'.022'08996073—dc20   94–26421
                                                          CIP

Printed on acid-free, 250-year-life paper
Manufactured in the United States of America

To my parents,

Arah Griffin Merritt and Elmer Merritt,

who never went beyond the third grade,

and to my children,

John, Katharine and David,

all of whom went to graduate school.

CONTENTS

ILLUSTRATIONS

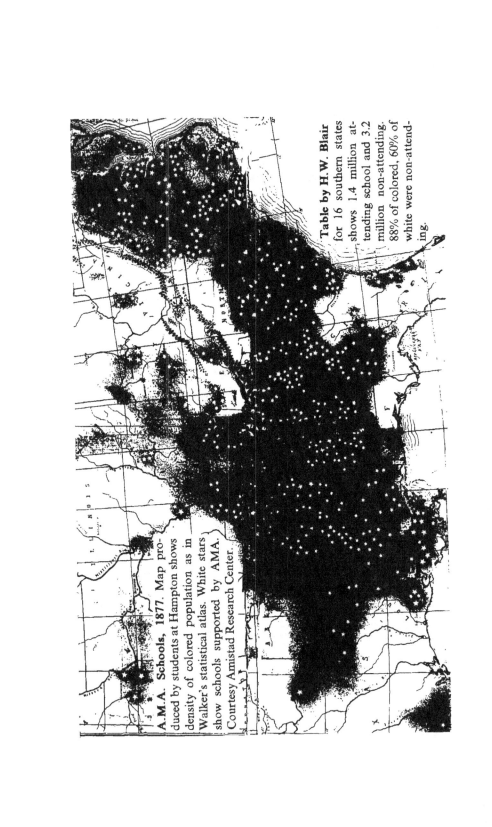

A.M.A. Schools, 1877. Map produced by students at Hampton shows density of colored population as in Walker's statistical atlas. White stars show schools supported by AMA. Courtesy Amistad Research Center.

Table by H.W. Blair for 16 southern states shows 1.4 million attending school and 3.2 million non-attending. 88% of colored, 60% of white were non-attending.

PREFACE

Although W.E.B. DuBois and Booker T. Washington disagreed about many things, they were one in their praise of the American Missionary Association (AMA). DuBois, raised free in the Congregationalism of New England, and Washington, born a slave in Virginia, were both products of—and later teachers in—AMA schools. These two men, giants among black Americans, and so different in their approaches to the struggle for equality, were effusive in their praise of AMA teachers. Washington called what they did "one of the most thrilling parts" of our history, and DuBois said unequivocally, it was "the finest thing in American history."

The record of what they believed was the finest event in our history might have been irretrievably lost, however, had it not been for one man, William Frazier, treasurer (in the 1950s) of the Board of Home Missions of the Congregational Christian Churches. Frazier found the letters written by the teachers of the freedmen to the officers in New York. They were mouldering in an attic storeroom, about ten percent already destroyed by rain from an open window. This collection measured over eighty shelf-feet, unsorted and uncatalogued. Frazier recognized their worth and successfully argued for their safekeeping. The collection was sent to Fisk University, an AMA school founded in Nashville in 1866.

Dr. Wesley Hotchkiss, Secretary of the AMA, appointed Clifton Johnson archivist of the surviving papers. In the 1960s Johnson removed the collection to Mufreesboro, Tennessee, for safekeeping. It was here that the work of microfilming was begun and where I first saw the papers, thanks to a research grant from Dr. Hotchkiss.

It was an incredible thrill to be the first person to read all of the papers. Knowing the kind of organization the AMA was, I assumed that some of the teachers must have been black. It was my mission to find those African Americans. It could only be done from internal evidence, because the AMA was truly color-blind and did not identify its teachers by race, as the Freedmen's Bureau did. It was not an easy task. A glance at the Index (where African Americans are identified by bold face type) will show that I identified over six hundred African Americans, thus undoing the carefully color-blind work of the AMA!

After the papers were sent to Dillard University in New Orleans (formerly Straight University), I spent months there completing work on my doctoral dissertation. I was often there at night alone except for the security guard in what was now called the Amistad Research Center, reading those marvelous letters from white and black teachers. As they poured out their struggles and fears and dreams for the black persons in their care, I was often moved to tears.

Unfortunately, the AMA collection is a one-way story. We have the letters of the teachers, but the letterbooks of the AMA that contained copies of the replies from the AMA officers are lost. Only occasionally is there a gleam of the reactions of Lewis Tappan or George Whipple in notes they wrote on the margins of the letters they received from the field. Nevertheless, what was saved is a treasure trove of the story of a "Crusade of Brotherhood"; the attempt—almost a frenzy of effort—to prepare millions of former slaves for citizenship before the withdrawal of Federal troops and the dismantling of the Freedmen's Bureau.

Fortunately, the AMA Archives also contain the monthly AMA journal, the *American Missionary,* and the Annual Reports, which enable the historian to identify policies and fiscal conditions not contained in the letters. The map of AMA schools in 1877 opposite the first page of this preface is from four frames of a microfilm of the *American Missionary.*

The AMA was well aware that once protection of the Union armies was removed and the Democratic Party was again in control of the South, the black people would be at the not-so-tender mercies of the same people who had refused them education before the war.

There was never enough money, but the AMA did the best it could. And it did more. It was responsible for the desegregation of coastal passenger shipping lines in the North; it introduced the Negro Spiritual to the world, America's indigenous contribution to the world's music; and it was largely responsible for the establishment of a public school system in Washington, D.C., and the

South, which neither whites nor blacks there had experienced before the war.

The conventional wisdom is that "New England school marms" taught the freedmen. Many did. But many came from other northern states, and one-third were men. Many were African Americans.

Whenever possible the AMA hired educated African Americans for the work. Many of them had been educated at Oberlin College (which accepted both women and African Americans!), their tuition often paid by abolitionists like Arthur and Lewis Tappan and Gerrit Smith.

In desperation—as Reconstruction came to a close—the AMA teachers raised up their own African American teachers from the former slaves, realizing that southern school boards would not hire Yankee teachers for black schools.

Most of them were heroes—the men and women who braved the enmity of the white South, the raids of the Klan, the sneers of the southern press, the unhealthy conditions among which they lived and worked, the long hours of classes: days, evenings, and weekends. This study salutes them all, but limits itself to the African Americans among those brave and dedicated persons, who worked for less money than they could have made elsewhere, and, when able, worked without salary at all.

Initially the AMA established schools while it intentionally refrained from establishing churches. God's truth, in the view of its workers and missionaries, was not limited to religious doctrines. His truth would come to the opening minds of all His children, white or black, who learned to read and write. His truth would continue to enlighten open minds through a liberal curriculum in common, high and normal schools and in universities that freedmen could afford to attend.

The AMA founded "universities" that began by teaching reading and writing and gradually expanded to high schools and normal schools. College level and graduate courses were added as their pupils grew. No one received a full college degree until it was earned, but all were taught using the same curricula in use in the best schools of the North.

A hundred years before the "black is beautiful" movement of the 1960s, the AMA instilled in its African American pupils a sense of pride. Students graduating from AMA universities in the 1870s delivered orations with such titles as "The Ancient Glory and

Future Hope of the African Race," "Elements of True Manhood," and "Crispus Attucks." In 1877 the commencement exercises at Straight University ended with the singing of "Hold Up Your Head Like a Man."

Eighty years before *Brown v. the Board of Education of Topeka, Kansas*, the AMA journal printed these words: "It is not enough to build two school houses equally good . . . on opposite sides of the street, one for white children and one for black, as is proposed in some, perhaps, in all of the Southern States. The moment this is done, a brand is put upon the colored children. . . . Two civilizations cannot grow up side by side and keep the peace; we tried that and failed. We cannot afford to try that experiment again."

The AMA experiment offering color-blind education for all had some significant results. Some of the African American teachers became officers in the Republican governments that flourished until the removal of federal protection. Some of the students became world famous. Its colleges provided oases of sanity in the South, where both races could meet and work together for a better America. Out of those meetings came studies that undergirded *Brown v. the Board of Education*. It was an utterly unselfish crusade. It was truly the finest thing in American history.

Month in and month out the AMA faced problems and overcame obstacles. So great was the need for schools and teachers that, year after year, the AMA spent more than it received with faith that increased contributions would close the fiscal gap. Garrisonians were insisting that the abolitionist's work was done once the slaves were freed. Efforts to establish more schools in the South were being blocked by white racists and black power-hungry preachers. Through it all the officers and workers of the AMA remained steadfast in their conviction that emancipation without education would be damaging if not disastrous. They were Christian abolitionists engaged in a crusade. They could not rest until, in community after community, schools and colleges were established and they could assert in confidence: "His Truth Is Marching On."

Clara Merritt DeBoer, Ph.D.

ACKNOWLEDGMENTS

I am deeply grateful to Dr. Wesley A. Hotchkiss, former executive officer of the American Missionary Association, for insights and aid.

I extend thanks also to Dr. Clifton H. Johnson, former Director of the Amistad Research Center, for his hospitality while I was working in these archives in Murfreesboro and New Orleans.

Special thanks is due Andrew Simons and Rebecca Hankins, archivists at the Amistad Research Center, now at Tulane University in New Orleans. Their assistance in obtaining illustrations for this volume was invaluable.

My thanks are also due to Dr. Tilden Edelstein, formerly Associate Professor of History, Rutgers University, for his encouragement in this work.

I am grateful to the American Association of University Women, who offered me a fellowship, and to the Ford Foundation. When the Ford Foundation offered me a grant, I gave up the AAUW award knowing that it would be given to another woman. Without the aid of the Ford Foundation, I would not have been able to complete the research.

As indicated in my preface, I am indebted, as are all historians, to a man I never met: the Rev. William Frazier, Treasurer (in the 1950's) of the Board of Home Missions of the Congregational Christian Churches, which included the Division of the American Missionary Association. It was he who "discovered" the boxes containing the files of the nineteenth century AMA in the attic of the Board's office building at 287 Park Avenue South in New York City. They, along with other records compiled by the Amistad Research Center, comprise the richest source of African American history extant.

And I am indebted to my husband, John C. DeBoer, without whose loving care and computer expertise this publication would not have been possible.

Clara Merritt DeBoer

LIBRARIES AND ARCHIVES VISITED

Amistad Research Center, New Orleans, Louisiana
The Anti-Slavery Society for the Protection of Human Rights, London, England
British Museum Newspaper Library, London, England
Dillard University, Will W. Alexander Library
Howard University Library, Washington, D.C.
Frederick Hosmer Johnson, Jr., Papers, Norwich, Vermont
New Haven Colony Historical Society
New York Public Library
New York Public Library, 135th Street Branch, Schomburg Collection
Oxford University, Bodleian Library
University of Pennsylvania, Van Pelt Library
Presbyterian Historical Society, Philadelphia, Penn.
Rutgers University Library, New Brunswick, N.J.
Church of Scotland, Overseas Council, Edinburgh
Edinburgh Central Library, Scotland
National Library of Scotland, Edinburgh
Syracuse University, George Arents Research Library
Union Theological Seminary Library, New York, N.Y.
United Church of Christ
    American Missionary Association Office, New York
    Board for Homeland Ministries Library, New York
    Congregational Library, Boston
    Connecticut Conference Office, Hartford, Conn.
    First Congregational Church (UCC), Washington, D.C.
    New Jersey Association Office (UCC), Montclair, N.J.
    New York Conference Center (UCC), Lisle, N.Y.
United States Library of Congress
United States National Archives
Yale University
    Beinecke Rare Book and Manuscript Library
    Sterling Library
    Divinity School Library
    Divinity School, Day Mission Library

LIST OF ABBREVIATIONS

AAS	American Abolition Society
AASS	American Anti-Slavery Society
ABCFM	American Board of Commissioners for Foreign Missions
ACS	African Civilization Society
ACUS	American College & University Society
AFAC	American Freedmen's Aid Commission
AFASS	American and Foreign Anti-Slavery Society
AGB	Amos Gerry Beman papers, Beinecke Lib., (Yale U.)
AHMS	American Home Missionary Society
AM	*American Missionary*
AMA	American Missionary Association
AMAA	American Missionary Association Archives
AME	African Methodist Episcopal Church
AMEZ	African Methodist Episcopal Zion Church
ARC	Amistad Research Center
BFAS	British Freedmen's Aid Society
BFASAPS	British & Foreign Anti-Slavery & Aborigines Protection Society papers, Rhodes House, Bodleian Library, Oxford
BFASS	British and Foreign Anti-Slavery Society
BFRAL	Bureau of Freedmen, Refugees, & Abandoned Lands
CBW	Charles B. Wilder papers, Sterling Lib., (Yale U.)
DAB	*Dictionary of American Biography*
EE & MP	Envoy Extraordinary & Minister Plenipotentiary
EFW	Edward F. Williams papers (ARC)
FAUC	Freedmen's Aid Union Commission (of Great Britain & Ireland)
GAR	George Arents Research Library (Syracuse U.)
GERA	Georgia Equal Rights Association
GSC	Gerrit Smith Collection (GAR)
HUL	Howard University Library

JNH	*Journal of Negro History*
MSC	Moorland-Spingarn Collection (HUL)
NEFAC	New England Freedmen's Aid Commission
NEFAS	New England Freedmen's Aid Society
NFSTC	National Freedmen's Savings & Trust Company
NFRA	National Freedmen's Relief Association
NLS	National Library of Scotland, Edinburgh
NS	New School (Presbyterian)
OS	Old School (Presbyterian)
PFRA	Pennsylvania Freedmen's Relief Association
PHS	Presbyterian Historical Society
PHFMS	Parent Home & Foreign Missionary Society (AME)
PS	Peter Still papers (Rutgers U. Library)
RC	Roman Catholic
SAM	*Supplement to the American Missionary*
UCBHM	United Church Board for Homeland Ministries
UCC	United Church of Christ
UMS	Union Missionary Society
VFA	Voluntary Freedmen's Association
WFAS	Western Freedmen's Aid Society
WMC	Wesleyan Methodist Connection

His Truth Is Marching On

I

OVERVIEW OF AMA WORK
DURING THE CIVIL WAR

The Constitution of the United States recognizes him as a person. *In the days of Thomas Jefferson, Virginia and other States designated him as a* citizen. *The prowess of Small and other colored individuals, and the good conduct and courage of the colored troops, have proved him to be a* soldier *and a* hero. *The eloquence of Douglass and of other sable speakers, has shown that he can be an* orator. *The piety of thousands of colored men evince that he can be a* Christian. *If, then, he is a person, a citizen, and capable of being a soldier, an orator, and a Christian, none but an idiot or a blockhead would assert that he is not a MAN.*
                        —Lewis Tappan, February, 1865

It is important at the beginning of this study to introduce Lewis Tappan, author of the above words, and to give some perspective to the American Missionary Association (AMA), of which Tappan was a founder and leader.

Lewis Tappan—administrative genius of the abolition movement, business man (who founded the company now known as Dun and Bradstreet), and churchman—was the unpaid Treasurer of the AMA for almost two decades and its most respected spokesman. Unlike the Garrisonians, who believed their mission was accomplished when slavery was abolished in the United States,[1] Tappan and the AMA did not rest at emancipation but went on to attack "caste," institutionalized racism that treated African Americans as something less than human beings. In his February, 1865, call for an end to America's discrimination against the black man, Tappan went on to say:

3

If then, the Negro is a man and a citizen, he is entitled to the treatment of a man and a citizen, and unless he is recognized and treated as such, he cannot be safely elevated in the scale of being. It will be in vain that he is liberated, that arms are put into his hands, that he is educated, that he is religiously instructed. And it will be worse than in vain, because if unacknowledged as a man entitled to all the prerogatives of a man and a citizen he will be a dangerous person in the community—the more dangerous in proportion to his intelligence, native and acquired.

As a missionary Association, having in view the intellectual, moral and religious good of men and especially of the people of color, and particularly the recently emancipated, and those who in the providence of God, and the march of events, are speedily to be emancipated, we claim that our colored brother should be treated in all respects as a man and as a citizen, by the churches, by the Government, and by the people.

At present, he does not receive such treatment either from the churches, the Government, or the people; to their shame be it spoken! Churches refuse him admittance to their pews and communion on equal terms; Government does not award to him the pay and honors due to his valor, nor shield him from the insolence and cruelty of others; and the people ostracize him from the esteem, and confidence, and emoluments of his country.

If the United States aims to be a righteous nation, and a power and example of civil and religious liberty to the nations of the earth; if its churches feel the obligation of christianizing its people, and aiding in the evangelization of the world; if the people expect the blessing of heaven upon their efforts to secure peace, respect, and honor to themselves and their posterity, let them first conquer themselves, and then award equity to those who are with themselves common inheritors of civilization and Christianity, and the joint subjects of retributive justice on earth, and at the bar of God.[2]

The AMA was founded in 1846 as an abolition organization by churchmen—black and white, mainly Congregational and Presbyterian—as a protest against the practice of denominational and interdenominational mission agencies of accepting money from slaveholders. Having tried unsuccessfully, as supporters of these agencies, to reform them from within, they finally saw no alternative to establishing a new organization that would not be thus tainted. The AMA was closely allied with the American and Foreign Anti-Slavery Society (the Tappanite wing of the abolition movement) and shared offices with it for many years in New York City. Lewis Tappan was a key officer in both organizations.

The AMA still exists today as a mission arm of a Protestant denomination, the United Church of Christ, that is a successor through church union of the Congregational churches of the nineteenth century.

Although it is not—and was not—primarily an educational organization, it did more to educate the freed slaves than any other organization, including the Freedmen's Bureau. The AMA's financial contribution to the education of African Americans through 1893 was twice as much as that of the Freedmen's Bureau during this period and second only to the aggregate of all the funds expended by all the Southern states and cities.[3] In 1867 almost one third of all the teachers reported by the Freedmen's Bureau at work in the South were commissioned by the AMA.[4]

"New England School Marms"?

The prevailing myth has been that "New England school marms" were the teachers sent to the South. In fact, as this study shows, many were from the Middle West, about one-third were men, and many were African Americans from both the North and the South. The AMA is best known for its educational work on behalf of African Americans, establishing some 500 schools and colleges including Fisk, Hampton, Atlanta, and Howard. This reputation is deserved. But this study focuses on what African Americans did in and through the AMA; some 500 African American abolitionists were discovered. In contrast to other abolition organizations, the AMA was established with four African Americans on its policy-making board of twelve men.[5] William Lloyd Garrison's American Anti-Slavery Society was criticized by blacks such as Samuel Ringgold Ward and Frederick Douglass for using African Americans only in clerical positions. The Quakers, too, lacked African Americans in policy-making positions, leading Levi Coffin, a white Quaker abolitionist, to join the AMA.[6]

The AMA through its spokesman Lewis Tappan viewed the Civil War (as Abraham Lincoln also viewed it) as the retributive justice of God. Its cause was slavery—in the upholding of which the North shared guilt with the South. Although the numerically inferior South had dominated American politics for much of the country's history, it was with the connivance of the North that this was so.[7]

Although as men of peace the officers of the AMA deplored the war, they were nevertheless fearful that a speedy end to the conflict would result in a compromise with slavery and the perpetuation of the evil institution. Immediately after the outbreak of the rebellion, which he saw as begun by the South, Tappan called for "Immediate and Universal Emancipation" by executive decree as proposed by John Quincy Adams in 1842.[8]

To the cry of what to do with the thousands of African Americans who would be pouring into the North as a result of the war, Tappan answered that they must be treated humanely, in fact, must be loved as brothers. If the freed people were "kindly and justly treated; if paid fair wages for their services;" they would "prove valuable, contented, and happy citizens." To those who argued in favor of expatriation, Tappan declared that "the colored people must remain here." It was "both physically and morally impossible that four or five million of our people" could be transported to "foreign parts." They were "native Americans" with "more natural rights to remain here unmolested and in the pursuit of happiness" than the millions of immigrants who had "a peaceful habitancy" here.[9]

The AMA followed the Union armies and established schools wherever and as soon as the military situation permitted. Thus the progress of the war dictated that work begin in coastal Virginia, proceed to coastal South and North Carolina, include Washington, D.C., and move to the West as the war sent refugees into cities like St. Louis, Memphis, and Cairo.

In some cases the Association felt the army was slow to allow them access to the freedmen. In April, 1865, for example, AMA Secretary Strieby attempted to persuade Secretary of War Stanton to give teachers passes to Richmond, arguing that at the very least the Association would give clothing to the women and children of enlisted colored men. Black enlistment would be encouraged when the men saw their children being educated and their families cared for. Although Secretary Stanton insisted he wanted schools for black children as much as Strieby did, he said it could only be done "consistently with public interests." Asked if he thought the schools established so soon after the armies entered Savannah and Wilmington were "prejudicial to the public interest," Stanton said that Savannah was as quiet as Oberlin twenty-four hours after Sherman took it, but that Richmond was "entirely different," that "the military necessity demanded a different course there." Although Strieby recognized that there was probably some truth in Stanton's remarks, he nevertheless felt that the real reason was "that Richmond is nearer Stanton's immediate supervision, and that the same technicality, that refused 'ration and shelter' to teachers in the District of Columbia, rules in denying passes to Richmond."[10]

The coming of the war not only opened up a vast new field of work for the AMA, but it affected those fields already established (like the Mendi Mission in Africa and the mission among African American expatriates in Canada) and fields about to be established, as in Haiti.[11] The long-cherished dream of making Mendi a truly African mission by staffing it with African American missionaries and teachers was still in the future. A step was taken, however, in the sending forth of Elymas Payson Rogers (black poet and minister of the Plane Street Presbyterian Church, Newark, New Jersey) to survey the Yoruba territory and report back on the work of Christian missions in Africa, making recommendations for the AMA's future there. His untimely death at Cape Palmas, Liberia, deprived America of one of her educated black sons and ended Roger's dream of becoming a missionary to his fatherland as well.[12]

Although the AMA is best known for its educational work among the freedmen in the South, it had been a strong abolitionist mission organization for fifteen years before the outbreak of the Civil War. That war was to change the AMA's priorities.

The work in the Mendi Mission went on during and after the Civil War, but the emerging needs of the southern fields threatened to cut off supplies of both funds and personnel for Mendi.

Eventually Mendi was transferred to the United Brethren mission board.

The mission to Haiti was abandoned after the death of the Rev. John W. Lewis, an African American minister from New England, shortly after he led a band of about thirty people—mostly fugitives from South Carolina, many of whom also died of fever—to Haiti in 1861. Never an advocate of colonization, the AMA had commissioned Lewis as a missionary. He and his thirty followers were organized as a church in New York prior to embarkation, and they were to form the nucleus of a mission on the island.[13]

The AMA relinquished its Canadian work, allowing the commission of Lewis C. Chambers to lapse in 1863. The migration of African Americans from Canada to Haiti and back to the United States had already largely depopulated some black communities.[14] Mary Shadd Cary, African American missionary teacher and editor supported by the AMA in Canada for several years, gave up teaching in 1863 to recruit black troops for the Union forces, a position she filled with her customary enthusiasm.[15]

During the war years the work in the home field changed drastically also. The number of missionaries among the antislavery aided churches of the West was rapidly reduced, and the teachers and missionaries among the freedmen rapidly increased.[16] In 1860 there were 112 home missionaries and 4 colporteurs as the entire Home Missions Department of the AMA (in the United States). In 1862 there were 93 home missionaries and 3 colporteurs—in addition to teachers of freedmen who by this date had begun to be commissioned. In 1865 there were only 17 home missionaries and 2 colporteurs.[17] In 1862 the AMA had 15 teachers and several other missionaries among the freedmen in Virginia and South Carolina. The following year there were 83 teachers and over 20 black assistants in Virginia; North Carolina; South Carolina; Washington, D.C.; Cairo, Illinois; St. Louis, Missouri; Columbus, Kentucky; Memphis, Tennessee; and surrounding areas. In 1864-65 there were 250 missionaries and teachers among the freedmen including some in Arkansas, Mississippi, and Kansas.[18]

The financial condition in the country generally and the curtailment of home missions work in the West because of the new field among the freedmen, had led the AMA to close the Western

Agency at Chicago.[19] Then the war in the West caused thousands of refugees to pour into cities like St. Louis, Memphis, and Cairo. The Association attempted to supply with workers those points in the West where freedmen were not so well protected as in the East. Help in that area was forthcoming when the Western Freedmen's Aid Society was formed at Cincinnati in January, 1863, with the Rev. C.B. Boynton, pastor of the Vine Street Congregational Church as Secretary and Levi Coffin, Quaker abolitionist, as General Agent. In 1867 that organization merged with the AMA.[20]

A committee was appointed at the Sixteenth Annual Meeting of the AMA in October, 1862, to consider the freedmen. Their report contained earnest appeals for money for schools and churches as well as requests for ministers and teachers. It was not "a permanent demand," its authors said. "In a few years the freed slaves will be able and willing to support in a great measure their own institutions." But their needs were "imperative" in 1862, "and as a matter of economy as well as humanity, they should be speedily met."[21]

Already by 1862 the AMA had provided "many thousands of elementary books" to the various stations where educational work was in progress among the freedmen. At Fortress Monroe—in addition to elementary texts—books on geography, arithmetic, and grammar were also in use. The Association's colporteurs had also distributed religious and anti-slavery tracts in the Border States, especially among the soldiers stationed there. Two pamphlets written by Lewis Tappan were circulated by the thousands: *The War: Its Cause and Remedy*, and *Immediate Emancipation: The Only Wise and Safe Mode*. The project of placing a copy of the Scriptures in every cabin was also under way. A Bible would serve as "an incentive" to learn to read.[22]

The AMA requirements for teachers of freedmen were competence in their field and adherence to "evangelical" senti-ments. Generally, membership in an evangelical church was required, but this stipulation was sometimes, if rarely, waived. Teachers from all such churches were hired. An exception was close-communion Baptists, whose exclusivity was the deterring factor.[23] It should be understood that in the nineteenth century the term "evangelical" meant something quite different from what it means at the close of the twentieth.

> Modern readers who associate the term "evangelical" with
> conservative fundamentalism must understand that at the
> time the AMA was born the term "evangelical" was used to
> distinguish the "mainline" denominations from Unitarian-
> ism.... The "Unitarian departure" was still a fresh and
> painful rupture for Congregationalists, requiring a more
> careful dotting of i's and crossing of t's than heretofore in
> New England theology.[24]

In so far as the AMA was concerned, the teacher who went
South to teach must be equipped with those qualities of character
and devotion to evangelical Christianity which would enable him or
her to impart genuine religion along with the alphabet and the
multiplication tables; the Bible in one hand must undergird the
grammar in the other. Unless that were the case those millions who
had been kept from both education and the pure gospel by slavery
would be a literate but immoral addition to America's mobile
society. Oliver Otis Howard, head of the Freedmen's Bureau and
later an officer of the AMA, congratulated the Association on the
quality of its teachers; and while mistakes were made and commissions extended to some workers whose devotion to Christianity and
the elimination of caste were less than wholehearted, the record was
generally a good one.

Qualifications for southern work were spelled out plainly in
the circular sent each applicant for an appointment as a teacher of
freedmen. The teacher must have (in this order): (1) "*A missionary
Spirit*" for work "to be carried on in a country devastated and
society demoralized, and generally made hostile by war;" no one
need apply "who is not prepared to endure hardness as a good
soldier of Jesus Christ—to do hard work, go to hard places, and
submit if need be, to hard fare." The men (and women) at "the
Rooms" (AMA headquarters in New York City) realized that the
only "adequate preparation" for such a life was "a true missionary
spirit. None should go, then, who are influenced by either romantic
or mercenary motives; who go for the poetry or the pay; who wish
to go South because they have failed in the North." (2) "*Good
health.*" The hard work, "the tax of brain and nerve" that might be
required, meant that only those in good health could conscientiously be sent by the executive committee. "This is not a *hygienic*
association, to help invalids try a change of air, or travel at others'

expense." (3) "*Energy.*" Not only should the teacher carry out the requirements of the school room and the directives of superintendents, but he or she should be a self-starter, able to see the possibilities for service and act upon them without another's direction" to seek to do good for Christ and his poor, by ministering to the physical wants of the destitute; by family visitation and instruction; in Bible reading and distribution, in Sabbath School teaching and in Christian missionary labors generally."   (4) "*Culture and Common Sense.*" It was "a mistaken mischievous idea" to think that "almost anybody can teach the freedmen. Nowhere is *character*, in the school and out of it, more important." In the South "more than at the North should the teacher have resources in himself, on which he can fall back in the absence of those helps, which school laws and a correct public sentiment here afford." Only those persons "least likely to make mistakes" should be commissioned. (5) "*Personal habits.* Marked singularities and idiosyncracies of character are specifically out of place here. Moroseness or petulance, frivolity or undue fondness for society, are too incompatible with the benevolence, gravity, and earnestness of our work, to justify" a commission. (6) "*Experience.*"[25]

An additional word was prepared for the prospective white teacher on the subject of caste by Lewis Tappan in 1867. Those who could not "conquer their prejudices . . . evince indisputably that they are unfit for the high and responsible office of superintendent or teacher, and should be dismissed from the post they so unworthily fill."[26]

From the beginning of its history and throughout the period of Reconstruction, a major task for the AMA was the search for black men and women eligible and willing to serve as officers, teachers, and missionaries. This was true for all fields that involved black persons: Mendi, Jamaica, the South, North, and West.[27] They operated under the tacit principle that a black person should be given a position if possible even though he might be less well educated or prepared than an available white man or woman. In their anxiety to appoint black persons and demonstrate the black man's abilities, they no doubt made some mistakes in choosing black teachers as they did in choosing white ones, but here, too, the record is a good one. Lewis Tappan denied charges that he gave preferential treatment to African Americans, but he was always looking for black persons to staff the Mendi Mission and was less likely to question a black man's motives before aiding him than a white man's.

Emancipation and Politics

The AMA accepted neither General Butler's "contrabands" nor General Wood's "vagrants" as properly descriptive of or fair to former slaves separated from their owners by the war. "Refugees" was a better term, but "freedmen" would be better still. The abolition of slavery could not come too soon.

Both General Fremont's proclamation freeing the slaves in Missouri (August 31, 1861) and General Orders No. 11 (May 9, 1862) issued by Major General David Hunter at Hilton Head, South Carolina, declaring the slaves in the Department of the South (Georgia, Florida, and South Carolina) "forever free" because "slavery and martial law in a free country are altogether incompatible," were applauded by the AMA. President Lincoln's subsequent repudiations of these acts of emancipation were deplored by the AMA. The men at the Rooms found "some comfort" in the fact that Lincoln's words seemed to mean that he did have the power to free the slaves as John Quincy Adams had argued, and was telling the rebels that he might be forced to use his presidential prerogative. (As early as 1842 Adams had said, "In case of actual invasion, or actual war, whether servile, civil or foreign, not only the President of the United States, but the commander of the army, has the power to order universal emancipation of the slaves.") So far as Lewis Tappan was concerned, Fremont had the power. The slaves were freed, and no one—not even Lincoln—had the power to re-enslave them.[28]

The AMA also denounced the additions to Illinois's constitution which denied the rights of mulattoes and blacks to migrate to or vote in that state. This work by an "overwhelming Democratic" convention sounded to the *American Missionary* editor as a dictum from Illinois's southern section known as Egypt. He called on all religious men in Illinois to vote against the constitution and for "Exact and equal justice to all men."[29]

The AMA rejoiced as the churches became less and less timid in their position against slavery, as it had rejoiced when the American Board of Commissioners for Foreign Missions declared itself on the side of the national government and against slavery in 1861 and 1864.[30] Lewis Tappan gloried in the separation of church and state, hoping it would ever be thus in the United States—but declared it was "the province of the Church to act beneficially upon the State"; whereas the opposite had "been the fact in this country for the past generation or two." Undeniably the Church had often "sided with politicians" against the interests of Indians and for the interest of slaveholders. He hoped that such times would be forever in the past.[31]

The Association also noted the contrast between Protestantism and Roman Catholicism in their attitude toward slavery. In the early days of the war there were many of New York's Irish population who enlisted in the Union Army. That this situation later changed and that the terrible draft riots of 1863 took place they saw as not unconnected from the fact that the Vatican was the sole European power to recognize the Confederacy.[32]

Black AMA Officers in New Positions

During the Civil War years there were no African Americans serving as officers or on the Executive Committee of the AMA. Amos N. Freeman had left the pastorate of the Siloam Presbyterian Church in Brooklyn to become pastor of the Talcott Street Congregational Church of Hartford (James Pennington's former pastorate). Charles Bennett Ray was active in the Congregational Association of New York and had resigned his post with the AMA. Henry Highland Garnet had formed the predominantly black African Civilization Society in 1858, and until the outbreak of the Civil War was preparing himself to lead a group of missionaries to Africa.

Garnet and Lewis Tappan shared the honors of addressing the meeting held at Cooper Union to celebrate the Emancipation Proclamation in 1863.[33] The Association "greatly rejoiced" in Lincoln's action, calling it "a step in the right direction." Although the Proclamation did "not go as far as we should have been glad to have it," the *American Missionary* editor declared, "yet it has gone quite as far as we expected. . . ."[34] During the terror of the draft riots of that year Garnet escaped the wrath of a mob when his daughter removed the nameplate from their door and white friends hid him in their stable. The committee of white merchants set up to provide relief for the victims of the mobs chose Garnet to take charge. Some 6,392 persons were aided through his office. Charles B. Ray and others also assisted in that effort. Biblical language came naturally to Garnet's pen when he wrote the address thanking the merchants for their help in a time of trouble.[35]

Garnet encouraged black men to enlist in the Union forces and volunteered his services as a chaplain to the black troops on Rikers Island. Rallies were held in black churches telling the people the truth about bounties and the rights of families to receive them. "Runners" had recruited black soldiers and had cheated them out of their due bounty money. Garnet was able to obtain evidence against the "runners," making government action against them possible. Probably these efforts on the behalf of African American soldiers were the cause of his being attacked while crossing the Hudson on the Cortlandt Street Ferry. He served as mediator between the troops and the government, acting as the agent of the Union League Club in helping to solve the problems of the troops on the Island. Garnet continued in this work until the Twentieth, Twenty-sixth, and Thirty-first Regiments of United States Colored Troops left for the field. He organized a Ladies' Committee for the Aid of Sick Soldiers, and started a hospital kitchen on Rikers Island. These activities were carried on in addition to his regular pastoral duties at Shiloh Church.[36]

In April, 1864, Garnet accepted a unanimous call to the pulpit of the Fifteenth Street Presbyterian Church, Washington, D.C., and began work there the following June. The Chaplain of the House of Representatives, the Rev. William H. Channing, asked Garnet to address the House on Lincoln's birthday in 1865; and he thus became the first black man to enter the halls of Congress in other than a menial capacity. William J. Wilson, black AMA teacher in Washington, attended the service and described the profound impression Garnet made on his listeners:

> Men who went to the house to hear a colored man, came away having heard a MAN in the highest and fullest sense. Many who went there with feelings of curiosity, came away wrapped in astonishment. Not only a man, but a great representative man has spoken, and they were amazed.[37]

One of the vice presidents of the AMA also attended that service in Washington. Dr. Joseph P. Thompson wrote in an article in the New York *Congregationalist* that "the simple announcement" that Henry Highland Garnet would speak in the Hall of Representatives "told the whole story" of four years of war. "Within the very building where the Fugitive-Slave-Law was passed, where a Senator was stricken down by a ruffian slaveholder," said Thompson, "a negro of unmixed blood, born of a Maryland slave, could preach upon 'the Political Pharisee,' who 'binds heavy burdens upon other men's shoulders, but touches them not with his own finger.'" Thompson continued:

> I knew Mr. Garnet would acquit himself well. He had stood in my own pulpit, with a quiet, manly bearing set off with most immaculate linen. He is a good sensible preacher, and a true gentleman, having no extravagance of manners. His sermon at the Capitol was credible to his intelligence. . . . Two points were worthy of special note. First his demand that since emancipation had come by necessity, enfranchisement should come by justice. That was exceedingly well put, and the great audience felt it. The other point was, that the sooner the negro should cease to be the subject of special legislation, the better for him and for the country. Give him his rights, give him a fair chance, and leave him to make his own way in the world, without tutelary legislation. . . .
>
> But after all, it was not the sermon that made the occasion, but the occasion that made the sermon. My heart sang other hymns than those rendered by the choir, my mind discoursed other thoughts than those uttered from "the speaker's desk." That large assembly in that hall, listening with serious and sympathetic interest to words of plain and stinging truth from the lips of a slave-born negro, was a sermon worth going to Washington to enjoy.[38]

Although there were no black AMA officers during the Civil War, black persons were important in the promotion of funds and in the big task of teaching and "elevating" the freedmen. The AMA did not have to tool up in order to prepare for the work among the freedmen; its institutional machinery already had two decades of experience. Suddenly the need for money rose astronomically. Now that the AMA's abolitionist position had been justified in part at least by the actions of the Federal government, money would have been more easily obtained had not the financial condition of the country dictated otherwise.[39]

Early in 1862 AMA agent William L. Coan (white) took William Davis and William Thornton (two black men from Virginia) on a lecture tour of the North; and both of the latter spoke at the AMA anniversary meetings in Boston in May. Over 200 barrels of clothing were received as a result of the Davis tour. Davis also spoke at the 1863 Annual Meeting of the AMA.[40]

Less than three months after the sending of Lewis C. Lockwood to Fortress Monroe to do whatever he could for the freedmen's welfare, AMA Secretary Simeon Smith Jocelyn visited the Fort and went immediately to Washington, where he was successful in his request to President Lincoln to supply the contrabands at the Fort with a doctor.[41] On the back of Jocelyn's letter Lincoln wrote: "If Genl. Wool is of opinion that the services of a surgeon are needed for the colored persons under his charge, and will select a suitable person, and put him to the service, I will advise Congress that he be paid."

Jocelyn reported to the Association that he found the refugees's "love of freedom strong. . . . Their desire for learning, and the aptitude of children and adults to learn . . . remarkable." He was particularly struck by the "passion" of the adults to learn to read the Bible. The refugees were "grateful" to those seeking their liberty and education and had "a keen discernment of character." For them the cause of the Rebellion was not ambiguous. They served as the "telegraph," giving information of "the movement of the enemy; —they dig trenches, throw up embankments, and, having more to gain in victory, and more to dread in defeat, than any white soldier, would fight our battles with unwonted daring." Jocelyn found them industrious and temperate. Although "the religious knowledge, experience, character, unusual intelligence and gifts, of numbers among them" were surprises, he pointed out that the majority were former residents of the Hampton area and had more advantages than slaves generally enjoyed.[42]

Repeatedly during the Civil War the nation was counselled by the AMA to repent its mistreatment of all men—American Indians, poor whites North and South, and especially the black man—and to abide by "the principle on which our fathers professed to establish" the country: "THE EQUALITY OF MAN BEFORE THE LAW." This was the way to peace. What but good could be the result of right action? Tappan called upon the government to destroy "all political distinctions between white and colored citizens, as such, "and to place colored soldiers upon the same footing as white soldiers.[43]

Just before the institution of the Freedmen's Bureau, Charles B. Wilder, Army Superintendent of Contrabands at Fortress Monroe, was again hindered by army officials unsympathetic with his purposes of encouraging "the self support and elevation of the race." He appealed to AMA Secretary George Whipple. Because the AMA had had "more to do with giving character and success to these model arrangements than all others in the country," Wilder concluded that Whipple was "the person of all others" to ask Secretary of War Stanton "to put these matters right."[44]

When the war was a year old, and again immediately after it was over, Tappan called for an antislavery amendment to the Constitution "to satisfy those who have believed that that instrument sanctioned the anomalous evil," and to take from any state the power of that evil's revival.[45]

Among the resolutions passed at the Annual Meeting of the AMA in Brooklyn in October, 1865, were the following:

> 3.. That the idea of emancipation which carries with it no protection of person and property, no advantage of the laws and institutions of the land—equal and impartial—is delusive and pernicious. In this age, and in this nation, there can be no meaning to liberty which leaves a man stripped of all civil rights, and free only as the beasts of the forest are free. Emancipation and liberty are but empty and mocking words if they do not convey the idea and rights of citizenship; and we protest against excluding men from the rights of citizenship, civil or political, on account of their color.

> 4. That the National Government by freeing the slaves lays itself under the highest civil as well as moral obligation, to protect them from the violence or wrongs that may be practiced upon them by their former masters or others; to give them attainable access to the use of the soil; and to guarantee to them, most fully, all the rights implied in the use already granted them of lands abandoned by rebel

owners, including the produce of the cultivation of those lands.[46]

NOTES

1. (DeBoer 1994, xii-xiii)

2. *AM*, IX (February, 1865).

3. (Drake 1957, 198). Drake included figures from J.L. Curry, *Education of the Negro Since 1860* (New York, 1894). For tabulation of contributions see (DeBoer 1994, 20).

4. (DeBoer 1994, 3-4).

5. (DeBoer 1994, 16, 86-87)

6. (Brown 1874, 393-399). See also (DeBoer 1994, 87).

7. Lewis Tappan, "The Rebellion," *AM*, V (October, 1861), 227-228; "The Prospect Before Us," *AM*, VIII (April, 1864), 90-91; "Our Public Affairs," *AM*, XI (August, 1867), 178-180.

8. Lewis Tappan, "The War—Its Cause and Remedy," *AM*, V (June, 1861), 130-132.

9. Lewis Tappan, "The Question at the Door," *AM*, V (August, 1861), 179-182; "The New Englander," *AM*, VI (May, 1862), 106-107.

10. M.E. Strieby, Washington, D.C., April 12, 1865, to George Whipple, AMAA.

11. For details of the Mendi Mission see (DeBoer 1994, 103-152). For the AMA Canada missions see (DeBoer 1994, 153-206).

12. *Fifteenth Annual Report of the American Missionary Association* (New York, 1861), p. 6.

13. *AM*, VI (July, 1862), 145; John W. Lewis, New York, January 30, 1861; February 5, 1861, to George Whipple; see also J. Theodore Holly, New York, November 11, 1862, to George Whipple; *AM*, VI (June, 1862), 123-124; August Wattles, Washington, D.C., August 9, 1862, to George Whipple, AMAA. For Lewis Tappan on colonization, see *AM*, II (September, 1858), 226-227. See also (DeBoer 1994, 97).

14. (DeBoer 1994, 184-187).

15. Silvia G.L. Dannett, "Mary Ann Shadd Cary: The Fourth Estate Newspaper Woman, Canadian Pioneer, and Lawyer," in *The Negro Heritage Library, Profiles of Negro Womanhood*, I (1619-1900), 157; See also (DeBoer 1994, 182-183).

16. *Nineteenth Annual Report* (1865), 35.

17. *Nineteenth Annual Report* (1865). Seven commissions of missionaries and both those of the colporteurs were allowed to expire. Of those remaining four devoted their time to work in Missouri and Kentucky; two worked among the freedmen in Kansas and Missouri; one worked in the Egypt section of Southern Illinois; one each among German immigrants, with a Welsh church, and in Indiana.

18. *Nineteenth Annual Report* (1865), 15-34.

19. *Sixteenth Annual Report* (1862), 47, 48, 49.

20. *AM*, VII (March, 1863), 59.

21. *Sixteenth Annual Report* (1862) 51-52.

22. *Sixteenth Annual Report* (1862), 44-45.

23. The "evangelical" criterion was removed in 1881, having been in disuse, and Unitarians and even non-church members were employed as early as 1922.

24. (DeBoer 1994, 14).

25. *AM*, X (July, 1866), 152.

26. (Tappan 1867, 10-11).

27. See, e.g., *AM*, XX (November, 1876), 244; Alexander, New Orleans, Louisiana, May 15, 1876, to Strieby, AMAA; Bassett, Philadelphia, Pennsylvania, November 11, 1868, to Gen. S.C. Armstrong, copy in AMAA of original on file at Hampton Institute. E.D. Bassett was principal of the African High School for Colored Youth in Philadelphia.

28. *AM*, V (October, 1861), 229.

29. *AM*, VI (June, 1862), 132.

30. *AM*, VIII (December, 1864), 292.

31. "The Duty of the Church," *AM*, VIII (December, 1864), 291-292.

32. *AM*, XI (December, 1867), 276-277; see also XII (January, 1868), 14-16.

33. New York *World*, January 6, 1863; *AM*, VII (February, 1863), 25-29.

34. *AM*, VII (February, 1863), 34-35.

35. (Smith 1865, 59-61); see also Lewis Tappan on Garnet and the riots: *AM*, VII (October, 1863), 225; (November, 1863), 250-252.

36. (Smith 1865, 57); Minutes of the Session of Shiloh Church, PHS; (Ottley and Weatherby 1967, 121-122).

37. (Smith 1865, 65-67).

38. New York *Congregationalist*, February 22, 1865; *AM*, IX (April, 1865), 90.

39. *Fifteenth Annual Report* (1861), 10.

40. *Sixteenth Annual Report* (1862), 7, 42, 43; *AM*, VI (April, 1862), 83; (July, 1862), 147-148; (November, 1862), 250; VII (July, 1863), 48; (December, 1863), 269.

41. Copy: S.S. Jocelyn, Washington, D.C., November 26, 1861, to Abraham Lincoln, AMAA.

42. *AM*, VI (February, 1862), 34-35.

43. *AM*, VIII (April, 1864), 90-91; IX (July, 1865), 154-156; see also V (June, 1861), 130-132; (August, 1861), 178-182; VI (May, 1862), 106-107; (August, 1862), 178-180; (September, 1862), 204-206; VII (May, 1863), 112-113; (July, 1863), 154-156; VIII (March, 1864), 58-61; (April, 1864), 90-92; (May, 1864), 122-124; (August, 1864), 194-196; (December, 1864), 267, 290-292; IX (February, 1865), 28-32; (April, 1865), 82-83.

44. Wilder, Fortress Monroe, March 20, 1865, to Whipple, AMAA. Capt. Wilder was heading a program in which the freedmen were cultivating confiscated lands near the James River and also building "model homes" for themselves; see *AM*, VII (July, 1863), 148.

45. *AM*, IX (July, 1865), 155.

46. *Nineteenth Annual Report* (1865), 8.

II

TEACHERS IN VIRGINIA

Your late generous donation to the A M Association was promptly acknowledged, but I had not time to tell you how timely it was. We had just given outfits, to four teachers who were on the verge of departing for Fortress Monroe. . . .

One of the four teachers is Thomas Tucker, a native of Africa, converted at our Mendi mission, and now, at the age of 20, a first rate scholar & noble . . . Christian. He has been 6 years at Oberlin. Poor Oberlin! Straightened for means, and yet doing more good than any other seminary in this land. A colored young woman there [Sara C. Stanley], Thomas informs us, is one of the best scholars. Colonize such persons! Why, they are to be the teachers of our children . . . & exemplars of all that is beautiful and excellent—for aught we know.

—Lewis Tappan to Gerrit Smith, December 2, 1862
Gerrit Smith Collection, GARL

My reasons for asking to engage in the work of instructing the Freed people of the South are few and simple. I am myself a colored woman, bound to that ignorant, degraded, long enslaved race, by the ties of love and consanguinity; they are socially, and politically, "my people," and I have an earnest and abiding conviction that the All-Father, whose loving kindness gave to me advantages which his divine wisdom withheld from them, requires me to devote every power with which he has endowed me to the work of ameliorating their condition, to advancing the civilization of a people, who though, through long years have been victims of oppression and brutality are yet susceptible of high cultivation, and for whom, I feel assured, that an inscrutable providence has appointed a destiny far greater and more glorious than any political charlatan or statesman has yet conceived of, a destiny as Christian men and women rejoice to contemplate—of intellectual power and spiritual greatness, of holiness perfected in the fear of God.

- - -

I never realized until now what peculiar elements of character are requisite to make us efficient instructors to those people—what foresight, penetration, keen discernment, ready apprehension of their innumerable phases of dispositions and temperaments, tact in the adoption of means and measures, and above all, hearts filled with the sanctifying love of Christ, and rich in the graces of the Holy Spirit. It seems to me that God has committed to us, the missionary teachers, the future of these people, the destiny of immortal souls is in our hands, plastic minds are to be molded by our hands, for good or evil, in beauty or deformity . . . . Oh! "who is sufficient for these things?"

—Sara G. Stanley, 1864 letters, AMAA

What to do about the slaves, now refugees "turned loose" by the war's general upheaval, was a problem immediately tackled by Lewis Tappan, treasurer of the American Missionary Association. Perhaps the solution lay in transporting those uprooted ones to the North for resettlement. In that vein he wrote on August 8, 1861, to Major General Benjamin F. Butler, commander at Fortress Monroe, Virginia, about the "contrabands"—as General Butler had termed them.[1]

The logistics of carrying out Tappan's suggestion must have staggered the man on the scene. Tappan's letter had been written on the day Hampton was fired by the rebels. On the day prior to this Butler had ordered Hampton's evacuation as no longer defensible by his forces, which had been depleted to reinforce the Army of the Potomac after the severe losses of Bull Run and Bethel.[2] Nevertheless, Butler's reply was "prompt and courteous." Since there was no probability that the refugees would be re-enslaved, Butler thought it best that they remain where they were; however, gifts of clothing would be appreciated, shoes in particular.[3]

Work Begins in Hampton

On September 3, three months after the colorful Zouaves of the Union forces first entered Hampton, Virginia, and less than a month after it had been temporarily reoccupied by rebel forces and burned under the orders of Confederate General McGruder, the Rev. Lewis C. Lockwood arrived there—the first missionary of the AMA to the freedmen. He found "a charred ruin": only half a dozen houses and a large, recently-erected building outside town remained.[4]

Lockwood was a product of western New York State, coming from that progressive white Congregational Church in Butler that had opened its pulpit to African American Samuel Ringgold Ward. The Butler church had also welcomed Antoinette Brown, the first woman seminary graduate, after her completion of the theological course at Oberlin in 1856. Lockwood had been employed by the Young Men's Christian Association of New York City, and was recommended to the AMA by that organization to serve as a missionary to the refugees at Fortress Monroe.[5]

Lockwood's mission was well received by General Wool, officer in charge, and joyfully welcomed by the Rev. C.W. Denison, Chaplain of the hospital. The contrabands greeted him "with deep, half-uttered, emotions of gladness." He compared their "heart-worship with formalism," and found their gentle chanting "like, and yet unlike, the chanting of the Litany responses by the boys of Trinity Church, New York." To Lockwood their singing was "enchanting," although he had not heard them at their best. Their "prime deliverance melody . . . was in this style:

'Go down to Egypt/Tell Pharaoh

Thus saith my servant Moses, Let my people *go*,'

accent on the last syllable, with repetition of chorus, like a warning note, in the ear of despotism."[6]

Lockwood was given permission to open schools for the freedmen as well as to carry on missionary work. He arranged for three Sabbath services: one in the summer home of ex-President John Tyler, one in the hospital chapel at the Fortress, and one in a building two and a half miles from the Seminary in which he was given quarters. He expected aid from Chaplain Machett and some of the soldiers in staffing the Sabbath schools.[7]

The contrabands received rations from the government and many were in government service. Reimbursement was not direct but in the form of rations and clothing, the men in charge of the departments hiring them at $5 per month (half what was given to whites), paying the money to the Quartermaster. Much of what they made was placed in a fund for the women and children and those unable to work.[8] Some were self-employed at fishing, clamming, and oystering. They were variously quartered in houses near the Seminary, former slave quarters, and some tents in the Fortress. Winter would bring with it great need for bedding and warm clothing. There were few complaints about the food; for many it was better than they had received in slavery. But there was strong feeling that those men who worked at least as hard as the white laborers should receive equal compensation. Clothing was very much needed for the women, the six hundred children, and the self-employed men—none of whom received clothing from the government.[9]

Lockwood intended "the inculcation of industrious habits, order, and good conduct in every respect." He would impress upon them the fact of their heightened visibility and their responsibility for the progress of liberty. He was pleased that many already understood that they were serving as examples of the results of freedom. He asked for prayers for "the wisdom and grace" to qualify him for his "peculiar and momentous responsibilities. . . ."[10]

Lockwood shared the services of worship with exhorters (religious leaders formerly slaves) among the contrabands, hoping that way to help in the "moral and intellectual development" of both leaders and people. Carey, Hubbard, Hill, William Davis, Peter Herbert, and William Thornton were the names of several leaders. Such men had been encouraged by Fremont's good showing in 1856, and were sure when Lincoln was elected that their freedom was not far off. So fervent had been their prayers and meetings that some slaveholders blamed them for Lincoln's victory. These were people who had lived in and around Hampton before the war. Lockwood found them more intelligent than refugees from interior parts of the state.

The freedmen generally had "a great thirst for knowledge," and Lockwood ordered a thousand primers only to find that he could use fifteen hundred for the eighteen hundred people in the area whose ranks were being added to daily. Many were anxious to be able to read the Bible for themselves. On September 15, "a high day in Zion," he opened Sabbath school in ex-President Tyler's house near Hampton, with the reading of the ABC card. This Sabbath school, like all the Sunday Schools sponsored by the AMA, included reading as a part of the curriculum.[11] On September 17, 1861, Lewis C. Lockwood established the first day school among the freedmen.

Mary Smith Peake

The first teacher of the freedmen hired by the AMA was a woman, but she was no Yankee schoolmarm. Mary Smith Peake was a free citizen of the State of Virginia, and according to the racial classification arising from the "peculiar institution" of slavery, she was black. She was born Mary Smith Kelsey in Norfolk in 1823. Her father was an Englishman "of rank and culture." Her mother was a free mulatto. Peake had taught privately in Hampton before the war. Several of the male leaders among the people had been her pupils: William Davis, William Thornton, and her stepfather, Thompson Walker.[12] Thus it was that a "black" woman had the honor of teaching the first day school for the freedmen, and her school in the Brown Cottage was the seed from which Hampton Institute would grow.[13]

As Lockwood found black persons capable of teaching, he set up additional schools. One such person was Peter Herbert; another was Mrs. Mary Bailey, a free woman who was assisted by a Miss Jennings and a bright boy named James who acted as monitor in a school in the Fortress.

Mary Peake's school near the Seminary showed rapid progress in a very short time. At the end of two weeks she offered to teach an additional school for adults in the afternoon. She was teaching her morning pupils writing and arithmetic in addition to reading. Lockwood thought it a "model school" in the circumstances. Although Peake had volunteered her services without pay, he strongly urged that she be reimbursed. After one visit to her school, he was moved to declare: "This is not a day of small things, though the beginning of days, but already a day of great things. To God be all the praise."[14]

At the Annual Meeting of the AMA a special offering was received for Mrs. Peake, and the Association began to pay her a regular salary. She communicated her thanks to the Association along with her gratitude for the work begun by Mr. Lockwood, characterizing the condition of the people around the Fortress before his arrival using the Biblical figure of sheep without a shepherd.[15]

A Christmas concert was held at Mrs. Peake's school in the preparation of which she was helped by Mr. Foster, the soldier who was the superintendent of the Sunday school her pupils attended. Mrs. Peake's fair-complexioned, five-year-old daughter Daisy was the "star of the evening." The program was unique. *For the first time black children performed in Virginia in a public demonstration of their talents.* It was the beginning of a new day for the Old Dominion and her black citizens.[16]

Mary Peake refused to take the advice of Brigade Surgeon Rufus King Browne that she rest. In January she wrote, thanking the Committee for the clothing and bedding sent with Mr. Coan. Her school was improving, although two children had died since AMA Secretary Simeon Jocelyn had visited it in the fall. Enrollment had reached fifty-three in the day school and twenty at night.[17] She continued to teach her classes even from her bed in the room she occupied above the schoolroom in the Brown Cottage. She died of tuberculosis on Washington's birthday, 1862, aged thirty-nine years. Lockwood, in telling her story, acknowledged that he was a learner in Mary Peake's presence.[18]

All the men with whom Mary Peake served at Camp Hamilton were lavish in their praise. Even when one discounts the Victorian's love of sentiment, one is awed by the evidence of the affection bestowed on the black teacher before and after her death. Two ministers wrote accounts of her life for publication. A brigade surgeon wrote an elogium, and a regimental doctor wrote a poetic tribute. George H. Hyde, who replaced her as teacher, was grateful that he had experienced "the last of her beautiful life." Even in death, he said, "the radiance of her life" yet illumined "the society of her race." She had been "the instructor of all among us who know anything."[19]

Lockwood wrote in March that Mrs. Peake was missed "more and more" each day: "She was indeed a queen among her kind." He had learned that the home and its furnishings that she had lost in the fire at Hampton almost equalled "the best in that aristocratic place." Yet she had been content to live in one room above the school, which Lockwood likened to the New Testament upper room of the Last Supper. There she had erected to herself "a monument more enduring than brass or granite, by impressing her own image upon a group of susceptible pupils," in whom she would live again. "We neer shall see her like again."[20]

Dr. Browne, as late as March 8, could not bring himself to describe her illness except to give it a name: phthisis pulmonalis. "In no other woman," he said, "however light the skin, have I seen a more comprehensive sense of duty or more activity and self-sacrifice for the benefit of others." When he visited her he "felt a new revival of my respect for human character . . . the august name of Providence and the faith in salvation." Browne found words "ineffectual" to describe the effect on his heart, "when with my hand tenderly taken between hers, in a low whisper she thanked me for my attention and invoked the blessing of God upon me." He was depressed and humiliated that his "art" had "so little hold on life."[21] Simeon S. Jocelyn called Mary Peake a saint, and Brown Cottage became a sacred place.[22]

Birth of Hampton Institute

After the building that housed the school in the Fort burned and one officer refused to allow Lockwood further access there, Hyde suggested that the Fortress school and his (Mrs. Peake's) be combined. Lockwood agreed: "And who knows but this seminary may yet be a good industrial & boarding colored school." Prophetic words—for this was the beginning of Hampton Institute.[23]

The more Lockwood heard of the songs of the freedmen, especially those about Joseph and Moses and the delivery from Egypt—songs that had been banned in slavery—the less anyone could convince him that even in that "mild region of slavery" slaves had "no desire for liberty, when they secretly pour out their own souls" in such music.[24] he was also often much moved by the facility and natural beauty of the public prayers and sermons of the unlettered exhorters—so much so that he sent many verbatim records to New York. He described exhorter Davis as "an Apollo," so eloquent that his speaking "melted every heart."[25]

A subject Lockwood found as "thrilling" as it was "novel" was the fact that fewer than half of the "married" contrabands were lawfully joined. He set out to convince them that a lawful marriage—even years after the fact of actual marriage—would elevate them in the eyes of the white community.[26] September 22, 1861, he began solemnizing the relationships of those who had "taken up with each other." With the aid of Chaplain Fuller of the Sixteenth Massachusetts Regiment five couples were married in the morning and six more in the evening. On the following Sunday twenty-one additional couples were joined in three separate services, accompanied by instructions on the responsibilities of marriage and family life. Lockwood requested one hundred engraved marriage certificates "to help deepen the sense of importance of the rite."[27]

On the basis of a promise of two dollars per month pocket money, black persons working for the government had subscribed $125 toward a building for school and church services. In the face of such generosity, Lockwood hoped Northerners would be moved to contribute. His original estimate of the cost of the building was $500, but the current prices of materials locally raised that figure to $1500. Lockwood suggested it might be less expensive to prefabricate it in New York and ship it.[28]

The Army Resists Lockwood

There was resistance to Lockwood's efforts among the refugees on the part of local white residents, of course, and some army officials as well. Some of the latter reacted from prejudice; this was particularly true of Quartermaster Captain Tallmadge and his assistant, a Sergeant Smith. Despite the commendable refusals of Generals Butler and Wool to return slaves to their former owners, some persons were remanded to slavery—a situation that kept the contrabands continually restive.[29]

Although the men of top rank at Fortress Monroe seemed sympathetic toward the refugees, some of their officers who had direct contact with the people were not, and defrauded them of wages and supplies.[30] Lockwood's complaints (that the refugees were not getting their just compensation) in articles to the generally sympathetic New York *Tribune* were not being published. He asked the Executive Committee to investigate and to persuade their friends in Congress to appoint a commission to investigate.[31]

Lockwood's remonstrances to the Executive Committee and to abolitionist congressmen, led to the appointment of Charles B. Wilder (a member of the Executive Committee of the AMA) as Superintendent of Contrabands at Fortress Monroe.[32] But there was doubtless backlash also in Wool's ordering Lockwood and Hyde from the Seminary. He declared that he had been in the school business long enough, that they could quarter themselves. The reminder that the government was not only quartering but transporting and subsisting missionaries at Port Royal was to no avail.

The Seminary was to be turned into a hospital under "wily-serpent-like" Dr. Cuyler and his "tool," Dr. McKay, its resident superintendent. These were pro-slavery men who had the ear of General Wool. McKay denounced the experiment at Port Royal as "cruel to South Carolina," an unwarranted violation of her laws. He also said that Lockwood's work "in unfitting the people . . . for a return to slavery to which they were doubtless soon destined" was wrong—to master and slave alike. McKay also declared that he knew who Lockwood was and he knew about the Committee in New York that had sent him, one of whom [Lewis Tappan] was "identified with the rankest abolitionism." Having been "shut out" of the Seminary and burned out of the Fort, Lockwood thought he should go North and lay "bare before the public the *whole iniquity.*"[33] Lockwood and the Executive Committee were certainly involved in the agitation that resulted in the appointment of a Congressional Committee to look into the condition of the freedmen.[34]

Lockwood succeeded in stripping Tallmadge of "his power to hurt the colored people," and Sergeant Smith was removed for misuse of supplies. Having won those battles, Lockwood was determined to put the pro-slavery doctors *"hors de combat."* He was especially determined after Dr. McKay had sent an armed guard with "gun in hand" house to house, rounding up black women to clean the Seminary. They were promised 12 1/2 cents in wages, but were not paid.

Reforms had been made, however, by the Congressional Committee in the matter of wages. Compensation was to be graduated "by merit & not by color," and the money given directly to the laborer himself. Lockwood had gone before the Commission to criticize Wool for evading "as far as possible all responsibility in reference to the treatment of these poor unfortunates."

Lockwood requested colored preachers for the area because it would be easier for them to obtain board. He also suggested that colored matrons be sent to teach the women and girls the arts of homemaking. Such women would help immensely to elevate the refugees. Such simple habits as family meals were unknown among the slaves, as they had been accustomed to snatch food by the handful whenever it was available. He wanted both teachers and matrons to be able to sing and read music. The kind of woman he sought would have those qualifications.[35] When no colored teacher seemed forthcoming, Lockwood begged for any teacher "male or female, white or colored," they would try to find quarters.[36]

The name of Port Royal seemed always to be before the public. That was a sore point with Lockwood, who urged the Committee to tell the story of Fortress Monroe in papers with a large circulation like the *Independent*, the *Tribune*, and the *Times*. It was not a coincidence, to his mind, that the squeaky wheel received the most money.[37]

John Oliver Begins Work at Newport News

John Oliver (black) was inspired to apply to the AMA for a commission to teach the Freedmen after hearing William Davis speak in Boston, and wrote immediately to William L. Coan.[38] Oliver, a carpenter by trade and a native of Petersburg, Virginia, had been studying for the ministry for two years, supporting himself and an aged mother by teaching school. A bachelor, he was a member of the Twelfth Baptist Church of Boston, and came highly recommended by his pastor, Leonard A. Grimes. William Coan was impressed and indignant that the Educational Commission in Boston had refused to send Oliver to the South (although he had certification) because it was against their policy to send black persons.[39]

The AMA Executive Committee in New York planned for Oliver to begin work at Newport News, but Lewis Lockwood thought it best that he spend some time first as an assistant to Charles P. Day, then in charge of the school at Fortress Monroe. After having been crowded for a time in Brown Cottage for church services, the old court house in Hampton had been fitted up for their use. Oliver saw powerful symbolism in that fact in which God had made "the wrath of man to praise him." The court house, which had been "the slaves bastile" [sic] was "changed into a place of peaceful worship dedicated to God." At the opening service attended by about a thousand persons, Lockwood spoke of Africa's early history, of her admirable past and her learned sons. Oliver was moved by the discourse and certain that its effect upon those people who knew nothing of the history of their fatherland was great indeed.[40]

In June Oliver started work at Newport News, establishing two schools, one of seventy pupils and another of forty. He alternated his time between them, spending three days at each place each week. For a time he also conducted an evening school for over a hundred adults at the camp ground, but a great influx of troops there ended that project. Many of the refugees at Newport News were ill, and it was almost impossible to persuade doctors to care for them. Oliver did what he could, but he pleaded for a doctor from the North.[41]

The troops that had arrived at the fort at Newport News were those under the command of General Ambrose E. Burnside, for whose leadership of men Oliver had no respect. Burnside's quartermaster Oliver characterized as cut from the same cloth as all quartermasters. Quartermaster R.G. Wormsley of New York State had become rich in the army. He had the temerity to tell Oliver that the black man was degraded and that slavery was his natural condition. Oliver aroused Wormsley's anger by asking in reply if he had ever seen any people so rapidly "demoralized" as the American soldier. Burnside's troops had acted more like wild animals than men when they first arrived. At the Parrish farm (the site of one of his schools) they had robbed the black people of everything in sight and had beaten those who had nothing for them to steal. Several soldiers attempted to beat one black man who had a knife and defended himself with it. He was put in the guard house but was removed and killed. Another man—harmless and old—was killed by soldiers also. Oliver declared that "the Blood of Two black men must ever be upon the heads of the New York 51st Regiment." If all the soldiers in the Union army were like those under General

Burnside, then he was convinced that the entire force was "beyond redemption."

Another act of barbarity was performed by minions of McClellan who descended upon the refugees, weapons in hand, and dragged off the men because the General needed more laborers. Many of the women were left hysterical as well as in want, not knowing where their husbands were taken or what they would do when their pitiful stores of food were exhausted.[42]

George W. Cook, a black teacher supported by the AMA in Norfolk, found it necessary to erect with his own hands a navy hospital building moved to the site, in order to have a place in which to hold his school. His wife also taught a school, but was supported by the parents of her pupils who paid a dollar a month for each child. Lewis Lockwood did not envy Cook his place of work. Norfolk—the home of four thousand African Americans before the war and to which an additional thousand refugees had gravitated—was a more difficult post than Hampton. There was a much larger concentration of whites and a more intense and active opposition on their part to efforts made on behalf of the contrabands. George Cook's school numbered about a hundred pupils and was expected to more than double when books were available for additional students.[43]

Oliver at Norfolk

When John Oliver returned to Virginia for a second tour of duty in the fall of 1862, he went to Norfolk. His assessment of George Cook was anything but favorable. As he saw it, Cook spent about an hour of each day at the school and the rest of the time was engaged in trade. The school was actually in the hands of his sister's brother from North Carolina, a man named Dempsey Ferber.[44]

As a first step in his work in Norfolk, Oliver held a meeting of the black residents of the city and organized a society with the purpose of helping the newly arrived freedmen. He had also distributed five barrels of clothing sent to him by his pastor to the people at the "pesthouse," a dormitory for the neediest. There he had found 380 people in the worst condition imaginable. He begged AMA Secretary Simeon Jocelyn not to put his letter aside before he determined to do something for the people in need in Norfolk before the onset of really cold weather.[45]

Within two weeks he was able to report that the benevolent society that he had started among the black residents had raised some five barrels of clothing and forty dollars to help the refugees. He encouraged the contrabands to do all they could for themselves and assured them that if they did not struggle for liberty it would "never be thrust upon them." As a result of his efforts among them, he had been falsely accused by a secessionist Baptist minister, Richard Allen, of fomenting an insurrection.

Oliver described the whites of Norfolk as exhibiting "the most violent and open secession proclivities," unchecked because of the absence of any military force in the area. For that reason he had great difficulty in persuading any of the black churches to allow him to use their buildings for schools. The whites were so intent on keeping Union forces from using the city as a base that they burned buildings that were designated for government use. That being the case, the black churchmen were aware that their churches would be easy targets for incendiaries if they opened them to Oliver. Therefore, in an effort to persuade the Norfolk people to change their minds about the use of their churches, and to show some progress for the mission, Oliver started a school in the black Methodist Church building in Portsmouth.

It was difficult to change people's minds, because the result of Lincoln's Emancipation Proclamation in the fall of 1862 was inimical to the interests of the black persons in the area. At first they thought it meant they were free and held a mass meeting of rejoicing on the first of January. More than five thousand people had gathered in Norfolk for the celebration, not realizing that they, being residents of Virginia, were specifically exempted from freedom by the President's decree, since they were in an area where the Union armies had prevailed. The Emancipation Proclamation made it clear that in this part of Virginia, as in Washington, D.C. itself, slaves were still slaves or contrabands—not yet freedmen. As a result of that proclamation "human life" was "most terribly insecure" in the area. "Norfolkites" were "burning every building that the Northern unionist[s]" had been using.

Work Begins at Portsmouth

The Portsmouth navy yard was also "in ashes" and Southerners were hiring members of the New York 99th Regiment "to mob and rob the colored people at all times day or night." They were also hired to seize slaves and take them outside the lines where they were turned over to their owners or to agents.[46]

Oliver visited nearby Portsmouth and started a school there. It was immediately popular. In ten days there were 130 in attendance, and the school that had been started in the basement filled the entire church building. Oliver also started a Sabbath school at the same place. He expected the school to exceed Hampton (150 pupils) in size. Feeling in Portsmouth's white community was "exceedingly bitter" against his school. Oliver asked for an assistant. Charles Wilder had told him that some ladies were being sent to teach in the Hampton area. Oliver would not mind working with ladies, he said, but wondered if they would object to a black associate. The Methodist Church had no pastor and had asked Oliver to secure one through the AMA. They wanted a black Methodist.[47]

The AMA sent a white Methodist minister, the Rev. Gorham Greely, and a white teacher, Harriet Taylor. By the time she arrived in February there were more than two hundred pupils. Boarding places were found for Greely and Miss Taylor with black families in the town. Oliver stayed on at Portsmouth long enough to get them settled, but he had already determined to establish a school in Norfolk before returning to the North.

Taylor had nothing but praise for Oliver's work in the school. She was particularly pleased with the orderliness she found. Both she and Greely were anxious that Oliver remain; the school was very large, and Greely would have his hands full in the church. The building held a congregation of about seven hundred and was filled to overflowing for services. Oliver was set on establishing a school in Norfolk where he had failed before, but he was also concerned about leaving the Portsmouth school. He pointed out to the Committee that they must have noticed that Greely was hard of hearing. Such an affliction was a stumbling block to efficiency in the schoolroom. Oliver suggested that the Association send another man and another female teacher as well, leaving Greely free for church work. Three teachers would have more than enough to do in the school.[48]

Harriet Taylor wrote John Oliver shortly after he left for Norfolk and confirmed his fears. She also wrote the men at the

Rooms in New York that order had disappeared from the school at Mr. Oliver's departure. She was able to control the girls, but certainly a man was needed for the boys, who took outrageous advantage of Mr. Greely's hearing impairment. Charles Wilder agreed that another man should replace Greely in the school. For the school's sake the best man would be John Oliver; although he did not recommend that Oliver be returned there.[49]

By March 1 Oliver had made arrangements to begin a school in Norfolk. In May he wrote from Boston that several young men there wished to send him back to the South at their expense and asked for a recommendation from Simeon Jocelyn.[50]

Thomas De Saliere Tucker

Another black worker in Virginia was a product of the AMA's Mendi Mission in Africa. Tucker, now in his second year at Oberlin, offered to serve as a teacher to the freedmen under the AMA. He came with the highest recommendation from his teachers. Not hearing from the Association as soon as he thought he should, Tucker suggested that he be given a year's trial work, unaware that all original appointments of the AMA were on a trial basis.[51]

He was sent to aid Charles P. Day (white), teacher at Fortress Monroe. Day and Tucker lived in what was, ironically, the former summer home of President John Tyler, who had been unable or unwilling to persuade the United States Navy to provide homeward passage for the *Amistad* Africans.[52]

An incident on the way to his new post provided Tucker with a view of life outside the rather special world of Oberlin and an opportunity to comment on American mores. When buying his ticket for the passage from Baltimore to Fortress Monroe, he met American racial prejudice:

> I gave the clerk a $5 bill for a cabin berth. He asked me if I were a colored man. I replied that it seems so. He returned $2.50, remarking that I could not be admitted into the cabin. Bro. King interposed by saying that I had come along in the company and they desired I should be admitted to the same fare. Whereupon, he asked Br. King if he would be knocking round with a colored boy, a pretty business to be doing with "niggers" etc. He spoke quite abusively but I said nothing,

for I must say, though I felt a little pained, yet, I considered
it below my honor to reply to a man who knew not the first
principles of civility. I rather pitied him and wished that he
had been brought up a gentleman.[53]

The advance notice of the Emancipation Proclamation
brought little joy to the Fortress Monroe area, for it was one of the
Congressional districts to be specifically exempted. Many of the
slaves were in danger of being remanded to slavery, although they
had been for some time, in effect, free. The only answer Charles
Day and others in the area could see to prevent a return to slavery
would be to send such persons north. Some of the children could be
saved by sending those with musical ability to Horace Waters in
New York. Waters had proposed educating a group of children in
music and providing for their needs at the same time. Day also
suggested that a few of his pupils taken north would greatly help in
the raising of contributions for the cause by firsthand demonstrations of their progress.[54]

When Day fell ill, the weight of both primary and advanced
departments of the school were put on Tucker. Day wanted to close
the school while he went north for a vacation, opening a night
session with Tucker and a third arrival, J.N. Bebout (white),
sharing its work. Bebout preferred having his own school, but was
willing to help Tucker if he proved incapable of handling the night
school alone. Bebout announced himself "very much pleased with
the children: In fact better than with the teacher (but perhaps I may
do no better)."[55]

Thomas Tucker described the opening of the evening school
for adults enthusiastically. By the second evening seventy-four
persons had enrolled and been stirred by his exhortations to take
advantage of all education had to offer them. He had also made a
census of the black persons at Fort Hamilton, a tedious job he was
glad to see finished. His work had turned up 1,227 people.[56]

Tucker found that almost every staple cost more in Virginia
than in the North: "Living in this place is almost fabulously high,
notwithstanding the economy of our household. . . ."[57]

Tucker had seemed surprised to find Charles Day a rather
young man. His relationship with Day was warm, but his initiation
into corporal punishment in the classroom was unsettling. It was a
subject that he had discussed with the men at the Rooms before

leaving for the South. They had evidently warned him that Day believed in spanking children; they had also written Day to be sensitive to the mental hurt such punishment might inflict on Tucker. Day was amused, for Tucker had himself whipped a pupil on his first day in the classroom. Tucker remarked on the incident: "I in all seriousness repeated the reply of Christian to Apollyon, 'Rejoice not over me O mine enemy for when I fall I shall rise again.' I *did whip* the first day but I was extremely sorry." He attributed his "fall" to his ignorance of the "vices" in which the children had been raised. He supposed that "in governing children as well as adults much of our success depends on our ability to read human nature." In that department he considered Day "decidedly superior." With his experience Day "ought to know more of human nature than an African" who had been "engaged in mere theoretical pursuits for the last six years." He thought he had a "decent stock on hand . . . of mere book knowledge . . . and could any amount of intellectual acquirement suffice to make a man practical at the same time, perhaps I might say without egotism that a direct transition from the Students room to practical life in the common walks of men would insure me success." Despite the fact that he disagreed with Day, he loved him.[58] Actually, Day was an exception among AMA teachers, who overwhelmingly abhorred the strap.

Tucker reopened the day school at Hampton in February, 1863, during the prolonged absence of Charles Day, hoping that the children were not "demoralized by their long vacation." He described himself as unable to take part in Brother Litt's protracted meetings, "the state of my head being such that it cannot endure any mental excitement," although his "prayers and wishes" were with the revival. His head was slowly mending and his eyes—which had been sore from a cold—were better. It is probable that Tucker's desire to absent himself from the revival meetings of Missionary Litts had more than mere physical discomfort behind it. Although such meetings had been dear to Mendi Missionary Thompson's heart, that was not the case with many of the other missionaries—particularly John S. Brooks, who saw and criticized much in Thompson's revivals in Africa that he had abhorred in black religious orgies in Canada. And it had been John S. Brooks who had been Tucker's mentor and friend at the Mendi Mission.[59]

Two other schools headed by African Americans were
started in the area. Samuel Simpkins had forty pupils and Lucinda
Spivery, a young lady "freed by the war," had eleven, one of whom
was Daisy Peake, daughter of Mary and Thomas Peake. Mr. Peake
had removed Daisy from Day's school because he had spanked her.
There was opposition against Day after Lewis Lockwood left the
mission to recruit black soldiers and seek an army chaplaincy
among them. Lockwood had evidently been strong enough to hold
the people together during his work there. Even he, however, had
spoken often of the sectarianism among the blacks who had always
been residents of Hampton and environs, most of whom had been
"close communion Baptists." His efforts to persuade them to accept
open communion were, he thought, successful. After he left, the
leaders among the black exhorters excluded Day from the
church.[60]

Charles Day arrived one day after Tucker had opened the
school. He was disappointed with the amount of work done by
Tucker and Litts with the older people in the night schools, and was
himself overwhelmed with the sole responsibility for the two
hundred children in the day school when Tucker spelled Brother
Litts at the Fort school for a week. The religious interest of the
people seemed to be growing, "although the ignorance & conse-
quent jealousy of the people hinders the work very much. They all
desire to preach but few to practice." This was, Day admitted, "the
dark side of the picture, not intended for their enemies.[61]

Help arrived in the form of Mrs. J.N. Coan (white), causing
Day to chortle: "Everything is going on swimmingly with me now:
day schools & night schools & every thing pertaining to the mission
here."

An agitator named Watkins was at work persuading the
people to emigrate to Haiti. Day expected he would persuade five
hundred to go, for he had no opposition.[62]

Then Tucker fell in love. Charles B. Wilder, officer in charge
of the contrabands, said: "Mr. Tucker is not of much of any use to
the cause here;" and Day commented that "Mr. Tucker is of no
consequence, except to wait on the colored ladies." Mrs. Coan was
more charitable. Although she did not think that Tucker was a fit
teacher "for this place" and seemed to have lost interest in his
school to the extent of allowing Mrs. Coan's daughter Jennie to

take almost complete charge of it, still she was sorry to be forced to say so and hoped her remarks would go no further; "for Mr. Tucker is so much of a gentleman in the house and a very pleasant man." Perhaps it was his desire to start a school of his own at Norfolk that kept him from being interested at Fort Monroe.[63]

Tucker at Norfolk

Tucker began his school in a black church in Norfolk enthusiastically. He wrote the AMA asking if they were willing to aid him; if not, he was determined to "carry it on myself, & depend for success on God & people." Although he did not think he would need outside aid, his optimism was poorly founded.[64] James H. Fairchild, principal of Oberlin, in his concern over Tucker's future, wrote George Whipple that the ten dollars per month and rations that Tucker received for his work among the freedmen would scarcely prepare him financially to return to Oberlin. In the winter of 1862 Tucker had earned twenty-five dollars a month as a teacher in Michigan. Fairchild pointed out that twenty dollars a month was "rather below the ordinary wages of good teachers" in Ohio. Satisfied that the AMA had done everything for Tucker "that could be asked," Fairchild proposed two possible plans whereby Tucker might finish his education: one of one year and one of two years' duration. He estimated the expenses of each and urged the longer plan, for it would cost the AMA no more and would give Tucker the chance to teach for two winters in the United States. Tucker "cheerfully" agreed to the longer course, though he preferred the shorter.[65]

The most singular letter from Tucker in the AMA Archives is one written in October, 1863. It included hints at thoughts of staying in the United States, but more important perhaps it serves as an illustration of the multifarious roles played by the men at the Rooms in New York that included counselor, friend, father confessor, *in loco parentis.*

> Your reference to my spiritual consecration in view of my future usefulness was read with interest. I am keenly alive to the practical necessity of a thorough change of heart; a fervent and whole-soul consecration, an ardent devotion to the cause of Africa, spiritual and temporal. Whenever I reflect, so far as a youth can, on all the Providences connect-

ed with my coming to, and residence in this country, thus
far, I cannot resist the conviction that he intends for me
some work in life. To be sure all men know that they were
not made to be drones; yet there are times when we are, as it
were, divinely impressed with a sense of *the* path marked out
for us in life. I feel that my only highest goodness and
happiness will consist in spending my life for benighted dear
Africa.

Some people were amazed that he would consider going back to
Africa. With the excellent education they said he had, he should
remain in America and work for the elevation of Africa here:

Their arguments are generally ingenious and plausible
enough; but I think it generally requires not much philosophy and logic to detect the sophistries employed. At all
events, unless I can see plainer indications of Providence
allotting me a sphere of duty in this country, to Africa I will
return.

The men in New York must have been hard put to answer the last
portion of his letter:

You have ere this seen Miss Spivery at the Rooms; what do
you think of her? Her health is so poor that I don't think it
will do for her to study. But should I love her ever so much,
ought I to make a wife of her in her comparative ignorance?
This is a thorn in my side. I confess to a strong love for her;
but this latter consideration harasses me much. It seems to
me as though I *never* could be happy with an ignorant
spouse. Of course, I suppose you will not insinuate this to
her. If you can advise her in any thing relating to her
improvement I would be greatly pleased and obliged.[66]

It is evident that as early as April of 1863 the men at the
rooms were aware of Thomas Tucker's feelings about Miss Spivery
and requested word from Charles Day about her. Day had
employed her for a time as an assistant at the Hampton school.[67]
It does not appear that Thomas DeSaliere Tucker, grandson of an
African king, married former slave Lucinda Spivery. It may be,
however, that Lewis Tappan (whose handwriting is in the notes on
Day's letter linking Tucker and Spivery) or someone else in the

AMA saw to it that she did receive higher education. From 1866 to 1870 she was a commissioned teacher of the Association. The handwriting, style, and grammar in her letters would indicate a thorough grounding in at least a common school education.

In the spring of 1864 Tucker was approaching his last year at Oberlin. He asked Lewis Tappan to obtain a principalship for him upon graduation in a colored school in Brooklyn. If that were not possible, he would be willing to work in a Southern city like New Orleans. Although he would "teach in any capacity—for the elevation of the freedmen," he would prefer "the higher English studies and the classics," having found that it was "more congenial" to his "taste to deal with maturer minds and higher studies." He also sent along his measurements so that Tappan could purchase a black suit for him. He wanted black, not being fond of "fashionable colors."[68]

Tucker estimated that the expenses for his last year at Oberlin would be $170 more than he could earn. He regretted that he would "detract from rather than add to" the funds of the Association "for the elevation of the American and foreign heathen." Still he hoped that his education would be "used to the good of humanity."[69]

He spoke with Selig Wright, "your indefatigable missionary to the contrabands of the Southwest," about working with him and argued that the two courses remaining to be completed at Oberlin were "so easy" that he could "well afford to be absent." He wanted to go to Natchez. He was sorry to report that Charles Jones, fellow Mendi student in America, had joined the army, thus losing sight of their object in coming to the United States: preparation to enable them to return as workers in their "benighted country."[70]

Whether or not he worked with Wright is not recorded in his letters; probably not, for he earned forty dollars per month at his winter job. After expenses he had $83 toward his final year's expenses and needed $140 more. He planned to teach a few years in order to repay the AMA and provide for a theological course also perhaps.[71] He therefore applied to the Executive Committee for a position as teacher, and they learned that he did not intend to return to Africa.

His last letter in the archives, written less than a year after criticizing fellow African Charles Jones for wanting to stay in

America, reflects the concern expressed by Mendi missionaries Mary Mair and John S. Brooks that there was little hope for the Tucker children so long as they remained within the power of the polygamous Tucker family in Africa, who dealt in slaves and rum:[72]

> Far from any desire to forget and forsake Africa; I still yet, as I have in the past, cherished the deepest sympathy for my native land. . . . My family influences in the Sherbro, as you well know, are very extensive. Returning there I would be subjected to trials and temptations which you perhaps can not well conceive of in this country. As your Sherbro mission is the only one you have in Africa, and as I could not return and labor there without great *disadvantages*, I preferred to be where I could be most efficient. I could willingly go to such a place as Shengay, Sierra Leone— anywhere where I can be farthest from my relatives.

Indeed, he had applied to both the Church Missionary Society (English) and to the United Brethren, but "unavoidable circum-stances" in the first instance and "limited finances" in the second had prevented commissions in those missions; far from neglecting his native land, he had "steadily kept her in view." Only when it seemed that fate had decreed that there was no place for him to work in Africa and that his talents could be put to better use in the United States, did he decide to remain here. "I shall be egotistic enough to say that I desire to render my life *eminently useful*, and shall, to this end, be governed by a sense of *duty*, and not by *selfish* inclinations." Nevertheless, if after his explanation the Committee felt that he should return to his home district in Africa, he would do so. As for the theological course they wanted him to take, he would do that also; although he felt that he had already spent enough of his life at school.[73]

Tucker's career from this point until his death in 1903 was apart from AMA sponsorship. He taught school in Kentucky and New Orleans, where he also edited several newspapers. He practiced law and served as the first president of Florida State Normal College, later Florida A. and M.[74]

Resettlement Programs

In 1863 Charles Wilder was given authorization to locate the freedmen on confiscated lands of the secessionists in the Hampton area of Virginia. The AMA rejoiced at the news and at the fact that the government had decided to accept black men into the army. This meant that the government would also be forced to protect and subsist the women and children of the soldiers. The turning of plantations over to freed people would also mean that money would be needed to provide seeds and equipment as well as teachers.[75]

Although the men at the Rooms in New York were some-what skeptical of land schemes, having seen the failure of Gerrit Smith's attempts to settle free African Americans in New York State in the 1840's, they nevertheless argued for the distribution of confiscated lands among the freedmen. A committee was formed headed by Lewis Tappan and including George Whipple, R.R. Graves, and Seth B. Hunt "to act as a *Commission*" for those wishing to invest in confiscated lands with the above purposes in mind and to prevent such lands from falling into the hands of speculators.[76]

Black Teachers More Numerous

By 1864 Captain Wilder could report advancement of the work among the freedmen to the point where he believed "a much larger proportion of the colored population in Eastern Virginia [could] read than the white." Wilder, a New Englander, said, "As in old times, the church and schoolhouse went up side by side, so now let the light of science and the light of the Gospel go together to heads and hearts."[77]

As General Benjamin F. Butler moved away from the Hampton area toward Richmond, more refugees poured in, overwhelming Wilder and prompting his request for agricultural experts to superintend and help get the soil prepared and seed planted.[78]

The resettlement program, however, came too late for some. The crowded condition of the freedmen at such stations as the Rope Walk at Norfolk speeded the spread of disease. When some five hundred of such refugees were placed under the oversight of AMA worker H.S. Beals at Taylor Farm, Virginia, many were in no condition to work at all and "the mortality" from "fever, measles, dysentery, small-pox, whooping-cough" etc. was "alarming." One quarter of them were ill on arrival and thirty-three died shortly thereafter. Beals did not regret the millions spent by the Sanitary Commission for the wounded soldiers, but he begged some "cordial for the fevered and burning lip—a barrel of farina" for the sick and dying freedmen.[79]

By 1864 the AMA had 250 workers in the South. Of the 64 AMA teachers and missionaries in the Norfolk-Portsmouth area of Virginia listed in the Annual Report for 1864, at least the following were African Americans: Blanche V. Harris, Sallie L. Daffin, Clara C. Duncan, Sara G. Stanley, Edmonia G. Highgate, William Henry Morris, William D. Harris, the Rev. John N. Mars, and the Rev. James Tynes. In the Fortress Monroe-Hampton area William H. Hillery was an African American among the 25 workers there.[80] In addition to these regularly commissioned persons, there were several other local black people who received some aid from the Association, including Amos Wilson, Mrs. Mary Ann Scott, and a Mrs. Corpru. Beginning too late in the year to be included in the report of 1864 were commissioned teachers Robert W. Harris and James E. Edwards.

Professor William H. Woodbury, AMA superintendent for the Norfolk area, and the teachers there decided to establish a school run entirely by black teachers to hold up as an example. The school—like all AMA schools—would be open to children of all races, but the situation in the South demanded a demonstration of African American competency. Blanche V. Harris, educated at Oberlin College, was the principal and Sallie L. Daffin, Clara C. Duncan, and Edmonia G. Highgate would assist. Harris called her entire staff "most excellent ladies." The school had 230 pupils (children and adults), 80 of whom had never been to school before. When Harris visited the families of her students, she found such "patience and kindness" exhibited that she became the learner "of simplicity, love and faith." The colored women in the area, with the help of the teachers, formed a Sewing Circle in order to help the many needy families in Norfolk.[81]

The plan was interrupted by illness. Miss L.S. Haskell (white), a teacher in another school, became ill and was replaced by Sallie Daffin. Then Harris, who had overtaxed herself in her ministrations to the sick and needy, became generally run-down and incurred heart trouble. So Miss S.S. Smith (white) joined Misses Duncan and Highgate. Smith felt that it was more than coincidence that when the all-black staff was announced, the trustees of the Methodist Church in which it was held moved it from upstairs to the basement, a very close and unpleasant place. She was proud of Blanche Harris for having given up her original fine school room in the public school building in order to head the experimental school in the Methodist Church on Church Street. Yet except for the illness of the women involved, the loss of the all-black staff was perhaps for the best; for it was being whispered abroad that the reason for its establishment was that the black and white teachers could not work together. Smith was "very glad" to be working with the black teachers whose abilities she had seen tested, and for whom she felt "the most sincere regard."

To Blanche Harris her illness was "a severe chastisement" indeed, frustrating her "cherished plan" and compelling her to resign as a teacher. But she still planned to do something for "my benighted and long-oppressed race" while at home in Oberlin, and hoped to be able to return to the work soon.[82]

When the Methodist basement proved too damp, the school was moved to the Bute Street Baptist Church and added to the school taught there by Samuel A. Walker and Maria E. Bassette (probably both white). Clara Duncan became ill, Edmonia Highgate was transferred to Portsmouth, and their places were taken by Sara Stanley (black) and Frances Newton (white).[83]

Sallie Daffin

When Haskell was called home by the illness of her mother, Sallie Daffin was asked to take her school of intermediate pupils. In addition to teaching that day school of forty students, Daffin also worked in the evening and Sabbath schools. She was amazed at the truthfulness of the students and the trust in God evinced by the old people. She felt her own faith weak by contrast. "Whatever sacrifices" she had made in leaving home to work with the freedmen, she knew that she was "the spiritual gainer in a three-fold measure." She found it "a source of unbounded pleasure" that people subject to the "driver's whip" all their lives and called "'incapable of supporting themselves,' should so readily yield to the genial influence of mild persuasion, and by their actions indicate an independence that would do credit to many of our most refined and intelligent minds."[84] In visiting among the sick and poor families in Norfolk's black community, she found that she had "experienced the beauty and truthfulness of the words: 'It is more blessed to give than to receive'."[85]

Although most of the teachers went north for a vacation, Daffin continued her school, since her commission was only for six months. Because the other schools were closed, hers was greatly enlarged and she found it necessary to open doors and use two classrooms to house the overflow. Because of the diligence with which her pupils pursued their studies, she looked forward "with the most sanguine hopes to the time when many of these hitherto benighted sons and daughters of Africa shall shine as stars in the Christian and literary world." She was working for ten dollars per month, and even poor housing arrangements did not prevent her from applying for another commission—this time for a year.[86]

In October, 1864, the army shifted large numbers of refugees. These and many other disrupting changes caused by the military made a school report useless. Daffin visited the "Rope-Walk" (where the newly arrived refugees congregated) one Sunday and helped the stewardess there start a Sabbath school. One old man, asked if he'd like to learn to read, replied, "Yes *Marm*. I know that I have the living witness in my breast, of being a child of God, but I want to be able to read His word for myself."[87]

Because the schools were reorganized in December, she promoted most of her pupils to the "high school," and was very discouraged trying to begin again. Since Daffin's letters were always filled with joy in her work, her discouraged letter that month prompted George Whipple in the New York office to write the following note on her letter: "Regret that the school has been interrupted & say a few words of cheer, she is a good teacher."[88]

Asked by Secretary Whipple to write candidly about the schools, she replied that to do so would require criticism of some persons "it would seem almost improper to censure," and asked him to forget that she had complained.[89]

Daffin had despaired that order would ever return when the schools were reorganized, but was again hopeful by the beginning of the new year, 1865. So many of the pupils had had a long vacation that it had taken them a while to be reaccustomed to the discipline of school. She had visited forty families in December and found many of them "in destitute circumstances." The evening school was going well, the interest at least as great as the year before. The Sabbath school numbered over 140, and the school at the Rope-Walk was "also in a state of progression." She spent her spare time at the hospital across the street from the Mission House writing letters for the sick and wounded and assisting William Harris teach in a school for them. Many of the soldiers there had learned to read while convalescing. The experience prompted her to write: "There is, I think, abundant evidence of an increasing desire on the part of *our* people to become educated; and I hesitate not to affirm that if we have the same advantages afforded us as the whites, we will convince those who deny the fact that we are inferior to none." She was commissioned for a year and received a raise in salary to fifteen dollars a month.[90]

In late January, 1865, Daffin felt the need of a short vacation and asked to spend a few days at home in Philadelphia, since she had not taken a vacation in the summer. She had spent the week between Christmas and New Year's working with the wounded soldiers and was tired. Her vacation was much appreciated and she returned to the work "refreshed and invigorated." While in Philadelphia she had been offered a very fine position, but could not "conscientiously" accept it. She felt, in fact, that she would never again be content to teach a Northern school. Blanche Harris had written her that she wanted to return to work. Daffin asked that if possible she and Harris be sent somewhere together—perhaps to Savannah. "I have a peculiar love for pioneer work."[91]

Despite the inconvenience of a crowded building the work went on—not so orderly as before, but still the children were interested and were learning and the average attendance was greater. She visited the Naval Hospital and spoke with many of the wounded from the battle of Fort Fisher and distributed tracts to the convalescents.[92] This was her last report from Norfolk. On April 9, 1865, she wrote from Wilmington, North Carolina, to which she had been transferred.

Edmonia G. Highgate

Edmonia G. Highgate was one of the most interesting of the African American teachers associated with the AMA. She was probably exceeded in courage and self-confidence only by Mary Shadd Cary, an AMA missionary commissioned earlier to teach escaped slaves in Canada.[93] She was involved with the AMA in some way for at least eight years, for a part of that time serving as a money-raising agent for the Association. The lecture circuit was not often braved by women of any color in the nineteenth century, but a black woman who travelled alone was special indeed. Highgate was a resident of Syracuse and worked in Binghamton, New York, when she applied for a commission to teach the freedmen. Not quite twenty years old, she had been teaching black children for two and a half years "in what might well be called missionary fields of labor." She described herself as "strong and healthy" and said she knew "just what self denial, self discipline and domestic qualifications are needed for the work and modestly trust that with God's help I could labor advantageously in that field for my newly freed brethren."[94]

She had been principal of Public School No. 8, Binghamton, and was described by the Superintendent of the Board of Education there as having given "satisfaction as to *scholarship, punctuality, diligence, & aptness to teach.*" D.H. Cruttenden added that she also enjoyed "the confidence of the Christian community" of Binghamton.[95]

Because she was away from Syracuse teaching, Highgate asked a good friend, Ira H. Cobb, to obtain the "certificate of Christian Character" she needed signed by her pastor and "a recommendation of my fitness for this particular work signed by at least two ministers or other competent persons." She admitted that her religious orthodoxy had been questioned by some but that she had written out all her beliefs and the result had met the approval of her minister, Michael Epaphras Strieby (white), and his wife. Appended to this letter was a note from Mr. Strieby, recently appointed Corresponding Secretary of the AMA, saying that the roundabout method of certificates of character could be dispensed with in the case of Miss Highgate. She was a member of his church (Plymouth Congregational Church of Syracuse) and "had had a good deal of experience in teaching," and in his judgment "would make a most admirable teacher among the Freed-men, and all the more so, that she has some of the African blood in her own veins."[96]

She was "truly glad" to be "approved" having been moved to enter the work "simply by a desire to be a pioneer in trying to raise them up to the stature of manhood and womanhood in 'Christ Jesus.'" She was willing to go to any post—rural or urban—except for Port Royal or the adjacent islands. She would be more than happy if she could go "'without any pecuniary compensation' from your excellent society," but she had to contribute to the welfare of a widowed mother and brothers and sisters. She was, however, willing to make the sacrifice of giving up a position that paid twice what she expected to receive in the field.[97]

Highgate arrived at Norfolk, had dinner at Prof. Woodbury's house, settled in at Rev. John M. Brown's, and went to the Rope-Walk to see the new arrivals—some five hundred refugees. She was intensely moved by their want and by their preference for freedom, albeit with rags, to slavery. She immediately wrote to two Sewing Circles to send her boxes of clothing. Her first Sunday in Norfolk she attended a Class Meeting at 6:30 a.m. and visited two other Sabbath schools in addition to the one in which she "was duly installed teacher." She began work in day and night school the next day, and on Tuesday—when her school had to close at 11 a.m.— she "improved the time by visiting all the schools here and two in Portsmouth." She expressed herself "delighted with the work and more than repaid for coming down to press the soil wherein the *monster Slavery* has its grave."[98]

Jermain Wesley Loguen declined to accept a bishopric in the A.M.E. Zion Church in 1864 because he feared that he would be stationed in the South. Yet he visited Virginia, making "a dashing raid into Norfolk, Va., and vicinity," and commented on AMA schools where he claimed there were "only three colored teachers" in the "admirably conducted schools." There were actually seven black teachers in the AMA schools in Norfolk and Portsmouth at the time, one of them an ordained minister. Loguen did, however, spend "six of the happiest days" of his life at Norfolk, and then went on to Hampton, accompanied by Miss Edmonia G. Highgate, whom he described as "an old tried friend" and "General Agent as well as teacher in Portsmouth and vicinity."[99]

Loguen was very complimentary to the AMA schools and personnel, but spoke as if all the AMA teachers were white:

> Our white friends seem to be endeavoring by these
> latter efforts to remove the blot from the country's escutchen
> [sic]. But I am convinced that the work is ours. They may be
> pioneers while we are gathering influence. But we must come
> forward, make sacrifices, and take our own position for the
> elevation of our people. We must help each other while it
> costs us something to do so. If we do not we shall be
> ashamed hereafter that we have not done so.[100]

Highgate went with Loguen to see the AMA orphanage at Ferry Point, Virginia, under the care of Rachel G.C. Patten and Mary Jane Doxey. When Highgate was principal of the Colored Industrial School in Binghamton, New York, she had sent boxes of clothing to the orphanage. Patten was anxious for Edmonia to join the orphanage staff and was joined by Miss Doxey and W.O. King, the one man at Ferry Point.[101]

Highgate had mixed feelings about the orphanage. She had been sent with Miss Smith, a white teacher (mentioned above) at Norfolk to a school in Portsmouth, where she served as "general visitor," taught in the night school and the industrial school, and sometimes instructed the monitors with Smith. Obviously she did not feel her talents were being put to the best use. Prof. Woodbury did not think she should go to the orphanage, and she would be "the last person by word or deed to so act as to show disrespect to our tried friend." She was afraid she would not be able to remain in the South longer than her current commission and wanted to make the best possible use of the time, asking if it were permitted that she use part of her salary to buy shoes and clothes for the needy freedmen.[102]

The men at the Rooms decided with Woodbury, and Miss Highgate was happy, for she was soon to be "nicely situated in one of the graded schools in Norfolk." Secretary Whipple's plan to send about $100 worth of material and shoes to the orphanage in place of spending her own money also pleased her. The teachers made it a policy to ask a small amount for any clothing distributed if the people could afford to pay. She acknowledged also the receipt of "a very rich box" from the Colored Ladies Society of Syracuse.

She was glad that Michael E. Strieby had been elected Corresponding Secretary of the AMA, a position in which he could "do more general good for this great cause," she wrote Strieby, "but it seems very strange for me to think of you otherwise than *my pastor.*"[103]

The last communication she sent from Norfolk was her report for the month of May: "The most earnest months of my existence were the two last which have just passed into God's eternity. I have been enabled to get to so many of my people who have spent most of manhood's and womanhood's freshness in slavery in this region of heart-breaks!" Her report ended with a statement that she had just returned from two hours teaching at the Rope-Walk (4 to 6 p.m.): "I have my reward in advance in all phases of this excellent work. My evening class of men . . . afford me decided recreation. Oh how inspiring the thought that these dear souls are 'forever free.'"[104]

Her position as principal of the Norfolk school was cut short by a breakdown and dangerous illness which forced her to rest for several months. Although her doctor forbade her return to teaching before December, she persuaded the men at the Rooms to accept her service as collecting agent in the fall of 1864. She wanted to fill the time doing something for the freedmen.

Since she was well known in Oswego County, New York, Highgate began there as a lecturer, telling the story of the work among the freedmen in which she had herself a personal role. She restricted herself to "country places" where male agents did not canvass. In addition to the money raised she interested people in the work of the Association and sent in their boxes of clothing for the freedmen and money for subscriptions to the *American Missionary.*

The winter weather made her work in the northern counties of New York very difficult. Roads were often impassable and she was once snowed in at Oswego for three days. She reminded the AMA officers that she was only lecturing until an opening appeared for her to teach again. Unfortunately, she missed a letter telling of an opening in Savannah. When the possibility of a position at Havre de Grace, Maryland, arose, she told them to send her post haste, not to wait until complete living arrangements had been made. She knew her people well enough, she said, to be certain she would not starve. Besides, she was capable of doing pioneer work. "I can go in alone," she declared.[105]

Clara C. Duncan

Clara C. Duncan secured her commission in AMA service through Blanche Harris. She was twenty-four years old and unmarried in 1864, an orphan paying for her own education at Oberlin, and had done household work as well as teaching for two terms to pay for her board and expenses at school.[106]

An unpleasant occurrence on the voyage between Baltimore and Fortress Monroe prompted Samuel A. Walker (who accompanied Misses Duncan and Maria E. Bassette to Norfolk) to action. Duncan had been refused her breakfast on the boat, and her companion was called names for associating with a "nigger wench." Immediately upon landing Walker reported the affair to General Wild and eventually to General Butler. The result was that the man involved (Rollin of the Bay State Line) was dismissed and orders were issued that henceforth any passenger paying for a meal be served at tables regardless of color.[107]

Clara Duncan was impressed by the decorum in her Primary School, held in the carpenter shop on Bute Street. She found only one case of insubordination in which she "inflicted corporal punishment." In addition to the day school she aided Edmonia Highgate at the Rope-Walk school between 4 and 6 each afternoon.[108]

In June her school moved into the Bute Street Methodist Church (AME) of Rev. John Mifflin Brown. He was also corresponding secretary of the Mission Department of the AME Baltimore Conference and editor of the AME organ, *Repository of Religion and Literature*. He had been a student of George Whipple at Oberlin, and was in charge of the AMA Mission House No. 3 (48 Bermuda Street) in Norfolk, where Sallie Daffin, Clara Duncan, Blanche Harris, and Edmonia Highgate lived. In 1864 John M. Brown and James F. Sisson (white AMA missionary who became a minister in the AME Church) instructed the exhorters of the Methodist churches in Norfolk and Portsmouth: Sisson in the English branches, and Brown in Theology.[109]

When Prof. William Woodbury returned to the field after taking his wife home to Holyoke, Massachusetts, for the birth of their son; Clara Duncan wrote of her happiness, saying that she loved the professor, who had been like a father to her, and quoting other teachers as saying that it seemed like home again since his return. While Woodbury was away she had written him about the "unpleasant atmosphere" in the Mission House, that a woman (Mrs. Brown) with four children and no interest in the cause was scarcely the one to have charge of the residence. She repeated her desire to give all—even her life if need be—to the cause, but thought her silence on the subject would not help. She so loved the Woodburys and looked forward to their return with the baby. Despite the problems "at home" the work had done her much good and had made her "a better christian."[110]

When Edmonia Highgate became ill, Clara Duncan accompanied her home to Syracuse. Highgate was deranged much of the time and allowed no one but Duncan to care for her. Miss Duncan was sorry not to remain in the field, but Highgate had become steadily worse until Duncan could sleep neither night nor day. William D. Harris, African American teacher at the Gosport Naval Yard, went with them as far as Baltimore, but his presence so upset Edmonia that he left them there. Clara Duncan wrote from Elmira, New York, between trains, that when they arrived at Miss Highgate's home (Syracuse), she would be only a day's ride from her own home which she had not visited in three and a half years; and she had Prof. Woodbury's permission to visit. At home in Pittsfield, Massachusetts, she found that she really needed a rest after the trying experience.[111]

Clara Duncan returned to Virginia to work at Whitehead Farm with Frances Littlefield (white) where some one hundred families had been settled on small plots of land. Although she had been fearful of two women working alone in the country, she found teaching there more pleasant than in the city; still the white tents and sounds of artillery practice reminded her that the country was at war. The soldiers in the night school seemed more eager to learn than others of the refugees.[112]

She continued at Whitehead Farm with Littlefield until the end of March, leaving then in order to return to Oberlin in time for the summer session. She was returning to school on the advice of Prof. Woodbury and knew it was for the best. She was to stay with the Dascomb family for a while at Oberlin. Clara would miss her friends in Virginia, but would be better prepared to labor there again after finishing her college education. From Prof. Woodbury she had had nothing but kindness and hoped he would be long spared for the work he did so well. She hoped to work again with Miss Littlefield whose cheerfulness and "self-sacrificing spirit" had done so much to make their home at the farm pleasant.[113]

Sara G. Stanley

Sara G. Stanley was twenty-five years old and unmarried when she applied for a position as teacher of the freedmen under the AMA. She was a resident of Cleveland, Ohio, and a member of the Westminster Presbyterian Church (Old School) there. She had a common school education and had attended Oberlin College for three years. Her letters attest to her facility of expression and excellence of vocabulary. Edmonia Highgate called her "my gifted friend" with reason. Thomas Tucker, from the African Mendi Mission and her fellow student at Oberlin, wrote a letter of recommendation for her. In it he wrote that "Ladies of color of high intellectual culture and personal accomplishments as she, can both serve the Freedmen as teachers, and at the same time be a strong vindication before the Southern secessionists of the equality of the races."[114]

Sara Stanley had taught in the Ohio public schools "at intervals during eight years," occasionally interrupted by family duties. She held a first-class teaching certificate in all subjects (Orthography, Reading, Arithmetic, Geography, English Grammar) in Brown County, Ohio.

She arrived at Norfolk, Saturday, April 9, 1864, and began to teach the following Monday. She found her sixty pupils "all eager to learn, and far more docile and tractable than I supposed possible for such illiterate and undisciplined children to be." She found them "very easily governed" because of "their affectional nature . . . kind words and gentle talk possessing far more potency, and producing a more permanent effect, than a stern deportment or rigid discipline."[115]

An interesting contrast in black and white soul-searching arose among the AMA teachers in Virginia. Rachel G.C. Patten and Mary Jane Doxey, white teachers in charge of the orphanage at Ferry Point, were both painfully aware of the contrast in comforts between their crowded hospital-home and Prof. Woodbury's Mission House in Norfolk. They were convinced that Woodbury had acted in a prejudiced manner toward some of the black teachers when they arrived—by putting them in a separate residence and neglecting to make them comfortable. Patten was a very outspoken lady, who told AMA Secretary Whipple she did not care if he put her long letters aside for a month, if he finally read them. Writing was a necessary catharsis for her, and he owed her an hour now and then, she declared! The only—or at least most charitable—reason she could think of for Woodbury's later warmth toward the colored ladies (a word she used advisedly), was that he had earlier had periods of mental derangement! She thought that William L. Coan, on the other hand, had shown Christian love and thoughtfulness toward the ladies in question.[116]

Quite the opposite feelings were entertained by Sara Stanley and Edmonia Highgate. Their regard for Prof. Woodbury, expressed in letters in his absence from the Mission, was too effusive and intense to have been feigned. Truly the light had gone out of the Mission when he was away. And they felt strongly that Coan was prejudiced against them as colored women. This is only one of many, many occasions when the lost letters written from the Rooms in New York to the workers in the South would have been interesting! How Secretary George Whipple must have pondered such questions and how carefully he must have worded his replies.[117]

Stanley also thought that Fannie Gleason, the matron of the Mission House (the one headed by Prof. Woodbury) in which she lived, was prejudiced against "her co-laborers of African extraction."[118] Stanley was probably correct in this assumption, and it remains inexplicable why Gleason was kept on in AMA employ. The post of matron was a hard one to fill efficiently and many of the missionary wives wore themselves out in it, but expediency did not overcome AMA reaction to caste prejudice wherever proved. Nevertheless, Stanley did not wish to leave the Mission House:

> If we could entirely set aside the fact of individual responsibility, we might, in consideration of her former surroundings, and the fact that her intellect and training has not perhaps been as thorough and extended as some others of us, pass by this expression of her feelings with indiffer-

ence. But as the character of nations, committees, societies, depends upon the character of individuals composing them, there can be Truth, Honesty, Equity, in the whole, only as these qualities inhere in individuals.

Oh! Mr. Whipple if we could have in this work only earnest, Humble, true hearted Christians—regarding all mankind as brothers, God's children, Christ's redeemed; feeling not that the great desire of all hearts should be to wear a Saxon complexion, but to be "clothed upon with righteousness," how blessed it would be, and what an outpouring of God's love, and the inexhaustible riches of his grace, it would receive.[119]

Stanley committed some great sin—at least in her own eyes, and afterward Secretary Whipple was kind to her during the month she spent in New York before going home to Cleveland.[120] Whatever it was—perhaps her own prejudice against and superior attitude toward Miss Gleason—she was forgiven by the men at the Rooms, and her next place of service was St. Louis, Missouri.

The men at AMA headquarters in New York showed great compassion in the way they handled delicate problems involving their female teachers. Although they seemed to have little patience with men who became involved in sexual mishaps, they went out of their way to aid the women with such problems. They were even careful to delete references from letters in the files, blacking them out, making it difficult for the researcher to discover such instances. Several of the white teachers either became pregnant or were accused of the fact by associates. In all such cases, the men at the Rooms cared for the women in question. One, after recovering her health, returned to the work of the AMA and continued in it until her death many years later.

William Henry Morris

Something more than a good educational background was needed for the work in the South. Some of the best prepared in so far as education was concerned—white and black—lacked the strength of character required. William Henry Morris was an able African American who failed as an AMA teacher. At Ashman College (later Lincoln University, Oxford, Pennsylvania) he maintained his position at the head of his class; he was a member of the Presbyterian Church (OS), and a successful Sabbath school teacher. He was "fond of learned language" but "capable of expressing his ideas in good plain English," and he sought the AMA commission "con amore." Unfortunately, once it was obtained he was not diligent in carrying out his duties. He was located at Baxter Farm No. 1 about ten miles from Norfolk. But he was overfond of the city and often appeared there during school hours, leaving his school in the hands of an untrained monitor, whom he had hired without permission and whose salary he charged to the Association. He quarrelled with everyone in authority: the overseer at the farm, whom he accused of breaking into his closet to steal clothing he had asked the AMA to send the freedmen; Prof. Woodbury, whom he accused of treating him poorly because he was black; Capt. O. Brown, Army Quartermaster for the area, who said that Morris would be removed from Baxter Farm if he caused another furor without good cause; Rev. John M. Brown (black), A.M.E. Church pastor in Norfolk, who was upset on learning that Morris was performing wedding ceremonies and who suggested (after hearing complaints from the colored teachers of Morris's neglect of duty), that he remain on the farm for a solid month without leaving. And one can be fairly certain that when he sent the bill asking for payment for the wages of his "servant," the men at the Rooms were somewhat less than cordial toward him.

On one of the last of his visits to Norfolk, Morris demanded lodging at the Mission House at 48 Bermuda Street, headed by Pastor Brown, where there were no extra beds, and crowded into the bed occupied by Brown and his son.

Prof. Woodbury said that, far from being mistreated because he was black, Morris had been treated too leniently for that reason; a white man would not have been allowed such latitude. Asked if he would like more black teachers, Mr. Woodbury said if they were like Morris, definitely not; but if they were like Misses Highgate and Harris, the more the better.[121]

In 1865 Morris, then living in New York City, asked the Association for another position, saying that "having been employed in this capacity by the AMA it is scarcely necessary for me to give you a lengthy enumeration of details relative to myself, etc."[122]

William D. Harris

William D. Harris was thirty-seven years old and had followed the trade of plasterer for seventeen years when he applied for a commission to work in Eastern Virginia or North Carolina. He described his education as the best he could get in North Carolina where he was raised. He taught a "select school" in that state for two years and a "common District school" for four successive terms and was the superintendent of a Sabbath school for five years.[123]

He was immediately hired and sent to Portsmouth. The day after his arrival he visited seven "model schools" in Norfolk and briefly addressed each. He also assisted in William L. Coan's evening school of seven hundred pupils. After filling in for ill teachers and assisting others, he was put in charge of Gosport and Newton schools.[124]

James F. Sisson (white) had enrolled fifty-six students in the Gosport school. Harris and his assistant, Amos Wilson, a black preacher recently released from slavery, set out to enlarge it by visiting. At the end of one week there were 75; by the end of March, 122. Harris thought at first—unlike most other AMA teachers—that the light colored children learned on the average more easily than the others, although the smartest boy and girl were both "quite dark." Weather was an enemy: "The snowstorms, high chilling winds and the raw damp atmosphere, has been a formidable barrier against bare feet and scanty clothing." Illness was also an adversary, and smallpox cut down on school attendance. He suffered from two important lacks: books and advanced students to act as monitors.

Although the people at Gosport wanted a Sabbath school and those at Newton an evening school, neither could be started right away; so he invited them to Sabbath school and evening school at the Methodist Church on North Street where he worked regularly. He did organize a Sabbath school in Gosport in April with 130 members. Sisters Edmonia Highgate and H.R. Arnold (white) and Brother John N. Mars taught with him there.

He taught four days a week in the Gosport school (held in the basement of the Methodist Church), two sessions per day. In addition to Amos Wilson, he had the help of Mrs. Mary Ann Scott; neither had much education, and he felt the need of a capable assistant. Trouble with rock and brick-throwing white boys, who lay in wait for the black children, was settled when the army provost marshal sent colored troops to round up the hoodlums and put them in the guard house.

Because of the great poverty all around him, Harris appealed to friends in Cleveland for aid. One group sent $15 and the black Freedmen's Aid Society $25.[125]

When Harris heard rumors that the schools would soon close and pass into government hands, he asked to be allowed to remain instead of taking a vacation and thus keep the school open as long as possible. He applied for a recommission to Portsmouth; although he would go anywhere sent. Since Rev. Mars had obtained an army chaplaincy and would leave his school, he asked them to send his brother, Robert Harris of Cleveland, Ohio, as an assistant. He wanted to continue in the work, but his salary was insufficient for the support of his family, and he asked for a raise.[126]

Harris gave the Gosport school a vacation during August, but he was kept busy calling in their homes and maintaining his three Sabbath schools" (1) 8:30 a.m. at Whitehead Farm, about 150 members; (2) 10:00 to 12:00 at the Encampment of the Second United States Colored Battery, about 50 in attendance; (3) at Gosport, 2:00 to 3:30, with about 125 people. His Sabbath schools would have been larger if he had more teachers; the two outside the city made it especially difficult. Misses R. Veazie and E. Eliza Lewis (both white) helped him greatly at Gosport.

When the military assigned the mission staff quarters too small to house them all and it was suggested by them that Harris could live elsewhere, he hoped that the change "was not instigated by a policy founded in injustice and Prejudice against Color" because a black man lived with white teachers. He was glad that "our noble Superintendent [Rev. Bell] who represents the pure and holy principle of the AMA is not in sympathy with such a policy, but I fear it is about to become a Rebel military necessity."[127]

In the fall Martha L. Kellogg (white) went—at her own request—to Gosport to help Harris. But the military rearrangement of schools resulted in her removal together with about fifty of the most advanced pupils of the school, and "Gosport School" was "shorn of its strength." Harris was also assisted by Elizabeth P.

Worthington of Vineland, New Jersey. Superintendent Bell wrote to Harris's pastor, A.N. Hamelyn of the Delaware Circuit, Ohio, on his behalf. As a result Harris was given a commission to preach the gospel by the Quarterly Conference of the Wesleyan Methodist Church.[128]

After the removal of General Benjamin F. Butler from command of Virginia, Harris saw many unhappy changes taking place. There seemed to be "a gloomy, unsafe, and unsettled feeling pervading" the Department, "Loyal hearts are sad disloyal spirits are jubilant." Colored children were turned out of *all* the public school buildings, "which were built by the sweat blood and tears of their unquestionable loyal parents, to admit children whose parents are of *extremely doubtful* loyalty." Rations of some of the teachers of the freedmen had been cut off but were still given "to thousands of semiLoyalists, many of whom are too proud to go for their rations themselves, but hire some col[ore]d person to draw for them." A frightening fact was that black soldiers on provost duty were "dying off very suddenly and strangely." Still it made his heart glad when the black community celebrated the anniversary of the Emancipation Proclamation with a march through town "buoyant with hope, liberty, education, and a glorious future." The freedmen ended the celebration with a dinner to which they invited the teachers.[129]

At the end of March, 1865, Harris, J.M. Brown, Sallie Daffin, and Cornelia A. Drake (white) visited New Bern, North Carolina, and vicinity, looking over the work there. It was going home for Harris, and he met many old friends. The trip convinced him that the AMA was the best organization to carry on the work at the South: "The AMA and representatives ... stand highest—first and best adapted to this great work, and—I would to God they possessed the whole ground. . . . I would have all work in and through this one channel." He did not think that he was prejudiced, "but I cannot have so much faith in sudden conversions from military necessity—besides think of the Unitarian seed, now being sown, hitherto unknown among this people." The other societies did not seem to care "for the spiritual interest of the people."

There was much work to be done at New Bern; fully half the children were unschooled. On Roanoke Island he was much impressed with the improvements made by the people in a little over a year. "They were building houses—fences—clearing —grubbing—planting (not plowing, because they have no plows) fishing—and sawing lumber by hand etc." Anyone visiting Roanoke and calling the black people lazy "must be egregiously blind & prejudiced." Harris gave the people on Roanoke the ultimate compliment when he said that he did not think a New England Yankee could be found who would work as faithfully in such circumstances. If those people could manage so well—on half rations and working soil that was almost completely sand—just think what they would be able to do on good land: "what a blessing for them and what a source of wealth to the nation, if they had what they so much need, and what is so abundant—viz *Land Land good LAND.*"

Although Harris repeated his willingness to work anywhere the AMA should direct, he thought that experienced workers might be the ones most profitably sent into the many new fields opening up as a result of the war. He thought he might be of better use to the Association in North Carolina, for example.[130]

Harris summed up the momentous history of April, 1865, as it affected his life:

> The vacation in all the schools for one week. The taking of Neimeyer Building by the Q.M. and thus ejecting five schools. the vacuum left by the Teachers leaving for Richmond. The excitement and great joy produced by the rapid and stupendous Triumphs of our victorious armies, and then the overwhelming sorrow—sadness—gloom—and darkness, that fell, so suddenly upon us, by the horrible death of our beloved President, have caused some irregularity in the general work in this Department— Indeed I think it would be passing strange if these events coming in the short month of April did not effect [sic] us.[131]

The war was over—or so it was supposed to be; and although Harris observed that Richmond was quiet under the command of General A.H. Terry, "mob-spirit" prevailed in Petersburg and Portsmouth. He made a prophetic statement:

> It is very plain to me that if the military authority is entirely withdrawn from the South under the present policy of the

Govt.—that we shall loose [sic] nearly everything that we
have gained by this terrible war. A dark cloud begins to
gather over the south, which may assume such proportions,
as may ultimately break, in a renewal of hostilities—and
another war ensue. Indeed it is my humble opinion that the
war is not really over, but only assumes at present a different
phase and unless we curtail the political power of the Rebels
and increase the power of the loyal people by giving the
negro the ballot, the South may yet succeed in ruining our
great Republic. To ignore the rights of God's poor in
Reconstruction—is to insure our destruction, is my faith. O!
that our statesmen may have the wisdom to see, and avert in
time, the impending evil.[132]

When Harris finished the school year in Portsmouth that June, it
was for the last time, but he returned again to Virginia to serve
simultaneously the AMA and the AME Church in Richmond.

Robert W. Harris

Robert W. Harris, younger brother of William D. Harris,
was twenty-four years old when he applied "for an appointment as
a Teacher of the Freedmen of the South." Like his brother William,
he was a plasterer by trade, but had been working on the railroad
for a year. He was not married, but contributed to the support of
his widowed mother and a younger brother and sister. His only
experience in teaching had been the private instruction of slaves
when he was a youth in North Carolina.[133] He asked to be sent to
work with or near his brother. In response to the circular sent by
the Association to all prospective workers, he tried to raise some
money toward his own support or to find others who would, and
was successful in obtaining $25 and promise of future aid from the
Freemen's Aid Society of his home town of Cleveland, Ohio.[134]

After helping "in conjunction with Br. Bill," to get the lady
teachers settled and canvassing the town of Portsmouth for pupils,
assisting in organizing a night school, two Sunday Schools, and a
Bible class, visiting among the poor and destitute, and asking the
Freedmen's Aid Society for clothing for them—he was assigned the
school on the Providence Farm, four miles from Portsmouth. His
pupils were the children of refugee farmers, squatting on the former
farms of white Virginians, living in self-built cabins or in the old
slave quarters. The homes of the former owners were occupied by

government officers, who hired the refugees, paid their wages (too low for adequate support for the large families), and distributed government rations.

No one near the school could afford to board him; so Robert Harris lived at the Mission House in Portsmouth, walking to and from his school each day until he found a room that cut the distance in half. He felt that he was imposing, however, for the family was very poor—a freedman, his wife, and six children—all of whom he was teaching to read.

His school room was the Colored Methodist Church, which had been used by the rebel soldiers as a stable for their horses; the floor, seats, window sashes, and "nearly everything combustible were torn up and burned by them." The people had replaced the windows and hoped to make further repairs. The children sat on logs until given benches by the government. His hopes to have a blackboard, some desks, and—most important of all—a floor, were answered by gifts from the North.[135] Harris conducted the Sunday school, which numbered about one hundred members. Although he could not begin a large night school until he arranged for a room nearer the church, he did teach about fifteen people in his room each night.

Harris was grateful for the clothes, especially the shoes, sent for the refugees, and hoped by the end of February that the worst of the bad weather was over. The most destitute of the people were the families of soldiers: "Nearly all the young and able-bodied men are in the Army and Navy, and they render but little aid for the support of their families." And rations had been reduced also. Harris spent much time writing letters to men in the service asking for money, only to receive answers from "the poor soldiers" asking in turn "for postage stamps and saying they have not been paid off."[136]

With warm weather many of the older children were needed by their parents to work on the farms; so the evening school he organized helped them. The harassment of white "rowdies" was foiled by the threat of calling for a guard of soldiers. "They have a wholesome dread of soldiers, especially *colored* soldiers."

Calling was a difficult and time-consuming process, for the families were scattered. His Sunday school consisted of 150 persons by the end of April—almost all the residents within four miles of his school. He saw "no signs" of laziness among the people and "little sickness. The hope of peace gave impetus to their "industry of all kinds, and all are working with renewed hope and energy." There seemed to be an awakened religious interest as well. He understood that was "nothing unusual at this time of year, sympathizing with external Nature the religious instincts awaken and blossom with the opening of Spring. Let us hope that it will also bring forth fruit in one season."[137]

He was grateful for the opportunity of being able to help the freedmen, and his request for a commission for the next school year to return to Providence Farm was favorably answered.

Harris returned to Virginia and taught in the Providence Church School for the school year of 1865-1866. Before leaving home for the field he collected used clothing to distribute among the freedmen. He taught both day and night schools, the latter to accommodate those who worked during the day. He had little insubordination, but used "the birch" when necessary, or deprived the children of recess or compelled them to stand for a long time. One of the best forms of punishment for tardiness and other faults, he found, was ridicule. Most pupils would rather be whipped than called tardy. Tardiness was the prime problem in Harris's school as it was in all the freedmen's schools. One difficulty, of course, was the fact that very few of the people had clocks. Another problem was irregular attendance, for which innumerable excuses were found.

Threats were made to burn down the school, and he had a guard posted for several days during the Christmas holiday season when there was much drinking among the lower class whites. Some of his pupils were attacked on their way home from school and their books stolen. And the whites refused to sell him wood to heat the school.

Harris did not let the people lose sight of the fact that he was laboring for their spiritual as well as mental elevation. He felt that "a spirit of true devotion" was exhibited at religious services, though there was still "considerable extravagance in their demonstration," which he thought nevertheless was "better than coldness."

The white land owners refused to employ the freedmen or to rent land to them, and still complained that the blacks would not work. To Harris their "perversity" was astounding. With hundreds of competent black men eager for work, the whites had formed a company to import white laborers. They were willing to pay wages to white men but not to former slaves. Such attempts had been made before but had always failed, "the whites refusing to put up with such accommodations as the Negroes have been accustomed to."

Harris found that teaching the freedmen to read was in effect teaching them a foreign language, for their speech was so different from the language of books. For this reason he found it "beneficial to have an exercise in articulation at every recitation."

He tried to make arrangements with the Association to borrow money to purchase a horse for the next year's work, in order to accomplish more visiting among his scattered constituents without so much physical drain on himself. But the following year he was assigned work in his home state of North Carolina at Fayetteville.[138]

William Hillery

Schools were established by the AMA wherever there was shelter available; often in the beginning such buildings were rude with gaping holes where windows had been. Places to house schools were scarce in cities, like Hampton and Atlanta, that had been burned, but they were also scarce in places like Savannah where few of the southern owners had left. The Army took for its own use most of the available buildings confiscated from rebel leaders. The benevolent societies were given what was left or else they used black churches, old slave marts, railroad cars, etc. Under President Johnson's rapid plan of general amnesty the property of rebel leaders was returned apace, forcing the benevolent organizations like the AMA either to build their own schools or at least to buy the property for them and accept the help of the Freedmen's Bureau in the erection of schoolhouses.

In the country, schools were often run on plantations, the owner (if there) giving the use of a building or a room in his own house for the work. Such schools were taught by AMA female teachers working either singly or in pairs. When no owner was in charge, the school might be taught by a male teacher who also had general oversight of the freedmen working the plantation grounds.

The Rev. William H. Hillery had such a position on the Whiting Plantation near Portsmouth, Virginia.

Hillery, later (1876) an AMEZ bishop, first worked under AMA auspices in 1864.[139] He was unable to begin school immediately at the appointed place, Whiting Plantation, because the school was unfurnished. When he did begin, it was without stoves or windows in a building made of "rived slabs, or rails made thin." Both walls and floor were generously supplied with cracks. By October he closed the school in order to have walls lined for more warmth, but had caught cold before he reopened. By Christmas he had an old "broken down" stove in the school room, but was still without heat in his own room, and his books and clothes and bedding shipped—he supposed—long since had not yet arrived.[140]

He taught day and night schools and a Sabbath school as well. Religious excitement compelled him to close the school for two months in February, which time he spent in visiting the families. The news of the capture of Richmond and Lee's surrender was received with jubilation by everyone.[141]

Hillery continued teaching at the Whiting Plantation until June 30, 1865, after which he toured the schools and churches of the area before returning home to New York State. Asked to give his observations on the people among whom he had worked, Hillery admitted that they were different and that only truly dedicated teachers and missionaries would be successful. He thought that black teachers had the greatest chance of working successfully without frustration. The religion of the freedmen was a problem: "The most prominent embarrassments to be met is their peculiar notion of God & Religion, with their odd and cruel right of the Husband and Father."

He thought the Association was missing an opportunity by closing schools for the long summer. This was an observation made by many of the missionaries, white and black. After the crops were planted, there were two months of comparative idleness—when the children might well be in school. But there were good reasons why the Association usually closed schools in the summer. Cholera and yellow fever were often raging plagues during those months, and children were more often than not called from school during the growing months—at least in the rice-growing areas—to keep the birds from the fields. In addition, northern teachers needed rest and relief from the oppressive heat of the southern summer.

Although George Whipple thought that Hillery had done good work at Whiting Plantation (where the latter had been both teacher and spiritual leader in addition to managing the accounts of the farm and distributing rations), the Association did not intend to continue work there and hesitated too long before making another assignment. Hillery accepted work in East Tennessee under the auspices of the AMEZ Church for the next two years. He regretted the misunderstanding, having desired to continue under the AMA. He therefore offered to teach a school for the Association in the vicinity of the Greenville, Tennessee, church he served.

In 1867 after nearly four years of preaching, more than half of the time in the South, Hillery was more impressed than ever with the desirability of an educated ministry. He had had to work so hard at his position among the freedmen that he had had little time even for private study. Hearing that the AMA had twenty scholarships for theological study at Oberlin, he applied for one. But the Association grants did not cover all expenses. Although Hillery received a favorable reply from George Whipple, he may not have been able to accept it; he wrote that he would forego Oberlin for another year if the Association would return him to Whiting Plantation, where the people asked for his return.[142]

NOTES

1. (Lockwood 1863, 53); General Wool, who replaced Butler at Fortress Monroe, preferred "vagrant" to "contraband." *AM*, VI (January, 1862), 17. Evidence points to Lewis Tappan as the author of the Appendix to Lockwood's rather pathetic pamphlet. Pages 53 through 64 are in Tappan's style, and were obviously added to explain the background of Mary Peake's work. Fortress Monroe, on the north entrance to the James River, was considered too strong to be attacked by Confederate forces.

2. (Lockwood 1863, 24-25).

3. General Butler, Headquarters, Department of Virginia, Fortress Monroe, Virginia, August 10, 1861, to Tappan, AMAA.

4. (Lockwood 1863, 16, 24-26).

5. Word had been sent to the New York YMCA by Chaplain P. Franklin Jones, 1st Regiment, New York Volunteers, stationed at Camp Butler, Newport News, Virginia. See the *SAM* (October 1, 1861), 241-243.

6. Lockwood sent the words and music to New York, where they were published by Horace Waters, see *AM*, VI (January, 1862), 12.

7. *SAM* (October 1, 1861), 243-244.

8. *AM*, V (December, 1861), 294.

9. *AM*, V (November, 1861), 259-262.

10. *SAM* (October 1, 1861), 244.

11. A regular primer was used to teach beginners. The teachers also used *The Freedman* and the *Freedmen's Journal*, published by the American Tract Society as well as Sunday school lessons like the *Pilgrim Series* of the Congregational churches. For information about *The Freedman*, see *AM*, VIII (January, 1864), 17.

12. (Lockwood 1863, 5, 14)

13. This was not the first school among black children in the South, of course. In 1852, Mrs. Margaret Douglass had instructed free black children in Norfolk. She was fined and imprisoned for that act of courage. See *AM*, V (December, 1861), 287.

14. *AM*, V (November, 1861), 257,259.

15. *AM*, V (December, 1861), 288-289.

16. Lockwood, Fortress Monroe, January 4, 1862, AMAA.

17. Peake, Fortress Monroe, January n.d., 1862, to Jocelyn, AMAA.

18. (Lockwood 1863, 40).

19. Hyde, Fortress Monroe, February 28, 1862, to Whiting, AMAA.

20. Lockwood, Fortress Monroe, March 6, 1862, AMAA.

21. Letter from Dr. Browne copied in Lockwood, Fortress Monroe, March 8, 1862, AMAA.

22. *AM*, VI (July, 1862), 147.

23. Lockwood, February 27, 1862, AMAA.

24. *SAM* (October 1, 1861), 248.

25. *AM*, VI (January, 1862), 14-17; (February, 1862), 30-32.

26. *SAM*, (October 1, 1861), 249.

27. *AM*, V (November, 1861), 256, 258.

28. Lockwood, December 23, 1861, AMAA.

29. *AM*, V (November, 1861), 259-259.

30. *AM*, VI (August, 1862), 180. Lockwood named Captain Tallmadge and Taylor and a Sergeant Smith as three army men who worked against the interests of the freedmen.

31. Lockwood, January 3, 1862; January 6, 1862, to the Executive Committee, AMAA; *AM,* VI (February, 1862), 30-32.

32. Whipple, Washington, D.C., March 10, 1862, to Jocelyn; March 11, 1862, to Tappan and Jocelyn, AMAA; *Sixteenth Annual Report* (1862), 40. See also CBW.

33. Lockwood, March 11, 1862, AMAA.

34. Lockwood, March 12, 1862; February 11, 1862, AMAA.

35. Lockwood, March 18, 1862, AMAA.

36. Lockwood, April 12, 1862; Tyler House, East Hampton, April 18, 1862, to the Executive Committee, AMAA.

37. Lockwood, Tyler House, April 28, 1862, AMAA.

38. Oliver, Boston, Massachusetts, February 5, 1862, to Coan, AMAA.

39. L.A. Grimes, Boston, Massachusetts, May 3, 1862, Testimonial for John Oliver; Coan, Boston, May 3, 1862, to Jocelyn, AMAA.

40. Oliver, Newport News, June 2, 1862, to Jocelyn, AMAA.

41. Oliver, Newport News, July 6, 1862, to Jocelyn, AMAA; *AM*, VI (August, 1862), 184; *Sixteenth Annual Report* (1862), 43.

42. Oliver, August 5, 1862; July 27, 1862, to Jocelyn, AMAA.

43. Cook, September 17, 1862, AMAA.

44. A black man named Peter Cook was supported by the AMA at Yorktown: *Sixteenth Annual Report* (1862), 42; Oliver, December 19, 1862, to Jocelyn, AMAA.

45. Oliver, December 5, 1862, to Jocelyn, AMAA.

46. Oliver, December 19, 1862; January 14, 1863, to Jocelyn, AMAA.

47. Oliver, January 26, 1863, to Jocelyn, AMAA.

48. Taylor, February 24, 1863, to Jocelyn; Oliver, Portsmouth, February 28, 1863, to Jocelyn, AMAA. *AM*, VII (April, 1863), 82.

49. Wilder, Fortress Monroe, March 6, 1863; Taylor, March 5, 1863, to Jocelyn. Greely also realized the need for another man to

control the male students: Greely, March 2, 1863; March 4, 1863, to Jocelyn, AMAA.

50. Oliver, Boston, Massachusetts, May 11, 1863, to Jocelyn; Thornton K. Lathrop, Boston, June 2, 1863, to Jocelyn. Oliver's active association with the AMA would seem to have ended with his opening of the Norfolk school. He was in Philadelphia in 1863, in charge of an employment office for black persons; September 26, 1863, to Jocelyn. In April of 1865 he reminded George Whipple that he had requested a post under the AMA whenever Richmond and his native city of Petersburg should fall into Union hands. That had happened: "You know that I can open the way, and I think I have some ability for the work. I want to go South this time to stay," Boston, April 6, 1865, The last letter in the archives is one written on a trip from Richmond to Boston. He was involved in helping a group of freedmen in Goosland County erect a building for school and church purposes. He asked if the AMA would help by sending them a teacher. He recommended a black young lady named Marie H. Mundruon [sp?] for the post, Boston, October 31, 1866, to Strieby, AMAA.

51. Fairchild, Oberlin, Ohio, October 18, 1862, Testimonial for Thomas Tucker; C.H. Churchill, Oberlin, October 17, 1862, Testimonial for Thomas Tucker; Tucker, Oberlin, November 4, 1862, to Whipple, AMAA.

52. (DeBoer 1994, 32).

53. Tucker, November 27, 1862, AMAA.

54. Wilder, December 28, 1862, to Jocelyn; Day, December 1, 1862, to Whipple, AMAA.

55. Bebout, December 18, 1862, to Jocelyn, AMAA.

56. Tucker, December 24, 1862, to Jocelyn, AMAA.

57. Tucker, January 17, 1863, to Whiting, AMAA.

58. Tucker, December 24, 1862, to Whipple, AMAA.

59. Tucker, January 31, 1863, to Jocelyn, AMAA.

60. Peake, Camp Hamilton, February 3, 1863, to Jocelyn. The opposition was led by Peake and William Thornton. At first William Davis took Day's part, but eventually he too joined the ranks. By 1865 the agitation against Day was too great to withstand further. See also Thornton, September 14, 1863, to Jocelyn; Davis, April 26, 1863, to Jocelyn; Coan, Norfolk, May 4, 1864, to Whipple (regarding the sensitivity and jealousy of Davis); Davis, Camp Hamilton, February 24, 1865; March 10, 1865, to Whipple, AMAA.

61. Day, February 12, 1863, to Jocelyn, AMAA.

62. Day, April 3, 1863, to Whiting, AMAA.

63. Wilder, April 10, 1863; Day, April 14, 1863, to Whiting; Mrs. J.N. Coan, Camp Hamilton, April 8, 1863, to Whipple, AMAA.

64. Tucker, April 15, 1863, to Jocelyn, AMAA.

65. Fairchild, Oberlin, Ohio, April 29, 1863; May 18, 1863; July 14, 1863; September 12, 1863, to Whipple, AMAA.

66. Tucker, Oberlin, Ohio, October 5, 1863, to Whipple, AMAA.

67. Day, April 27, 1863, to Whipple, AMAA.

68. Tucker, Oberlin, Ohio, May 8, 1864, to Tappan, AMAA.

69. Tucker, Oberlin, Ohio, June 5, 1864, to Tappan, AMAA.

70. Tucker, Oberlin, Ohio, September 7, 1864, to Whipple, AMAA.

71. Fairchild, Oberlin, Ohio, July 4, 1865, to Whipple, AMAA. In 1863 Tucker had received $50 from the AMA and $25 from the

Ohio Congregational Education Fund; in 1864, $50 from the AMA; the balance he paid himself.

72. (DeBoer 1994, 124-130, 136).

73. Tucker, Oberlin, Ohio, July 15, 1865, to Whipple, AMAA.

74. Copy: *Hall of Fame Honorees, Florida Agricultural and Mechanical University*, AMAA. Tucker enrolled in Straight University's Law Department (an AMA-founded school) in 1871 and graduated in 1882: Copy: from a letter of Horace Mann Bond, Dean of the School of Education, Atlanta University, November 10, 1962, to Dr. Anna Arnold Hedgeman, Consultant, United Church Board for Homeland Ministries, AMAA.

(Ferris 1913, 777-778) states that Tucker's performance at Florida State Normal College did not live up to expectations and the real burden of administration fell on the shoulders of the vice president, Thomas Gibbs, son of Jonathan Gibbs. After the death of Professor Gibbs, the college "went to pieces" under Tucker, said Ferris. Tucker was replaced by Nathaniel Young, another Oberlin graduate (as were both Gibbs and Tucker).

75. *AM*, VII (March, 1863), 58.

76. Circular, "Sale of Confiscated Real Estate at the South," (New York, January 14, 1865); New York *Tribune*, January 16, 1865; New York *Independent*, January 19, 1865.

77. Beals, March 20, 1864, in *AM*, VIII (May, 1864), 125.

78. *AM*, VIII (July, 1864), 172; *Independent*, June 9, 1864.

79. Beals, Taylor Farm, May 16, 1864; June 21, 1864, AMAA; *AM*, VIII (August, 1864), 187-188.

80. *Eighteenth Annual Report* (1864), 26.

81. Harris, Norfolk, March 30, 1864, to Whipple, AMAA.

82. Harris, April 9, 1864; Oberlin, Ohio, May 24, 1864; January 30, 1865; April 10, 1865, to Whipple; June 24, 1864; February 13, 1865, to Strieby, AMAA. Her next place of service for the AMA was Natchez, Mississippi.

83. Bassette, April 30, 1864, to Woodbury; Bassette and others, Teacher's Monthly Report, Bute Street Primary School, April, 1864, AMAA.

84. Daffin, March 14, 1864; March 30, 1864, to Whipple; Woodbury, March 17, 1864, to Whipple; Daffin, Teacher's Monthly Report, Fenchurch Street Graded School No.4, April, 1864; June, 1864; Daffin, April n.d., 1864; July 4, 1864; July 20, 1864, to Whipple, AMAA.

85. Daffin, August 1, 1864, to Whipple; Teacher's Monthly Report, July, 1864, AMAA.

86. Daffin, September 7, 1864; September 1, 1864, to Whiting; August 29, 1864, to Woodbury; Teacher's Monthly Report, August, September, 1864, AMAA; *AM,* VIII (October, 1864), 259.

87. Daffin, October 29, 1864, to Whipple, AMAA.

88. Daffin, December 2, 1864, to Whipple, AMAA.

89. Daffin, December 18, 1864, to Whipple, AMAA. Daffin was probably referring to Mrs. J.M. Brown, the matron of the Mission Home in which she boarded.

90. Daffin, December 24, 1864; January 1, 1865, to Whipple; see also William D. Harris, Portsmouth, July n.d.; August 10, 1864, to Whipple, AMAA.

91. Daffin, February 20, 1865, to Whipple, AMAA.

92. Daffin, March 1, 1865, to Whipple, AMAA.

93. (DeBoer 1994, 160-183).

94. Highgate, Binghamton, New York, January 18, 1864, Testimonial for Edmonia Highgate, AMAA.

95. D.H. Cruttenden, Binghamton, New York, January 26, 1864, Testimonial for Edmonia Highgate, AMAA.

96. Highgate, Binghamton, January 22, 1864, to Ira H. Cobb; Strieby, Syracuse, January 27, 1864, to Jocelyn, AMAA.

97. Highgate, Binghamton, January 30, 1864; February 17, 1864, to Jocelyn; Syracuse, March 19, 1864, to Whipple, AMAA. Because her school ended March 18th, she supposed it would be too late to go south until the fall. If so, could she act as AMA collecting agent, raising money and clothing for the freedmen meanwhile? She had done so for the NFRA of New York City the year before. They had paid her $1.00 a day plus expenses, and she had sent them $155 clear in 6 weeks.

98. Highgate, Norfolk, March 30, 1864, to Whipple, AMAA.

99. For Loguen's earlier associations with the AMA see (DeBoer 1994, 16, 58, 92, 208, 217-220).

100. Loguen, Syracuse, May 9, 1864, in *Wesleyan*, and reprinted in *AM*, VIII (July, 1864), 175-176.

101. Patten, Ferry Point, April 29, 1864, to Whiting; King, Ferry Point, April 30, 1864, to Whipple and Strieby, AMAA.

102. Highgate, Portsmouth, April 30, 1864, to Whipple, AMAA.

103. Highgate, May 19, 1864, to Strieby, AMAA.

104. Highgate, June 1, 1864, to Whipple, AMAA.

105. See Highgate letters: October, 1864, to February, 1865; also N. Goodell, November 21, 1864, AMAA. Her next place of service was Darlington, Maryland.

106. Duncan, Oberlin, Ohio, February 24, 1864; March 1, 1864; March 9, 1864, to Whipple; Mrs. M.P. Dascomb, Oberlin, March 2, 1864, to Whipple, AMAA.

107. Walker, March 28, 1864; Duncan, March 30, 1864, to Whipple, AMAA; *AM*, VIII (May, 1864), 123-124.

108. Duncan, June 1, 1864, to Woodbury; Teacher's Monthly Report, Primary School, Carpenter's Shop, Bute Street, May, 1864, AMAA; *AM*, VIII (August, 1864), 188.

109. Brown, Baltimore, Maryland, May 1, 1864, to Whipple; Norfolk, September 18, 1864, to Whipple and Strieby; Sisson, Portsmouth, March 7, 1864, to Whipple, AMAA. See also articles from the *Repository of Religion and Literature*, cited in *AM*, VI (February, 1862), 38; VIII (March, 1864), 56-57.

110. Duncan, July 1, 1864, to Whipple; Teacher's Monthly Report, June; August 1, 1864, to Whipple; August 29, 1864, to W.H. Woodbury, AMAA; *AM*, VIII (October, 1864), 233-234. Her complaints must have been made in regard to Mrs. J.M. Brown, who was matron of Mission Home No. 3 where Duncan lived.

111. Duncan, October 2, 1864; October 17, 1864, to Whipple; Harris, Portsmouth, October 4, 1864, to Whipple; February 2, 1865, AMAA. Duncan made her home with Mrs. Mary O'Solimon in Pittsfield.

112. Duncan, December 8, 1864; February 1, 1865; February 9, 1865, to Whipple; February 3, 1865, to Strieby, AMAA.

113. Duncan, February 22, 1865; February 9, 1865; April 1, 1865, to Whipple; March 2, 1865, to Strieby; March 29, 1865; June 9, 1865, to Whiting; Oberlin, Ohio, June 9, 1865, to Strieby, AMAA.

114. Tucker, Cleveland, Ohio, February 22, 1864, to Whipple, AMAA.

115. Stanley, Teacher's First Class Certificate, Brown County, Ohio; Cleveland, Ohio, January 19, 1864; March 14, 1864, to Whipple; J.A.Thome, Cleveland, Ohio, March 3, 1864, to Whipple; George H. Wyman, Cleveland, Ohio, March 3, 1864, to Whipple; Moses A. Hoge, Cleveland, Ohio, February 29, 1864, Testimonial for Sara G. Stanley; A. Crooks, Cleveland, March 7, 1864, to Whipple; Stanley, April 28, 1864, to Whipple, AMAA.

116. Patten, May 14, 1864; June 6, 1864, to Whipple, AMAA.

117. Stanley, July 21, 1864, to Woodbury, with note added by Edmonia G. Highgate; August 29, 1864, to Woodbury, AMAA.

118. Stanley, October n.d., 1864; October 6, 1864, to Whipple; see also Fannie Gleason, November 6, 1868, AMAA.

119. Stanley, October 6, 1864, to Whipple, AMAA.

120. Stanley, New York, January 26, 1865, to Whipple; Harris, February 2, 1865, AMAA.

121. Martin, Oxford, Pennsylvania, November 11, 1863, to Whipple; Morris, Baxter Farm No. 1, February 24, 1864, to Whiting; March 12, 1864, to Whipple; March 28, 1864, to Woodbury; April 15, 1864, to Whipple; April 18, 1864, to Woodbury; May 2, 1864, to Whiting; May 2, 1864, to Whipple; Teacher's Monthly Report, May, 1864; Woodbury, March 29; April 8, 1864; to Whipple, AMAA.

122. Morris, 24 Bible House, New York, April 22, 1865, to Whipple, AMAA. The address might mean that Morris was working for the ACS.

123. Harris, Brooklyn, New York, February 13, 1864, AMAA. Harris was born June 6, 1827, and was married, with four children.

124. Harris, March 1, 1864, to Whipple, AMAA.

125. Harris, April 1, 1864, to Woodbury; April 30, 1864, to Whipple; Teacher's Monthly Report, Gosport Navy Yard School in Portsmouth, April, 1864, AMAA.

126. Harris, July, 1864, to Whipple, See also Harris, May 4; May 31; June 30; July 1, 1864, to Whipple; Sisson, March 7, 1864, to Whipple; Mars, July 1; July 29, 1864, to Whipple, AMAA; *AM*, VIII (July, 1864), 173-174; (October, 1864), 235.

127. Harris, October 4, 1864, to Whipple; see also July n.d.; August 10, 1864, to Whipple, AMAA; *AM*, VIII (September, 1864), 212.

128. Harris, August 10; December 3, 1864, to Whipple; March 6, 1865, to Whiting; Kellogg, October 29, 1864, to Whipple, AMAA.

129. Harris, February 1, 1865, to Whipple, AMAA.

130. Harris, April 6, 1865, to Whipple, AMAA.

131. Harris, May 1, 1865, to Whipple, AMAA.

132. Harris, letters May through June, 1865, AMAA.

133. Robert W. Harris, Cleveland, Ohio, August 26, 1864, to Whipple; September 2; September 19, 1864, to Strieby, AMAA.

134. Harris, Cleveland, Ohio, September 30; October 10; October 15, 1864, to Strieby, AMAA.

135. Harris, November 29; December 29, 1864; February 3, 1865, to Whipple. The pastor of Providence Church was James Tynes: Brown, October 27, 1864, to Whipple, AMAA.

137. Harris, Providence Church, near Norfolk, April 1, 1865; April 29, 1865, to Whipple, AMAA.

138. See the letters of Robert Harris, June through October, 1865, AMAA.

139. (Smith 1922, 104, 109). In 1872, Hillery was secretary of the Eleventh General Conference of the AMEZ Church at Charlotte, North Carolina, at which Robert Harris was the recording secretary, and by which J.W. Hood, J.J. Clinton, S.D. Talbot, J.J. Moore, S.T. Jones, and J.W. Loguen were elected bishops.

140. Hillery, New York, May 11; August 14, 1864, to Whipple. Hillery was 21 in 1864, married, with no children. His salary was $18 per month, plus rations. Ten dollars of his pay went to his wife Susanna at Caroline Depot, Tompkins County, New York. Hillery, Downey's Farm, September 6, 1864; Whiting's Plantation, October 4, 1864, to Whipple; Teacher's Monthly Report, Whiting Plantation School, Elizabeth County, October, 1864; Whiting Plantation, October 21; November 4, 1864, to Whipple; March 2; May 29, 1865, to Whiting, AMAA.140.

141. Hillery, letters for 1865, AMAA.

142. Hillery, letters for August, 1865 through September, 1867, AMAA.

III

TEACHERS ELSEWHERE IN THE SOUTH

Sir: I have a great desire to go and labor among the Freed-men of the South. I think it is our duty as a people to spend our lives in trying to elevate our own race. Who can feel for us if we do not feel for ourselves? And who can feel the sympathy that we can who are identified with them? I should like to go, as soon as possible: for I feel as though there is much work to be done, and I would like to do my share. I would have gone upon my own responsibility but I am not able. And the times being so unsettled, I thought it would be safer for me to be employed by some Society. Then, I shall not be troubled about my livelihood for it cramps ones energies to have to think about the means of living. . . . I teach the common English branches. . . . I shall be ready to leave Newport as soon as I can settle my present business. I have a Select School, but I believe I can do more good among the Freedmen.

—Mrs. E. Garrison Jackson, 1863,
AMAA

South Carolina

The second area of work in the slave states made possible by the Civil War was South Carolina. During the winter of 1861 aid in the form of books and school materials was given to a Methodist army chaplain, the Rev. Dr. Strickland, stationed in the Sea Islands, and a group of soldiers, plus one black man, who were teaching the people there to read.

Early in 1862 James A. McCrea (white AMA missionary) was sent to Beaufort, where he established both religious services and a school in the African Baptist Church. The Association also aided the Rev. Mansfield French with books and supplies, which were distributed among the various islands where teachers and superintendents were at work. John Conant was sent to Port Royal in June as a missionary-teacher. He joined forces with McCrea at Beaufort and established two day schools on neighboring planta-tions. In the fall of 1862 the Association sent two more teachers to Beaufort and two others to Hilton Head.[1] The Association missionaries in the Beaufort area were referred to as "Gideonites," and one of them expressed the hope that they might prove worthy of the name.[2]

Chaplain Mansfield French gave the AMA a description of the former slaves at work on the plantation near Beaufort where he was involved in a project of setting up a "model" cabin on each plantation. Each cabin was to have a four-paned window, a table for family meals, a mirror to encourage neatness. Materials were to be provided the women for making bed ticks and pillows. Sheets, towels, and soap were to be provided. French had the pleasure of baptizing five children, three of whom belonged to the families who had left Charleston on the *Planter*. One was Robert Anderson, the infant son of Robert and Hannah Smalls.[3]

The first black worker in South Carolina to receive monetary aid from the Association was "Uncle" Cyrus White, who taught gratuitously at St. Helena Village for seven months beginning in the fall of 1863 before one of the missionaries suggested that he receive some small remuneration for all the help that he had been to the school there.[4]

The Rev. William T. Richardson was the Superintendent in charge of AMA work in the islands of South Carolina and Georgia in 1865. There were 26 schools and 34 teachers in his jurisdiction and some 2,060 students, 700 of whom were adults.[5]

Mr. E.H. Freeman, a black resident of Newark, New Jersey, taught a school on Cane Island, South Carolina. At the end of the school year, Superintendent Richardson thought Freeman had done well and would make a good minister if he had the opportuni-ty to study theology.[6] The Rev. Theophilas G. Steward, also from New Jersey, an AME minister and member of the African Civilization Society, was aided by the AMA at Beaufort.[7]

During the final weeks of the war several black missionaries and teachers from the North were added to the force of AMA workers in South Carolina: Thomas W. and Mrs. Laura J. Cardozo were sent to Charleston; Mary Still was sent to Beaufort; H.H. and

Mrs. Lizzie R. Hunter to Charleston; Paul Gustavus Barnswell and Jonathan Jasper Wright to Beaufort. Because most of this work began after the surrender at Appomattox, their accounts are included below in the Reconstruction section of this book.

Washington, D.C.

AMA work began in Washington, D.C., in May, 1862, when the Rev. Danforth B. Nichols (white) went there as a missionary. At the suggestion of H. Hamlin of the United States Treasury Department and vice president of the National Freedmen's Relief Association (NFRA) at Washington, Nichols was soon appointed Superintendent of Contrabands in the District by General James S. Wadsworth, military governor. Nichols reported that there were eleven thousand resident free African American persons and some twelve hundred or more refugees from the slave states. The number could not be definitely given, for the population was in a very transitory state. Many arrived destitute; and although most of the men could find work with the government, there was great need of help for the women, children, and the ill. Of the latter there were many, and the mortality rate in the miserable hospital facilities was high. Nichols praised the work of the NFRA at Washington for the hospital it had established, and said that both the NFRA and the American Tract Society of New York were doing admirable work in the field of education in Washington.

Nichols was enabled to move the contrabands from the crowded quarters at "Duff Greens Row" to a much more healthy location in the suburbs—the military barracks at Twelfth Street and Vermont Avenue, formerly occupied by Captain Barker of the George Brinton McClellan Dragoons. A new well provided "an abundance of good cold water," but many of the refugees were preyed on by "land sharks ... politely called hackmen," who charged them eight dollars to transport them to the new location.

Arrivals who were able-bodied, including women with no more than one child to care for, were placed almost as soon as they arrived. Before emancipation in the District, many of the servants there were supplied from Maryland. Emancipation having cut off that supply, there was a great demand for domestic help. A school was built at the camp and a laundry, in which women who could not otherwise pay their way might find employment. Nichols found most of the refugees anxious to work and help in whatever way they could—there were very few "shirks" among them.[8]

Perhaps the most disturbing experience that Nichols had in those early days among the black people of Washington happened on a sightseeing tour he took with a friend. For the first time he saw his country's capital through the eyes of a black man, and the experience made him heartsick.

> One would hardly believe after having visited the different rooms at the Capitol beholding the beautiful and suggestive specimens of sculpture & reading the appropriate mottoes... both speaking of equal rights and equal privileges, that a practice so hostile to teaching prevailed but so it is, and for those who know how to *reconcile* the *irreconcilable* we leave this subject to dispose of as best they can.
>
> I called on a brother beloved in the ministry of reconciliation this morning to go with me and show me some of the things which as yet I had not seen about the Capitol. This brother was well-dressed, and acted the part of a perfect gentleman, not differing from the so called gentility as far as I could judge in any particular, he was a good Latin, Greek and Hebrew scholar, and even conformed to the ways of the world more than myself ... and yet with all his conformity to those so called conventional rules of genteel life, he failed to be popular he was shunned by the masses he even had to go into the Representative Hall by a side door ... passing from the Rotunda several voices dressed in Uniform too called out "*a nigger has no right here*" no nor no where else according to the same class. Oh how that word of taunt sent the dagger to his heart. I endeavored to turn it off by explaining certain emblems in the old Representative Hall. Oh how my heart bled for him. No wonder then my brother that you desired me to take another street rather than the Pa. Av. upon leaving the capitol. Now who will not say that to act thus towards one whose skin is but one shade darker than the white mans, is evil and ridiculous as *cowardly & unchristian*. But there is comfort in the truth which comes from the Proverb: "Every dog has his day." What is down now will be up after a time. Only wait and the lower strata of the earth will come to the surface. Time will make all things right to him that can wait. Then black man pray on & hope on and clouds and darkness will give place to sunshine.[9]

Rachel G.C. Patten and Mary Jane Doxey (both white) went to work in the Contraband Camp as AMA missionaries in the summer of 1862. Their reports gave the distaff view of the situation there, which often differed sharply from Nichol's observations. For Christmas Day, 1862, Mrs. Abraham Lincoln presented the refugees in Washington with a gift of "forty-five turkeys, apples, cranberries and other good things." There was a feast prepared for all the camp, with toys for the children. Rachel Patten wanted the Executive Committee to be sure to include Mary Lincoln's benevolence in the *American Missionary*, so that she could send a copy to the White House. Her object was to induce Mrs. Lincoln—who was, Patten thought, "a true union Lady and no secesh as was reported in the North"—to do more for the refugees. Mrs. Lincoln had promised to visit the camp, but the small-pox there kept visitors away. It was a virulent epidemic, one-fourth of the nearly four hundred cases had died. Even two of Nichol's children were ill with it.

Another great day of celebration was Emancipation Day, January 1. Just as the missionaries were distributing special treats of food and toys, the news came. There was a great tumult, the people shouting, "We are no more slaves! No more contrabands!"

Two of Washington's leading African American women had been of great help to the AMA missionaries: Mrs. Elizabeth Keckley, Mrs. Lincoln's dressmaker, and Mrs. William Slade, wife of the black clerk of the Treasury Department. Patten said that both women, active workers among the poor and oppressed, deserved the thanks of the Association.

It was small wonder that so many died, housed as they were in tents without adequate protection from the cold. Patten and Doxey had boarded until mid-December with the family of Dr. Lorenzo D. Johnson, surgeon at Lincoln Hospital, but could stay there no longer when the Johnsons needed their room. They moved then to the building where they dispensed clothing at the camp. It was "more like a very common stable" than a house, through whose generous cracks the wind whistled. But the missionaries at least had an adequate supply of blankets, and they felt guilty that such was not the case for the people in the tent hospital.

Rachel Patten visited all the small-pox cases in the camp as well as some outside. Many were ill with other diseases also. While

Mary Jane Doxey was occupied distributing food and clothing and jobs, Patten walked in "shoe deep" mud, caring for the sick. When she thought of the work they did and saw the way they lived, she realized that no one could have forced her and Doxey to do what they did. Dr. Johnson had told them that he thought God had sent them. Patten's reply was that if He had not, then they wanted to return "as soon as possible."

During a terrible storm the roof of the men's hospital collapsed. Some of the dying men could not be moved even then. One was the former slave and namesake of Colonel John Washington of Harper's Ferry, and though he spoke well of his master, he loved freedom more. After he died Rachel Patten expressed the wish that his master might some day meet him in heaven, but believed that entry there for the master would be less assured than it had been for the slave.[10]

Dr. Lorenzo Johnson, surgeon of Lincoln Hospital and member of the executive committee of the NFRA, had interested himself in the education of the black people in the area. Since emancipation he had been unable to prod into action the commissioners appointed to do something about educating the colored people of the capital. Their excuse was that they were waiting for the mayor to act. Johnson said that the truth lay in the fact that it was "an uphill, unpopular work to educate colored people, slaves or free, South of Masons & Dixons Line." Myrtilla Miner had opened a school some years before [in 1851] and had succeeded in earning "the confidence and the patronage of the *aristocracy* among the colored people—(for *we* have our Fifth Avenue Colored people, as well as *you* white folks)."[11] But Miner had charged a high tuition; so few could afford to attend her school. Then her health had broken down and she left, but not before trying to raise money for an academy or high school for girls. Harriet Beecher Stowe gave a thousand dollars to the fund, but all that had been done was the purchase of property (which was in the hands of trustees) and an act of incorporation.

The educational advantages for African Americans in the capital were few and poor, wrote Johnson. There were Sabbath schools and "pay schools such as they are, conducted by the Colored people." And "the 'Am. Tract Society' as if to redeem it from the imputation which attaches to them, of not doing as much as they might for the colored race, sent some rather pugnacious young men" to Washington, "to educate all our 'contrabands.'" The men had been mostly Princeton students, who began more schools than they could handle, and all of which had since been closed. Johnson had taken charge of one such school. At about that time the NFRA was organized, and Johnson was on its education committee. The principal teacher in the school of about fifty pupils was Lizzie Smith (black). Dr. Johnson and Miss Smith continued to teach two night schools for a time also. They made theirs "a true missionary school," inviting all to come whenever they could, regardless of age or sect, in the hope that all those kept from education in slavery might at least "be able to read the Word of God and thus learn of Christ."

Dr. Johnson's time was so completely taken up by his work at the hospital that he had very little opportunity to visit the day school and had just stopped the evening sessions. In all he guessed that some five hundred different persons had been given primary books and "more or less instruction." "We have taught old ladies looking through their glasses with their grandchildren to read. A mother came with her babe and held it in her lap, while learning her alphabet." He had "tried to create the conviction that Education *must* follow Emancipation."

The present opportunity that was slipping away concerned Dr. Johnson. All the schools like Miss Miner's that would *someday* be built would not answer the current need. The black community needed a school for all ages, one open at night as well as in the day so that working people could attend. "We want what might be, with great propriety termed a free Colored Mission School—with the understanding that if they *will come* they *may*, without money or price—there to find the books and the blackboard." If they could pay, then they should. And it was Johnson's experience that they would.

He asked the AMA to undertake just such a mission school. Lizzie Smith—"a remarkable girl," who had taught black children "the rudiments of learning" for several years—owned a two-story house on a large lot that would serve for such a school. It was in a good locality, and Smith (who taught a small pay school in her father's house) would lease it for less than they could rent else-where. The NFRA was unable to undertake the project. If the

AMA would underwrite it, he thought that the Misses Patten and Doxey might serve as its teachers.[12]

The Association was favorably impressed by Dr. Johnson's proposal. In 1864 the AMA had a school in operation at Lincoln Hospital, taught by Laurie Gates. The next year it was described in a local paper as having been provided with a "comfortable school room" by Dr. Lorenzo D. Johnson.[13] Such were the beginnings of the Lincoln Industrial Institute, not officially established until the days of Reconstruction, but built upon the work begun around Lincoln Hospital by Dr. Johnson and Lizzie Smith.

Dr. Johnson had also alerted AMA missionary Isaac Cross to a virgin field for his endeavors in Washington, D.C. Associated with every hospital in the District were about fifty black workers—washerwomen, ditch diggers, teamsters, etc. No one seemed interested in the spiritual or educational welfare of those people. Johnson suggested that Simeon S. Jocelyn bring along for them from one to three hundred primers when he came to Washington to investigate Johnson's school proposal.[14]

In 1864 the AMA had aided 16 missionaries and teachers in the Washington area and was operating 7 schools with over 700 pupils. The longest established of those schools was that of Mr. and Mrs. William J. Wilson (black) at Camp Barker. It had a student body of more than 200 and was held in a building purchased from the American Tract Society.

William J. Wilson had been born in slavery on a southern plantation, but had been principal of Public School No. 1 for colored children in Brooklyn, New York, for about twenty years when he resigned in 1863. He had had opposition from several sources, all of it—according to James McCune Smith, who recommended him to the AMA—unjustified. About ten years before his resignation, Wilson had become a correspondent for *Frederick Douglass' Paper*, using his pen name "Ethiop." Wilson's pastor had complained to the school board that Wilson was neglecting his pupils by spending his time writing. A Mr. Cardozo from South Carolina, whom Wilson had befriended, had worked against him, collecting signatures from parents.

Wilson had also made some strong antislavery speeches at Cooper Institute during the winter of 1862-1863 which "excited the wrath of a Copperhead-Celtic member of the local Board of

Education," who vowed to remove Wilson from his school and place his own nephew there instead. The case was referred to the local board by the school board of the city. Wilson's removal was voted at an illegal session of the local board during the absence of the president (Wilson's friend). Before the city board acted, Wilson resigned.[15]

He went on an exploratory visit among the schools for freedmen in the Washington area and consulted with the education committee of the NFRA at Washington for whom he contracted to teach one of their schools temporarily and applied for a commission in an AMA school. His wife was also employed in another of the NFRA schools; their daughter was with them, and they all wished to work together. Wilson was happy to find Henry H. Garnet in Washington, a man who would be "invaluable to us all."[16]

Appointed to the school at Camp Barker, Wilson applied for a position for his daughter there as well.[17] School began Monday, June 27, 1864, with 72 pupils; on Tuesday there were 125, and by Friday 150. The condition of the buildings was deplorable, and Wilson found it impossible to imagine how his predecessor had managed without a privy or how the children could be taught "the principles of *morality & religion* or even *self respect*" if such matters were not attended to. There was no equipment save an empty building at Twelfth Street, sadly in need of whitewash, a few broken seats and blackboards. There was also reason to complain about salary. His was fifty dollars per month, his wife's twenty. Their board cost forty dollars, leaving only thirty dollars of wages for all other expenses.[18]

James B. Johnson (white), a clerk in the Quartermaster General's Office, had kept up the Sabbath school and evening school at Camp Barker Chapel in the time between the departure of the American Tract Society and the arrival of the AMA missionaries with the help of the Association of Volunteer Teachers for Colored Schools. The Boston Tract Society had supplied the school with copies of the *Freedman*. The Sunday school averaged 150, three of his teachers came from Johnson's department; two others were from the Internal Revenue Department. Johnson thought that Wilson was doing well in the day school.[19]

The matter of the privy was a continuing problem. Without a fence it was erected only to be overturned and smashed. Books were a simpler matter. Wilson ordered Montieth's No. 2 *Geography* and the Marcus Wilson series of readers. He thought the Wilson primer especially good for beginning readers. Salary continued to be a sore point. His wife's board now cost more than she received as pay.[20]

When the school had reached more than two hundred pupils, Wilson declared it too large for his wife, Mary A.G. Wilson, himself, and their daughter, Annie. When offered white teachers temporarily, he asked for colored help. Colored teachers would prove to the freedmen that they had the ability to be elevated: "Colored people must be taught to do our own work, being assisted only by the dominant class. This is as essential as the work to be done," Wilson said. "As long as the dominant class are to fill among us the first places, even when it can be avoided & we to be regarded as minors and recipients of favors we shall be but the same helpless & dependent people, slaves."[21]

Wilson had applied to the Pennsylvania Freedmen's Relief Association (PFRA) for the post of Superintendent of their work in the Washington area before accepting the AMA school, desiring a wider sphere of influence than that offered by the schoolroom and feeling that his years of experience had prepared him for such a position as well as some white men in like offices. The time had arrived, he felt, for competent black men to be given "positions of trust and responsibility." He applied again for the job with the PFRA and received a favorable reply. But that society was on good terms with the AMA and would not consider him so long as he was employed by the Association. The AMA was "doing a good work" and the PFRA was glad of their "co-operation."[22]

Wilson was convinced that AMA Superintendent William L. Coan discriminated against his school in the matter of supplies and repairs. Since the Camp Barker School was the oldest AMA school at Washington, and in Wilson's opinion "second to no similar school" there, it should have at least "equal facilities." Wilson was also against Coan's plan to "break it up," that is, divide the school into several classes. Wilson wanted it kept together under himself as principal.[23] For his part, Coan was embarrassed in not being able to make important and expensive repairs to the Camp Barker building without authority from New York, authority which never seemed to arrive.[24]

After five months Wilson was still trying for a raise in salary, but he had received permission for pay for assistant teachers. Replying to George Whipple's statement that competent black teachers were hard to find, Wilson suggested Julia B. Landre, who was assisting them at the school as being "well qualified for an *assistant teacher.*" Landre, like Mr. and Mrs. Wilson, was a member of Henry Highland Garnet's Fifteenth Street Presbyterian Church. The daughter of a widow, she taught music, and Wilson thought her "indispensable."[25]

In January, 1865, Wilson was given a ten-dollar raise in salary. The school numbered 225 and was the largest in Washington. Wilson was proud of the fact that he and his wife had recruited that number "by our own personal efforts and influence."[26]

Landre was commissioned as a regular teacher in the spring. When it had looked as if she might give up and look elsewhere for a position, Wilson had recommended Sarah Thomas, a cousin of Dr. John H. Rapier, African American surgeon of the Freedman's Hospital.[27]

To Secretary Whipple's inquiries about their work in the Sabbath School, Wilson replied that they did none—that he and his wife did the work of four persons in the day school and many wondered how they survived as it was. In her "spare time" Mrs. Wilson recruited pupils for the school. He and his wife also taught two evenings a week for the Voluntary Freedmen's Association, for which they received ten dollars.[28]

Georgia

Savannah, Georgia, fell to the Union forces under General William Tecumseh Sherman on December 21, 1864, and within a few days an education association of colored people was organized with the help of the Rev. John Watson Alvord (white) and the Rev. James Lynch (an African American Methodist preacher originally sent out by the NFRA but now working on his own). The Rev. William T. Richardson, AMA Superintendent in South Carolina, arrived in Savannah on January 9, 1865. He approved of the organizational efforts by Alvord and Lynch and helped them as they put their school into operation on January 10 "with some five hundred scholars."

Meanwhile the Rev. Samuel W. Magill, a native of Georgia who was the AMA's agent in Connecticut, had been appointed by the AMA to establish schools in Savannah with northern teachers. He arrived on the scene in February to find that the black Education Association of nine persons had affiliated themselves with the AMA "for aid and counsel" with the approval of Richardson, expecting the AMA "to foot the bill" when the $800 they had raised was exhausted. Although none of them except Lynch could so much as read and write, and none had experience in managing a school, all four buildings in Savannah appropriate for schools had been turned over to them, and they had been given the power to determine curriculum and hire teachers.

Magill wrote of his fears engendered by the segregated, exclusively black nature of the Education Association. Shortly thereafter he was asked by General Rufus Saxton to serve as director of education for the city. He faced a situation in which fifteen unqualified black teachers had been appointed by the Education Association and would need to be replaced. Teachers he had secured could not be brought to Savannah because no place could be found for them to stay. Nevertheless he did secure one building from the Association and began a school of his own there. By the end of the first week he had 150 children and 70 adults enrolled, and simultaneously the Association asked him to take over the direction of their schools. He promised to do so as soon as possible, but expected trouble from the "Catos." "Leading men among the negroes, especially their preachers are jealous of their honors & influence and as they have started on the principle of managing things themselves & admitting their white friends only to inferior places," he thought it would be difficult to change things.[29]

The winter was a severe one, and many of the freedmen were among the greatest sufferers from Sherman's liberating—but literally devastating—march to the sea.[30] Refugees housed in the school chapel at Beaufort, South Carolina, died at the rate of three or four a day. Many were without food or fire or clothing to protect themselves from disease and cold.[31]

The first black AMA worker, the Rev. Hardy Mobly, arrived in Savannah in April, 1865.[32]

Maryland

Two African American teachers were at work for the AMA in Maryland while the Civil War was still in progress. Edmonia G. Highgate, who had worked for the AMA in Virginia, organized a school for the Association at Darlington, Maryland, having told the men at the Rooms in advance that she intended to get the school started, supply it with a competent teacher, and then resign. She felt that the work of educating the freedmen was the responsibility of African Americans in so far as possible, and when black persons were capable, they should have positions of the first rank. It was not her place simply to teach a school of fifty children, especially since she had an offer for $50 a month plus board at Richmond. Highgate appointed her mother teacher of the Darlington school without asking the permission of the Association.[33]

Mrs. E. Garrison Jackson, native of Concord, Massachusetts, began to teach an AMA school at Port Deposit, Maryland, in April, 1865. John W. Martin, African American Secretary of the Public School Committee, had applied to the Association for a teacher and described her as a noble teacher, "second to none." So pleased was he with Mrs. Jackson that he begged the AMA to send a like teacher to the black people of Delaware City, Delaware.[34]

Missouri

Sara G. Stanley was happily at work in St. Louis, Missouri, in March, 1865, and hoping to forget herself "and the poor little world within my own heart" in her work. She was more than pleased with the cordial reception the colored people of Missouri had given her in view of the fact that she had often impressed the people with whom she worked—and George Whipple as well—as being haughty. Like so many other fellow workers, Stanley found it difficult to tell George Whipple how much his kindness, his love, his fatherly counsel had meant to her.

She remembered enviously the abundance of supplies she had used in Virginia, for her present school (in an unattractive, poorly-lit church basement) was without either maps or blackboards. These aids she considered "indispensible" for illustrating the lessons; illustration was "the most effectual method of instruction, especially among minds so materialistic and untrained as the freed people's." She hoped that her rather weak disposition would bear up under work that required "an earnest unselfish spirit, strong in love for God and Humanity, and not least, a vigorous body."[35]

Kentucky

Although Kentucky did not leave the Union, slavery still existed there and its "anomalous condition . . . rendered it more difficult to labor for the colored people there than elsewhere." At Camp Nelson a large group of black persons assembled during the war, including several thousand black troops. Working among them, aided by the AMA and the Western Freedman's Aid Committee at Cincinnati, was a black preacher with some education, the Rev. Gabriel Burdett. There was much suffering at the Camp, some 43 persons dying between Christmas, 1864, and January 20th.

African Methodist Episcopal preacher Reedy was supported by the Association in Louisiana.[36]

The AMA responded to the campaigns of the war in the West by sending workers to Cairo, Illinois, and to Memphis, Tennessee, in 1862. In 1863 work was begun at St. Louis and across the river at Brooklyn, at Camp Shiloh, President Island, and in the vicinity of Corinth, Mississippi. AMA work began in North Carolina at New Bern in 1863, and in Florida in 1864. There seem to have been no African American workers at any of the above points during the Civil War, however, except for Robert Morrow at the freedmen's school at Camp Lotten, North Carolina.[37]

NOTES

1. *Sixteenth Annual Report* (1862), 44-45; *AM*, VI (April, 1862), 89.

2. Miss M.A. Wight, July 19, 1862, AMAA; *AM*, VI (September, 1862), 211.

3. French, June 23, 1862, AMAA; *AM*, VI (August, 1862), 184-185; for the story of Smalls and the *Planter*, see (Simmons 1887,165-175).

4. E.S. Williams, St. Helena Village, January 8; April 23, 1863, AMAA; *AM*, VII (April, 1863), 88-89; (June, 1863), 139; *Seventeenth Annual Report* (1863), 32, 43.

5. *Nineteenth Annual Report* (1865), 24.

6. Freeman, June 1, 1865, to Strieby; Richardson, Beaufort, June 8, 1865, to Whipple, AMAA.

7. See the chapter below dealing with the AMA and its relations with the AME Church.

8. Nichols, Washington, D.C., June 16, 1862, to Whipple, AMAA; *AM*, VI (June, 1862), 138; (September, 1862), 209-211.

9. Nichols, Washington, D.C., May 31, 1862, to Whipple, AMAA.

10. Baker, August 16, 1862, to Jocelyn; Patten, January 21, 1863, to Jocelyn, AMAA.

11. The color-blindness of the American Missionary Association makes determination of the race of its associates often difficult. Until this quotation was found, the writer was convinced that Lorenzo Johnson was white.

12. Johnson, March 12, 1863; Dr. C.B. Webster, Contraband Hospital, May 8, 1863; see also undated clipping, "From the Last Annual Report of the Freedmen's Relief Association;" Printed circular, AMAA.

13. Johnson, May 20, 1863, to Jocelyn, AMAA; *AM*, VII (November, 1863) 242; Washington *Chronicle*, June 29, 1865; *Eighteenth Annual Report* (1864), 11.

14. Johnson, May 28, 1863, to Jocelyn, AMAA.

15. *Eighteenth Annual Report* (1864), 11; James McCune Smith, New York, June 2, 1864, Testimonial for William J. Wilson; Certificates of Character for William J. Wilson, July 1864, AMAA. The Cardozo mentioned was not Francis Lewis Cardozo, but may

have been his brother Thomas or another relative. Wilson also wrote for the *Anglo-African Magazine* under the name "Ethiop."

16. Wilson, Brooklyn, New York, August n.d., 1863; March 19; April 28; June 6, 1864, to Jocelyn, AMAA. For H.H. Garnet and his work for the AMA, see (DeBoer 1994, 50-51, 59-68).

17. Wilson, June 16; June 19, 1864, to Jocelyn; Isaac Cross, Near Navy Yard, Washington, D.C., June 6, 1864, to Jocelyn, AMAA.

18. Wilson, July 4; July 19, 1864, to Whipple; Principal's Monthly Report, Camp Barker School, July, 1864, AMAA.

19. Johnson, July 18, 1864, to Whipple, AMAA. Later Johnson was treasurer of Howard university.

20. Wilson, August 6; August 27; October 1, 1864, to Whipple; October 12, 1864, to George E. Baker, AMAA.

21. Wilson, August 30, 1864, to Whipple, AMAA.

22. Wilson, October 26, 1864; copy: J.M. McKimm, Philadelphia, n.d., to W.J. Wilson; Principals's Monthly Report, Camp Barker School, October, 1864, AMAA; *Eighteenth Annual Report* (1864), 11.

23. Wilson, November 5; November 15, 1864, to Whipple, AMAA.

24. Coan, November 16, 1864, to Whipple, AMAA.

25. Wilson, December 7, 1864; January 23, 1865, to Whipple; Garnet, 1864, Testimonial for Julia B. Landre; Wilson, March 1, 1865, to Whipple, AMAA. Brooklyn *Union*, February 20, 1865. The first entry in the Register of the Fifteenth Street Presbyterian Church made by Garnet, was to record the fact that Julia B. Landre came to the church by transfer of membership from Zion Methodist Church of Boston, July 8, 1864, Records of the Session and the Church Register of the Fifteenth Street Presbyterian Church, 1841-1868, M-SC. Wilson and his wife came by letter from the Siloam Presbyterian Church of Brooklyn, New York, January 20, 1865.

Wilson, "for many years" an Elder of the Siloam Church, was affirmed a Ruling Elder (proposed by William Slade, Elder), by vote of the church, March 27, 1865.

26. Wilson, January 22, 1865, to Whipple, AMAA.

27. Landre, March 23, 1865, to Strieby; April 24; May 4, 1865, to Whipple; Wilson, March 11, 1865, to Whipple; Rapier, Freedmen's Hospital, December 28, 1864, to Whipple, AMAA.

28. See Wilson letters, March through June, 1865; Landre, June 12; July 13, 1865, to Whiting, AMAA.

29. Magill, January 28; February 3; February 16, 1865, AMAA; William T. Richardson, January 31, 1865, in *AM*, IX (March, 1865), 59; Richardson, January 10, 1865, to Whipple, AMAA.

30. Magill, January 28, 1865, AMAA.

31. Richardson, January 31, 1865, in *AM*, IX (March, 1865), 59.

32. Mobly's work for the AMA will be covered in the Reconstruction sections of this study.

33. Highgate, March 10, 1865, to Strieby; March 13; March 31, 1865, to Whiting; Teacher's Monthly Report, March, 1865; April 13, 1865, to Whipple; May 12, 1865, to Whiting; Mrs. H.F. Highgate, June 1, 1865, to Whipple, AMAA. Edmonia's brother died as a result of wounds received at the battle of Petersburg.

34. See letters of Mrs. E.G. Jackson for 1863 and 1865; of Martin for 1865 and 1869, AMAA.

35. Stanley, Cleveland, Ohio, March 1, 1865, to Whipple; St. Louis, Missouri, March 25, 1865, to Whipple, AMAA.

36. Burdett, January 20, 1865, to John G. Fee, AMAA; *Nineteenth Annual Report* (1865), 29.

37. *Seventeenth Annual Report* (1863), 42-47; *Eighteenth Annual Report* (1864), 17; see also Monthly Report of the Misses Gill, Burness, and Smith of the AMA, and Robert Morrow of the government, for February, 1864, AMAA. The school was begun by Morrow on December 4, 1863.

IV

OVERVIEW OF AMA WORK
DURING RECONSTRUCTION

We owe him the best education—in art, science and reli-
gion—which our civilization affords, and he will repay us by
intelligent toil, by cultured art, and above all, and richer than all, in
the example of a religion that is emotional, spiritual and practical.
            —*American Missionary*, XIV (March, 1870)

In fifty years the negro race will have artists, poets and
merchants in the first rank.

                —General Clinton Bower Fisk,
                    American Missionary, XI (July, 1867).

Undeniably, 1865 was a watershed year in the life of the
American Missionary Association for many reasons, some of which
(like the ending of the Civil War and the beginning of Reconstruction) it shared with the entire country. The establishment of the
Bureau of Freedmen, Refugees, and Abandoned Lands (BFRAL,
referred to hereafter as the Freedmen's Bureau), with the installa-
tion of General Oliver Otis Howard, a Congregational layman, as
its head was intimately connected with the work of the Association
at the South, as well as a national event.

There were other incidents in that memorable year that were
more limited in their national effects but of great importance for
their effects on the AMA. The Annual Report of the Association
for 1865 declared that the decision of the National Council of

for 1865 declared that the decision of the National Council of Congregational Churches made in Boston in June "had as direct a bearing upon the immediate interests of the Association as any other event" that had occurred during the year. At that meeting the decision was made to recommend to the churches the raising of $750,000 for benevolent purposes for the year, $250,000 of which would be given to the AMA for its work among the freedmen. With this decision the Congregationalists joined the Wesleyan Methodists, the Free-will Baptists, and the (Dutch) Reformed Church as the denominations *officially* recognizing the AMA as their "special instrumentality for reaching the freedmen."[1]

Another important change in 1865 was in the area of personnel. Lewis Tappan, having served gratuitously as treasurer of the AMA for nineteen years and before that as corresponding secretary of the Union Missionary Society, resigned. He pleaded advancing years as the cause. Tappan did not leave the organization, of course, and was immediately elected one of the vice presidents, but he would no longer be one of the men at the Rooms, involved in the day to day details of the work.[2] Tappan's resignation left George Whipple and Michael Epaphras Strieby as corresponding secretaries and William E. Whiting as assistant treasurer. Edgar Ketchum was elected to replace Tappan, but the detailed financial work was done by Whiting.

Still Unsectarian

The AMA had been from the beginning a New England institution, although many of its members, like Arthur and Lewis Tappan, had been transplanted from the rock-bound coast. It had always been a largely Congregational institution, although many of its members were temporarily or conveniently (or even uncomfortably) called Presbyterian because of the Plan of Union. It was only a matter of time until what was implicit would be explicit—until the people who traced their religious origins in America to Plymouth Rock would be establishing churches throughout the South like Plymouth Congregational Church in Charleston, South Carolina, and Pilgrim Congregational Church in Woodville, Georgia—both predominantly black.

Having denominationalism thrust upon them however, did not change the unsectarian nature of the AMA. Officers and members still included non-Congregationalists like vice presidents Seymour Straight (Baptist) and the Rev. Sella Martin (black Presbyterian) and General Clinton B. Fisk, a member of the executive committee (Methodist). Straight and Fisk contributed liberally to establish the institutions of higher learning named after them in New Orleans and Nashville. Unsectarianism had always characterized Congregationalism. Travelling lightly in so far as theology and ecclesiastical baggage were concerned, Congregationalism provided inclusive community churches under whose liberal banner all evangelical Christians could find a home.[3]

Expanding Religious Work

The immediate reaction of the Executive Committee of the Association to the decision of the National Council was to plan for the extension of its religious as well as its educational work among the freedmen. District secretaries and state agents were appointed as collectors for the fund. One of the agents at work in New York state was Edmonia G. Highgate, African American Congregationalist from Syracuse and former AMA teacher among the freedmen in Virginia.

In disbursing funds from the Congregational churches, the AMA planned to send out approximately three hundred teachers, "mostly ladies," who would work in night and Sunday schools in so far as possible in addition to their regular teaching. "In every group of five day-schools, a female missionary would be employed for house to house visiting, whose special province would be the teaching of "practical, everyday religion, the kind of teaching most needed by this people." In larger districts composed of about twenty schools, a minister would be sent to advise and counsel the teachers and missionaries and to organize churches. The men chosen for the latter posts must be creative and prudent, able to adapt themselves to the various conditions of life in the area in which they found themselves for the greatest good of the freedmen. "With arrangements thus adapted to this peculiar field and people, and withal thoroughly religious in all their parts, we begin at the foundation of society, and hope to impart to schools, homes, and people an elevating and Christian power."

The AMA was confident at the beginning that the southern states would eventually establish public school systems like those in the North. When that happened, the above plan would make it possible for the Association to turn over its educational work to the states, and "still have left to it a network of *religious* effort ramifying the South"[4] Although the churches established would work closely with the schools in the neighborhood, the schools would not be parochial ones inculcating denominationalism and requiring their pupils to attend Congregational churches.[5]

The special connection of the Association with Congregationalists had no effect on its unsectarian choice of teachers. It did not discriminate among the evangelical churches in selecting educational personnel. Teachers representing the following denominations were at work in the AMA schools of the South in 1865: Congregational, Methodist (Wesleyan, AME, AMEZ, etc.), Baptist (several national churches), Orthodox Friends, Reformed (Dutch) Church in America, Episcopal, and Presbyterian. And the funds committed to the AMA by the Free-will Baptists and the Wesleyan Methodists would continue to "be sacredly and impartially used according to the design of its donors."[6]

Expanding Educational Work

During Reconstruction the AMA increased its workers among the freedmen to a peak of 533 in 1870, gradually changing its emphasis from fundamentals (teaching reading and writing) to normal education (teaching black future teachers) as qualified students became available. From its beginnings the AMA had envisioned the preparation of African Americans for the Mendi Mission in Africa and the eventual education of the slaves after freedom. During Reconstruction both facets of this hope began to be realized through the products of its higher institutions in the South.[7]

In order to expedite the work, two additional branch offices were opened: in Cincinnati (the Middle Western Department) and Chicago (the Western Department). General oversight was still exercised by the New York office (which handled the Eastern Department and all other missions) and a general field agent was added to co-ordinate the work and keep the men at the Rooms informed. The Western Freedmen's Aid Society (WFAS) under Levi Coffin and others, operated out of Cincinnati and merged its work into the AMA in 1867. The AMA and the WFAS had cooperated in their endeavors before 1867 and particularly since the solicitation efforts of Levi Coffin and Sella Martin in Europe.[8]

Land and Civil Rights

The Association continued its belief in the need and the right of the freedmen to secure lands of their own. To that end it advocated the provision of homesteads for the freedmen and suggested that capitalists invest in land rather than cotton and sell to the freedmen, thus keeping them from becoming perpetual serfs[9] Although there were never enough funds to carry out even the work of education, the Association nevertheless accepted and administered monies contributed for the purchase of confiscated and abandoned southern lands for the freedmen. Consistent with its philosophy of man, however, the AMA did not believe in building segregated black rural communities any more than it sanctioned urban ghettoes. In fact, it compared unfavorably the "slow progress" of such segregated rural projects as Hilton Head and Port Royal with the "rapid advancement" of the people where the population was mixed. The Rev. Gustavus D. Pike was an AMA agent for land purchases for freedmen. He and the men in New York were convinced that black farmers would only receive just due for their labors if they owned their own land. When hired out to former slaveholders, they were all too often defrauded out of any payment for their work and were, as de facto slaves, worse off physically than before emancipation.[10]

The AMA backed the work of the National Freedmen's Savings and Trust Company as proof of the economic good sense of the freedmen. When the bank failed during the depression of the 70s, the Association realized the great loss it meant for those black persons who had entrusted it with their savings.[11]

The Fifteenth Amendment met with the whole-hearted approval of the AMA. President Grant's proclamation as well as the proclamation of Secretary of State Hamilton Fish were published in the *American Missionary.* [12] Full civil rights for African Americans had always been a part of the program of Christian abolitionists. They could see hope for such reforms only in the Republican party.

Teachers in the South feared the consequences of a national Democratic party victory. With the resurgence of local and state

Democracy it was obvious to most that the removal of the protection of the federal government would mean the removal of rights for the freedmen as well. If that were to happen, the only hope for the African American would be in his "elevation" through education and religion to a model citizenship and the recognition of that fact on the part of the white citizenry.

AMA work continued throughout Reconstruction in Jamaica, Africa, among Chinese immigrants on the West Coast, and among the Indian Americans.[13] The AMA was asked by the Department of the Interior to submit names for Indian Agents and as a result four of its former workers among that minority group were assigned areas of work. One Indian Agent, Edward Parmelee Smith, AMA General Field Agent, also served as Commissioner of Indian Affairs for two and a half years until his resignation in December, 1875.[14]

Role of Women

The Association emphasized the importance of the woman's role in family and national life in a series of articles in the *American Missionary* and gave particular note to the responsibilities of the African American women of the South. Since all the women could not be teachers, however, calls were made for experts in various industrial fields to give their services to prepare black women for industries, hospitals, etc. in the South which were hiring only white women.[15]

During Reconstruction also the Association saw fit to add a woman to the staff at the Rooms in a position other than merely clerical, and secured the services of Delia E. Emerson to act as a Corresponding Secretary and also to make extended trips through the South and report her observations on the work and suggestions about personnel.[16] This action came in recognition of the fact that letters from New York meant a great deal to the missionaries who were often "strangers in a strange land" in the South, despised by native whites as "Yankee nigger teachers," and isolated from congenial society. Such letters were so missed by former AMA teachers that they continued to write the men at the Rooms after leaving the AMA for other work.[17] But, with several hundred teachers in the South, George Whipple and the field agents could not possibly write each one a personal letter each month. Samuel

Hunt was Secretary of Education for a time in the 1870s, but he did not have Whipple's (or Jocelyn's or even Tappan's) talent for filling a worker with encouragement through the medium of a letter. Delia Emerson helped answer that need and in 1883 became the head of the newly organized Department of Women's Work of the AMA.

The Association voiced its appreciation of the importance of women, North and South, when it admitted that perhaps more space should be given to discussions of "Freedwomen" and their particular needs, rather than restricting itself to the inclusive term "Freedmen."[18]

Soon after the end of the Civil War Lewis Tappan advocated a national system of education. To arguments that such a step on the part of the federal government would be a usurpation of state and individual rights, Tappan replied that it was "the duty of every government to provide against crime, pauperism, and wretchedness," and there was no better beginning toward that end than providing for a national school system. The South was seen by the Association as neither "loyal" nor "pacific" in 1871 and the North as fooling itself when it thought that the rebellion was over. Obviously, many parts of the South were determined against establishing public schools, Texas courts having even declared such schools unconstitutional. In the face of such intransigence the AMA declared that the federal government must establish common schools "where the States neglect or refuse to maintain them." If Congress did not already have the power to establish a national school system, Lewis Tappan advised the people to provide a Congress with such power. O.O. Howard concurred in this and looked upon the proposed Bureau of Education as the natural successor of the Freedmen's Bureau. In 1872 the AMA advocated the passage of the National Education Bill with provision for federal aid to schools. The AMA also advocated an education bill to give public land for school purposes.[19]

Even without the disruption of the war, many orphans had been produced by the South's ruthless division of families under slavery. The Association established orphanages at Wilmington, North Carolina, and at Atlanta, Georgia, during Reconstruction. Arrangements were also made for some orphans to live with families in New England and the West.[20]

End of the Freedmen's Bureau

Another year of tremendous import to the work of the AMA was 1870. On July 1 of that year the aid of the Freedmen's Bureau (which had been of considerable help in renting and erecting buildings for schools) was withdrawn when Congress refused to extend its life. While individual AMA teachers and superintendents had evinced distrust of individual Bureau officers and chafed under the attenuated slowness that seems to characterize all workings of bureaucracy, the Association generally praised the accomplishments of the BFRAL and declared that the monuments the often misrepresented Bureau had built to education in the South would some day be appreciated even by white Southerners.[21] The AMA recognized the weaknesses of the Bureau both in the lack of power accorded General Howard and in the insufficiency of funds given him for the task.

> But the means at his command have been, from the first, so exceedingly limited, both in the funds needed and in the use of abandoned lands, that less has been accomplished than was expected; and, at this date, the manifold pardons granted to the rebels, their rapid re-possession of abandoned lands, and the speedy re-organization of State governments in the South, cripple alarmingly the power of the Bureau. . . .
>
> These measures of the Government, and these strides of the Southern States towards the resumption of their former power have other bearings upon the interests of the freedmen. . . . Our teachers and missionaries were warned months since, by the former slaveholders, that as soon as the military were withdrawn, no teacher of the colored people would be tolerated. These intimations are being realized.[22]

The withdrawal of Bureau aid accelerated the removal of "Freedmen's societies, once so numerous" from the field, "leaving most prominent as a great national organization, the American Missionary Association."[23]

Just how long Congress would continue the BFRAL appropriations for black schools in the face of southern resistance was always a question, and the return of the Democratic leaders of the South to Congress spelled the institution's doom. Howard, as head of the Bureau, had never felt confident in its longevity and expected President Andrew Johnson to maneuver its demise and

Howard's ouster. Johnson did cater to the demands of the southern Democrats to remove from effective posts those Bureau agents like General Rufus Saxton, who were determined to provide the freedmen with "forty acres and a mule," and tried to replace Howard with John Mercer Langston.[24]

William S. Tilden, AMA Superintendent at Washington, D.C., argued that Howard was not the best man for the position of Bureau chief—that it should have gone to an avid pre-war abolitionist, which Howard had not publicly shown himself to be. Such a remark, of course, is evidence of political naivete. It would have been politically inexpedient, to say the least, to have appointed one of the pre-war "ultraists" like Lewis Tappan or George Whipple to the post. It was rather flirting with disaster to give the post of Assistant Commissioner to General Clinton B. Fisk, who boasted that as agent in charge of Kentucky he was "very grateful to God" that he had "so administered the Freedmen's Bureau in Kentucky, as to meet almost the unqualified disapprobation of Kentucky."

Howard was a moderate abolitionist who appointed some able black men to Bureau offices. Perhaps another in his place might have done a better job. As Fisk told the AMA at its anniversary meeting in Boston in 1867, however, those in the ordered cities of the North had little knowledge "of what the duty of administering the Bureau was. It was about all there was of law, order and society in the South." Fisk had jurisdiction over five states where "there was no law." The soldiers of the South returned to burned cities and plantations, "desolated lands and poverty." People of both races crowded into cities "doing nothing, waiting for the government to tell them what to do." In the tremendous task that Fisk had, to prepare the land for production and to care for the needs of thousands of people, "the most efficient aid" received was from the teachers of the AMA.[25]

In the chaotic state of the post-war South, Howard welcomed the aid of northern philanthropy and operated on the general basis of expending Bureau funds to undergird the work of benevolent societies engaged in black education in proportion to the size of their own efforts. Because the AMA did more of such work than other societies, it received more aid. The total amount received from the Bureau by the AMA was $213,753.22, most of which was for rentals of buildings. When buildings were furnished by the BFRAL, they were to revert to the federal government should they ever be used for any other than school purposes.[26] And the AMA, realizing that the majority of Americans could not be persuaded that government aid should be either enlarged or long continued, asked those who cared (generally church members) to support their efforts.[27]

Deficit Budgeting

Despite Bureau aid and the added contributions from Congregational churches, the AMA operated on a deficit budget throughout the period of the Civil War and Reconstruction. In 1861 the debt was $13,576.26. It rose to $87,726.59 in 1868 and gradually dipped to a low of $55,481.26 in 1873. This dip was at least partly the result of the selling of the Iowa lands of the Avery bequest, beginning in 1870—a financially unwise move in the long run, but viewed a necessity in the urgency of the moment.[28] The debt rose again to a high of $96,559.20 in 1875. The society resorted to borrowing money from its members and from its employees, both those who had assets and those whose only liquid assets were their salaries.. In the latter cases teachers were asked to wait for their salaries when they could, receiving them with interest later. In 1867 a circular was sent to all workers asking for such sacrifices.[29]

The large debt had in fact arisen partly out of the aid given by the BFRAL in building schools. In order to take the greatest advantage of such help, the Association had borrowed money to purchase land (not provided by the Bureau) on which schools could be erected. The two disastrous fires, at Chicago in 1871 and in Boston in 1872, not only occurred in areas where the AMA had received many contributions, but also siphoned off benevolent contributions from other sections of the country to help repair the damage in those two cities.[30]

The Association sought in 1872 to dispel optimistic rumors "that large sums were contributed from many sources for the education of the freedmen." It was difficult to estimate what the southern states were doing. Considering the impoverishment of the whites there and their lack of interest in the "elevation" of the blacks, little was being done. The AMA could speak more definitely of the work of "religious bodies at the North," however. For the year 1871-1872 the following contributions were made:

Presbyterian Church (North)	$ 50,081
Baptist Churches	49,000
Episcopal Church	15,000
Methodist Episcopal Church	34,059
Peabody Fund: *conditional pledges* for the previous year to all work in the South, white or black. By the end of June, 1872, "most had been paid."	106,000
American Missionary Association	209,970[31]

The Peabody Fund was used "mainly for the whites," but even if all of its contributions were used for blacks, its contributions together with those of "four of the large, wealthy and liberal denominations," amounted to less than that expended by the AMA. And although much had been made of the contributions of the people of Great Britain to the work in America, that amount was "comparatively little" compared to the $100,000 given to reimburse the slave masters in the West Indies.[32]

    The urgent need for the AMA to do all it could toward the tremendous task of educating the freedmen called for the employment of great numbers of teachers. However, the limitation of funds resulted in the hiring of fewer teachers—particularly African American ones—than would probably have been the case without such limitation. Increasingly the AMA commissioned only those teachers who could afford to work without salary or who could secure their support from some other source—usually their home churches. Since the northern black teachers who applied for commissions were unable to support themselves without salary and came from churches unable to aid them, they did not have this avenue to jobs in the South.

Higher Education

    Another change that began to be marked in 1870 was the shifting away from common school education toward an emphasis on higher education—especially the education of teachers. In 1870 there were 533 workers commissioned by the AMA, 105 of whom were black (34 from the North and 71 from the South). There were 19,500 students in day schools, 2,348 in night schools, and 16,234 in Sabbath schools. Work was carried out in 16 states and the District of Columbia, in "200 distinct fields." This work represented a 20% drop in primary and intermediate pupils, about the same number of grammar (high school) students, and a 100% increase of students in normal courses. It included five regular college students for the first time.[33]

This trend continued. The AMA expected that the South would eventually establish a public school system, but whether it did or not the northern benevolence could not be expected to staff it with northern teachers even if southern boards would hire them. Since the South would not educate black teachers, the AMA would do what it could to prepare teachers for whatever kind of black schools would be established. As the common schools were phased out (becoming parts of regular school systems or taught by AMA students as pay schools), the requirements for the teachers who were needed rose while their numbers fell. While there were numbers of African Americans, North and South, who were capable of teaching the primary children, there were few with the education requirements for teachers of high school, normal school, or college students who were willing to accept the danger and low salaries obtaining at the South.

Transition

The peak year for AMA teachers was 1870. In 1871 there were 309 missionaries and teachers, 63 common schools, and 21 Graded Schools with normal departments, and 7 chartered institutions. In the ten years from 1861 to 1871, 3,470 missionaries and teachers had been commissioned. They had taught 164,723 pupils in 343 day schools and 156,376 in night and Sunday schools. By that date "more than *a thousand*" students from AMA normal and higher institutions had also taught schools not counted in the above tabulation.[34]

The decline in numbers of common schools and workers sustained by the AMA in the South did not continue unabated, however, When it became obvious that schools simply would not be established for African Americans in certain areas, the Association began other schools. In 1881 there were only 50 AMA schools altogether in the South and 230 teachers. In 1890 there were only 6 chartered institutions of higher education (Berea and Hampton having become independent). But in 1890 there were again 21 normal and graded schools, 53 common schools, and 340 AMA workers; and "some twenty thousand of the brightest youths of the race" were in training. Expansion was aided by gifts: Daniel Hand, $1,000,000 in 1888, $500,000 in 1842; and the Charles M. Hall (of aluminum fame) bequest in 1914 of one-sixth of his fortune.[35]

The 1923 *Who's Who: A Directory of Workers of the American Missionary Association, 1922-23,* showed that there were 580 workers in the following categories:

Negroes	278
Whites	259
Puerto Rican	14
Japanese	10
Chinese	10
Indian	7
Hawaiian	2

The removal of the evangelical requirement in 1881 was evident in the religious classification of the workers:

Congregational	357
Methodist	98
Presbyterian	32
Episcopalian	20
Lutheran	4
Unitarian	4
Church of God	2
Mennonite	1
Disciples of Christ	1
Seventh Day Adventist	1
Christian Scientist	1 [36]

In 1904 seventeen of the AMA's schools were headed by African American principals who were graduates of its institutions. In 1930 a black *woman*, Dr. Mary E. Branch, was elected president of Tillotson College, Austin, Texas. She brought the college out of the sad state of decline into which it had fallen, and before her untimely death, had raised the enrollment beyond five hundred and paved the way for the future union with Samuel Huston College (Methodist) to form Huston-Tillotson College on the Tillotson campus.[37]

NOTES

1. *Nineteenth Annual Report* (1865), 12-15; "Action of the Council;" and "$750,000!" printed circulars distributed by the AMA, AMAA; *AM*, IX (October, 1865), 227-229, includes extracts from the circular letter of the National Council; see also *AM*, X (August, 1866), 179.

2. *Nineteenth Annual Report* (1865), 7; *Twentieth Annual Report* (1866), 6; for Tappan's resignation, see *AM*, IX (December, 1865), 277; for the story of the Union Missionary Society, see (DeBoer 1994, *passim*).

3. See a booklet produced by the Congregational Christian Churches in mid-twentieth century: Rev. L. Wendell Fifield, *What It Means to Be a Member of the Congregational Church* (New York, n.d.), 2-4:
      "The basis of membership in a Congregational Church is a statement of purpose rather than a statement of creed. . . . As experiences and intellectual capacities change, . . . it is inevitable that creeds should change. . . .
      "Furthermore, the Congregational denomination is clear that the basis of the first church, that is, the group of disciples who were gathered about Jesus, is to be found in their purpose to be with Him and to be like Him. The intellectual statement of His nature and of His work came as a result of that fellowship. It did not precede it.
      "We consequently believe we are true to fundamental Christian principles when we admit into our membership any who express a purpose to live a Christian life as that Christian life is interpreted by their own best judgment. . . . People of different

shades of intellectual thought about religion work happily together in the Congregational fellowship.

"At no time are any statements made which do violence to this intelligent desire to know the truth. No member is ever told that he must believe any specific religious tenet in order to be a good church member."

4. *Nineteenth Annual Report* (1865), 14-15; see also the letters of Edmonia G. Highgate, AMAA.

5. The AMA was critical of the Roman Catholic Church and of Protestant Churches that differed in this regard.

6. *Nineteenth Annual Report* (1865), 14; see also *AM*, X (September, 1867), 204-205.

7. *AM*, XIV (June, 1870), 121-128. There were 300 workers in 1865, 353 in 1866, 528 in 1867, 532 in 1868 and 1869: (Woodworth 1878); (Strieby n.d.); *AM*, XVI (January, 1872), 12-13; by 1869 the Eastern Department alone had furnished the South with 314 teachers from its schools: *Twenty-third Annual Report* (1869), 51.

8. For the origins of the WFAS, see *AM*, VII (March, 1863), 59; see also Levi Coffin Report, XI (January, 1867), 9; for the teachers commissioned by the various departments, see the *Twenty-first Annual Report* (1867), 15.

9. *AM*, XIII (April, 1869), 83-85; (May, 1869), 108; XI (April, 1867), 90-91; XIV (July, 1870), 157; XVII (January, 1873), 2-3.

10. W.F. Eaton, Beaufort, South Carolina, April 4, 1865, to Whipple, AMAA; *AM*, XIII (May, 1869), 110-111; XII (September, 1868), 207-208; XIV (March, 1870), 60-61.

11. For a report of Gen. Howard on the bank, see *AM*, XIII (November, 1869), 243-245; *The Republican* (Norfolk) *Extra*, November, 1867, AMAA. See also the *Twenty-ninth Annual Report* (1875), 16.

12. XIV (May, 1870), 109-111. For the view of a black teacher on the Fifteenth Amendment, see M.L, Hoy, Prince Frederick, Maryland, May 16, 1870, AMAA.

13. For the phasing out of the work in Jamaica, see (DeBoer 1994, 191-193). In 1874 the work in the Sandwich Islands (modern Hawaii), long self-sustaining, was relinquished, but was resumed in 1904. In 1883 work was enlarged to include the poor whites of the Central South; in 1890 the Indians of Alaska were included; in 1899 work began in Puerto Rico: see *Thirty-Seventh Annual Report* (1883), 51; *Sixtieth Annual Report* (1906), 1050107. The work in Siam was relinquished and the property given to the AMA missionary on that field: *Twenty-eighth Annual Report* (1874), 7; see also *AM*, XVI (January, 1872), 12-13.

14. William F. Cady, Department of the Interior, Office of Indian Affairs, Washington, D.C., September 9, 1870, to Whipple; E.P. Smith, Department of the Interior, Office of Indian Affairs, Washington, D.C., to Whipple, AMA Archives. Smith also wrote, with regard to his term as Commissioner: "I had some advantage in my Indian experience, but I had the disadvantage of being put into a machine with all the old forces still in operation. . . . I leave with the satisfaction of knowing that my two & a half years at this desk has not been altogether in vain. I *know* that the whole Indian outlook has changed front, and that matters have come now to such a footing that only a patient continuance in well doing is required to solve the whole question. . . . I have the rather melancholy satisfaction also of knowing that I'm from $1200 to $1500 out of pocket by being Indian Comr. . . ." For biography of Smith see (Armstrong 1993).

15. *AM*, XIII (March, 1869), 59-60; (May, 1869), 108-109; (July, 1869), 161-162.

16. See, e.g., Emerson, Selma, Alabama, December 7, 1875; Tougaloo, Mississippi, December 23, 1875, to Strieby, AMAA.

17. See letters of Lewis C. Chambers and William D. Harris, for examples, AMAA.

18. *AM*, XVIII (April, 1874), 87-88.

19. *AM* IX (August, 1865), 180; XV (February, 1871), 39; XVI (April, 1872), 90-92; XVIII (February, 1874), 37; (July, 1874), 158; XV (February, 1871), 38.

20. Lewis Tappan contributed $3,000 to one asylum. *AM*, X (June, 1866), 122, 127; (October, 1866), 226; *Twentieth Annual Report* (1866), 25; *Twenty-fifth Annual Report* (1871), 54: by 1871 the Brewer Asylum near Wilmington, North Carolina, and Washburne Memorial Asylum at Atlanta were no longer needed.

21. *AM*, XIII (September, 1869), 203; XIV (July, 1870), 162; XVII (February, 1873), 37-38; for the Howard investigation and his vindication, see XVIII (July, 1874), 157; *Twentieth Annual Report* (1866), 11; *Twenty-first Annual Report* (1867), 62; *Twenty-second Annual Report* (1868), 25; *Twenty-third Annual Report* (1869), 15-16.

22. *Nineteenth Annual Report* (1865), 11-12.

23. *Christian Union*, cited in *AM*, XV (July, 1871), 150.

24. Gen. Charles H. Howard, Charleston, South Carolina, November 7, 1865; November 22, 1865, to Hunt, AMAA. In deference to Howard, Langston refused Johnson's offer. For Saxton's removal, see (Howard 1907, II, 283-284; cf. (McFeely 1970); although McFeely admits that the White House was in control of the Bureau (23), he puts the blame for Saxton's removal on Howard (227), a charge he makes without substantiation.

25. *AM*, XI (July, 1867), 147.

26. *United States Government Document, 41st Congress, 2nd Session, House of Representatives, Report No. 121*, 362-378.

27. *AM*, XIX (February, 1875), 25-26.

118

28. *AM*, XIV (February, 1870), 36-37; (September, 1870), 202-203; Lewis Tappan, Saratoga Springs, New York, June 11, 1862, to Whipple; June 13, 1862, to Jocelyn; June 13, 1862, to Whipple; June 17, 1862, to Jocelyn; June 18; June 28, 1862, to Whipple, AMAA.

29. The debt was $93,232.99 in 1876 and $62,816.90 in 1877. *AM*, XI (July, 1867), 150151; XII (September, 1868), 202-203; see printed circular, Edward P. Smith, New York, April 25, 1867, to Gabriel Burdett; and replies on printed form from Burdett, Kentucky, May n.d., 1867; E.H. Freeman, Franklin, Tennessee, May 23, 1867, to Smith; see also printed circular: Whipple and Strieby, New York, October 8, 1869, AMAA.

30. *AM*, XV (December, 1871), 282-282; XVI (May, 1872), 110; XVII (January, 1873), 13.

31. The AMA figure was the money allocated to the freedmen out of total expenditures of $327,997.67; *Twenty-sixth Annual Report* (1872), 8, 15; a resolution was passed to ask the churches (Congregational) to give $500,000 for the work of the AMA for 1873; *AM*, XVI (August, 1872), 183-184; (October, 1872), 231. For the Peabody Fund, see (Drake 1957, 198-200).

32. *AM*, XIII (April, 1869), 82; XVII (February, 1873), 28.

33. *AM*, XIV (July, 1870), 162; XIII (May, 1869), 98: in 1869 the AMA had 492 workers in the South, 100 of whom were African Americans, 51 from the North, 49 from the South.

34. *AM*, XV (July, 1871), 148.

35. In 1946 the Hall bequest was valued at $8 million. (Brownlee 1946, 279).

36. (Woodworth 1890, no pagination); (Brownlee 1946, 274-279).

37. *AM*, LVIII (January, 1904), 35; (Brownlee 1946, 192-194); (Brownlee 1963, 55-56).

V

THE REACTION OF THE SOUTH

We are not only opposed by the rebels, but by the great majority of the professors of religion among the Unionists; we therefore feel our labor is to educate the whites as well as the blacks.

—from a teacher in Baltimore, 1866
AMA Annual Report

Twice I have been shot at in my room. Some of my night scholars have been shot but none were killed. The nearest military protection is two hundred miles away.

—from a teacher in Louisiana, 1866

Miss Wells, a graduate of Mt. Holyoke, was one of these heroines who followed the army before peace was declared into one of the bitterest and most conservative parts of the South. She began her school which she named "Trinity" at Athens, Alabama. The Ku Klux lined up around her school, fired volleys of shot and beans through her windows on either side of the chair on which she was sitting. After repeated threats, the school was burned over her head. The Association, unwilling for her to run further risk, urged retreat. This the brave woman refused to do. She established a brick yard, set the negroes to making bricks and under her direction they built the school house which served them for many years. Another teacher in North Carolina was ordered to leave but she replied, "I was sent by the American Missionary Association and when it says "Go!" I will go and not before.

—*Congregational Milestones*
(New York, ca. 1919)

The removal of the protection of the federal government with the demise of the Freedmen's Bureau was followed by an increase in violence against the persons of teachers as well as freedmen. There was also an increase in the destruction of property devoted to the education and religion of the African Americans in the South. But violence did not wait for 1873. Wherever federal troops were removed, the opportunity for violence with impunity against the freedmen and their teachers was possible. Tennessee, a state that had never really experienced federal occupation, witnessed the Memphis massacre of 1866, to which AMA superintendent Ewing O. Tade was a witness, and during which the Lincoln Chapel he had built with his own hands was burned. At Memphis forty-six black persons were killed, two whites, five black women raped, ten others maltreated, one hundred robbed, ninety-one cabins, nine churches, and twelve schools burned.[1] The Memphis *Avalanche* reacted to the news that the northern teachers had fled Memphis:

> Another lesson has been taught the white fanatics. It is that we want none of their "school-marms" among any of our population, white or black. It is said they have all left in a great fright. A happy riddance we have. They were nuisances. Women, who could come down South to teach negroes are unfit for any but negro society. The South never learnt anything from New England. The Pharisaical religion, the morals, the "isms" of that land of hickory hams and wooden nutmegs have never obtained a foothold among us and never will. These "isms" are sprouts to be planted among us by those "school-marms," and the South will rejoice when the last one has left us.

Such blatant hate was not limited to Memphis. The leading editorial of the Norfolk *Virginian* reacted similarly to the departure of the northern teachers.

> The negro "school-marms" are either gone, going, or to go, and we don't much care which, where to, or how—whether it be to the more frigid regions of the northern zone, or to a still more torrid climate; indeed, we may say that we care very little what land they are borne to, so not again to "our'n" even though it be that bourne whence no traveller returns. Our grief at their departure is, however, lightened somewhat by the recollection of the fact that we will get rid

of a most abominable nuisance; and here the theory of compensation comes in to compensate and console us, and dry up the fountains of our tears.

Our only fear is that their departure will not be eternal, and like other birds of prey they may return to us in season and again take shelter, with their brood of black-birds, under the protecting wings of that all-gobbling, and foulest of old fowls, the well-known buzzard yclept Freed-men's Bureau.[2]

In 1866 the AMA school at Camp Nelson, Kentucky, was broken up and the teachers driven away by "Regulators." Kentucky had not left the Union and had escaped much of the war, but the violence there in 1866 was horrible indeed.[3]

Edmonia G. Highgate, having acquired a position in the government schools in New Orleans, Louisiana, reported in December, 1866, having been shot at and her students as having shared the same fate, although none had died. She had left the city to rest "after the horrible riots in New Orleans in July," and had established a school in Lafayette Parish, Vermillionville, two hundred miles from New Orleans and military protection.

Under General Banks of the Freedmen's Bureau a public school system had been established in Louisiana, supported by taxes. In 1867 "the old rebel School Board" set out to segregate the schools in New Orleans. In a series of discussions on the proposition by leading African Americans of the city, members of the black Louisiana Educational Association, the group of citizens who backed Highgate's school for indigent children, deplored the move as one that would lead to inferior buildings and inferior teach-ers—the result wherever separate schools for black children were tolerated. Highgate said she "would rather starve" than teach a proscribed school. If her school were turned over to the old board, she would resign and return to the country and once again risk rebel bullets. "If we are true to ourselves and consistent and persistent in demanding rights," she said, "we shall, sooner or later, obtain them."[4] Highgate died young. The cause is now unknown, but the AMA officers presented her mother with a sculptured bust of Edmonia—a most unusual action on their part.

Lawlessness prevailed in Texas. Committees appointed by the State Convention to investigate, reported that as of June 1868, there had been 939 murders since the end of the war. During that period 379 freedmen had been killed by whites, as compared with 10 whites killed by freedmen. Violence against loyalists in the state had increased with the institution of General Hancock's rebel government. The only loyal senator in 1866, A.O. Cooley, was assassinated and Wheelock H. Upton, a Union leader in Western Texas, was hanged by a mob—both in July, 1868. Many Union supporters were forced to flee the state.[5]

Missouri, like Kentucky, never left the Union and was also a place of violent activity aimed at teachers and freedmen.[6] "Flattery and intimidation" were pursued in Missouri to persuade the freedmen to vote Democratic. Barbecues and public dinners were given, and when they failed, men were whipped and even murdered. Many did not vote at all out of fear. Those who voted Democratic did so "through fear or flattery." The freedmen were promised equality and even friendship if they voted Democratic, while the alternative—"no labor or patronage"—meant "starvation." A similar situation was reported in North Carolina by AMA superintendent Beals, where many Wilmington blacks were forced to join Democratic clubs or lose their jobs.[7] In Louisiana Governor Warmouth admitted that the freedmen were not protected by the courts and were killed by whites with impunity.[8]

By 1870 "secret and systematic violence" was the order of the day in many parts of Georgia. An AMA teacher (male) was warned to leave a town near Atlanta and did so when the mayor refused to give him protection. A few miles away another teacher was beaten and hanged until almost dead and given five days to leave. Another teacher (black) in the same area was shot for holding a school. All three incidents happened within a few days of each other. Similar situations occurred in Mississippi and Texas.[9]

An AMA student was beaten by the Ku Klux Klan in Alabama for teaching a school.[10] On Easter Sunday in 1873 in the Grant Parish massacres, 148 black men were trapped in the Louisiana court house to which they had been lured, and which was then set afire. It was the estimate of a white Louisiana Republican that 5,000 black members of his party had been killed in Louisiana from the end of the war to 1873.

Two male Methodist teachers from Ohio teaching at Corinth, Mississippi, disappeared. Others were beaten, threatened, and had their schools burned.[11] One AMA missionary in Mississippi received the following letter:

> 1st Quarter, 8th Bloody Moon—Ere the next quarter be gone! Unholy teacher of the blacks, begone, ere it is too late! Punishment awaits you, and such horrors as no man ever underwent and lived. The cusped moon is full of wrath, and as its horns fill, the deadly mixture will fall on your unhallowed head. Beware! When the Black Cat sleeps we that are dead and yet live are watching you. Fool! Adulterer and Cursed Hypocrite! The far-piercing eye of the grand Cyclops is upon you! Fly the wrath to come.
>
> Ku Klux Klan[12]

The General Assembly of North Carolina in 1871 was described as "completely under the control of the Ku Klux"; and the Congregational Church of Dudley, North Carolina was burned by incendiaries on February 21, 1871.[13] In South Carolina the Hamburg massacre posed the question of "the ability of a southern state to protect its black citizens."[14] The teacher in the day school held in the AMA chapel at "New-Ruhamah," Monroe County, Mississippi, was "driven off" and the pastor warned to "desist from further preaching." Elsewhere in Mississippi three female and three male teachers "were driven off by the Ku Klux Klan."[15]

AMA teacher John O. Stevenson (white) at Port Lavaca, Texas, was threatened with death by the Klan in 1868 and slept in a different house each night to escape them.[16]

While few AMA teachers were actually harmed physically, some of their buildings were destroyed by incendiaries. Emerson Institute (Mobile, Alabama) was burned April 16, 1876; Lewis High School and Norwich Chapel (Macon, Georgia) on December 13, 1876; Straight University (New Orleans) February 16, 1877; Beach Institute (Savannah) February 26, 1878. These were large institutions; many small buildings were destroyed all over the South.[17]

In its haste to establish a "white man's government" in the South the southern "Democracy" (leadership of the southern Democratic Party) allowed those who thrived on terror and hate to people the Klans and drive the black man from the polls. Southern African Americans lived in much less security than in the days of slavery. Even the cruelest slaveholder had an investment in his

slaves and would seldom kill one. But emancipation had changed
that, and no loss of investment stayed the hand of the violent.[18]

Still, it was not so much the extremes of terror and violence
that caused many African Americans to look elsewhere than the
South for the future of their children; it was the day-to-day
oppression—the commonplace variety of violence—of the white
race that refused to allow the freed slave to live in dignity, earn his
bread, and educate his children. In the life of Gabriel Burdett,
AMA missionary and trustee of Berea College, can be traced the
rationale for the great emigration of African Americans to Kansas
and the West at the end of the century. Burdett was a native of
Kentucky, where he had spent thirty-four years of his life as a slave
and two as a soldier in the Union Army. An unusual man, Burdett
had managed to acquire an education of sorts and taught in the
lower forms at Berea College as well as in a district school. In 1867
he reorganized the Camp Nelson Church of Christ (an independent
organization with congregational polity) that had been begun by a
white missionary and broken up by white mobs. He re-established
the school that had been destroyed by "Regulators." He was
responsible for organizing it as a Normal School, leaving the
district school (then taught by his daughter) to provide the
fundamentals of education for the children of the area. He was
determined to make Camp Nelson a viable black community.

Burdett was the Republican elector from the seventh district
of Kentucky (Henry Clay's old area) and a leader of his people. The
overwhelming defeat of the Republicans there in 1876, however,
discouraged him to the point of eventually leaving Kentucky for the
West. He could see no future for the colored people of Kentucky so
long as their white oppressors there forced on them a "mere mud
sill" existence. For twelve years after the war he worked in the
Camp Nelson church, itinerated, founding other churches and
schools, exhorting the people to vote Republican. And all that time
he saw his people move backward instead of forward. They were
too few to make a Republican victory possible and too many to
reform the sharecropper system. The white land owners could pick
and choose among those hungry for lands to till and charge them
more rents and plowing fees for the privilege than they made from
their share of the crop. Burdett reasoned that if enough African

Americans left the state, those who were left might be able to make a decent living.

Unable to provide for his large family on the salary given him by the AMA alone (the people at Camp Nelson church were unable to keep their promise of aid) Burdett determined to take his children where they could grow up without the foot of the oppressor ever on their necks—where a man was always a man. To that end he asked and received AMA aid to move his family to Kansas in 1877.[19]

NOTES

1. Tennessee's ratification of the Fourteenth Amendment exempted that state from much of congressional Reconstruction. For the Memphis massacre, see *United States House of Representatives, 39th Congress, 1st Session, Report No. 101, Memphis Riots and Massacres*, particularly the testimony of the Rev. Ewing O. Tade on May 25, 26, and 31, 1866: p. 12 tells of the burning of Lincoln Chapel; p.6: the report of E.B. Washburne, from the Select Committee on the Memphis Riots, that the riots began on the afternoon of May 1st, with the Irish—aroused by the press—attacking the blacks. See also *AM*, X (June, 1866), 133; (October, 1866), 222; *Twentieth Annual Report* (1866), 37.

2. For this and the previous quotation see *AM*, X (August, 1866), 174; Norfolk *Virginian*, July 2, 1866; cf. Norfolk *Journal*, June 1, 1867.

3. See the report to General Howard, cited in the *Twentieth Annual Report* (1866), 38; *AM*, XIV (January, 1870), 2.

4. Highgate, February 8, 1866; Vermillionville, Louisiana, December 17, 1866; New Orleans, September 27, 1867, to Strieby; unidentified newspaper clipping, 45720, AMAA.

5. *AM*, XII (September, 1868), 204-205; Robert C. VanDyne, Jr., Clinton, DeWitt County, Texas, July 18, 1873, AMAA.

6. *AM*, XIII (April, 1869), 86.

7. *AM*, XII (September, 1868), 203-204.

8. Letter of Governor Warmouth to the President, *AM*, XIV (January, 1870), 12, 17-18.

9. *AM*, XIV (January, 1870), 12, 17-18; (January, 1870), 18-19; (December, 1870), 282; XV (March, 1871), 60-61; (June, 1871), 132-133 (the editors apologized for including so few KKK "outrages" in the magazine); XVI (February, 1872), 39-40; XX (October, 1876), 218-219.

10. *AM*, XVII (January 1873), 5.

11. *AM*, XVII (June, 1873),129; XVIII (October, 1874), 222-225, 229.

12. *AM*, XII (August, 1868), 183.

13. *AM*, XV (February, 1871), 27; (April, 1871), 74-75.

14. *AM*, XX (September, 1876), 196.

15. *Twenty-fifth Annual Report* (1871), 55, 60; *Twenty-sixth Annual Report* (1872), 63; for other KKK activity see *AM*, XII (September, 1868), 196; XIII (October, 1869), 230-232; XIV (December, 1870), 283; XV (February, 1871), 28, 37-38; (April, 1871), 84-85; (November, 1871), 256-257; XVI (February, 1872), 39-40.

16. *Twenty-second Annual Report* (1868), 76.

17. (Drake 1957, 176).

18. The violence continued long after the official end of Reconstruction; for example, three schools were burned in 1899: *Fifty-third Annual Report* (1899), 35.

19. See the letters of Burdett and those of John G. Fee, AMAA.

VI

AFRICAN AMERICANS
IN THE ADMINISTRATION OF THE AMA

It has occurred to me that some advantage might be gained by the identity of the A.M.A. with the public interest of the colored people through so important an organ as the National Convention of Colored Men which is to be organized in this City on next Wednesday the 13th inst. If you think with me I shall be glad to be your Delegate to said Convention. . . . I myself have strong hopes that much good will come out of it as I shall thus be enabled to speak of a work very near my heart and pay a tribute to the work of the A.M.A. which it deserves and which the leading men among our people ought to know it deserves.

—Sella Martin (African American Vice President of the AMA),
Washington, D.C., January 7, 1869,
to AMA officers in New York City,
AMA Archives

None of the old "great" African American abolitionists was in a position of authority in the administrative councils of the AMA during Reconstruction. However, John Sella Martin, a younger African American spokesman, became a special AMA agent and lecturer in Europe, a member of the Executive Committee, and a vice president of the Association.

John Sella Martin

Martin's name is sometimes rendered J. Sella Martin, but most often as Sella Martin. He was a tall, handsome man with light

Courtesy of Moorland-Spingarn Research Center,
Howard University, and Amistad Research Center

Sella Martin

coloring. On one occasion when he had to have his head shaved because of a skin problem, he said he would be glad when his hair grew out again because people thought him Chinese instead of colored. He was elected to the Executive Committee of the AMA at the annual meeting in 1864 and was also a featured speaker at the meeting. He arrived in London in May, 1865, and spent the better part of three years as AMA collecting agent in Europe. In 1868 he was elected a vice president of the AMA.[1]

It was as a member of the Executive Committee that Martin made the suggestion in 1865 to send representatives abroad to solicit funds for the work among the freedmen. Other benevolent organizations in the United States had already done so. Since the latter did not begin working among African Americans until the end of the Civil War, and since the AMA had spent "more than twenty thousand pounds sterling" in establishing "schools and missions" among the freedmen of Jamaica since 1846, the Association felt it had a prior claim on the benevolence of Great Britain.[2]

Sella Martin was born in Charlotte, North Carolina, September 27, 1832, the child of his master. Most of his years in slavery were spent in urban areas where he learned to read. Unlike most fugitive slaves, Martin escaped from the deep South, in December, 1855. He received some training in theology under a Baptist minister in Detroit, Michigan, and tried the lecture circuit in Illinois and Michigan under the tutelage of Hezekia Ford Douglass. He first served the Michigan State Baptist Association in Buffalo, New York, and was introduced to Boston church circles by Kalloch, the abolitionist pastor of Tremont Temple, in 1859. He served as pulpit supply of the white First Baptist Church of Lawrence, Massachusetts, until he was called to his first black charge, the Joy Street Baptist Church of Boston. Subsequently he moved to New York and the pulpit of Shiloh Presbyterian Church.[3]

Martin was chosen as the AMA's major agent in Europe. He was a good choice. Martin was an eloquent speaker and, though a man of spirited temperament, he had great stores of patience and tact and had been, moreover, a pastor of a church in Bromley-by-Bow, London, for six months in 1861, and was therefore no stranger to London churchmen.[4] While in England in 1863, Martin had earned the money to free his sister and her children from slavery. On his return trip he had offered his services to President Lincoln toward achieving the aims of the war.[5]

Although he found some freedmen's societies in England had not heard of the AMA, Martin managed "by personal visits and bushels of tracts and letters" to reach "every Freedmen's Aid Society in England, and the three great Central Associations, as well as the National Committee formed of delegates from them" had "adopted" the AMA as one of the recipients of their benevolence.[6]

Shiloh Presbyterian Church was unhappy at having their pastor away so long in Europe. Having paved the way for collections in England and Scotland and having cleared up some misunderstandings about the nature of the AMA (which its name and Garrison's opposition had not helped), Martin returned home late in 1865. Martin found it necessary to explain the non-ecclesiastical (i.e., non-denominational) yet religious nature of the AMA because Garrison claimed that the American Freedmen's Aid

Commission was the only non-ecclesiastical organization. Martin must have done a good job because, during a five-month period at the end of 1865, nearly 20% of the financial receipts of the AMA had come from Great Britain, to say nothing of quantities of clothing and blankets.[7]

Faced with finding someone to reap where Martin had sown, the men at the Rooms and on the field recognized that Martin was the best man for the post and sent him back the next spring.

Between his first and second trips to England for the AMA Martin joined Henry H. Garnet and John M. Langston on a visit to Washington to "watch the interests of their race in legislation." While there they interviewed General O.O. Howard, having heard that he was opposed to Negro suffrage. Howard declared that he was for equal suffrage for all men and wished that an educational requirement might be made, but feared that the opposition in the South to the education of the freedmen was "forcing us to adopt at once universal suffrage," even though this would result in an uneducated electorate.[8]

Lewis Tappan and Michael Strieby wanted to make Sella Martin the AMA Secretary for Europe on his return in 1866. For some undiscovered reason this was not done. Perhaps the fact that a Western Secretary had just been appointed and the appointment of another so soon would seem injudicious. Perhaps it was because Dr. William W. Patton had volunteered to serve in Europe and would object to serving under Martin. In any case Martin was the principal agent in Europe, with a house in London, having resigned his pastorate at Shiloh Church.[9]

Financial Stringencies

Because of the work of Sella Martin in Great Britain during 1865 and the efforts of John C. Holbrook who followed him, receipts for the AMA mounted from a pre-European tour sum of about $1,000 a week to as much as $10,000 a week. This prompted the Association to invest more heavily in land for school buildings than it otherwise might have. Then, early in 1866 when expenses were running $1,000 per day, receipts from Europe almost stopped and receipts from the United States were curtailed to a low of $500 per week. This caused the secretaries in New York to look forward with something like terror to the expenses of June when teachers must be paid and sent home, and to mid-July when the $5,000 overdrawn in May might have become $25,000 or $30,000.[10]

Part of the difficulty in Great Britain lay in the internal squabbles of the Freedmen's Aid Union Commission of Great Britain and Ireland, many of whose members were Quakers. A schism in that body took place in 1866, but by that time Martin was convinced that the European secular arm of freedmen's aid had about run its course and it was time to impress the Congregational Union of England and Wales, the Free Church of Scotland, and the Presbyterians generally with the religious nature of the AMA's work. It was the general consensus of the AMA men in Europe that the Quakers were interested only in the physical relief of the freedmen. Once that problem was largely cared for by the sending of blankets and clothing, the European Quakers were no longer interested. They were certainly not persuaded of the freedmen's need for intellectual enlightenment, nor were they interested in religious education of any kind not distinctly Quaker in nature.[11]

The AMA representatives were snubbed in Europe by William L. Garrison, who denounced them as "ecclesiastical" on the one hand while accusing them on the other hand of taking unfair advantage of the American Freedmen's Aid Commission by collecting funds from the Congregational Churches of New England! The AMA counted on Levi Coffin to offset Garrison's moves against them among the Quakers of England. When Garrison told the British people in 1867 that they should no longer contribute to the work among the freedmen, James Thome thought the result would be "unfavorable" in England but would not affect the work in Scotland.[12]

When Martin asked for an assistant to help with the work in Europe, the AMA suggested the Rev. James A. Prince, African American Congregational minister. This was probably the Jacob A. Prince ordained by a "Convention of Christian Brethren" in Geneva, New York, in October, 1849. Probably he worked there with the same group of Congregationalists that Samuel Ward and Henry Garnet had both served. It has not been discovered why Thome was commissioned instead of Prince. In 1859 Prince was pastor of a church in Brooklyn. This may have been the predominantly African American congregation personally aided by George Whipple.[13]

Several white representatives of the AMA assisted Martin
during his three years in Europe: Dr. William W. Patton of
Chicago; John C. Holbrook, pastor of the Congregational Church
at Homer, New York; and James A. Thome, pastor of a Cleveland
Congregational Church. It was James Thome who was to achieve
the closest relationship with Sella Martin. In the beginning Thome
was concerned over what seemed Martin's wish that they work
separately—one in England, the other in Scotland or on the
Continent. Martin was being cautious, having been hurt by what he
considered the patronizing attitude of Dr. Patton during their work
together.[14]

James Thome, White Assistant

Thome had liked Martin at once and had found all the good
things the men at the Rooms had said about him were true and
more. But Martin's apparent reserve had kept the men apart.
Thome could not understand the reason for it and theorized—
correctly—that possibly neither was at fault.

Martin's sensitive nature and delicate health (he suffered
from recurring bouts of malaria) exacerbated his disappointments,
and when funds seemed to be acquired more slowly, his spirits were
low indeed. It was at just such a low point of spirit that he received
an added blow from the men in New York which seemed to
question his honor and deny their trust in him. He was seen riding
on a first-class coach by an English woman who reported the news
to the AMA with the added fillip that contributions for the
freedmen given by Englishmen were being thus abused.[15]

In probably the most eloquent writing of his career, Sella
Martin defended his very occasional use of first-class accommodations when ill and travelling all night between engagements with no
chance for rest. That he had never abused the Association's funds
but on the other hand had done everything possible to save money
was Martin's affirmation. He had undertaken to work for the
AMA for the same low salary he had received at Shiloh Church
when he could have had twice that amount from another society,
and had even resorted to renting out a room in his London house in
order to cut expenses.[16]

It was during this nadir of Martin's relationship with the
AMA that he and James Thome came to know and have the

highest admiration for each other. Thome minced no words in telling the men at the Rooms that Martin's allegiance was probably lost forever and Thome knew where to put the blame. Men could only do their best work when they were trusted, Thome declared. When they really got to know each other, the white slaveholder's son from Kentucky and the African American slaveholder's son (and former slave) worked joyfully in tandem. Each appreciated the other, and their letters were testimonials of their friendship. Loving Martin, Thome nonetheless saw his weaknesses for the work they were in. Martin refused to do alone what was for him the demeaning work of "button-holing" individuals and "begging" for their contributions. He would accompany Thome on such visits to business men, but Thome knew he would not do it once Thome returned to America. Martin's bouts of despair when things were going slowly, Thome thought, must be balanced by a partner with more optimism—one willing to do the hard work, bear the onus of the labor, and let Martin receive the applause of the crowd for his eloquence on the platform.[17]

Thome might have been surprised to know how well Martin understood both Thome and himself as he explained to the men in New York:

> If ever a field was laboriously and conscientiously and I may add intelligently worked this was by Bro. Thome. You mention ... Bro. Holbrook as possessed of superior begging qualities and experience ... but I claim as much for Mr. Thome.
>
> It is impossible for you to know the work that was done in this field in the way of soliciting while Bro. Thome was here ... both of us being hard at work and myself working all the harder because I did not like the work but felt your fetters....

Words of praise from his good friend, the Duke of Argyle, pleased Martin, but

> I deprecated his reference to me at the time and under the circumstances more than I can tell you. Besides its appearing to be invidious to my colleague it was based upon

an imperfect analysis of the respective forces of bro Thome
and myself. Bro Thome had taken the 'unshowy' but
indispensable part of facts and figures and left to me to deal
in *oratorical claptrap,* the thing above all others to take with
popular audiences if mixed in the proportion of one grain of
good sense and pertinency to about ten grains of showy
points and emphasis. Now of the many many kindnesses I
have received from Mr. Thome not the least was this habit of
his of yielding his preferences for argument and appeal and
sacrificing his greater fitness for such work that he might
serve the cause with statistics and leave me free to serve it
better than I otherwise could in argument pathos and
appeal. I regard this habitual self denial in the presence of
constant demonstrations of popular approval while I was
speaking in which bro Thome was as demonstrative as the
rest as among the strongest proofs of his greatness of mind
and as the chief means of producing the results so far
attained. It requires those as well mated as Bro Whipple and
yourself and as bro Thome and I to work harmoniously
while one constantly labors at the figures of mathematics
and the other sky-larks in figures of speech. I know that
when men lose themselves in their work such harmony
always takes place. . . .[18]

The settlement of the *Alabama* claims was much desired by
Martin, the reason a rather complicated one. During the reforms
that followed the strife in the weaving industry in England which
arose partly as a result of America's Civil War, a fund (called
Lancashire) was raised to supply hospital care and medical
attention for the families of weavers in Lancaster. The Civil War
had created havoc in Lancashire, 85% of whose cotton came from
America's South. With the removal of many of that category of
worker the funds had not been exhausted. A considerable amount
was therefore available, and Martin, among others, urged that it be
sent for work among the freedmen. However, the Derby Government expressed the conviction that such a gift would seem to be a
bribe for a favorable settlement in the *Alabama* controversy. Lord
Derby thought a better use for the Lancashire fund might be a
hospital for workers in the Midlands. Because he was on good
terms with Ambassador Charles Francis Adams (who had invited
him to evening gatherings at his mansion on four occasion) and a
good friend of Mr. Horan, the secretary of the American legation in

London, Martin was sure he would hear as soon as any decision was made. (Adams had been a member of Tappan's American and Foreign Anti-Slavery Society.) But the *Alabama* claims were not settled until 1872.[19]

Martin proposed establishing freedmen's aid committees on the continent—particularly in countries where his French could be used: Switzerland, France, and Russia. But America and the problems of the freedmen were farther from the Continent than from Great Britain, and the latter had not Great Britain's feeling of guilt concerning slavery. Europe's own problems were closer to the people. The 1860s saw rumors of war, cholera epidemics, famine in India, and unrest in Greece. The Protestant leaders of France like Theodore Monod were pessimistic, and Martin declared that no help could be expected from the Roman Catholics, "who had never been taught to give." There was also the disadvantage arising out of the French aversion to the congressional approval given in the United States to the execution of Maximilian by Juarez.[20]

Cassius Marcellus Clay, American Minister to Russia, did not recommend attempts to raise money there in 1867. The Russians were still "suffering" financially as a result of emancipation, and "Greece and the Turkish wars are giving them more active objects of charity than our remote Blacks of a different religion." A black man representing the Garnet League had already canvassed the country with Clay's patronage and had left an agent there. Obviously, Clay did not want to present another soliciting black man at court.[21]

Sella Martin and James Thome represented the AMA at the Anti-Slavery Conference held in Paris August 26 and 27, 1867. The dates of the Conference seem to have been specifically changed to coincide with an evangelical conference in Holland and thus to keep as many evangelical leaders as possible away from Paris. Despite that fact and the presence of Garrison, Martin's address to the Conference stressed the importance of "those evangelical principles which have made the English-speaking race what it is." He said that the AMA was following "the wisest policy in sending the Bible along with the spelling book." Martin continued:

> Mr. Garrison says his Society is the largest non-ecclesiastical Freedmen's Aid Society in America. The term ecclesiastical we do not accept, because we are supported by, and employ

in, our work, members of every evangelical sect. But the
term 'religious but non-sectarian' we can and do accept. We
are not unmindful of the advantages to the world that are to
grow out of the civilization and Christianization of the
freedmen in commercial, social and political points of view.
Europe and the north will get better cotton and more of it
from free men than they did from slaves, and the corresponding increase of their export trade to clothe and satisfy
these people, whose daughters must dress, and whose wives
will demand luxuries, will not be the least of their gains.

In addition to commercial advantages, the freedmen would serve to
bind the North and South together if they were "educated and
made prosperous." And perhaps most important of all, they would
perform the Christianization and civilization of Africa and end the
infamous slave trade still flourishing, and still costing England and
France millions every year to furnish patrol squadrons.[22]

Martin Returns from Europe

When his work in Europe neared completion, Martin asked
for a position in the South, either as Southern Secretary or in a
pastorate in Mobile, Charleston, or New Orleans. Although he was
a Presbyterian minister when he went to Europe, Martin declared
himself a Congregationalist in spirit.

The AMA hoped to secure Sella Martin for the pastorate of
the Plymouth Congregational Church of Charleston, South
Carolina, founded in 1867, and foundering under a series of
unfortunate pastorates. Although Martin agreed to visit Charleston
and look over Plymouth Church, he said he was wary of ecclesiastical marriages arranged by others. He would never again take a
church unless the initiative to call him came from the church in
question. When Martin accepted the pulpit of the Fifteenth Street
Presbyterian Church in Washington, the call to Plymouth was
extended to John T. Ford (white).[23]

In Europe Sella Martin had been accorded "the friendship of
John Bright and the Duke of Argyle, preached in the pulpits of the
most distinguished clergymen of various denominations, and was a
favorite orator on all Scotch and English platforms." He had a

private interview with Queen Victoria and was generally welcomed by British society. But in Washington an attempt was made to keep his daughter from public school because of her "slight tinge of colored blood." After a description of the lionizing of Martin in Europe, Dr. W.W. Patton, editor of *Advance* and fellow AMA agent with Martin in Europe, declared: "This is the man whom the City of Washington cannot recognize! Whose daughter must not be suffered within her white public schools!"[24]

Martin continued his interest in the AMA, offering to attend the National Convention of Colored Men (January 13, 1869) at Washington, as the representative of the Association, thus enabling him to "speak of a work very near my heart and pay a tribute to the work of the American Missionary Association which it deserves and our people ought to know it deserves."[25] At the National Labor Convention a year later, he introduced a resolution of thanks to and of confidence in the AMA that was adopted by the convention.[26]

Martin left the pastorate of the Fifteenth Street Church in the spring of 1870 to become the editor of the *New Era*, a venture in which he was assisted by Frederick Douglass as corresponding editor. In his farewell message to his congregation, Martin said:

> It may be that my departure from the pulpit will help toward the solution of some questions I have raised in it, one of which is, whether it is not better to break up colored churches along with the colored schools, and join with our white brethren, like Gen. Howard and his colaborers, who are ready to receive us as brethren in the church of Christ.

The editor of the *Independent* concurred:

> We trust the day is not distant when such a thing as a colored or a white church or school will not exist in any part of the United States. . . . It must come through a perception of the folly as well as wickedness of the caste spirit, and the growth among men of every complexion and race of that true feeling of brotherhood which Christianity enjoins. The time must come when the thought of a church or school for white people or black exclusively will seem as absurd as it would be now to propose separate schools and churches, for tall people and short people, or for people with blue eyes, in

distinction from those whose eyes are black. To this complexion it will come at last, and the sooner the better.[27]

The Martins moved to New Orleans in 1871, where Mrs.
Martin was in charge of the Industrial School associated with the
Hathaway Home for the Poor and Friendless. Although Martin
had hoped to continue with the newspaper, his wife's doctor had
ordered her farther south for her health. Martin suggested that he
might serve the AMA either in Mobile or New Orleans. He chose
New Orleans, the place where as a slave he had had his own
oystering and fruit business. The AMA reported the needs of Mrs.
Martin's Industrial School, where needle work of all kinds and
machine sewing were taught. A Medical Dispensary was also
provided, under the charge of Dr. James Newman, "a colored
physician of eminence."[28]

Martin's last years were spent as an active worker in the
Republican Party. The "chronic wasting disease" from which he
suffered brought him an early death. He was only forty-four years
old when he died in 1876 of an overdose of laudanum, taken for the
relief of pain.[29]

Charles Bennett Ray

Of the original African American AMA officers, Charles B.
Ray lived the longest; and although he spent his life in New York
City, his relationship with the Association ended thirty years before
his death. The AMA followed the plan—born in part out of
financial necessity and in part out of a reaction against paternalism—of putting seed money into projects and expecting aided
mission churches to become self-sustaining after a few years. This
had been its program with Ray and his Bethesda Congregational
Church in New York, and aid to Ray as a city missionary had been
ended in 1855. As his work changed from general missionary
endeavors to those of a settled pastor with his flock safely housed in
a building, Ray resigned his AMA office in 1856, becoming more
and more the Congregational minister, entering into the work of
the denomination locally, and depending upon it for aid to his
struggling congregation.

Sometime in 1874 Ray wrote an anonymous paper entitled,
"Origin and Future of the American Missionary Association by a
Colored Minister," in which he deprecated the story of the AMA's

origins as presented in a New York newspaper account of the 1873 annual meeting. The newspaper story stated that the AMA had arisen from the American Home Missionary Society because of the latter's refusal to take an antislavery stand. Mr. Whipple should know better, argued Ray; the AMA could not grow out of a home mission board, for it was itself both a home and foreign missions organization. It had in fact grown out of the Union Missionary Society (UMS), a largely black institution. Ray expressed irritation at the Oberlin influence behind the founding of the AMA, particularly the activities of Asa Mahan. Oberlin students had been *persona non grata* with the established mission boards because of their antislavery sentiments and unorthodox Christianity; and Mahan wanted a channel for his Oberlin-trained ministers and teachers, Ray wrote. There were two obstructions, Ray thought, to using the largely African American UMS as that channel: Oberlinites might object to being sent out by a society with an African American president (Pennington); and a heavily black society would not attract contributions in any large amount.[30]

Ray's Critique of the AMA

Ray seemed resentful of George Whipple as an Oberlinite, and, as far as Ray was concerned, a Mahan appointee. Whipple was universally loved and was evidently warm and charismatic by nature, which makes Ray's antagonism that much less understandable. Ray had served as recording secretary for the UMS Executive Committee, a fact he thought worthy enough to mention in the 1874 paper. He was a proud man, impatient with African Americans who allowed whites to do their thinking for them. At the time the AMA was established, the office of corresponding secretary was temporarily left vacant, until the services of Whipple, mathematics professor at Oberlin, were secured. Ray probably wanted that office. In any case, he allowed his paper to be published by Theodore Bourne, who—less retiring than Ray—used his own name and Ray's anonymous article to blast the racial policies of the AMA, arguing that "white men engineered the Association, and that from the outset the places of trust, honor and emolument" had been filled by them. He had been "assured" that no African Americans had served it as officers "for years past." Mr. Bourne contrasted the AMA with what he claimed was his own creation, the African Civilization Society.[31]

Bourne asserted that the African Civilization Society had begun with a board half black and half white, many whites gladly serving in subordinate positions. Had the AMA followed such an example, said Bourne, Africa would have been civilized and Christianized long ago. Since the major purpose of the African Civilization Society was "the civilization and evangelization of Africa, and the descendants of African ancestors in any portion of the earth, wherever dispersed," it would seem that Mr. Bourne's criterion for the redemption of Africa had been met by *his* institution. Bourne's remarks were scarcely to the point. The African Civilization Society had ceased to function; and when it was in operation, several of its officers were also officers of the AMA. The Society had also become an almost all-black group in its latter days, as it changed its emphasis from Africa to the education of the freedmen. Many African Americans (Pennington, Garnet, and Crummell are examples) were as bent on the "civilizing and Christianizing" of Africa in the nineteenth century as were the white evangelicals; however much they praised Africa's past greatness, they saw African animism as something to be overcome before Africa could join the modern world—a move they saw as not only desirable, but necessary.[32]

At its beginnings the AMA had had a heavier African American representation than any antislavery organization—religious or secular. Its difficulty in so far as black membership was concerned in its later years lay in its denominational affiliation and that denomination's dislike of segregated churches. There were few black Congregationalists in 1874 and most of them were in the South, less than ten years removed from slavery. Ray did not write the racial portion of the criticism, but he may have agreed with its position. Yet Ray was co-editor of the *Colored American* when that paper criticized the practice of putting black men in positions of honor simply because they were black. "Colored men, to be as other men, must be left to combat the same vicissitudes, and by the same necessities of the case, be goaded on to the efforts and enterprise common to other men." The editorial concluded: "To cast up 'the highway' and 'gather out the stones' is the business of our friends, but to improve and elevate our condition, emphatically the business of ourselves."[33]

Ray's suggestion in 1874, however, that there was no longer a need for the AMA, that its work among the oppressed peoples might better be absorbed by the AHMS and the ABCFM, thus removing from those organizations any excuses to neglect such work, had much to recommend it. Was there any longer any need for compartmentalizing the special claim of brotherhood, for dividing the work at the South between the AMA (largely black) and the AHMS (largely white)? On the other hand, however, the continued presence of the AMA after the Civil War and the abolition cause was over, resulted in a Conference of the South (a regional administrative body) in Congregationalism which was predominantly African American. This fact—while long a sore point with determined integrationists in the denomination and a seeming accommodation to the racial dictates of the South's segregation formulae—nevertheless gave southern black Congregational churchmen an organization that was black (albeit loose and largely social as was the genre of the denomination's structure).

Within eight years of Ray's suggestion, the AMA had made plans to divest itself of its African missions by giving them into the care of the ABCFM or to some other denomination; to take over the ABCFM's Indian work in the united States; and to become a home missions society in fact.

The cooperation on a national level of Congregational churches which began with the establishment of the National Council of Congregational Churches in 1865, resulted in some pressures for consolidation between the home societies—the American Home Missionary Society (which became in the 80s the Congregational Home Missionary Society) and the AMA—and for more efficient ways of raising funds.

The Mendi Mission was turned over to the United Brethren; another African mission was given to the Presbyterians; the international nature of the work was removed from the constitution; cooperative committees were established with the Congregational Home Missionary Society.[34]

Ray died in 1806, his funeral conducted by his old friend, former AMA officer Amos N. Freeman.[35] He and Freeman had made a pact that the survivor would perform this service for the other. Lewis Tappan had been dead for thirteen years, but one of his nephews was among the congregation. Ray, Freeman, and Tappan had worked together in the American and Foreign Anti-Slavery Society and in the AMA as brothers. Ray and Tappan had also shared a New England heritage and its concomitant Congregationalism. Each had served his denomination to the best of his ability as he saw it. The death of the white layman passed without notice in the Congregational Yearbook; the African American minister was eulogized.[36]

Greatness and Tragedy: the Black AMA Abolitionists

Ray and Samuel E. Cornish seem exceptions to the general tragic *denouements* of the lives of the original African American abolitionists associated with the AMA. Cornish was freed from financial cares by his marriage, and Ray seems to have found a comfortable existence in New York. Although Pennington was rehabilitated from the alcoholism that cost him the pulpit of Shiloh Church, and was at work at the end of his life in Jacksonville, Florida, his story is part of the tragedy of caste surrounding the eminent African American officers who were a part of the AMA. There was no room for such men in nineteenth-century America. As black men they were unwelcome in most white society; as *educated* black men they were not at home in the black community. As Congregational and/or Presbyterian ministers, they were almost anachronisms in an age when there were few black churches of either denomination. There were even fewer churches of African American membership that were willing or able to accept their educated ministry with its accompanying religion of reason. Nor were there many white churches strongly abolitionist enough to call an African American as pastor. Such churches that did exist were usually small and incapable of supplying a pastor with adequate support.

The lives of Pennington, Beman, Freeman, Garnet, and Martin became a kind of homiletic game of "Going to Jerusalem," as they moved from one to another of the available churches. Pennington, Garnet, Theodore Wright, and Sella Martin all served Shiloh Church (Presbyterian) at various times; Pennington, Beman, and Amos Freeman all worked for the black Congregational Church of Portland, Maine. Pennington and Beman served New

Haven's Temple Street Congregational Church; Pennington and Freeman supplied Hartford's black Congregational Church; Garnet and Martin were both pastors of the Fifteenth Street Presbyterian Church in Washington; Garnet and Samuel Ward served a small group of Congregationalists in Geneva, New York. Ward, in contrast to the others, also served white congregations at Butler and Cortland, New York, yet found his resentment of white oppression something he could scarcely control. Christian forgiveness came hard to Ward, who likened his feelings about slaveholders to the vindictive words of Psalm 109. White people who wondered at the bitterness expressed by black people against their oppressors knew very little about human nature, "else they would wonder rather that, what with slavery and Negro-hate, the mass of us are not either depressed into idiocy or excited into demons," Ward wrote in his autobiography.[37]

Ward's last days were spent in St. George Parish, Jamaica, where he died a poor man in 1866.[38] Yet Frederick Douglass had characterized Ward as the ablest prophet of black America, and both Douglass and Daniel Webster had praised Ward's oratory. To Webster he was "the ablest thinker on his legs before the American people." Ward had been a minister of the gospel, a teacher, a lecturer; he had studied medicine; he had been a newspaper editor and publisher and had studied law to augment that work:

> but I beg to say, that after smattering away, or teaching, law, medicine, divinity, and public lecturing, I am neither lawyer, doctor, teacher, divine, nor lecturer; and at the age of eight-and-thirty I am glad to hasten back to what my father first taught me, and from what I never should have departed—the tilling of the soil, the use of the hoe.
>
> I beg to conclude this chapter by offering to all young men three items of advice, which my own experience has taught me:—
>
> 1. FIND YOUR OWN APPROPRIATE PLACE OF DUTY.
> 2. WHEN YOU HAVE FOUND IT, BY ALL MEANS KEEP IT.
> 3. IF EVER TEMPTED TO DEPART FROM IT, RETURN TO IT AS SPEEDILY AS POSSIBLE.

He was a man born out of his time. He was America's native son, freed of the slave's chains but bound by prejudice, held down by an "ever-present, ever-crushing Negro-hate."[39]

Henry Highland Garnet had received a commission from the General Assembly of the Presbyterian Church to establish African American schools and churches in the South, while he was pastor of the Fifteenth Street Presbyterian Church in Washington.[40] At the fourth anniversary of the abolition of slavery in the District of Columbia, Garnet began his address by saying that it would no longer be presumptuous to call his audience "fellow citizens." "The history of 250 years has demonstrated the fact that the black race in America, or wherever dispersed, can neither be forever enslaved or blotted out, God is with us and we must be free," he said. His speech concluded with the resolution:

> That we are sensible of the fact that we are engaged in a stubborn war with numerous and unrelenting foes, which, by the help of God, we mean to fight out to the end on our native soil, aiming to complete the establishment of our rights and liberties; and that our weapons are the spelling books, the Bible, the press, and the implements of industry; and the Church of Christ; and our watchwords are UNCONDITIONAL LOYALTY TO GOD AND OUR COUNTRY.[41]

The men at the Rooms wanted to appoint Garnet as AMA lecturer and fund raiser in Europe, but were dissuaded by Sella Martin. Martin remarked that it would be too hard for Garnet to complete the myriad individual encounters that must be so persistently repeated in slow-paced Europe. It is unclear whether Martin was referring to Garnet's physical infirmities (asthma and a wooden leg) or to his psychological constitution, that would balk at the tedium involved and the magnitude of patience required—as Martin's own sensitive nature did.[42]

Garnet returned to the pastorate of Shiloh Church in 1867, where he remained (except for about two years he spent as president of Avery College) until his appointment by President James Garfield (who was an AMA vice president) as minister to Liberia in 1881. Although appointed by Garfield, Garnet was not confirmed by the Senate until reappointed by President Arthur.[43] In 1877 he became a life member of the AMA.[44] A good friend wrote of him that he was greatly disappointed at the end of his life in his people among whom and for whom he had given so much of himself. To Alexander Crummell it was almost as if he accepted the Liberian appointment in order to escape an unresponsive and ungrateful constituency. Thus the pre-eminent Henry Highland Garnet found his life incomplete and lamented at its close that even the freed people in the churches of the North fell short of enlightened Christian citizenship. Although his first allegiance had always been to the United States as his native land, he yearned to see Africa in the hope that in Liberia at least he would find the fulfilled black man of his dreams and expectations.

He preached his farewell sermon in Shiloh Church on November 6, 1881, and sailed six days later, reaching Monrovia two days before Christmas. He spent less than two months in Liberia. A bout of fever left him weakened, and the asthma from which he had suffered for many years took his life early in the morning of February 13, 1882. "They buried him like a prince," wrote Alexander Crummell, "this princely man, with the blood of a long line of chieftains in his veins, in the soil of his fathers." It was Crummell who wrote Garnet's eulogy, addressing him as the friend of his youth, "Statesman, Poet, Orator, Clergyman, Philanthropist!" and paying him this tribute: "Thus it was that for twenty years he was, what I have not heard of any other colored man, in any of the great cities, *the* man of New York."[45]

NOTES

1. See Strieby, March 18, 1865, to T. Lyman; Martin, March 20, 1865, to Strieby; Executive Committee Minutes, April 26, 1865; Martin, New York, April 29, 1865, to Whipple; L.A. Chamerozow, London, July 5, 1865, to Whipple, AMAA. See also *Eighteenth Annual Report* (1864), 7; *Twenty-second Annual Report*, 7.

2. *AM*, IX (June, 1865), 134.

3. The best account of Martin's life is in (Brown 1865, 241-245); there is a much abbreviated account in (Brown 1874, 535-536). (Woodson 1925) says incorrectly that Martin escaped from Georgia, but otherwise appears to be a resume of Brown's abbreviated account.

4. London *Morning Star*, April 27, 1863; see also a much enlarged account of Martin's speech before a meeting in St. James Hall, Pickadilly, printed by the BFAS, BFASAPS.

5. (Quarles 1969, 110-111).

6. Martin, Glasgow, Scotland, July 28, 1865, to Tappan, AMAA.

7. *Twentieth Annual Report* (1866), 4, 6, 10, 11, and for the AMA position of the necessity of religious teaching for the freedmen, 51-55; see also large portions of the July and September issues of the *AM* for 1866; IX (December, 1865), 276; X (April, 1866), 82.

8. (Howard 1907, II, 317).

9. Martin, New York, March 20, 27, and 29, 1866, to Strieby, AMAA. Martin had also been offered a secretaryship with the African Civilization Society.

10. Strieby, Homer, New York, May 21, 1866, to Holbrook, Patton, and Martin, AMAA. The receipts of the AMA were published each month in the *AM*; see X (January, 1866), 24, where receipts from great Britain include "friends in England and Scotland, by Rev. Sella Martin, $1,820.11."

11. Martin, London, June 9, 1865, to "My Dear Sir;" June 9, 1865, to Strieby; June 30, 1865, to Whipple; May 24, 1866, to Holbrook; Holbrook, November 4; November 21, 1865, AMAA.

12. Thome, Edinburgh, October 24, 1867, to Strieby, AMAA.

13. At the Prince ordination Garnet gave the ordaining prayer and Ward preached the sermon. Other parts were taken by J.W. Loguen and Amos Beman; see AGB Papers, Martin, January 7, 1867;

Thome, April 3; May 4; May 10; June 11, 1867, to Strieby, AMAA.

14. See the 1866 letters of Martin and that of March 9, 1868, AMAA.

15. Thome, Glasgow, November 8, 1867; Edinburgh, December 14, 1867, to Strieby; Martin, Glasgow, November 10, 1867; Edinburgh, December 20, 1867, to the Executive Committee, AMAA.

16. Martin, Glasgow, November 10, 1867, AMAA. Martin, like Garnet and E.P. Rogers, also wrote poetry; see "The Sentinel of Freedom," *Anglo-African Magazine*, I (November, 1859).

17. Thome, Edinburgh, February 17, 1868, to Strieby, AMAA.

18. Martin, March 9, 1868. Cf. Thome, April 3; May 4; May 10; June 11; October 24, 1867; January 14, 1868, to Strieby, AMAA.

19. *The Daily News* (London), May 25, 1867, 5; Martin, October 4, 1867; see also Martin, May 3; May 25; August 2, 1867, AMAA.

20. Martin, December 29, 1866; May 9; August 2, 1867, AMAA.

21. Martin, May 9; May 18; May 25, 1867; Clay, St. Petersburg, May 13, 1867, to Martin; May 13, 1867, to the AMAA.

22. (Woodson 1925, 256-261).

23. Martin, March 1; April 4; June 26; July 10, 1868, AMAA.

24. *AM*, XIV (February, 1870), 39. For accounts of Martin abroad, see *AM*, X (August, 1866), 180-181, (October, 1866), 230-233; XI (January, 1867), 8-9, (July, 1867), 156-157; XII (February, 1868), 36-38; (April, 1868), 87-89; XIII (September, 1869), 204-205; *Twenty-second Annual Report* (1868), 85.

25. Martin, Washington, D.C., January 7, 1869, AMAA.

26. *AM*, XIV (February, 1870), 39.

148 His Truth Is Marching On

27. *AM*, XIV (April, 1870), 90-91; see also XIV (April, 1870), 89-90; (May, 1870), 114, for citation from the *New Era*.

28. Martin, May 18, 1870, AMAA; *AM*, XV (October, 1871), 230.

29. New Orleans *Republican*, August 12, 1876, 3; August 16, 1876, 3, copies of newspaper clippings, ARC. Martin had not expected to live a long life, and had taken opiates for pain while in Europe: Martin, Glasgow, November 10, 1867, AMAA.

30. [Charles B. Ray], *Origin and Future of the American Missionary Association* [New York, 1874], 3, said that two-thirds of the UMS as constituted in 1842 was white. Actually one half of the officers were black: see (DeBoer 1994, Chapters II and III). He also reported that Lewis Tappan was elected a vice president at the initial meeting, neglecting to point out that Tappan declined an office. This work is attributed to Ray because the author identifies himself as a black Congregational minister who attended the organizational meeting of the AMA.

31. The writer believes that Theodore Bourne was white; therefore, this is the first time she was made aware that the African Civilization Society was "engineered" by white men. To this point she had thought that that honor went to Henry Highland Garnet, who is usually given the credit.

32. *AM*, III (January, 1859), 17; (Dabney 1949, 26, 29, 35-40, 58-59, 77, 100).

33. (Dann 1971, 321-322).

34. *Thirty-sixth Annual Report* (1882), 11, 16; *Thirty-seventh Annual Report*, 43-45; *Thirty-eighth Annual Report*, 33-36, which included a paper by Michael Strieby giving the following statement of agreement between the AMA and the AHMS: "Neither Society will establish in any locality a church that will not admit to membership colored persons suitably qualified, nor will it sustain any church that will not fellowship the neighboring Congregational churches or that will not unite with the local Congregational Conference or Association." In general it was agreed that the work

at the South would be carried on by the AMA and that at the West by the AHMS.

35. (DeBöer 1994, 16, 53-54, 87).

36. *Sketch of the Life of Charles B. Ray* (New York, 1887), 60; New York *Independent*, August 26, 1886; *Congregational Yearbook* (Boston, 1887).

37. (Ward 1855, 28-29).

38. F. Landon, "Samuel Ringgold Ward," DAB XIX (1936), 440.

39. (Ward 1855, 28, 34).

40. Mrs. Harriet E. Rogers, August 10, 1865, to Whipple, AMAA.

41. (Howard 1907, 321-322).

42. Martin, London, December 29, 1866, AMAA.

43. *JNH*, XXII (January, 1937), 72.

44. *Thirty-first Annual Report* (1877), 105. *Minutes of the General Assembly of the Presbyterian Church in the United States of America*, NS (New York, 1868), 151, Garnet's address is given as Pittsburgh, but he is still listed as pastor of Prince Street [Shiloh] Church; (New York, 1869), 383, Garnet is listed as "President, Allegheny City, Pennsylvania."

45. (Crummell 1891, 299-304).

From a photograph taken in the spring of 1866   FISK SCHOOL—WEST VIEW   Sketched by Hardy L. Keith, '01

VII

AFRICAN AMERICANS
AND THE AMA COLLEGES

The teachers in these institutions came not to keep the Negroes in their places, but to raise them out of the places of defilement where slavery had wallowed them. The colleges they founded were social settlements; homes where the best of the sons of the freedmen came in close and sympathetic touch with the best traditions of New England.
        —W.E.B. DuBois, *The Souls of Black Folk*

No denominational schools surpass those of this group [AMA] in educational standards or administrative efficiency. It is probable that no church board has equaled this association in the thoroughness of its self-examination.
        —United States Department of the Interior
        Bureau of Education, Bulletin 1916, No. 38.

The AMA's institutions of higher education, like its common schools, were open to all regardless of race, color, sex, or creed. One southern reporter, in a sneering yet half-complimentary review of Atlanta University, remarked that a student could be a member of the theological department without being "a member of any church." He thought that was "quite liberal."[1] While the Association was glad to find Protestant churches interested in establishing schools among the freedmen, it opposed those groups that insisted on a specific—or in fact any—church affiliation as requisite for matriculation. The privileges of AMA schools were available for anyone: white or black, old or young, church member or not. Denominationalism was never emphasized. "The majority of its college students, due to the distinctive historic religious affiliations

151

of the Negro, have never been Congregationalists. No attempt is made to proselyte and most of them go back to their own churches and there invest their increased talents." No other denomination has performed "such an unselfish service" or made "such a purely eleemosynary contribution . . . millions of dollars without hope or purpose of profit."[2] The work of the AMA during the Civil War and Reconstruction was the greatest adventure in brotherhood in the history of America.

Eight Chartered Institutions

January 1, 1866, the AMA reopened Berea College, Berea, Kentucky, that had been closed because of the war. It had been an integrated school at its founding in 1858 and was continued on that same basis.[3] In addition to Berea, seven other chartered institutions of higher education were established during Reconstruction: Hampton Normal and Agricultural Institute, Hampton, Virginia (opened in 1868 and chartered in 1870);[4] Fisk University, Nashville, Tennessee (Fisk School established 1866, Fisk University chartered August, 1867);[5] Atlanta University, Atlanta, Georgia (chartered October 17, 1867);[6] Talladega College, Talladega, Alabama (work begun 1867, chartered February 17, 1869);[7] Tougaloo University, Tougaloo, Mississippi (work begun 1869, chartered 1870);[8] Straight University, New Orleans, Louisiana (incorporated June 25, 1869, building occupied in February, 1870);[9] Tillotson Normal and Collegiate School, Austin, Texas (chartered 1877).[10]

Even to many of its own personnel the AMA seemed optimistic in calling its schools colleges and universities before there were any black students ready for collegiate education. It was done to give the African American students goals they might not otherwise have had, and to declare the Association's purpose of eventually preparing black students for all the professions.

Although open enrollment was a principle to which the AMA staunchly adhered, standards were not lowered in order to enable a boast of large numbers of black graduates. The first Fisk graduates—the first black college graduates in the South—given the A.B. degree were James Dallas Burrus, John Houston Burrus, and Virginia Ella Walker, in 1875. Three years later John H. Burrus and Virginia (Walker) Broughton were the first recipients of M.A.

degrees from Fisk.[11] Atlanta University granted its first six collegiate degrees in 1876; and that same year two girls, who had graduated from Straight's Normal Department in 1873, received degrees from that school's College Department after six years of study.[12] One of the six African Americans awarded the A.B. degree at Atlanta was Richard Robert Wright, twenty-three years old. He it was who gave General Howard the message for the North, "We are rising," when a lad in an AMA school. John Greenleaf Whittier made the incident the theme of a poem. Wright became principal of Howard Normal School (1876); earned an M.A. (1879); was principal of Ware High School (1890-91); president of Georgia State Industrial College (1891-1921); a banker in Philadelphia; trustee of Atlanta (1889-1898). He thought it of enough significance to include in the resume of his life in *Who's Who in America*, the fact that he addressed the AMA at its anniversary meeting in 1907.

The Theological Department at Straight was in operation for eleven years before it awarded its first B.D. There had been many students, but most of them did not have a basic college course before taking theological training; and "the theological and literary attainments of the students would never have justified" awarding the degree before 1881. "It is little less than a crime to confer an unmerited degree upon a young man. It would not only be a fraud, but a source of constant embarrassment to him." So declared the Annual Report in 1881. That year, however, A.E.P. Albert, an ordained Methodist minister who had studied at Atlanta University, was properly prepared and was awarded the B.D. degree.[13] It was twenty-six years after its incorporation that Talladega graduated its first collegiate class.[14]

Howard University

In addition to its eight chartered institutions, the AMA had much to do with the founding of Howard University, Washington, D.C. The first division of Howard to begin operations was the Normal and Preparatory Department. During Howard's first year (1867), the teacher of that department was Edward Franklin Williams, whose salary was paid by the AMA. From 1881 through 1884 the AMA also paid one half the salary of William W. Patton, president of Howard, as well as the salaries of the men in the

Theological Department.[15] By supplying half his salary, the AMA was also able to secure the post of tutor on Howard's faculty for African American George Collins in 1870.[16]

Howard University, though not officially established by the AMA, was begun with its blessing and by men who were backers of the Association and members of Washington, D.C.'s First Congregational Church. The idea was born November 19, 1866, at the monthly prayer meeting for missions at First Church. The university was named after Oliver Otis Howard, head of the Freedmen's Bureau and a member of the church; and its first president was Rev. Charles Brandon Boynton, pastor of First Congregational Church, but the office had first been offered to George Whipple, executive secretary of the AMA. Although nonsectarian like all the Association schools, many Congregationalists were involved in its leadership. In addition to Boynton, six of its first thirteen presidents were of the Pilgrim faith: Amzi L. Barber, F.D. Fairfield, William Weston Patton, Jeremiah E. Rankin, Stephen M. Newman, and J. Stanley Durkee.[17]

Although theological training for African Americans was the initial stimulus that resulted in the founding of Howard, theological studies did not begin there until January 6, 1868, when Danforth B. Nichols and Ebenezer W. Robinson began gratuitously giving "instruction twice a week to a number of men already accredited as preachers and others looking forward to that work." A short time later, a course of study was drawn up and lectures begun by General Eliphalet Whittlesey, a former Colonel of the 46th United States Colored Regiment and Assistant Commissioner of the Freedmen's Bureau, who was also an ordained minister.[18]

Funds were never allocated to the Theological Department by the federal government, as they were to the other departments of Howard. The AMA was its principal backer, although for a time it shared the support of the department with the Presbytery of Washington[19]

John Bunyan Reeve

The Theological Department was officially organized in 1870, and the AMA engaged John Bunyan Reeve, black Presbyterian minister from Philadelphia, in 1871, to serve as its Dean and Professor of Biblical Theology.[20] He also taught Greek Grammar and Testament, Theological Encyclopedia, English Rhetoric and Etymology. He had attended New York Central College at McGrawville, and Union Theological Seminary (N.S. Presbyterian) in New York City. He was given the Doctor of Divinity Degree by Lincoln University in 1870.[21]

Reeve attended the Annual Meeting of the Association in October, 1871, and spoke on the work at Howard. He said he was glad to co-operate in plans to start a church either near Lincoln Mission, or on University Hill in Washington, feeling the latter place certainly in need of one. A church was organized at the University in January, 1872, with an interracial charter membership that included Chinese immigrants, a freedman, a native African, a Creek Indian, J.B. Johnson (treasurer of Howard), and the daughter of a deceased African missionary. "It seems a little like St. Luke's description of the gathering on the day of Pentecost," commented the editor of the *Missionary.*[22]

Reeve's fellow laborers at Howard were happy with his appointment and considered him a pleasant and dedicated worker. For his part, Reeve was anxious that some religious training be given to women—not preparation for preaching nor training for minister's wives—but for religious work in the churches. He was sure that white men were unaware of the importance of women in black churches, where they outnumbered the men "five to one" and formed "the chief support, spiritually and financially."[23]

In the beginning instruction in the Theological Department was in the evening, most of the men spending a full day at work in the city before attending classes. By 1873, the number who could give full time to study had grown, and some day classes were held. But almost immediately the impact of the great industrial depression of 1873 was felt. It made its impress on the AMA as elsewhere. Money left New York faster than it arrived., and the officers found it difficult to meet commitments. Reeve found it encouraging when a new student arrived, not only armed with a fair educational background, but also with two hundred dollars of his own money. Perhaps because of the financial problems of the time and the fact that the AMA was not always able to send his salary on time, Reeve also served for a season as the stated supply of the Fifteenth Street Presbyterian Church.[24]

There were several white lecturers who assisted Reeve: Jeremiah Eames Rankin (Homiletics), Danforth B. Nichols (Biblical Geography, etc.), Eliphalet Whittlesey (Evidences, etc.), Lorenzo Westcott (Church History), John D. Butler (Sacred History). Messrs. Darwin and Michaelis E. Goldberg each taught Hebrew. Mr. Goldberg also taught vocal music, a subject emphasized by the department in order that the future ministers might be able to lead in congregational singing when necessary.[25]

By 1873 there were twenty-seven students altogether; and although it was with difficulty that they could be classified on the basis of preparation, there was "what may properly be called a Middle and a Junior Class." During the year 1873-1874, the AMA provided almost $600 in aid to indigent students.[26]Some of the enrollees of each class also took the English course at the University. Others were privately instructed in spare time by Reeve and the members of the Middle Class. This was done especially for older men who had felt called to the ministry but had been denied the advantages of education. It was a question of accepting them as they were (uneducated) or letting them go on preaching as they were.

As Reeve saw it, the "distinctive feature" of the Theological Department was its "undenominational character." Students were learning to go beyond "the men whose names have been battle-cries for centuries" (like Wesley, Calvin, and Luther) to "the sure word of God."[27]

During the year 1873-1874, there were 69 theologues under AMA auspices in the South, in classes at Atlanta and Straight Universities, at Talladega College, and at Howard University. Thirty of them were at Howard: seven Seniors, six middlers, eleven Juniors, and six unclassified. The Seniors had entered when the department was organized in 1870. Standards were raised at the beginning of 1874; so the students entering then or later received a "better general preparation" than previous classes.

Five denominations were represented among the students. Pastors of neighboring churches also attended the department's lectures. In that way, "a steady though indirect influence" was exerted on churches representing "an aggregate membership of three thousand souls."

The fall of 1874 saw a diminished number of students in theology at Howard, only seventeen, but all were classified students. The financial panic was at least partially at fault. Reeve had himself aided some students by advancing his own money. For financial reasons, Reeve resigned as Dean of the Theological Department at the close of the 1874-1875 school year. At least one other African American worked in Howard's Theological Department during Reconstruction. Alexander Crummell, D.D., was visiting Lecturer on Pastoral Work in 1877.[28]

African American Roles Elsewhere

The stories of the foundings of all the AMA schools are engrossing and filled with the names of men like General Samuel Chapman Armstrong, principal of Hampton; John G. Fee, long-time abolitionist and president of Berea; Edmund A. Ware, president of Atlanta; James Abram Garfield, trustee of Hampton and President of the United States. But these were all white men and their stories have been told elsewhere. There were black men involved in the establishment and early years of these schools, however, and some were members of the charter boards of trustees. Ambrose Headen and William Savery were trustees of Talladega. (Talladega's charter board was also notable for the inclusion of a woman member, Phebe M. Beebe, a teacher from Michigan). John J. Cary and W.W. Mallery were among the charter trustees of Fisk; Cary was treasurer of the Board in 1869, and Mallery was a member of Fisk's Advisory Committee in 1873. Gabriel Burdett was a trustee of Berea College. William J. White, Baptist minister of Augusta and editor of the *Georgia Baptist*, was a trustee of Atlanta University. Thomas W. Cardozo was a trustee of Tougaloo by virtue of his office as State Superintendent of Public Education for Mississippi, and John R. Lynch was a trustee of the same institution. John R. Clay, wealthy African American real estate dealer in New Orleans, was a trustee of Straight University. Col. James H. Ingraham, Dr. James T. Newman, Dr. Charles H. Thompson, Adolphe Zemar, and Samuel Wakefield were other black trustees of Straight. Before a generation had passed, some of the graduates of AMA schools would serve their alma maters as trustees. Joseph E. Smith was elected a trustee of Atlanta University in 1880 and remained on the Board until his death thirty-eight years later. George W. Moore was a trustee of Fisk in 1897 and a lecturer on Pastoral Theology at Howard University.[29]

African Americans played a larger role in the establishment of Talladega than of the other AMA colleges. Thomas Tarrant and William Savery returned from a freedmen's convention at Mobile in 1865, and started a school in the house of David White. A black educational association headed by Henry Knox then secured a separate building for it. In 1867 that school "was merged in the college founded by the American Missionary Association to provide education 'From which no one shall be debarred on account of race or color.'" The first building used by the college was Swayne Hall, an edifice William Savery had helped to build in 1852 when he was a slave carpenter.[30]

Its belief in the equal ability of the freedmen to learn incontestably proven in its schools in the South, the AMA looked for educated black men with the requisite moral character to head departments in its institutions of higher learning. The Association made no secret of the fact that acceptance of a position in one of its colleges meant financial sacrifices. Salaries were low, and satisfaction must come from the intangible rewards of teaching. Although there were no black presidents of AMA colleges during Reconstruction, there were several African American heads of departments and a number of instructors.

Straight University, New Orleans

In addition to John B. Reeve, whose story appears above in the account of AMA personnel in Howard University, the first dean of Straight's Theological Department was also a black Presbyterian minister, Charles H. Thompson. Thompson, who had been an AMA missionary in Ohio during his seminary years at Oberlin, and who had since held pastorates in Brooklyn, New York (Siloam Presbyterian), and Newark, New Jersey (Plane Street Presbyterian), also helped to found Central Congregational Church in New Orleans and served it as pastor.[31]

Two other departments at Straight were headed by African Americans. Dr. James T. Newman, physician in charge of the dispensary connected with the Hathaway Home in New Orleans, was chosen to head the fledgling Medical Department in 1872. Plans were underway for the purchase of a hospital building for the use of this department in 1874, the year that both the law and medical departments at Straight were asked to become self-sustaining. No doubt the demise of this early medical experiment was aided by the promise of Louisiana politicians that colored students would be accepted at the state medical schools.[32]

Louis A. Bell was the African American who organized the Law Department at Straight University in 1871. Bell's association with the AMA began in 1867 when John Watson Alvord of the Freedmen's Bureau recommended him to the AMA as a teacher. At that time Bell was a clerk in the Navy Department in Washington and a member of the Nineteenth Street Baptist Church of that city. Bell's father had been a man of some property in Washington; but when his considerable activities as an agent of the underground railroad were discovered, he was forced to flee, leaving everything behind. He made a new life in New Bedford, Massachusetts, where Louis was graduated from the collegiate class of the high school in 1860. Between that time and his position in Washington, Bell had taught school in California. Because a sister and his mother were dependent upon his support, the salary offered by the AMA "would be a sacrifice" he was "not unwilling, but unable to make."[33]

Between 1867 and 1871 when he began at Straight, Bell acquired an LL.B. degree. In 1873 when he was thirty-one, Bell was awarded an A.M. from Straight. He and several others read papers at the graduation ceremonies. Bell's was entitled, "Death Penalty," in which he took a stand against capital punishment. James T. Newman (who was awarded a Ph.D. by Straight in 1873) read a paper entitled, "A Defense of the Medical Profession." Leon Dewitt Stocking (who was awarded a bachelor of medicine degree) spoke on "Experimental Physiology." Sometime between 1867 and 1873 Bell was married. His wife lived in Philadelphia during his years at Straight.[34]

By 1874 Bell had established quite a department with the following lawyers as instructors: Prof. E. Filleul (Civil Law and Practice), H.C. Dibble (Constitutional Law and Statutory Construction), S. Belden (Commercial Law and Admiralty Practice in U.S. Courts), G.W. Carter and E.C. Billings (Criminal and International Law and Evidence), Louis A. Bell (Common Law and Equity). Bell was evidently a self-effacing individual; for, although he was the organizer of the department, when he restructured it in preparation for a self-sustaining program, he held an election of the law faculty. Professor Filleul was elected dean and Bell secretary of the law faculty.[35]

The law school at Straight proved popular with white men, several of whom joined its student body. But its primary purpose was to prepare African Americans for positions in local and national government. There were fifteen students in 1875. In 1873 there had been twelve to open the session:

P.P. Carroll (St. Bernard, La.)
C.C. Antoine (New Orleans)
Thomas J. Flanagan (New Orleans)
Louis A. Martinet (St. Martinsville, La.)
R.H. Isabelle (New Orleans)
A.F. Riard (Vermilionville, La.)
Victor Rochon (St. Martinsville, La.)
S.R. Snaer (New Orleans)
John E. Staes (New Orleans)
Eugene Staes (New Orleans)
Harry Lott (Alexandria, La.)
J.B. Lott (New Orleans)

Eugene Lucie and Charles A. Baquie also attended classes.[36]

Louis A. Bell died in the fall of 1874, and a search was made to find an African American to head the department in his place.[37]

The AMA hired Louis A. Martinet as instructor in French at Straight while he was a student in the Law Department. Martinet was an accomplished linguist and also taught Latin. He was active in the Louisiana Republican party and served as a member of the state legislature. At one point during Louisiana's political unrest, Martinet feared for his life if he returned to his home.[38]

Barnabas Root of the AMA's Mendi Mission, West Africa, taught Hebrew at Straight University, 1872-1873.[39] That same year Miss N.A. Ramsey was employed to teach in the primary school at Straight. A native of Petersburg, Virginia (her brother was Samuel Coles, AMA missionary), she was educated in Ohio.[40] There were also several students of Straight who taught in the primary school there.

Gabriel Burdett, former slave and Union soldier, taught in the primary school at Berea College after the war. Alice E. Peck, a native of Alexander, New York, headed the primary school at Berea from 1870 through 1877.[41]

Fisk University

African Americans were first employed by Fisk University in the music department. Notable among them was Ella Sheppard. Redeemed from slavery as a baby by her parents at terrible cost, Ella grew up in Cincinnati. She had a great aptitude for music, but was forced to enter her teacher's home after dark by the back door in order to keep secret the fact of a black pupil. She taught a pay school for black children at Gallatin, Tennessee, to earn money for a college education. When the sum total of her year's savings turned out to be six dollars, she nevertheless went to Fisk in 1867, where she managed to sustain herself by giving music lessons. After two years of such work, she was given a position on the Fisk faculty as teacher of music, a post she held until her husband George W. Moore (also a graduate of Fisk) accepted a position as AMA missionary in Washington, D.C.

Sheppard's greatest renown is as accompanist of Fisk's famed original Jubilee Singers. She travelled with the Jubilee Singers for five years in Europe, singing before Queen Victoria and many other European rulers and statesmen. Her greatest work for the AMA, however, was as a fitting wife of an outstanding Congregational minister who became Secretary of the Southern Field for the AMA, the first African American to hold such a post. Important in her own right, Mrs. Moore became the "pastoress" of Lincoln Industrial Institute, a leader in AMA Women's Work, and an effective public speaker. She "often responded to the American Missionary Association to speak upon its platform and never failed to greatly interest all who heard her. . . ." Several of her addresses were published by the Association.[42]

The organization and tour plans of the first troupe of Jubilee Singers brought Rebecca Massey to the faculty of the unofficial music department of Fisk University, Ella Sheppard was a very valuable member of that department, teaching voice and instrumental music as well as accompanying the choir and singing in her own right. Her absence with the Singers left a gap the AMA was unable to fill adequately with one person. Massey was able to take over the instrumental lessons but lacked both Sheppard's ability as a singer and her expertise as a teacher of voice. Massey was a product of Oberlin College. She joined Fisk's faculty in 1871 and was still there at the end of Reconstruction.[43]

James Dallas Burrus, one of the first collegiate graduates of Fisk in 1875, was hired that year as instructor of mathematics. When he resigned in 1877 to take graduate work at Dartmouth, that post was taken by his brother John Houston Burrus, who was also graduated in 1875. John, in turn, resigned in 1879 (when he received his A.M. from Fisk), and James returned with a master's degree from Dartmouth.[44] In 1877, Laura S. Cary, daughter of Fisk trustee John J. Cary, was graduated from the classical course at Fisk and made instructor of Greek.[45]

Student Teachers

Each of the "colleges" contained every level of education from elementary school through graduate programs, although some years had to pass before there were candidates ready for the collegiate departments. It was a general practice in the AMA colleges to employ the outstanding students in the normal department as teachers in the college primary school. This program was not without its critics, however; some parents in New Orleans, for example, argued that they had sent their children to Straight University common school to receive superior education and not to be taught by students.[46]

Among the student teachers at Hampton Institute were the following African Americans:

Sarah Brown (from Bladen County, N.C.)
(Miss) Henrie Jane Bullard (Charleston, W.V.)
D. Amos Ellet
Nancy J. Ellison (Beaufort, N.C.)
Marina Fulford (Beaufort, N.C.)
Hattie Lawrence Green (Wilmington, N.C.)
Eliza Anna Jackson (Charleston, S.C.)
Calvin Johnson
Harriet Kelley
George W. Taylor (Hampton)
Caroline Valentine

W.R. Watkins
Edward Whitehurst (Hampton)
Ella G. Willis
Samuel Cavino Windsor (Newbern, N.C.)[47]

Student teachers at Straight University included the following:

Amelia Jackson
Magnolia Millia
Amanda M. Perkins
Felix Perkins
Cora Smith
Alice Thomas[48]

Yancy Benjamin Sims was a student teacher at Talladega in 1867.[49]

Between 1869 and 1871 the following Howard University students taught in the AMA's school at the Lincoln Mission, Washington, D.C.:

Eleanora Page (from Washington, D.C.)
Sophia Graham (Washington)
Annie Levere (Detroit)
Fanny Shippen (Washington)
Ellen Fisher (Washington)
Ruth Fisher (Washington)
Furman J. Shadd (Washington)[50]
Thomas McCants Stewart (Charleston, S.C.)
Joseph W. Morris (Charleston, S.C.)[51]
S.R.J. Nelson (Washington)
Daniel Morris (Kilmarnock, Va.)
P.F. Morris (Washington)
George Copeland (Alexandria, Va.)
Simon Peter Smith (Columbia, S.C.)[52]
Charles A. Harris (Bladensburg, N.J.)
Isaiah Washington (Washington)
Inman Edward Page (Washington)[53]

E.H. Grasty (Danville, Va.)
N.D. Nixon (Washington)
J.E. Jenkins (Washington)
C.M. Milford (Washington)
T.W. Payne (Wilmington, N.C.)
M.F. Jordan (Norfolk, Va.)
Samuel Thompson (Alexandria, Va.)
John W. Dersey (Washington)
J.M. Brown (Washington)
Robert Hunt (Annapolis)
William J. Troy (Richmond, Va.)
Alexander Stanard (Augusta, Ga.)
T.E. Miller (Charleston, S.C.)
Hugh M. Browne (Washington)
J.E. Blenheim (Alexandria, Va.)
R.K. Morris (Washington)
Charles J. Malord (Bear Hollow, Va.)
James E. Hunt (Annapolis)
William H. Balis (Leesburg, Va.)
D.A. Sadgwar (Wilmington, N.C.)
William Middleton (Washington)
J.E. White (Washington)
J.W. Bell (Washington)
E.R. Russell (Washington)
John Shippen (Washington)
J.S. Evans (Washington)
Edward W. Turner (Washington)[54]
Arthur Smith (Washington)
Samuel Cook (Washington)

Faith in the Ability of African Americans

The AMA's faith in the ability of African Americans to fill all the roles of life is demonstrated in the structure of its schools. Although the major emphasis was placed, out of necessity, on the preparation of teachers; provision was made for ministers, doctors, lawyers, farmers, mechanics, seamstresses. Sometimes a lack of money meant that an expensive department—like the Medical Department at Straight—either had to be abandoned or asked to become self-sufficient, but the principle of equal education remained intact. And the institution of manual training in some of its schools, a recognition of the fact that blacks should also be prepared to enter trades from which they had been excluded for lack of training, did not alter the fact that the AMA's major role was in advancing the cause of higher liberal education for African Americans. The importance of that emphasis can be seen in the impact of its graduates upon the life of the United States as well as in evidence pointing to the uniqueness of its work, like the fact that its Law Department at Straight University was the only such school south of the Potomac open to African Americans.[55]

When the war and military Reconstruction had ended and Jim Crow was recognized and solidified in state laws, the AMA schools in the South remained islands of sanity in the midst of segregation—places where members of both races could meet and study together, and work for the implementation of the Law of the Land into the life of America. A reporter for the *Atlanta Constitution*, arguing against state aid for Atlanta University, wrote that in that institution "the mischievous doctrine of social equality is practically inculcated." He was upset by the fact that black and white, teachers and students, ate their meals together. Objections were also made against the Theological Department. Rather than lose state aid for Atlanta, the AMA was willing to close that department and transfer the students to another of its schools. [56]

NOTES

1. *AM,* XVIII (September, 1874), 198.

2. (Maurer, Atkins & Rogers 1925, 5).

3. See circulars: "Literary Institution, Berea Kentucky," April 2 and May 30, 1866, AMAA; *AM,* III (October, 1859), 234.

4. See circulars: "Hampton Normal and Agricultural Institute," 1868 and 1870; "An Act to Incorporate the Hampton Normal and Agricultural Institution, Approved June 4, 1870," AMAA. See also *AM Extra* (August, 1869), "Hampton Normal and Industrial Institute, Report of Special Committee." The report was signed by

Mark Hopkins, Alexander Hyde, B.G. Northrup, and James A. Garfield.

5. See manuscript: "Rules for the government of the Faculty of Fisk University," February 8, 1868; circulars: "Rules and Regulations of the Fisk University, Nashville, Tenn.," 1868; "Fisk University, Nashville, Tennessee," n.d.; "Fisk University and Normal School," 1869, AMAA.

6. *AM*, XIII (November, 1869), 245-246.

7. *AM* XIII (October, 1869), 224-225.

8. *Historical Sketch of Tougaloo University, Tougaloo, Mississippi* (n.p., n.d., but after 1887); Frank Woodworth, *Tougaloo University, Tougaloo, Mississippi* (n.p., n.d., but post 1887); *AM*, XIV (August, 1870), 172-174.

9. *AM*, XIV (August, 1870), 169-171; for the union of Straight University (AMA-Congregational) with New Orleans University (Methodist) to form Dillard University, see *Facing Facts* (New York, 1935), 4-5, AMAA.

10. *Thirty-first Annual Report* (1877), 71. In 1877 property and a charter were obtained for the Collegiate and Normal School. Normal classes were held during the year in a rented building.

11. *AM*, XIX (August, 1875), 182; *Thirty-second Annual Report* (1878), 60.

12. *Thirtieth Annual Report* (1876), 62; the six who graduated from Atlanta, along with four who completed the Normal Course and three who finished the "eclectic Biblical course" made a total of thirteen—the largest number sent out from Atlanta to that date. Most of them had received all their education in AMA schools. They were examined by the Governor of Georgia. Articles from the *Atlanta Times* and the *Atlanta Constitution* were excerpted on pages 62-63 of the Report.

13. *Thirty-fifth Annual Report* (1881), 76.

14. *The Negro—a Congregational Opportunity* (New York, 1921), 22, AMAA.

15. See the AMA Executive Committee Minutes, 1881-1884, AMAA.

16. Collins, September 24, 1870, to Smith, AMAA.

17. (Brownlee 1946, 199-200); (Logan 1969, 12-15).

18. Dwight O.W. Holmes, "Fifty Years of Howard University," *JNH*, III (October, 1918), 372.

19. (Brownlee 1946, 200).

20. Reeve, September 20, 1871, to Cravath, AMAA; *Twenty-eighth Annual Meeting* (New York, 1874),27.

21. *Twenty-seventh Annual Report* (1873), 27; (Logan 1969, 51).

22. See the Reeve letters to Cravath for 1871, 1872, AMAA; *Twenty-fifth Annual Report* (1871), 10; *AM*, XVII (January, 1873), 1.

23. Nichols, August 10, 1872; Reeve, June 29, 1872, AMAA; Of course, the men at the Rooms in New York knew about the theological training (at Oberlin) and ordination of Antoinette Brown (first seminary-trained woman minister) in 1856.

24. See Reeve letters for 1872-1875 to Cravath, AMAA; Records of the Fifteenth Street Presbyterian Church, M-SC.

25. *Twenty-seventh Annual Report* (1873), 26-27; Reeve, April 1; May 1, 1873, to Cravath, AMAA.

26. (Logan 1969, 52).

27. *Twenty-seventh Annual Report* (1873), 27.

28. *Twenty-eighth Annual Report* (1874), 26-27; *AM*, XVII (January, 1874), 6; Richard A. Tucker, June 19, 1874; Reeve letters for 1874 and 1875, to Cravath, AMAA; *Thirty-first Annual Report* (1877),47; (Logan 1969, 64).

29. *Twenty-third Annual Report* (1869),39; *Twenty-seventh Annual Report* (1873), 47; *Thirty-fourth Annual Report* (1880), 40; Wakefield, New Iberia, Louisiana, December 1, 1874, to J.A. Adams, AMAA. The author makes no claim of having identified *all* the African Americans who served AMA colleges during Reconstruction. Workers were not identified by race in the AMA reports. It was thanks to an account written by a white reporter in an Atlanta paper that I learned that most of Atlanta's trustees were "white Northerners" or "blacks," which led to Mr. White's identity. *Fifty-first Annual Report* (1897), 45.

30. Circular, "Savery Library, Talladega College, Talladega, Alabama," n.d., AMAA.

31. The story of Thompson and Central Congregational Church, New Orleans, is told below in the chapter on "Catos and Congregationalists."

32. See the letters of James T. Newman, AMAA.

33. See letters of J.W. Alvord, AMAA.

34. *AM*, XVII (August, 1873), 177-178.

35. See the letters of Louis A. Bell, AMAA, particularly, June 1, 1874, Straight University, to E.M. Cravath.

36. *AM*, XV (April, 1871), 88; Bell, June 1, 1874, to Cravath, AMAA.

37. Adams, October 6; October 31, 1874; Isabelle, February 18, 1875, to Cravath, AMAA.

38. See the letters of Martinet, AMAA.

39. Root, New Orleans, February 17, 1874, to Cravath, AMAA; for the story of Barnabas Root, see (DeBoer 1994, 130-137, 140).

40. Ramsey, Amite City, Louisiana, October 6, 1871, to General C.H. Howard; Mrs. R.A. Leslie (nee Ramsey), Osyka, Mississippi, June 8, 1874. One noteworthy fact is that Miss Ramsey received an extended and affectionate testimonial from a Roman Catholic priest for her work in human and race relations: John Scollard, St. Helena's Church, Amite City, January 1, 1872, to the Rev. Dr. Healy, Straight University, AMAA.

41. *Nineteenth Annual Report* (1865), 29-30; *AM*, XIV (June, 1870), 125; XX (February, 1876), 30.

42. *AM*, LXVIII (July, 1914), 223; (August, 1914), 287; XLIV (January, 1895), 10; (Moore 1912); *Negro Womanhood: Its Past* (New York, n.d.); Ella Sheppard Moore, "Historical Sketch of the Jubilee Singers," *Fisk University News*, II (October, 1911), 41-58. Although music was stressed at Fisk from the beginning, there was no formal Music Department until 1884.

43. See the letters of Rebecca Massey, AMAA; see also Spence, Nashville, Tennessee, January 7, 1874, to Cravath and other letters to Cravath in 1871.

44. See the letters of James Dallas Burrus, AMAA. See also Joe M. Richardson, "A Negro Success Story: James Dallas Burrus," *JNH*, L (October, 1965), 274-282, for the work of James and John Burrus at Alcorn University, where the latter became president in 1883. Richardson also explains that technically Dartmouth did not award a master's degree, having no graduate program as such, but gave Burrus an honorary Master of Arts. See also (Simmons 1887, 281-287); *AM*, XIX (August, 1875), 182; XX (February, 1876), 29; *Thirty-first Annual Report* (1877), 63; *Thirty-second Annual Report* (1878), 60.

45. *Thirty-second Annual Report* (1878), 59, 60; *AM* XXXIII (August, 1879), 232. John J. Cary was a cashier of the Freedmen's Bank in Nashville. Miss Cary, "attractive in person, cultured in

manners," died of typhus fever, June 28, 1879, aged 23. See also *Thirty-third Annual Report* (1879), 23.

46. Adams, October 27, 1874; Adams explained that it was hard for the people to believe (although true) that the Straight pupils taught better than the older public school teachers in the South. See also Thompson, New Orleans, October 27, 1874, AMAA.

47. Samuel Armstrong, Hampton, Virginia, April 22, 1870, to Smith, AMAA; *AM*, XV (May, 1871), 97; XXII (May, 1869), 99; XIV (June, 1870), 122; Ella G. Willis, Teacher's Monthly Report, Armstrong School, Elizabeth City, Virginia, for April, 1870; letters of Samuel C. Windsor, AMAA. Among the many Hampton graduates who taught in the 1870's were George E. Stephens of Beaufort, N.C., who taught at Bonsacks, Virginia; George W. Cole, at Tappahannock, Virginia; Ackrel E. White, among the Blue Ridge Mountains.

48. See schedule of classes at Straight University (1874); Adams, November 22, 1874; Ashley, March 3, 1874, to Cravath; Ashley, Report of Straight University, April, 1874, AMAA.

49. *Twenty-first Annual Report* (1867), 49.

50. All the names on this list were submitted by George G. Collins, Washington City, May 10, 1870, AMAA. Furman J. Shadd was 16 years old in 1869, when he gave an address at Howard's second anniversary: *AM*, XIII (August, 1869), 170. He became a member of the Mississippi legislature in 1871.

51. Thomas McCants Stewart and Joseph W. Morris were students under Francis Cardozo at Saxton School (Avery Institute) at Charleston. In 1873, during the time of unrest at Howard University when O.O. Howard had taken a leave of absence and John Mercer Langston was Acting President, Cardozo called the boys from South Carolina home, where they entered South Carolina University. See Simon Peter Smith, Washington, D.C., December 26, 1873, to E.F. Williams, EFW Papers, ARC. For a biography of Stewart see (Simmons 1887, 1052-1054); Stewart became a lawyer and was a professor in Liberia College. For Joseph Morris, see

(Simmons 1887, 162-164); Morris did not leave Howard in 1873, but graduated in 1875. After studying law at South Carolina University, he was principal of Payne Institute and then president of Allen University.

52. See the letters of Smith, EFW Papers, ARC.

53. Inman Edward Page also left Howard in 1873, when he became one of the first African Americans to attend Brown University. In 1878 he was employed as a teacher in the Lincoln Institute of Jefferson City, Missouri (see below), and two years later was made principal. See (Simmons 1887, 474-480).

54. See the letters of Edward W. Turner, AMAA.

55. *AM*, XV (July, 1871), 157.

56. *AM*, XV (April, 1871), 73-74; (August, 1871), 183-185; XIX (March, 1875), 51-52; (August, 1875), 183; XV (December, 1871), 283-284.

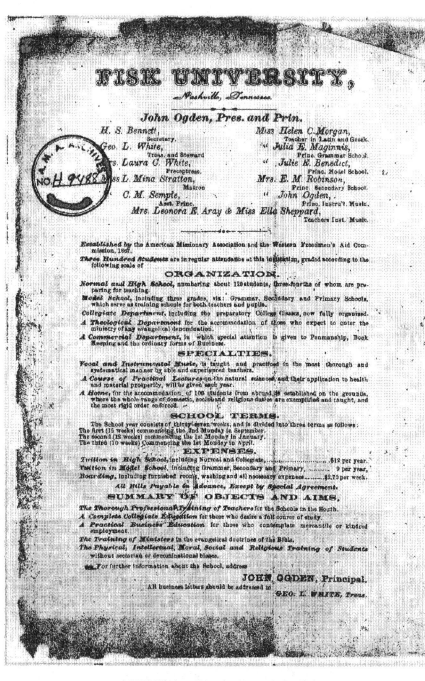

FISK UNIVERSITY,
Nashville, Tennessee.

John Ogden, Pres. and Prin.

H. S. Bennett,
Secretary.

Geo. L. White,
Treas. and Steward

Mrs. Laura C. White,
Preceptress.

Miss L. Mina Stratton,
Matron

C. M. Semple,
Asst. Princ.

Miss Helen C. Morgan,
Teacher in Latin and Greek.

Julia E. Maginnis,
Princ. Grammar School.

Julie E. Benedict,
Princ. Model School.

Mrs. E. M. Robinson,
Princ. Secondary School.

John Ogden,
Princ. Instru'l. Music.

Mrs. Leonora E. Aray & Miss Ella Sheppard,
Teachers Inst. Music.

Established by the American Missionary Association and the Western Freedmen's Aid Commission, 1867.

Three Hundred Students are in regular attendance at this institution, graded according to the following scale of

ORGANIZATION.

Normal and High School, numbering about 120 students, three-fourths of whom are preparing for teaching.

Model School, including three grades, viz: Grammar, Secondary and Primary Schools, which serve as training schools for both teachers and pupils.

Collegiate Department, including the preparatory College Classes, now fully organized.

A Theological Department for the accommodation of those who expect to enter the ministry of any evangelical denomination.

A Commercial Department, in which special attention is given to Penmanship, Book Keeping and the ordinary forms of Business.

SPECIALTIES.

Vocal and Instrumental Music, is taught and practiced in the most thorough and systematical manner by able and experienced teachers.

A Course of Practical Lectures on the natural sciences and their application to health and material prosperity, will be given each year.

A Home, for the accommodation of 100 students from abroad, is established on the grounds, where the whole range of domestic, social and religious duties are exemplified and taught, and the most rigid order enforced.

SCHOOL TERMS.

The School year consists of thirty-seven weeks, and is divided into three terms as follows:
The first (15 weeks) commencing the 2nd Monday in September.
The second (12 weeks) commencing the 1st Monday in January.
The third (10 weeks) commencing the 1st Monday in April.

EXPENSES.

Tuition in High School, including Normal and Collegiate, ... $12 per year.
Tuition in Model School, including Grammar, Secondary and Primary, ... 9 per year.
Boarding, including furnished rooms, washing and all necessary expenses .... $2.75 per week.

All Bills Payable in Advance, Except by Special Agreement.

SUMMARY OF OBJECTS AND AIMS.

The Thorough Professional Training of Teachers for the Schools in the South.

A Complete Collegiate Education for those who desire a full course of study.

A Practical Business Education for those who contemplate mercantile or kindred employment.

The Training of Ministers in the evangelical doctrine of the Bible.

The Physical, Intellectual, Moral, Social and Religious Training of Students without sectarian or denominational bias.

For further information about the School, address

JOHN OGDEN, Principal.

All business letters should be addressed to

GEO. L. WHITE, Treas.

1868 Fisk University Handbill
Courtesy AMA Archives, Amistad Research Center

VIII

AFRICAN AMERICANS
AND AMA HIGH AND NORMAL SCHOOLS

I am anxious to hear about the school. The "Morris Street School,"—Mr. Sumner's has been restored by order of the President, *and the School Commissioners here have rented it to Mr. Tomlinson from the 1st Jan. to 1st July 1867, for* Two Thousand Dollars. *Thus the Four Public Schools accommodating 2500 pupils have all been restored to the Rebels, and the colored people here will be completely destitute of all school accommodations by the end of this Term, for mine will be restored then too.*

Mr. Tomlinson says he intends to ask Gen. Howard for an appropriation of Fifteen Thousand *to build a school for Mr. Sumner, and Five Thousand to build one for our Asso. in accordance with the promise he made you. Mr. S. school expects to hold 1000 pupils, mine 400.*

> —Francis L. Cardozo, November 21, 1866,
> Saxton School, Charleston
> AMA Archives

In addition to its chartered colleges, the AMA also established many normal and high schools. In 1873 there were twenty-one of them:[1]

Graded and Normal Schools	Numbers of Teachers, Pupils, & Value of Property
Williston School, Wilmington, N.C.	10; 525; $9,000
Washburn Seminary, Beaufort, N.C.	3; 267; $1500*
Avery Institute, Charleston, S.C.	10; 317; $22,000
Brewer Normal, Greenwood, S.C.	1; 100; $4000

Lewis High School, Macon, Ga.	6; 518; $12,000
Beach Institute, Savannah, Ga.	10; 731; $12,000
Storrs School, Atlanta, Ga.	6; 434; $10,000
Emerson Institute, Mobile, Ala.	2; 135; $20,000
Swayne School, Montgomery, Ala.	6; 612; $15,000*
Lincoln School, Marion, Ala.	5; 300; $5000*
Trinity School, Athens, Ga.	2; 163; $3000
Burrell School, Selma, Ala.	8; 500; $7000
Howard School, Chattanooga, Tenn.	3; 368; $8000
LeMoyne Normal & Commercial	
School, Memphis, Tenn.	9; 291; $15,000
Normal School, Lexington, Ky.	4; 280; $8000
Ely Normal School, Louisville, Ky.	$20,000
(supported by the city in 1873)	
Union Academy, Columbus, Miss.	10; 376; $2000
Barnes Institute, Galveston, Texas	4; 183; $10,419
Rio Grande Seminary,	
Brownsville, Texas	3; ——; ——
Normal School, Pine Bluff, Ark.	3; 157; ——
Lincoln Institute, Jefferson City, Mo.	3; 236; $33,500*

*(* denotes that property title was in the hands of local Trustees, not the AMA.)*

Lincoln Institute, Jefferson City, Missouri

In January, 1866, the 62nd United States Colored Infantry, stationed at Fort McIntosh, Texas, subscribed $5,000 to establish a school in Missouri primarily for colored children. The soldiers had contributed $4000 and their officers the remainder. Captain R.B. Foster, a member of the committee appointed to oversee the plans who was also an officer of the 62nd Infantry, was authorized to try to raise additional funds. He secured $1325 from the 65th United States Colored Infantry, at Baton Rouge, Louisiana, and $2000 from the Freedmen's Bureau. The school was opened in September, 1866, in Jefferson City, Missouri, and named the Lincoln Institute. Its objectives were published in a circular seeking money for a building:

> If the colored people of this State are to have good
> common schools supplied with competent teachers; if they

This cut of Storrs School, Atlanta, was first published in *Harper's Weekly* of March 30, 1867. Courtesy Amistad Research Center.

Trinity School, Athens, Alabama. Courtesy Amistad Research Center

are to have the opportunity of a higher education in agriculture, the mechanic arts, law, medicine, theology, science, and literature, without going out of the State for it, and without awaiting for the slow process of such correction of public sentiment as will open our high schools and colleges to them—a process much hindered by their ignorance—it is simply a necessity of the case, that all the means available should be concentrated in an institution strong enough to be respectable and useful, and with elasticity to develop the departments of a university.[2]

Although Missouri's new Constitution provided for education of both races, the minority of the state who backed the law were "unable to give it general effect." Missouri had not left the Union and was not under the same kind of military occupation as other southern states. The only Bureau agent in Missouri at the end of the war was a disbursing agent at St. Louis. The AMA announced in 1867 that "in no other State in the Mississippi Valley have outlandish attempts to discourage, and even personally to injure, our teachers been more frequent." AMA personnel had been "compelled in some instances to flee from town to town to escape personal injury, while in others only a rare heroism has held them to their posts."[3] At the end of the year, the AMA school at Jefferson City was merged with Lincoln Institute.[4]

Because colored people could neither vote nor hold office, the AMA declared in 1869, the schools in Missouri were to be segregated and in the control of whites. Persons opposed to the education of African Americans were in power in most areas where schools were needed and refused to supply either buildings or teachers. The bright parts of the picture were that the State Superintendent, T.A. Parker, was "in full sympathy with the education of the colored children," and the new Bureau officers were helpful. James Milton Turner, later an African American minister to Liberia, held simultaneously an appointment from Parker and a commission from the AMA. He was engaged in finding out those places where local officials were neglecting the education of colored children. At Jefferson City the work was carried on jointly by the Trustees of Lincoln and the Public School Board.[5]

In 1871 Missouri voted some aid to Lincoln Institute, the only school of its kind for African Americans in the state, and the AMA sustained one teacher there. The new principal was the Rev. M. Henry Smith, former AMA worker at Warrensburg, Missouri. The AMA sold its property in Jefferson City and devoted the proceeds to the permanent endowment of a professorship at Lincoln, in 1873. Lincoln Institute grew eventually into Lincoln University, as its founders had envisioned[6]

Thomas W. Cardozo at Charleston

Saxton School, which preceded Avery Institute at Charleston, South Carolina, was headed first by Thomas W. Cardozo and then by his brother, Francis Lewis Cardozo. The AMA schools in Fayetteville, North Carolina, were also headed by African Americans, Robert D. Harris, assisted by his brother Cicero R. Harris. These were talented men and their work for the AMA deserves somewhat extended treatment.

AMA work in Charleston, South Carolina, was unique. While there were schools and even towns (like Fayetteville, North Carolina) where the AMA staff was entirely black, in Charleston the Superintendent was African American and his wife was the matron of the Mission Home where all the non-local teachers, white and black, boarded. In addition, Charleston was a stopping point for the steamers plying coastal waters, and the Mission Home there was a stop-off point for teachers on their way to places farther south. This made Charleston a most important post for AMA workers in the nineteenth century when most travel from New York to the South was by water.

Thomas and Francis Cardozo were Charleston natives, the sons of Jacob Newton Cardozo, Jewish economist and anti-nullificationist newspaper editor, and Lydia Williams, a free mulatto of mixed Indian and Negro blood. Both were well-educated men, Francis Cardozo was doubtless one of the best educated men of any color in the state.[7]

Thomas Cardozo was employed shortly before the close of the war and given permission before leaving New York to hire local teachers for the two buildings that would be under his care in Charleston.[8] There were ninety teachers in Charleston in April, 1865, under three Associations: the Freedmen's Aid of Boston, the

National Freedmen's Relief Association, and the American Missionary Association—all under the general direction of James Redpath, Superintendent of Public Instruction for the Military Department of South Carolina and Georgia. The idea proposed by Redpath (who was also the representative of the Boston Society) that each of the associations pay all of the teachers one month in three was declined by the AMA, in view of the fact that they had fewer teachers in the city than the other societies and would therefore be supporting "regardless of character" teachers who might indeed be "godless or Unitarians."[9]

Cardozo objected to Redpath's order not to open school sessions with scripture and prayer, which Redpath said was given because "the children did not pay strict obeisance." As a result of Cardozo's objection, all schools thereafter were begun with the opening exercises generally used in nineteenth century America. There were several night schools for freedmen in Charleston: the Garrison, the Saxton, and the Beecher. Cardozo named his the Lewis Tappan Night School. It was second in size only to the Saxton.[10]

The schools were carried on using New England pedagogical methods, which Cardozo characterized as the best. About seventy-five of the teachers were local people. All Redpath required of them was that they promise to treat the colored children the same as they would white ones. Cardozo also asked if they were church members and found that nine-tenths of them were. None were Roman Catholics. His chief objection to southern teachers was "their very deficient brogue; and non-yankee system of teaching."[11]

The rebels had removed almost all of the furniture from Charleston to Columbia, and Cardozo was fortunate in finding any to furnish the Mission Home. The first two teachers to share the residence with the Cardozos were Sarah A. Thayer and Vira Gould, white women from New England. Mr. and Mrs. H.H. Hunter, a black couple from New York, were also a part of the mission family. They and Thomas Cardozo did not get on well together, and the Hunters left to work at Hilton Head.[12]

Cardozo said that one northern teacher could do the work of two southern ones, but there were advantages in hiring local teachers. One was financial, and they could continue to teach, taking only a month's vacation, rather than the three months northern teachers took to escape the southern summer. He hoped "to get a still stronger foothold in Charleston in the fall." To that end he inquired if the AMA would support fifteen or eighteen teachers. He knew of several "very accomplished colored ladies in the North" who were anxious to work with him.

Cardozo found that he could economize to the extent suggested by Samuel Hunt (Corresponding Secretary for Education for the AMA)—that expenses of the Home for provisions other than those received in government rations not exceed five dollars per month per teacher—only if he were not called upon to entertain visitors and others not drawing government rations. The Rev. Ennals J. Adams, for example, had stayed at the Mission Home for four weeks while drawing no rations. The government had stopped the practice of issuing rations for missionaries and there were rumors that it would soon stop rations for teachers as well.

He found it necessary to explain some of the difficulties caused him by the presence of Adams as well as Adams's problems with the local Presbyterian Church, for whom Adams only preached on Sunday mornings. (The African Methodists rented the building for the afternoon.) As Cardozo understood it, the trustees and several influential men in the church had given Adams notice that they did not want him in the summer, since they wished to fill the pulpit then with a variety of speakers. Because Cardozo wanted to get along with all factions in Charleston for the good of his schools, it was unfortunate that those Presbyterians who did not want Adams thought that Cardozo was on Adams's side because he lived in the Mission Home.

It was also a problem that "the contending parties" in the church used the Home as a place to argue over their differences. Cardozo was surprised that Adams had arrived in the summer, since the heat seemed to prevent him from making calls. He was at home when Cardozo left for work in the morning and still there, "monopolizing a settee or a long bench," when he returned in the afternoon. It upset Cardozo to see a man sleeping about the house all day when there was more work than they all could do by keeping at it continually. If Charleston's heat was too much for Adams, Cardozo was sure there was much that could be done on the nearby islands. Cardozo had suggested—since Adams's board was such a burden to the expenses of the Mission Home—that he board among his congregation. This Adams did not wish to do.[13]

James Redpath was relieved of his position in Charleston, and Cardozo was glad to hear that the AMA was sending Francis Cardozo to Charleston; "May our whole family inhale a Missionary Spirit," he said, "as there is no limit to the work to be done here.

In August, 1865, Francis Lewis Cardozo arrived in Charleston, after having discussed with the men at the Rooms in New York news they had received of an indiscretion committed by Thomas when he was a teacher in Flushing, New York. Thomas evidenced relief that the story was finally known. His school board in Flushing had requested that he use his smartest female student to help in the morning with the younger children. This he did, tutoring her after school. When he found that she was "immodestly inclined," he asked that she recite at his home. Her mother, however, thought her progress in Mrs. Laura Cardozo's presence was slow and asked that he resume tutoring sessions at the school. He had every intention of being "more strict with her," but in an "unguarded" moment he "fell." In the future he would keep himself from such temptations. Although he loved his profession, he admitted that he had "forfeited all claims" upon the AMA. He was immediately relieved of his position and turned over accounts and property to his brother.

Thomas Cardozo then entered mercantile pursuits in Charleston. But his store was burned—perhaps by incendiaries—and his first reaction was to return to work among the freedmen. Indeed, while he had kept the store, he had, at Rev. Adams's request, headed "a flurishing Sabbath School." He could go to work immediately for the Freedmen's Aid Society, whose only criterion was that those they employed be "good *laborers.*" But he did not wish to be "identified" with a group that misused the Sabbath. True, he had sinned, but he had repented and he wished to continue in the work as a Christian. He asked if it were necessary to tell whatever benevolent society might offer him a position the whole reason for his leaving the service of the AMA.

The next summer he wrote from Baltimore, Maryland, where he had been teaching a school under the auspices of the Baltimore Association, which was doubtful of reopening many of its schools for the fall and winter session. Since he had gathered his school on his own, he hated to see it close and asked the AMA to accept him again: "I have always felt that to labor under the auspices of the Am. Miss. Assn. is to labor really in the vineyard of our Heavenly Father." He was a member of the Congregational Church in Baltimore, and his wife would join at the next communion. A month later, in a letter dealing with other business, he said, "I admire your style of saying *No* to an applicant very much."[14] His final communications with the AMA came in 1874 when, in his capacity as State Superintendent of Education for Mississippi, he served as a trustee of Tougaloo.[15]

Francis Lewis Cardozo at Charleston

Francis Lewis Cardozo, who replaced his brother as the superintendent of AMA work in Charleston, was born in that city, on the first of January, 1837. He attended local schools until he was twelve, was apprenticed to a carpenter for five years, and worked at the trade until he was twenty-one. Using his savings, and possibly with some help from his family and the AMA, he continued his education in Europe. He received his undergraduate education at the University of Glasgow where he took prizes in both Greek and Latin. He then attended Theological Hall Edinburgh for a year (1861). This was the seminary of the United Presbyterian Church of Scotland, a reform church that had split from the established church. The United Church had no relationship with slavery to its discredit, and was therefore in great favor with American abolitionists like Lewis Tappan. Cardozo also spent three years at the London School of Theology after which he was ordained and returned to the United States in May, 1864, accepting the pulpit of the Temple Street Congregational Church of New Haven, Connecticut.[16]

He resigned his pastorate the following July, and prepared himself to undertake work among the freedmen at Charleston. His congregation at New Haven regretted his departure, but "the more pious and intelligent of them" agreed with him that the large and "destitute" field of the South needed laborers.[17]

Although he deplored his brother's weakness in the Flushing incident, Francis expressed the hope that the AMA would forgive Thomas who Francis was sure was contrite. All the available

Francis Lewis Cardozo

intelligent colored persons were needed in the work of teaching the freedmen.[18]

Having been told by George Whipple that the teachers from the North would arrive on October 8th, Cardozo opened the school on October 4th with four local teachers on hand to classify pupils. On October 8 the 400 scholars had been divided into 10 classes, but there were only 4 teachers and no books. Cardozo unhesitatingly declared his embarrassed circumstances. He hired two additional local teachers and reclassified the school into six classes using the old books. On October 9 another hundred pupils had swelled the ranks to 500. His school had been visited by Reuben Tomlinson, Superintendent of Schools for Freedmen in South Carolina, who telegraphed the AMA to send teachers.

The local teachers were anxious to discover what the AMA would pay and compare it with the salaries of the Boston Society, and take positions with the society paying the larger amount. Cardozo hated to lose those he had chosen, for they were the best of the local teachers. He therefore reminded the men at the Rooms that rents in Charleston were three times what they were before the war with everything else correspondingly expensive.[19]

The northern teachers had not arrived by October 21st; so Cardozo was compelled to hire the twelve teachers he needed for his six to seven hundred pupils, or else lose them to other schools. Seven were hired permanently, five for a week, and two were teachers of the National Freedmen's Relief Association (NFRA), ordered to report to him by Reuben Tomlinson.

The following African Americans were employed by Thomas and Francis Cardozo in the AMA schools in Charleston:

Mr. W.H. Bruleigh	
Mr. A.H. Palmer	
Suil Miller	
Mrs. Antonia A. Barnet	
William O. Weston	hired by Thomas Cardozo 5/1/65
	rehired by Francis Cardozo 10/1/65
Joanna Weston	hired July, 1865
Frances Rollins (Philadelphia)	hired May 1, 1865; rehired Oct.
Mary F. Weston	hired June, 1865; rehired Oct.
Amelia A. Shrewsbury	hired June, 1865; rehired Oct.
Margaret Sasportas	hired June, 1865
Richard S. Holloway	January, 1866
Rosabella Fields	January, 1866
Harriet Holloway	January, 1866
Charlotte Johnson	January, 1866
Mrs. Catharine Winslow	January, 1866
Mrs. Moncuria Weston	January, 1866
Miss ——— O'Hear[20]	1867, assistant teacher

Mrs. Amanda Wall was also hired in January, 1866. She was the wife of Captain Orindatus S.B. Wall (black), Freedmen's Bureau officer in Charleston. The Walls were natives of Oberlin, Ohio, and Wall was the brother-in-law of John Mercer Langston.[21]

In 1865 the school was honored with visits from several illustrious persons: Major General Oliver Otis Howard, Major General Rufus Saxton, Rev. Rowland Howard (a brother of the general), and Rev. John Alvord (Superintendent of Freedmen's

Schools under Howard). Cardozo and the teachers were "encouraged and stimulated by the 'God bless you in your noble work' from such an excellent Christian" as General Howard. Cardozo felt the deep responsibilities and possibilities of his office. If he could impress the hundreds of young people in his care with the rewards of living Christian lives, he could not "aspire to a nobler work." There were already some young men he hoped would eventually undertake theological studies, and he hoped the AMA would provide aid for them.

Cardozo preached at various places on Sundays—once for E.J.Adams on the day he ordained his elders. When not preaching, Cardozo worshipped at Adams's church. This was natural, for Adams's congregation was made up of the black people now removed from the Presbyterian churches in the city, people Cardozo had known most of his life.

The political situation was "very confused and unsettled." The whites had been "entrusted with power too soon," they were "still disloyal at heart." They were "most treacherous" in their campaign to regain full civil control, and their feelings of "hate and revenge toward the colored people" seemed "fiendish" to Cardozo. They put every obstacle possible in the path of the freedmen and then pointed to their condition "as an argument for re-enslaving them."

The Saxton School

The freedmen's schools provoked them the most. The "Secession School Committee" had petitioned General Saxton to have the buildings restored to their control. Since they had no money and no desire to continue the schools, Cardozo supposed they wanted them back to close them. Yet the colored people were entitled to half of the school buildings, having been taxed for their erection. Cardozo counselled them to insist on one half, taking their case to the Supreme Court if need be. He saw possible trouble in the future when civil law was fully reinstated because the blacks had formed Leagues and were "determined not to submit so tamely as they did before the war."

Visitors came almost daily to the school. People like Levi Coffin were "agreeably surprised," but no rebels came. "They pass by on the other side, and mutter curses as they hear the children sing. . . ." One well-dressed woman had stood in the school door one day when the children were singing and had said, "Oh, I wish I could put a torch to that building! The niggers!"[22]

The teachers had named the school the Saxton School after their good friend in the Bureau who had provided them with it. Although the best building in town (the old State Normal School), it was without window panes or stoves. When cold weather came the BFRAL provided stoves and boarded up the windows. Cardozo had divided the school into the usual New England departments: primary, intermediate, and grammar. He expected future teachers of the primary pupils to come from the graduates of the grammar, or normal, department. He had promised the advanced pupils that they would receive certificates signed by Superintendent Tomlinson when they graduated, which had stimulated their studies.[23]

The Charleston Home

Properties were being returned so fast to their former rebel owners that Cardozo and the teachers had been forced to move three times by November, and were then living in the former home of R. Barnwell Rhett, the "notorious" editor of the *Charleston Mercury.* Although Rhett's residence, the house was owned by George L. Trenholm, ex-Secretary of the late Confederacy. Trenholm was not yet pardoned; so the house had not yet been returned and no rent had to be paid on it. One special annoyance that plagued the movement of the Home from one repossessed rebel house to another across Charleston, was that each house they moved into had privies that were the neighborhood scandal, so badly did they need cleaning. Prices for that noisome chore were astronomical in postwar Charleston.[24]

The constant necessity to watch expenses goaded both the AMA and its superintendents. Times were hard for everyone in Charleston, and Cardozo was grateful for the bale of blankets that arrived from England and the suffering they would help to alleviate. Clothing sent from the North was greatly appreciated, except for "the old boots which economical philanthropists always send." One particularly welcome box was a case of felt hats for girls. The children loved them, and Phebe Alcott (principal of the primary department) thought that they would soon "be known far and near as the Rhett house Regiment." The children were assessed twenty-five cents per month by the Freedmen's Bureau, but at Christmas time Cardozo found it very difficult to demand payment of the destitute. In order to supply all the children with books, he sold them below cost and provided them free to the fatherless and orphans.[25]

Stung by Samuel Hunt's reiterations about economy, Cardozo retorted that it was not economical to feed teachers less than they needed for proper sustenance. To quiet any fears that Hunt might harbor of their using benevolent contributions for luxury items, he presented a daily menu:

Breakfast: Hominy. Hash—made of fresh beef and potatoes. Coffee and Bread and Butter.
Dinner: Fresh or Salt Beef, Bread and Potatoes
Tea [the final meal of the day]: Bread & Butter and Tea

Fresh beef sold for eight cents per pound and salt beef for six and one-half cents per pound at the commissary. These were the cheapest meats available and the ones used "almost entirely." He also pointed out again and again that he could not be responsible for the cost of board if he did not have a supply of ready cash on hand. Food at the commissary had to be paid for in cash. Without cash, it was necessary to purchase from local merchants whose prices were fifty to one hundred per cent higher.[26]

Additional expenses of the Charleston Home arose from the fact that it was a convenient stopping-off place for those travelling on to the Sea Islands or farther south. Francis Cardozo was called upon to accommodate teachers of various other societies, army nurses, aides of General Howard, etc. Sometimes the teachers of other societies did not reimburse the Home for food and lodging after accepting his hospitality.[27]

By 1866 the price of beef had risen to twenty-three cents a pound at the commissary. In reply to compliments from the Rooms, Cardozo said he was pleased but wished they might also believe that he operated as economically as possible. When word came again that the expenses of the Home in Charleston were too great, Phebe A. Alcott replied in a manner which shows something of the spirit of the AMA teachers generally. She wrote to Hunt with verve and humor:

You told me once that I might feel at liberty to *write* whatever I should say if I could see you. We have just heard that you are troubled again about our expenses here. Now solely on my own responsibility, and without consulting a single member of the firm, I write to you. It may not be my business—yet in this work one feels that whatever affects the interests of our cause *is* our individual business.

Six dollars a week would not accomplish at the North *one half* of what it does here. We work as I believe few teachers are willing to work—because we love the cause and the Master—and not much for the loaves and fishes. We do not expect and *we do not have* more than the necessaries. We do not complain that we have no carpets nor curtains—that we live in a crowded unhomelike way, that we have to dress plainly and forego all society, that we use tin spoons and no tablecloths, that our parlor, *alias* pantry, *alias* dining room, *alias* reception-room, is dismal and bare in its appointments as can well be. But we must have good food—and by that I mean wholesome—not rich food. We do not have cakes and pies, nor often puddings. We have no fruit—seldom even dried apples. We have no butter on the table at dinner and few condiments of any kind beside salt. We must have fuel and light—but we are not extravagant in our use of them. We must have washing done, but it is certainly at less cost than it is obtained by teachers of any other society here. Mine does not cost more than one half of what it did in Baltimore—and it was not dear there.

Now in regard to work. When the schools were first opened teachers could deal with the children in masses—150 or 200 to a teacher. But the work has progressed the masses have *individualized.* We must deal with the children separately—see to each one personally. I think it would be time and money *wasted* for a teacher in our school here to undertake to teach 100 scholars or even 75. We *cannot* do it. I believe you have not six more *hard working* teachers in any one field than the six who occupy the third floor of the "Rhett House!" We are *driven* with work. Our session is longer than in any other school in the city. We distribute clothing many and many a day from the close of school until dark. We have had an evening school in our *parlor,* for recreation. We have a Sabbath School numbering now 200 scholars—for the success of which we feel responsible, the burden of which we bear. We have letters to write for the cause—and to show you that they accomplish something I will mention here that I rec'd last week the tenth valuable donation (a large package of new clothing from the church which sends me out—and the fourth which I have rec'd from that alone) for the benefit of the Freedmen. In addition I have rec'd quite a large sum of money from friends whom our school has interested which has been and will be used for its direct benefit.

I am not complaining. We rejoice to work—though *I would not work so hard* another year if I were permitted to labor here again. I do not believe it is right:—but we are dispirited when a letter comes hinting that we cost the Asso. too much. We cannot work with the spirit we need if we think there is dissatisfaction at 61 John St. I know you are straitened on every side but I doubt if you wrote another word about *economy* could you see just how things go here.

I have very high respect for Mr. Cardozo. He has such a hearty interest in and desire for the welfare of the school as I *know* you do not find in all your superintendents. His heart is in the work—and I believe he is faithful to the extent of his ability. Your teachers here agree in their respect and esteem for him.

Pardon my boldness if it seem bold. But it seems a matter of regret to me that you should—perhaps unwittingly—depress or depreciate a good man working faithfully and intelligently in our cause. I am sure that you have confidence enough in me to take this letter with all the candor and good faith in which I write.

Very respectfully yours,
Phebe A. Alcott

P.S. I add the inevitable "P.S." to say that I have been prostrated with sickness for the last two weeks—on account of overwork and therefore speak *ex cathedra.*[28]

Overworked Teachers

Cardozo was concerned about his overworked teachers who taught day school from 8:30 to 2:30, evening school from 7 to 9, and Sunday school from 12 to 1:30, besides making calls in the homes of their pupils and walking to and from school a mile away. He was grateful for such a splendid group of teachers, "a most noble and devoted set," who deserved "the highest praise."[29]

Francis Cardozo agreed with his brother Thomas about the comparative qualifications of northern and southern teachers. Thomas had declared that a teacher from the North could do twice the work of a teacher from the South and use better methods. At one point Francis hired Richard S. Holloway (black local teacher) who was needed for a class of boys the southern female teachers could not handle and for whom he had no northern female teacher to spare.[30]

His preference for northern teachers led to a misunderstanding with Samuel Hunt which upset Cardozo very much. Hunt had told Mrs. Amanda Wall and Louisa A. Alexander in error that Cardozo had requested New York not to send colored teachers, and their feelings had been unnecessarily hurt. Cardozo emphasized the fact that his request had been for *northern* teachers, and it was "perfectly indifferent" to him whether they were colored or white. He made the request as he did because northern teachers were "more competent" than southern ones. He asked Hunt, therefore, to correct his error in writing for the women involved: "I am sure you would not willingly do me the injustice of supposing me guilty of such unchristian conduct as requesting competent persons to be denied positions on account of their color." It should be obvious to Hunt that "such conduct would be specially foolish and suicidal" on Cardozo's part.[31]

By the end of November, 1865, there were almost 1000 students in the old State Normal School building: 200 on the first floor, 250 on the second, 425 on the third, and 80 in the dome. In setting up his school Cardozo put the northern teachers with the higher classes, the local colored teachers with the lower divisions, "where they may improve by the superiority of their *white* fellow-laborers, and whose positions afterwards they may be able to occupy."[32]

General Charles H. Howard thought that Cardozo would prove "an admirable Principal of the Normal School," and would do a great deal for the freedmen outside the school as well as in it. He was also sure that Cardozo could speak for himself, but he noticed that he needed more teachers than he had.[33]

Cardozo pronounced Saxton "the best school in the city, white or colored. If that sounded like "self-praise," he had the evidence of visitors—including James Redpath, former Superintendent in Charleston and no friend to the AMA. He credited the school's excellent reputation to two things: the student body, many of whom had had the advantage of some education; and the corps of "First Class," diligent, enthusiastic teachers from the North. Not only were the latter efficient workers in the schoolroom, but pleasant and harmonious residents of the Mission Home. Five of the six women living in the Home were white (Mrs. Wall had her own residence in the city), and one, Louisa A. Alexander, was an African American from Oberlin College.

Cardozo's desire that all of the teachers in Saxton School be AMA employees was not realized until the fall of 1866. He began with twenty-one teachers, fifteen of whom were AMA employees and six local people hired by the NFRA. In staffing the school for the 1866-67 year, he asked the AMA to employ all the teachers and include among them his sister and her husband, Mr. and Mrs. C.C. McKinney, who had been living in the North for several years and were teaching in Thomas Cardozo's former school in Flushing, New York. McKinney had taught school in Charleston, New York, and Cleveland, and had been in charge of both vocal and instrumental music at an Episcopal church in Cleveland. Mr. and Mrs. McKinney wished to return to Charleston and reside there permanently.[34]

The arrival of the McKinneys occasioned a discussion of the use of colored teachers in the freedmen's schools. Cardozo acknowledged the fact—pointed out by the AMA—that educated, capable colored teachers were hard to find, that by acting hastily they sometimes employed those who proved unworthy representatives of the race. Cardozo was sure that the McKinneys would help make up for such mistakes made in Charleston. And because so few intellectually prepared African Americans were available, when found they should be employed.[35]

Cardozo requested that the salaries of Mary F. Weston and Frances Rollins be raised to thirty-five dollars a month from the twenty-five they were receiving. They were equally as good as the NFRA teachers with whom they worked who received fifty dollars a month. Cardozo knew that the other societies in Charleston would gladly give them thirty-five dollars. At first Hunt refused to raise the salaries of the two local colored teachers, but when Cardozo said in that case they would have to be replaced with teachers from the North costing forty dollars per month, *plus board*, Hunt relented.[36]

Since it was a general rule in the North that each teacher should have fifty pupils in a class, and since Cardozo's average attendance showed less than that amount per teacher, Hunt asked why he could not get along with two less persons on his staff. Cardozo patiently pointed out—as he had before—that the rooms were sometimes too small to allow fifty in each, and one room was so large that it held 350 students, and therefore required the services of a principal to keep the various classes from impinging on each other. He was also well aware that one could profitably teach fifty children in the North, "but these scholars here are so undisciplined, and have never before enjoyed the advantages of a public school, that a teacher cannot do the same justice to them as if they had."[37]

General Saxton's Removal

Saxton's removal from Charleston was a blow to the freedmen. Captain O.S.B. Wall requested George Whipple to use his influence in Washington to keep General Rufus Saxton from being removed from his position. Saxton was disliked by "all the late Rebs and all the Negro-hating Union officers"—which described the majority according to Wall—because he was "unswervingly true to the Negro." Certainly Saxton was opposed to the President's policy and the orders given to General O.O. Howard regarding the freedmen on the Sea Islands: "how could it be otherwise when his very honor is at stake?"[38]

An interview with General Howard assured Whipple that if Saxton were removed it would be for the sake of his advancement. Saxton was nevertheless removed from the Department of South Carolina, Georgia, and Florida and from the position of Inspector of Settlements and Plantations. Word went around that Saxton had been released through the influence of General Grant, because he was "obnoxious" to the "Rebels on account of his devotion to the interests of the colored people." Governor James L. Orr and ex-Governor Aiken had had a special meeting with Grant during the latter's visit and requested Saxton's removal. General O.O. Howard gave the same reason for Saxton's replacement, but placed the blame squarely upon President Johnson, who was determined to remove all such officers in the South who were, in his opinion, too sympathetic with the freedmen and with northern sentiment.[39]

The African American community of Charleston was very sad indeed. Several meetings were held in Adams's church. At one, "an eloquent freedman" broke down during a speech in praise of the General, threw his arms about Saxton, and wept. Saxton was so moved that he said "he could not trust himself to speak." The people had collected pennies and nickels from five or ten thousand persons with which they bought Saxton some silver gifts worth one hundred dollars. The three thousand children in the schools gave him "a handsome copy of the Bible, a Photograph Album, and a beautiful Prayer Book." Saxton was replaced by General Robert K. Scott, who seemed to be pleased with the schools.[40]

Three-fourths of the pupils in the Saxton School were slaves before the war and about one-fourth free. The latter group had had the advantage of some education and were therefore more advanced. From that group Cardozo chose three young men and nine girls for special tutoring, and arranged through the AMA that the boys (Joseph Wilkinson, Arthur O'Hear, and Walter Jones) receive college educations in the North.[41]

Under Scrutiny

Cardozo was persuaded by Tomlinson to hold a public examination on May 31, 1866. A half-sneering, half-complimentary review that Cardozo termed "curious" was published by the Charleston *Daily News*. The audience was described as "expecting to be amused, and determined to be pleased." The reporter said that "the upper tandom of Charleston was there, for the Saxton School was "the *recherche* seminary to which all the aristocracy send their children." Because one quarter of the student body had been free before the war, the article insisted that they constituted "an aristocracy of color. This school must not, therefore be considered as giving a fair average idea of colored education in the city." Because it was planned to make this a normal school, only the best pupils had been kept. This was of course not true, although the reporter might have in some way learned what was to be the case for the following year. Cardozo had in fact zealously guarded all his students for fear they *would* go to the other schools. The reporter insisted that the selection process had resulted in "scarcely a single pure black" being seen in some of the classes. He could not leave off his story without giving the South's view of the teachers:

We take great pleasure in recording this interest everywhere manifested in behalf of the education of the colored people. No small credit is due for all this to the much-abused schoolmarms, for the self denial and philanthropy which induce them to leave their much vaunted and beloved New England, and visit this benighted Southern land, illuminating the night of our barbarism by the light of their countenance. . . .

Preaching to the heathen, instructing and civilizing them, appears an innate passion with the pious descendants of the Pilgrims. . . .What a pity our tropical climate and its concomitant epidemics make such sad inroad upon their health and spirits; and we do not think that in our selfishness, we ought to insist on their remaining here any longer than the present month. . . .

We regret the necessity of this hegira; for we could spare these Plymouth Pilgrims of progress. . . .

George Trenholm and other prominent white persons came. Others "respectfully declined being present at such an examination."[42]

Not all whites were so intransigent. Cardozo conferred with Julian Mitchell of the law firm of Whaley and Company, and was surprised to find him so liberal; and to learn that Governor Orr was in favor of a common school system for the state for both white and colored children, was a beginning "in the formation of a public opinion in favor of educating the colored people and giving them their rights."

Cardozo—in constant fear of losing the Normal School building—kept an abbreviated school in session during the summer of 1866, staffed by those on salary who would not increase the expenses. Despite that maneuver, the building was turned over to the Charleston School Board in September. An outbreak of virulent fever resulted in a quarantine and a delay in the arrival of the teachers from the North. Mrs. Minnie Cardozo, who had given birth to a son in August, came down with the fever. Scarcely a family was free of it.[43]

Avery Institute

Cardozo's second year at Saxton School was far from being as satisfying as the first had been. The Military Hall supplied for the school had to be shared with another school, but its greatest fault was that it was an acoustical nightmare. The 800 children filled it with disorder and din. The staff was not up to the standards of the previous year. Book orders were improperly filled. Only the promise that a Normal School was being built on land purchased by the AMA through the Avery bequest kept up the spirits of teachers and pupils. Avery was a Wesleyan Methodist supporter of the Association.[44]

In making plans for the Avery Institute being built in Charleston, Cardozo was anxious that the latest teaching methods be used. Professor Thomas N. Chase of Atlanta University recommended that a graduate of the Oswego Training School be hired if possible. Cardozo asked that all the teachers sent in the fall of 1867 be Congregationalists. Their combined help would increase the effectiveness of Plymouth Church's Sunday school. The Saxton teachers had all helped in E.J. Adams's church until the establishment of Plymouth Congregational Church (1867), the first church founded among the freedmen by the AMA. He also wanted at least one teacher to be a musician. The school had been without a good music teacher since his sister's health had forced the McKinneys to return North.

General Daniel E. Sickles, Bureau Commander of North and South Carolina, asked Cardozo in the summer of 1867 to serve on the Registration Board of Advisors for the two states. The purpose of the Board was to establish "rules and regulations for the proper execution of the Registration." The Board was composed of four men, one white and one black from each state.[45]

Returning to Charleston in the fall of 1867, after the first vacation he had taken since going there, Cardozo and his family were ejected from the first-class compartment of the Richmond and Friedericksburg Railroad. It was especially humiliating to Cardozo because both his wife and son were ill. The year before Louisa Alexander and Mrs. C.C. McKinney had had to pay more fare than the other teachers for their return fare North, because the Leary Line that took the others would not accept colored women except as steerage passengers.[46]

Cardozo found Avery Institute unfinished on his return, but promised for January. This year he *was* selective so far as the student body was concerned. Out of the first 600 applicants, he chose 250. Because the school would place its emphasis on preparation for teaching, there would be only one small primary class. This class would be under the teacher in charge of the Experimental Division (Practice Teaching); thus she would have both the most advanced pupils as well as the least advanced in the school. This arrangement would also mean that the teacher of the advanced students would have the required number of pupils (fifty).[47]

Cardozo announced in November that his friends had persuaded him to become a candidate for the Constitutional Convention. He had agreed, not because of any "desire for the turbulent political arena," but from "a sense of duty . . . being the *only educated colored* man in Charleston." Although it was not certain that there would be a convention or that the Republican ticket would win, yet both things looked probable. To prepare himself for that eventuality, he asked E.P. Smith to send him a book containing the constitutions of all the states. If Smith could think of anything else that he could study in order to prepare himself, he would appreciate the advice. He took it for granted that the AMA would not object to his being a member of the Convention. He meant to see that the school did not suffer in his absence.[48]

He made a trip to Washington in February and was present for "all the Impeachment excitement." That alone had made the trip worthwhile. He expected the Constitutional Convention would complete its work by the middle of March. They met March 10, 1868, as a State Nominating Convention, where General Robert K. Scott was chosen candidate for governor, and Cardozo candidate for secretary of state. He was elected, and resigned as AMA Superintendent.[49]

The school was moved into the new building on April 29, 1868. Francis Cardozo, who had worked so long and so hard for that day, turned the control of the school over to Ellen M. Pierce. The dedication took place May 7th, and Saxton School officially became Avery Institute. It was named in honor of the late Rev. Charles Avery, a Wesleyan Methodist of Pittsburgh, whose bequest of $10,000 enabled the AMA to purchase the land for the school and erect a Mission Home. Cardozo, the new Secretary of State for South Carolina, was in charge of the dedication ceremonies.

Governor-elect Scott was present, and Rev. Ennals J. Adams read selections of Scripture.[50]

Cardozo Becomes A Public Official

By the end of July Cardozo had taken charge of his new office and found the work "comparatively easy." He thought that the South Carolina legislature had done "a good deal of important work, notwithstanding all the pressures brought to bear against them." The members dispersed to their homes for the coming campaign, in which "the Rebels are all armed to the teeth and are going to muster the most desperate efforts to carry this State for Seymour and Blair."[51]

His new office did not make him forget Avery Institute. He attended the school's Examination in June, 1869, and was much pleased with both the affair and the new principal, Mortimer A. Warren. Governor Scott also liked Warren, and thought of the Institute as "in a measure his own offspring," having been Bureau Superintendent when the funds for the building were allocated. Cardozo asked the AMA for scholarships to Howard University for Avery students Joseph Morris and Thomas McCants Stewart. The following summer he asked the Association to hire three others, including Arthur O'Hear, who had gone from Oberlin to Howard where he was just completing his sophomore year.[52]

The AMA continued its interest in Cardozo, noting his public acts and offices. The story of the ejection of Francis Cardozo and C.L. Ransier (Chairman of the State Central Committee of the Republican Party of South Carolina) from the Eutaw House in Baltimore on account of their color, was carried in the *American Missionary*. The incident occurred during the meeting of the National Executive Committee of the Union League of America. The National Executive Committee had canceled its suite of rooms at the hotel and passed a resolution censuring the hotel-keeper.

In 1871, F.L. Cardozo was engaged as Professor of Latin at Howard university, commuting between that position and his work as Secretary of State for South Carolina. He was elected Treasurer of South Carolina in 1872. He was in that office when asked by E.M. Cravath to evaluate D.C. Cottle of Columbia. Cardozo said he did not know Cottle, but that he would interview him and "learn whether he is worthy of the important position of a teacher with the Association." He asserted his continued interest in education, especially for African Americans who needed it "so badly," pointing out that as Treasurer he had paid over $300,000 for schools in the past five months—more than his predecessor had expended in five years.[53]

Cardozo later accepted a clerkship in the United States Treasury Department during the Hayes administration. After six years there he became principal of the Colored High School of Washington, D.C. A former pupil, who learned his college Latin under Professor Cardozo at Howard, described him as "very dignified in bearing, and polished in manner." He was "a courtly gentleman who treated his classes with the greatest of kindness," and was "an educator of very fine talent." He was described by a historian who knew him as tall and fair. He was every inch a gentleman, a gentle man, sensitive to the feelings of his staff, patient, and slow to anger. If he erred it was on the side of being too trusting. He went to great lengths to protect his faculty from uncreative encounter.[54]

As an AMA Superintendent in Charleston, Cardozo had prepared himself to become Chairman of the Committee on Education of the South Carolina Constitutional Convention. Even the endless patience he showed with the always exacting and often exasperating Samuel Hunt (who seemed inordinately deaf to the written word), gave him practice in the tact requisite in political life. His experience running the Saxton School and the Mission Home on a circumscribed budget was not without influence in his offices in the state government of South Carolina.

The Harris Brothers at Fayetteville, North Carolina

Two other AMA African American teachers whose work resulted in the establishment of a normal school were Robert and Cicero Harris. They took charge of the AMA schools in Fayetteville, North Carolina, in the fall of 1866. Cicero was the third son who worked for the AMA of what must have been a magnificent family of ten children. He was twenty-two when he began at Fayetteville and, although he had had no previous teaching experience, was highly recommended by both his older brothers and by people in Cleveland, where he had stood at the top of his class at Central High School. Like his eldest brother William, he was a member of the Wesleyan Methodist Church.[55]

Robert Harris was AMA Superintendent in Fayetteville, teaching the Summer Intermediate School; and Cicero taught the Phillips Primary School. Robert did not recommend that their assistants be commissioned: "These native teachers are not competent to manage a school, or to give proper instruction to those who are beyond the Alphabet. We can only use them as assistants, and they are poor at that." He kept hoping for additional teachers from the North, but the financial reversals in the country adversely affected the income of the Association. Evidently the New York office repeated its offer to commission any local people he thought competent, for he flatly repeated his opinion: "These native teachers can not begin to fulfill the requirements of our Society." After all, what could be expected of persons paid only fifteen dollars per month? "It is 'poor teach' and 'poor pay.'"[56]

Robert Harris was concerned about other places without teachers and strongly urged the AMA to put workers at Smithfield and Goldsboro. He was backed in this wish by Samuel S. Ashley, AMA Superintendent for North Carolina; Mr. and Mrs. Bemis (white) and Mr. and Mrs. Nichols (white) were engaged for those points.[57]

During the school year 1867-68, the AMA schools in Fayetteville remained in separate buildings, awaiting the school promised by the Freedmen's Bureau that would be built on land purchased by the people of the city. The two hundred pupils of the Primary School met in Evans Chapel and the Intermediate School (limited to seventy because of lack of accommodations) convened in the old Academy nearby. The Harrises were now assisted by some of their more advanced students.

They were heartened by the election in November, 1867, when only 4 African Americans voted for the conservative Democrats, "although the latter confidently expected to receive at least 100 colored votes!" the results had "completely confounded" the whites, some of whom at least were beginning to see that the black man had ability and could think for himself. A few days before the election, John M. Langston had delivered "a most eloquent and telling speech . . . proving himself an able lawyer and eloquent orator."[58]

Like so many of the Association's teachers, Robert and Cicero Harris taught a night school and Sunday school in addition to their regular teaching. They were concerned with the spiritual as well as the intellectual advancement of their people. Robert Harris also organized a school in the country, twelve miles from Fayetteville, under one of his advanced pupils and named it the Whipple School after the AMA officer. He had sent out six such teachers from his school.[59]

The garrison of federal troops was removed late in 1867, leaving them without protection, but in little danger of direct attack, although the area was strongly Democratic and in no hurry to help with the building of Bureau schools for black children. There was cause for rejoicing, however, in that the three former students then acting as assistants had shown such promise that Robert Harris consented to their being commissioned by the AMA. Because the Association continued to have financial difficulties, the schools were closed in June, the local people being unable to sustain them further. Although the Harris brothers had a widowed mother to support, Robert wrote that their salaries might be held by the AMA "until the treasury is relieved."[60]

In 1868, Samuel S. Ashley became the Superintendent of Public Instruction for the state, and was, of course, still interested in the Association schools there. He thought (and earnestly desired) that the Fayetteville schools should be continued under their present leadership by obtaining $25 per month from the people, $10 for each brother from the Bureau ("the Bureau aid, you understand, must be for rent. But as the house is in the possession of the colored people the rent can go for teachers"), and the remainder from the AMA.[61]

The Howard School

Even after the Bureau building (called the Howard School) was erected, it could not be used because it was unfurnished. The people were unable to raise the necessary money, and Robert Harris appealed to the AMA to use their influence with the Bureau and wrote Washington himself for the cause. One of the difficulties lay in the fact that the local quartermaster was an intemperate man who neglected his duties. Finally an appropriation of $485 by the Bureau for desks, seats, and stoves, was received in February, 1869, but there was no money for blackboards, tables, chairs, curtains, shades, landscaping, or supplies. In order to have the bare essentials with which to work, Harris appealed to the AMA for $50. Probably William E. Whiting, Assistant Treasurer of the Association who was also a liberal contributor to its treasury, gave the money as his personal contribution. In any case, when the brothers reorganized their Sunday school, they named it the Whiting School.[62]

During the summer of 1869, the Harris brothers chose to remain in Fayetteville and keep their school open rather than return North. Their salaries and expenses for the summer would thus be less than if the Association were to pay their transportation to and from Cleveland. This was the last year of aid from the Association; Howard School reverted to state control, becoming the first state normal school for African Americans in North Carolina. Robert Harris was still teaching in Fayetteville in 1872.[63] He was also the recording secretary of the Eleventh General Conference of the AMEZ Church at Charlotte, North Carolina, June 19, 1872, where William H. Hillery (another former AMA teacher) was the secretary, and where Jermain Wesley Loguen (former AMA Missionary) and J.W. Hood (one of 84 Fayetteville citizens who had signed a petition asking the AMA to continue to support the Harrises in 1867), were elected bishops. AMEZ Bishop Cicero Harris (North Carolina Annual Conference), was secretary of the Twelfth Annual Conference of the AMEZ Church at Louisville, Kentucky, in 1876, where William H. Hillery was elected bishop.[64]

Perhaps if the AMA had sought earlier, it might have secured the services of all three brothers—William, Robert, and Cicero—in the ministry to Congregational churches in the South. But the process of planting churches was not a part of the AMA's program at the South until 1867, when Plymouth Congregational Church was established in Charleston, South Carolina. In any case, when it approached Cicero Harris to become a minister in a denomination in which the congregation was supreme, and where no bishops nor councils exercised control, it did so several years after he had experienced the power of the bishop's office:

> I thank you for this manifestation of your confidence and esteem. I am no sectarian, and I pray for the success of the Gospel wherever it is preached. For Congregationalism I

have ever had a special regard, and, were I to leave the church of my choice, would probably feel more at home in that church than in any other. Still, I am a Methodist, and have not yet come to the conclusion that I can serve the Master better in any other capacity. The majority of our people are Methodists or inclined that way, and tho' there is much ignorance and superstition among them, I think it best to remain with them and do all I can for their education and evangelization. "If the mountain will not come to Mahomet, Mahomet will go to the mountain."[65]

AMA Students Who Served as Teachers

African Americans, usually outstanding students of the normal or common schools in which they taught, were employed by the AMA as assistant teachers. Some of the following were graduates and were employed as regular teachers.

Louisa Broadfoot	Sumner Sch., Fayetteville 1867-69
Caroline Manuel	Phillips Sch., Fayetteville, 1867-68
James Middleton	Phillips Sch., Fayetteville, 1867-68
Fannie A. Wilson	Swayne Sch., Montgomery, Ala. 1876-77
Mary L. Hardaway	Swayne Sch., Montgomery, Ala. 1876-77
Lawrence Chestnut	Gainesville, Fla. 1872-73
William Webster	Gainesville, Fla. 1872-73
Julia Simpson	Howard Acad., Ocala, Fla. 1871
Sarah Lowry	Americus, Georgia 1869
Emperor Gordon	Bainbridge, Ga., 1868-1869
Levi Burkett	Bainbridge, Ga., 1868-1869
J.J. Gideon	Bainbridge, Ga., 1868-1869
C.H. Standley	Bainbridge, Ga., 1868-1869
J.J. Carter	Bainbridge, Ga., 1868-1869
Henry Jones	Lewis H.S.,Macon 1870-71
Emma Johnston	Union Acad. Columbus, Miss., 1874
Fannie Sadgwar	Williston Acad., Wilmington 1870
Mary L. Chadwick	Washburn Sem. Beaufort, N.C., 1867,'70
Lovey Mayo[66]	Washington Sch., Raleigh, N.C. 1874-76
Ida Ransom	Washington Sch., Raleigh, N.C. 1874-76
Sarah Dunstan	Washington Sch., Raleigh, N.C. 1874-76
Robert S. Taylor	Washington, N.C. 1869-70
Alexander Lightfoot	Washington, N.C., 1869-70

Collin C. Shaw	Washington, N.C., 1869-70
Miss M.A. Cadett	Washington, N.C., 1869-70
Maggie Cupps	Williston Acad., Wilm'ton, N.C. 1868-69
Martha Nixon	Williston Acad., Wilm'ton, N.C. 1868-69
Josephine Holmes	Williston Acad., Wilm'ton, N.C. 1868-69
Hattie Fulford	Morehead City, N.C. 1869-70
Laura F. Whittington	Hull Swamp, N.C. 1869
Sarah A. Crum	Avery Inst., Charleston, S.C. 1870-71
Ellen Waddy	Eastville, Va. 1869-71
Charlotte Middleton	Fayetteville, N.C. 1869

In addition to the above, Adella E. Cleveland and Julia Turner, both students of Atlanta University, were teaching at Beach Institute, Savannah, Georgia, in 1874. Michael Jerkins taught at Washburn Academy, Beaufort, North Carolina, in 1871 and 1872. And the future president of Wilberforce University, William S. Scarborough, taught at the AMA's Lewis High School, Macon, Georgia, 1875-76.

William S. Scarborough

Scarborough had attended Lewis High School as a student from 1867 to 1869. Then he went to Atlanta University preparatory school for two years before entering Oberlin. When he graduated from the latter in 1875, he was a thorough product of AMA and Congregational schools. His year of teaching at Lewis High was not very successful. His fellow teachers criticized him for the lack of order in his classes, and AMA Agent Delia Emerson (there was now a female officer in the Rooms in New York!) declared flatly that he could not teach. After studying theology at Oberlin for some months, he asked for a professorship in an AMA college, saying that the course "matters little whether it is Latin, Greek or Natural Sciences." Perhaps his experience at Macon kept him from securing such an appointment.

One of his biographers claims that prejudice kept him from the chair of Greek at Howard University in 1885, a strange charge in view of the fact that James M. Gregory (black) was Latin professor at Howard at the time and Martha Bailey Briggs had been principal of the Normal Department since 1873. Perhaps the real reason so many of the trustees voted against Scarborough was that he was a better author (he wrote Greek texts) than he was a teacher. In those days at Howard, the head of a department was primarily a teacher.

One noteworthy result of Scarborough's days at Lewis High was his marriage to AMA fellow-teacher Mrs. S.C. Bierce, who also joined him on the faculty of Wilberforce.[67]

NOTES

1. *Twenty-seventh Annual Report* (1873), 73-74.

2. Circular: "Lincoln Institute, Jefferson City, Missouri" (n.p., n.d.), signed by J. Addison Whitaker, Arnold Krekel, Wm. Bishop, Executive Committee, AMAA.

3. *Twenty-seventh Annual Report* (1873), 73-74.

4. *Twenty-second Annual Report* (1868), 69.

5. *Twenty-third Annual Report* (1869), 53-54.

6. *Twenty-fifth Annual Report* (1871), 60; *Twenty-sixth Annual Report* (1872), 71; *Twenty-seventh Annual Report* (1873), 87; *AM*, XVI (July, 1872), 147.

7. (Karp 1969, 203); (Simonhoff 1956, 203, 252, 265-267). Currently some members of the Cardozo family think that Jacob's publicist brother Isaac was the father of Thomas and Francis Cardozo. (Brown 1874, 495-496) states that Thomas completed his education at the Newbury Collegiate Institute.

8. Cardozo, April 11, 1865, to Whiting, AMAA.

9. Cardozo, April 29, 1865, to Strieby, AMAA.

10. Cardozo, April 29, to Strieby; see also Mansfield French, Beaufort, April 24, 1865, to Strieby; H.H. Hunter, Charleston, May 6, 1865, to Strieby, AMAA.

11. Cardozo, May 10; May 15, 1865, to Whiting, AMAA.

12. Cardozo, May 31, 1865, to Whiting; June 16; July 18, 1865, to Strieby, AMAA.

13. Cardozo, July 1, 1865, to Hunt; Adams, August 11, 1865, to Whiting; August 16; August 23, 1865, to Whipple; August 23; September 15, 1865, to Whiting. The O.S. Presbyterian Church sent an agent to take care of Zion Church on July 16, 1865, and Adams then began to gather another church.

14. See Cardozo letters for July to December, 1865, from Charleston, and for 1866 from Baltimore, AMAA.

15. Cardozo, Jackson, Mississippi, November 4, 1874, AMAA; (Karp 1969, 205) implies that Thomas Cardozo was guilty of embezzling $2,000 from the funds of Tougaloo University.

16. *The Theological Hall Calendar of the United Presbyterian Church* (Edinburgh and Glasgow, May, 1878), NLS, Edinburgh; (Mackelvie 1873, 693, 700, 303); (Small 1900, 51-52); (Robson 1900, n.p.). These list Cardozo as a student of Theological Hall in 1861, from Hutchensontown Church, Glasgow, and note that he went to America. There were 33 students at the Hall in 1861, and 4 professors.

17. Cardozo, New Haven, July 5, 1865, to Whipple, AMAA.

18. Cardozo, August 18, 1865, to Whipple and Strieby, AMAA.

19. Cardozo, Charleston, October 10, 1865, to Hunt, AMAA.

20. See Saxton School Monthly Reports and teachers' letters for 1865-1867, AMAA.

21. Amanda Wall, December 14, 1865, to Whipple; January 5; January 19, 1866, to Hunt, AMAA.

22. See Cardozo's letters for October and December, 1865, and Saxton School Superintendent's Report for December, 1865, AMAA.

23. See Cardozo letters for November, 1865, AMAA; See S.C. Hale, Hilton Head, South Carolina, November 25, 1865, for evidence of the fact that the Boston Association and the NFRA teachers there were not interested in grading the freedmen's schools, but Hale managed to get grading through despite them.

24. Monthly Report, Saxton School, April, 1866; Cardozo, April 2, 1866, to Hunt; May 2, 1866, to Whiting, AMAA.

25. Cardozo, January 27, 1866, December 2, 1865, to Whipple; Alcott, November 29, 1865, to Hunt; Cardozo, December 30, 1867, to Smith, AMAA.

26. Cardozo, December 30, 1865, to Hunt; December 30, 1865, to Whiting, AMAA.

27. Fidelia E. Morgan, Augusta, Georgia, December 12, 1866; Miss L.A. Jenness, Savannah, Georgia, November 2, 1865, to Hunt, AMAA; see also French, February 27, 1866, to Whiting. French described the Mission Home at Charleston as "a well ordered family. The table is a plain and economical one, showing a conscientious regard on Mr. C. [sic] part to the sacredness of the trust committed to him."

28. Alcott, March 27, 1866, to Hunt. White teacher Carrie Atkins, described Cardozo as a "very intelligent gentlemanly person & very desirous of promoting the happiness of his teachers but much annoyed at his deficiency of means to procure household comforts for them." October 24, 1865, to Hunt, AMAA.

29. Cardozo, January 27, 1866, to Whipple, AMAA.

30. Cardozo, January 27, 1866, to Whipple, AMAA.

31. Cardozo, January 13, 1866, to Hunt, AMAA.

32. Cardozo, January 13, 1866, to Hunt; Alcott, November 29, 1865, to Hunt, AMAA.

33. Howard, November 10, 1865, to Hunt, AMAA. He expected that BFRAL would be employing as teachers "colored persons who at least know how to read"—unless indeed the Bureau were "abolished."

34. Cardozo, December 2, 1865, to Whipple and Strieby; December 2, 1865, Testimonial for Mr. and Mrs. C.C. McKinney. For information on the "considerable strife" at Charleston between "the Boston and New York Associations," with Redpath favoring the Boston society, see W.T. Richardson, Beaufort, South Carolina, April 13, 1865, to Whipple, AMAA.

35. Cardozo, January 13, 1866, to Hunt, AMAA.

36. Cardozo, March 2, 1866, to Hunt, AMAA.

37. Cardozo, March 2, 1866, to Hunt, AMAA.

38. Wall, December 11, 1865, to Whipple; Circular No. 1, R. Saxton, Headquarters Asst. Commissioner of the BRFAL, for South Carolina and Georgia, Beaufort, S.C., June 10, 1865, AMAA. One paragraph of the letter reads: "To this Bureau is entrusted the supervision and management of all abandoned lands, the educational, industrial and other interests of refugees and freedmen, and the location of such as may desire it, on homesteads of forty (40) acres, where by faithful industry they can readily achieve an independence."

39. Cardozo, January 27, 1866, to Whipple, AMAA; (Howard 1907, 283).

40. Cardozo, January 27, 1866, to Whipple, AMAA. See also (Williamson 1965, 84) for a description of General Scott.

41. See Cardozo and Whipple letters May to September, 1866, AMAA.

42. *AM*, X (August, 1866), 175-176; Program of Public Examination, May 31, 1866, AMAA.

43. Letters of Cardozo to the AMA for March 10, 1866; August-October, 1866, AMAA.

44. Cardozo's letters and reports to the AMA for 1866 and 1867, AMAA; see also Reuben Tomlinson's complimentary report of Saxton School, cited, *Twenty-first Annual Report* (1867), 33.

45. Cardozo, June 8, 1867, to Smith, AMAA.

46. Cardozo, New Haven, Connecticut, September 16, 1867; Cardozo letters for September and October, 1867 from Charleston to the AMA. See also Reuben Tomlinson, State Superintendent of Education, BFRAL Report of Schools for Freedmen in South Carolina for the month of December, 1865. This is one of many BFRAL manuscripts in the files of the AMA. On this large chart of South Carolina schools, 21 teachers are noted as working in Saxton School (11 colored, 11 Northerners). See also similar report for January, 1866, where Tomlinson notes 12 colored teachers at Saxton. In December, 1865, the total of black teachers in all associations in S.C. was 35, 27 of them in Charleston, and 5 at Greenville. The BFRAL, unlike the AMA, regularly denoted the racial make-up of the teaching staffs. See also the letters and monthly reports of Louisa Alexander (from Oberlin), AMAA.

47. Cardozo, Philadelphia, September 26, 1867; Charleston, October 11, 1867, to Smith, AMAA.

48. Cardozo, November 4, 1867, AMAA. In addition to the Saxton School, Cardozo had the oversight of a plantation school under Miss S.J. Foster. She had about 50 day pupils and another 30 in evening school.

49. Cardozo, March 9, 1868, to Smith: unfortunately, the letter referred to in this letter ("sent last week"), containing an account of remarks he had made at the Convention on compulsory education, is not in the files; April 1; April 18, 1868, to Whiting, AMAA.

50. Cardozo, May 1, 1868, to Smith; May 2, 1868, to Whiting, AMAA; *Twenty-second Annual Report* (1868), 41.

51. Cardozo, Columbia, S.C., June to September, 1868, AMAA.

52. Cardozo letters June, 1870, to Smith, AMAA; *South Carolina Republic* story of Avery Examination, cited, *AM*, XIII (August, 1869), 171-172.

53. *AM*, XIV (June, 1870), 135; and XV (November, 1871), 251; also Cardozo, Columbia, S.C., June 7, 1873, to Cravath, AMAA.

54. (Simmons 1887, 430-431); Cardozo, October, 1866, April 24, 1867 and May 26, 1868, to Hunt; Miss H.C. Bullard, December 7, 1865; Jane Van Allen, February 23, 1866, to Hunt, AMAA.

55. Harris, July 10, 1866; Robert A. Johnson, Cleveland, June 25, 1866, Testimonial for Cicero Harris; H.B. Knight, Cleveland, June 21, 1866, Testimonial for Cicero Harris; Theodore Sterling, Cleveland, July 7, 1866, Testimonial for Cicero Harris, AMAA.

56. Robert Harris Financial Statement, November 1866; Superintendent's Monthly Reports 1866-1867; Teacher's Monthly Reports, Sumner School 1866-1867; Harris letters 1866-1867; Ashley, Wilmington, N.C., February 20 and 25, 1867, to Smith, AMAA.

57. Ashley, Wilmington, June 12, 1867, to Smith, AMAA.

58. Harris, Fayetteville, N.C., November 30, 1867, AMAA.

59. *AM*, XI (August, 1867), 174-175; XIII (July, 1868), 152.

60. Robert Harris letters 1867-1868; Financial Statement, November, 1867, to June, 1868; Teacher's Monthly Reports, Sumner School 1867-1868, AMAA; *AM*, XII (April, 1868), 162.

61. Ashley, September 29, 1868, to Smith; September 15, 1868, to Robert Harris, AMAA.

62. Robert Harris letters from Cleveland and Fayetteville, July 1868, to June 15, 1868; Robert and Cicero Harris Teacher's Monthly Reports through June, 1869, AMAA.

63. See his letters for 1869 and 1872, and the Monthly Reports for 1869 from Robert and Cicero Harris for 1869, AMAA; *AM*, XIII (October, 1869), 224.

64. (Smith 1922,104, 118-119); (Hood 1895, 111-113).

65. Harris, February 13, 1878, to Ashley, AMAA.

66. Mayo went on to Hampton to school and eventually was a teacher in Hampton's Indian Department, an honor shared with Booker T. Washington. Mayo was a very valuable worker at Raleigh.

67. See the letters of William S. Scarborough, Mrs. S.C. Bierce, Anetta Lynch, and Delia Emerson, AMAA. In so far as the author has been able to ascertain, Mrs. Bierce was white. See also (Simmons 1887, 69).

VOL. XIII.　　MARCH, 1869.　　NO. 3.

AMERICAN MISSIONARY ASSOCIATION.

FREEDMEN.

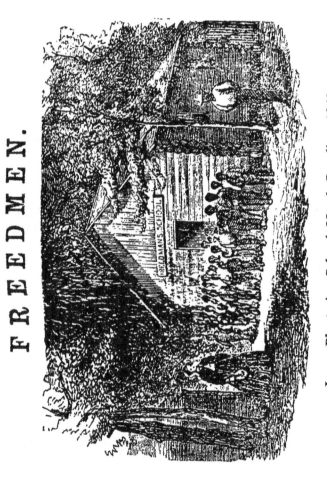

James Plantation School, North Carolina, 1869
Courtesy Amistad Research Center

IX

AFRICAN AMERICANS
AND THE AMA COMMON SCHOOLS

The North ought to insist that men and children shall have equal rights and opportunities in all public schools and institutions. The common school is peculiarly an American institution, an institution which our Fathers put among the fundamental things. It was called the common school, because it was the common heritage of American youth. Now, it is not enough to build two school houses equally good, two hospitals, two churches on opposite sides of the street, one for white children and one for black, as is proposed in some, perhaps, in all of the Southern States. The moment this is done, a brand is put upon the colored children. But in a Republic, whose fundamental law is that all the citizens are equal, we cannot consent to any such discrimination. . . . Two civilizations cannot grow up side by side and keep the peace; we tried that and failed. We cannot afford to try that experiment again.
C.L. Woodworth
American Missionary, 1876

The enormity of the task of educating four million people, the cost of sustaining northern teachers in the South, the reality of the entrenched prejudice against educating the blacks on the part of southern whites, the fear that the temporary protection of their work by the federal government would cease before the task was finished—all these considerations placed the AMA in a race against time and dictated the training of southern African American leaders.

At first local African Americans with some education were employed as assistants in the schools. Their work was generally unsatisfactory for several reasons. Usually their education, received

211

clandestinely under the South's prohibitory statutes, was not of the best. As teachers they knew nothing of accepted pedagogical methods and simply taught by rote. The southern black teachers also believed in corporal punishment and used the strap with great frequency, to the consternation of most northern teachers. It did not take long for the AMA teachers to see that using monitors chosen from among their brightest pupils who had experienced proper pedagogical techniques was a more effective procedure.

Classes to train teachers were begun as early as there were pupils and teachers available. Several difficulties were apparent almost immediately that threatened to keep the brightest pupils from receiving more than a common school education. Most of the black people were poor, and there was a great demand for teachers, especially in the interior sections where northern teachers had not gone. In the hope of making a living for themselves and their families, the brightest students were tempted to teach tuition schools in the rural areas. Generally, however, the promised tuition was not realized, and the young teachers had interrupted their own education, having gotten little in return for their sacrifices. To keep their promising students in school until ready to attend one of their colleges, the teachers encouraged the benevolent in the North to provide scholarships for them[1]

One of the surprises awaiting the northern teachers was that despite the laws and proscriptions against education for slaves, some had nevertheless learned to read. When asked how, many of this fortunate group said that their mothers had taught them. Mary L. Chadwick served as a monitor in the AMA's Washburn Seminary in Beaufort, North Carolina (while a student there herself) and then became a teacher of primary children. Her earliest letter to New York tells an interesting story:

> Mr. Beals tells me I must send you a statement of my part of the school. I cannot give much account of it until I learn more myself, which I intend to do. I learned my letters & how to read a little before the war—when I was a slave. . . . My Master once sent me for a book of Hannah More's. Instead of bringing the whol [sic] pile like the rest did, I fetched the one Massa wanted. He said why didn't you bring all the books. I said I seed it on the back, Massa. He said "Who learnt you to read? Bring me the cowhide" & gave me

three or four licks on the head. Since the Yankees came I learn fast, and when I could read "In the beginning was the word" I felt very proud. I love to teach in the school, & get $10 a month. My Master hired me out for $50 a year, and when I come and ask for a Christmas gift, he gave me 10 cents. I come again & say "Massa is that all?" He says "Ain't Missus gwine to give you a pie?"

I wish I could tell you how grateful I am to you for doing so much for us. I feel it—but seems like I cant express it.[2]

There is an historical myth that New England "school marms" educated the freedmen during and after the Civil War. Like most myths this one has a large hold on the truth. Probably the majority of the teachers were indeed women from New England, but there were also a large number of women from the Middle Atlantic States and the states of the old Northwest Territory—all of whom were still Yankee school marms, of course. But many of the teachers were neither women nor Yankees.

About one-third of the AMA working among the freedmen were men. If those men who were strictly pastors were excluded from the list, there was still a goodly proportion of men. The percentage of men was even higher among the African American teachers. Of the 467 AMA workers definitely identified as African American, 293 were men, although 80 of that number were devoted mainly to the work of pastors and missionaries.

Another difference between the white and black AMA staff members was their birthplace or residence at the time they were commissioned. Although there were very few white teachers who were Southerners, more than half of the African American workers lived in the South. More than a third of the black men and women serving during Reconstruction were products of AMA normal schools or classes.

Another myth appearing in writings unsympathetic toward the Union cause and/or abolitionism, is that the Yankee school marms were usually elderly spinsters. The overwhelming majority of them—like their African American counterparts—were young people, most of them in their early twenties. Of the unmarried black women, only Mary Still seems to have been middle-aged. Many of the black men were married, and over one-fifth of the black women were married.[3]

Like their white fellow workers, several of the AMA African Americans had attended or were graduated from Oberlin College. Three of the black men had been educated in Europe, and others came from Africa (two from Mendi, several from Liberia) and the West Indies.

Efficiency and economy rather than race dictated the placement of AMA teachers. During the war, of course, the availability of freedmen was the factor that determined that the beginning of the work would be in Virginia. Later there were other considerations. Comity arrangements with other educational societies resulted in some areas taken for work by the AMA and others relinquished to those societies. There were some states like Delaware, where the AMA did little, while almost all the work in Georgia—the most populous state in so far as blacks were concerned—was under its auspices.

For several years there were over one hundred workers in Georgia alone, yet there were few African American workers there, in contrast to the situation in Virginia. In 1865 there were 115 missionaries and teachers in Virginia—more than in any other state—sustained cooperatively by the AMA (95), the Free-Will Baptists (16), and the Presbytery of Mahoning (4); in 1868 there were 73, the AMA supporting 56, the Free-Will Baptists 17. By the end of Reconstruction, with the exception of a common school sustained at Carrsville, the AMA work in Virginia was concentrated at Hampton and vicinity. The only church established and maintained in Virginia by the AMA was Bethesda Church at Hampton, organized in 1869 and served by white pastors during Reconstruction.[4]

As other stations opened up, the work in Virginia was shared with other societies and AMA personnel sent elsewhere. Although the first AMA normal school in the state was not established at Hampton until 1868, it could immediately harvest the pupils who had been under AMA tutelage in Virginia since 1861. By 1869 Hampton was already sending out a crop of young African American teachers. In their first two years of teaching, many of them were supported by the AMA, thus giving Virginia a higher proportion of black teachers than would be true for Georgia, where work could not begin until 1865 after General Sherman had made his march to Savannah. It was true that Atlanta University was established in 1867 before Hampton was *officially* organized, but work in Georgia began four years after work at Hampton.

Other factors determined the percentage of black teachers to white in various areas. Generally speaking, teachers were sent to stations nearest to their homes in order to cut down transportation costs, whether those costs were borne by the Freedmen's Bureau, as they sometimes were, or by the AMA. Thus, teachers from Ohio, Michigan, and the other states of the Old Northwest, were more likely to be sent directly south to Kentucky, Tennessee, or the Southwest; and New England residents to those schools in the states along the coast. Of course, if a teacher paid his own way completely, and some did, then it was immaterial how far he or she had to travel to the field.

The tabulations below contain the names of AMA African American teachers, their places of residences or the school from which they were sent out to teach, and the places and dates of service. The lists below do not contain names of those whose work was limited to missionary labor, or who were not aided by the AMA, or whose work has already been noted above. (An asterisk [*] indicates that letters from the individual survive in the AMA Archives.)

ALABAMA

AMA work in Alabama during Reconstruction was centered at Talladega College, in Swayne School at Montgomery, and Burrell School at Selma. The following African Americans, in addition to those mentioned above, served in Alabama.

Sara G. Stanley* (Cleveland, Ohio), 1868, Mobile. This was the last of several stations of AMA work served by Stanley. She was married in 1868 to a Mr. Woodward (perhaps C.A. Woodward*, Cashier of the Mobile branch of the National Freedmen's Savings and Trust Company), a white man of Mobile.
Edmund Rivers (Talladega student), 1868-69, Mardysville. He was a first-year theologue at Talladega in 1875.
Albert J. Brown (Talladega student), 1868-69, Silver Run. In 1875 he was a middler theologue at Talladega.

Lindsey A. Roberts* (Rogersville, Tenn.), 1872, Athens
Samuel B. White* (Talladega graduate), 1873-18, Kingston; 1875-76, Kymulga.[5]
Marietta G. Hardwick (graduate of Talladega Normal Department 1876), 1877, Burrell School, Selma.

FLORIDA

Cecile H. Coleman* (Oswego, New York), 1871-72, Meginniss's Place near Tallahassee.
Emaretta McClellan (Jacksonville), 1870-71, Jacksonville.
Mr. _____ Bennett (Jacksonville), 1870-71, Jacksonville.
Mary Still* (a Philadelphian who moved to Florida in 1866), 1869-72, Stanton Institute, Jacksonville (taught a primary class).[6]

GEORGIA

When AMA missionary the Rev. Hiram Eddy was asked to describe what it was like to begin a school among the freedmen, he said that one word came to mind: "Chaos." "It is utter chaos. the numbers, the work, the eagerness, the profound ignorance, . . . make it a scene of confusion from which you cannot bid order arise by a word, but you are compelled to adopt the developmental theory of the universe & wait for order as a thing of growth." His experience at Macon had given him "a better idea of chaos" than he had ever had before. Sometimes the eagerness of the people to learn moved him to tears and painted "the curse of slavery in blacker colors." The need was so great. One AMA teacher visiting Georgia said that twenty thousand teachers were needed at once. At Augusta in May, 1866, there were 1062 pupils and 6 teachers. One of the latter understated the overwhelming job when he said, "We are doing quite a business."[7]

Georgia is difficult for the researcher to deal with in the Reconstruction period both because of its size and the large black population, and because of the peculiarly backward condition of many of the rural slaves. Even the freedmen in Atlanta seemed farther behind, there being fewer who could read there than in other southern cities.[8]

Georgia had its share of white opposition to the teaching of the freedmen. There were instances of violence and murder. W.T. Walker, a member of the Congregational Church in Atlanta, was murdered because he had the temerity as a colored man to work in the Republican party. Schools and churches were burned. Missionaries denounced the "free elections" as farces without the protection of federal troops.[9]

With the rest of the South, Georgia suffered from plagues of yellow fever, smallpox, cholera, and scarlet fever, which caused the schools to be closed periodically. A word that appears often in the letters from Georgia is "patience." One Georgia teacher asked the men in New York to send down a few cans of patience to the mission residence along with other staples.[10]

In addition to the names listed in the Annual Reports of the AMA, there were teachers hired on the local scene by the Superintendents, In 1865 a group of local teachers was supported in Macon:

Lavinia Martin	Miss E. Hitch
Mrs. Hitch	Ella Watson
William Cole	John Berritey
R.N. Mitchel	Henry Owen
Isaac Prince	L.M.A. Sellers
Louis Smith	Henry Taylor
Lewis Williams[11]	

Other African American teachers in Georgia during Reconstruction with their dates and places of service are listed below.

Louis B. Toomer*, 1865-66, Savannah. In the night school he assisted Hardy Mobley, the first African American AMA worker in Savannah, mentioned in a previous chapter. (Mobley arrived in Georgia before the end of the war.)
James Porter, 1865-66, Savannah, Oglethorpe School
Miss M.C. Deas, 1865-66, Savannah, asst. School No. 2
Miss ___ Jones, 1865-66, Savannah, asst. School No. 2
Miss ___ Porter, 1866, Savannah, asst., School No. 2
Louisa Alexander* (Oberlin student), 1867, Marietta
Miss Delonius Harris, 1867-68, Macon
James L. Hagerman* (New York City), 1868, Altama; 1870, Blackshear. (For 1869, see South Carolina.)

William Steward * (Bridgeton, N.J.), 1869, Americus
Sarah Lowry, 1869, Americus, assistant
Emmanuel McClellan *, Norfolk, Virginia, 1868-69, Attapulgus.
McClellan had attended the Normal Department of Wilberforce for
more than two years. He had also taught school at Norfolk,
Virginia and was a member of the AME Church there. He had lost
his right arm.[12]
William A. Jones * (Oberlin student, Elmira, New York), 1869,
Hopeton.
Anthony Wilson * (Elliott Bluff, Georgia), October 1868 to March
1869, Elliott's Bluff; March, 1869 to July 1970, Sapelo Island;
August 1870 to March 1871, Elliott's Bluff and Woodbine. Wilson
had some difficulty with Charley H. Marshall, who attempted to
steal Wilson's teaching job and even forged his name to checks at
the post office. Wilson later became a Republican member of the
Georgia legislature from Camden County. He continued to
subscribe to the *American Missionary*.[13]
Robert Carter *, 1869, Savannah, night school.
Hezekiah Brown *, 1869 Savannah; 1870, Ditmersville (Savannah)
Mrs. Hezekiah Brown, 1870, Ditmersville (Savannah).
J.D. Enos * (West Chester, Pennsylvania), 1869 Valdosta. As a
native Pennsylvanian, Enos had been a quartermaster sergeant of
the Third Regiment, U.S.C.T., 1st Pennsylvania Colored Volunteers. In 1870 he became the postmaster of Valdosta as well as a
teacher there.
Samuel Drinks, 1869, Valdosta, assistant to Enos.
Charles Anderson (later an ordained minister), 1869 Valdosta,
assistant to Enos.
Henry Jones, 1872, Atlanta. Although no letters from Jones
survive, other sources indicate he had a fine tenor voice and was
asked to join Fisk's Jubilee Singers, which he refused. He was also
teaching at Byron Station in 1872 and in Macon in 1871.[14]
Floyd Snelson *, 1872, Andersonville; 1874-77, in charge of school,
Golding's Grove (Dorchester Academy)[15]
George S. Smith * (Atlanta U. graduate), 1874, Byron Station.[16]
John H.H. Sengstacke * (educated in Europe), 1875-1904, Savan-
nah. He continued as teacher and minister until his death in 1904.
His most important role was as AMA minister.[17]
Emma Jackson, 1874-75, Golding's Grove.

Seaborn Snelson*, 1875-77, Golding's Grove.
Silas Daniels*, 1877, Golding's Grove.
George B. Snowden*, 1875, Golding's Grove; 1877 Belmont.
M. Blanche Curtiss* (graduate of Normal Department, Atlanta U.), 1877, Dalton; (1878, Livingston, Miss.).
Samuel B. Morse* (Atlanta U. student), 1876, Athens.[18]
John McIntosh, 1877, Athens; (later Dorchester Midway School). He became a member of the Georgia legislature. When he was a pupil at the AMA's Bryan School in Savannah, one of his teachers wrote of him: "I send you the name of one of my scholars—John McIntosh—as being the best boy in school—he has kept perfect lessons, has neither been late nor tardy, and has kept the rules of the school. His name is the first on the 'Roll of Honor,' he is 14 years of age—and was formerly one of the most uneasy of school boys."[19]
Susan V. White (graduate of Normal Department, Atlanta U.), 1877, Marietta. She was from Seily Pond, Georgia, and was an accomplished organist as well as teacher.[20]
Howard Bunts, Jr., 1877, Albany. He was a member of the Georgia legislature. Mrs. Bunts was teaching in the AMA building in Albany.

In addition to the teachers and ministers who served their people as employees of the AMA, there were other African Americans in Georgia who had some contact with the Association—like **Hamilton Brown***, the president of the Colored School Committee of Milledgeville, and **William Craft** "of antislavery note," who taught day and night schools in Bryan County, who was sent a subscription to the *American Missionary* by his friend **P.S. Porter***.

Rev. Wilkes Flagg, pastor of the Milledgeville Baptist Church and member of the School Committee, was the leading African American in the town. When the AMA teachers were refused lodgings by the whites of Milledgeville, they boarded with Pastor Flagg.[21]

William A. Golding*, member of the Georgia legislature, was an influential African American whose relationship with the AMA was close for several years. **Jefferson T. Long*** (1836-1900), member of the 41st Congress of the United States, from Georgia, had some correspondence with the AMA regarding both their educational and church work in Macon.

KANSAS

Because Kansas was a free state, schools there were open to African American children, and the only AMA workers in that state were missionaries.

KENTUCKY

Berea College in Kentucky was unusual in that it had a student body composed about equally of black and white students during Reconstruction.[22] After the war began, the AMA had workers at Camp Nelson, where black soldiers and their families were housed. For a time there was a possibility that the college would be re-established there rather than at Berea. African Americans working under AMA auspices in Kentucky during Reconstruction include those in the following list.

E. Belle Mitchell* (Danville, Kentucky), 1865-66, Lexington; 1866-67, Richmond. She later married a man named Jackson. In 1874 she was teaching at the Normal School at Lexington.[23]

William H. Miller* 1865-66, Lexington. In 1869 he was graduated at the head of his class at Lincoln University.

Sara G. Stanley* (Cleveland, Ohio), 1866, Louisville.

George G. Collins* (Oberlin), 1867, Danville.

Mrs. George Collins, 1867, Danville.

Louisa Alexander* (Oberlin), 1868, Greenville; 1869, Paducah and Henderson.

Moses T. Weir* (Oberlin), 1868, Elkton.[24]

C.C. Vaughn* (Dinsmore, Ohio), 1868-70, Cynthiana. Vaughn was born a slave in Virginia, and spent three years in the army during the war. He attended Liber College in Indiana, and Berea College in Kentucky. In the latter institution he did student teaching to help with expenses. He became a licensed Baptist preacher.[25]

Laura Henson (Cincinnati), 1869, Lagrange.

Arthur C. O'Hear (Graduate of Avery Institute, Charleston, S.C.), 1868-69, Greensburg.

Joseph H. Henson (Cincinnati), 1869, Shepardsville; 1870, Millersburg.

Miss N.A. Patterson* (Oberlin), 1869, Union Hall. The author thinks there is a strong possibility that the Miss Patterson from Oberlin, who taught for the AMA at Union Hall, Kentucky, in 1869, might have been Mary J. Patterson, the first African American woman to earn a collegiate degree, graduating from Oberlin in 1862. Miss Patterson had assisted Mrs. Dascomb at Oberlin, and Mrs. Dascomb was very close to George Whipple. In any case Mary J. Patterson applied for a teaching position with the AMA.

Elizabeth Henson* (Oberlin), 1869, Richmond; 1870, Kingston.

George Cary (Xenia, Ohio), 1869-70, Winchester.

Fannie Burwell* (Cleveland), 1870, Versailles.

Laura King (Berea student), 1871-74, Howard School, Lexington.[26]

Enoch Seales, 1870-71, Camp Nelson.

B.A. Imes (Oberlin), 1876, Camp Nelson.

Benjamin F. Lee (Bridgeton, N.J.), 1870, Danville. Lee became editor of the AME publication, the *Christian Recorder* and President of Wilberforce University. He was born in Gouldtown, New Jersey, 1841, and was educated at Wilberforce.[27]

LOUISIANA

The AMA sent teachers and missionaries into Louisiana during the Civil War. They were removed, however, or else absorbed into the school system inaugurated in that state by General Banks of the Freedmen's Bureau. The Bureau's schools were closed in the spring of 1869, and lack of funds and organization resulted in "but few and weak schools" under the school law of that year. A "low estimate" placed the number of unschooled colored children in Louisiana at 85,000.

The AMA declared that no state was in greater need of schools. Before 1869 public schools had not existed outside of New Orleans, and until the Civil War only the children of planters had been educated (abroad or in the North), the masses of the people—white and black—growing up ignorant. Even in the Bureau's 216 schools, only 12,309 pupils had been taught. When they were closed, Louisiana was indeed a mission field.

Baptist and Methodist mission boards joined the AMA in bridging the gap left by the closing of the Bureau schools. The AMA was "the chief agency," sustaining "more schools in the rural districts than all other agencies combined." During the year 1869-70, the AMA supported 50 teachers in the state. Yet, despite the efforts of the church groups and the local government agencies, 50,000 black children were without schools, while others walked as much as 12 miles a day to attend AMA schools.[28]

The following African Americans (in addition to those already mentioned above) were employed by the AMA in Louisiana.

Emma Brown*, 1870, New Orleans. The author thinks that the Emma M. Brown listed as an AMA teacher in New Orleans in 1870 may be Emma V. Brown of Washington, D.C.. Emma V. Brown had applied for a position with the AMA late in 1869, asking to be sent to Charleston, New Orleans, or Mobile. Emma V. Brown was warmly recommended by Sella Martin, O.O. Howard, and John Alvord.[29] Emma Brown became Mrs. Henry P. Montgomery.

Charles A. Austin (New Orleans), 1869-70, Monroe.

Rosalie Collyunna (New Orleans), 1869-70, Algiers.

Miss Isadore Fredericks (New Orleans), 1869-70, Algiers.

Edward North (Gretna), 1869-70, Algiers.

Mrs. H.W. Reedy, 1870, Baton Rouge.

Ellen E. Saville (New Orleans), 1870, Baton Rouge.

Emeline Hays (New Orleans), 1870, Carrollton.

Sarah E. Henry (New Orleans), 1870, Carrollton.

Eliza Pierce (New Orleans), 1870, Cottonport.

Frank Joseph (New Orleans), 1870, Gentilly Road.

Henry Lewis (New Orleans), 1870, Greenville.

Carrie R. McKinley, 1870, Gretna.

James Hogan, 1870, Gretna.

Mrs. Agnes Lewis, 1870, Hammond Station.

The Rev. S. W. Otts (New Orleans), 1870, Jefferson City; 1871-72, Algiers.

D.M. Williams, 1870, New Orleans.

John H. Collins, 1870, New Orleans.

Mary C. Comerford, 1870, New Orleans.

Mary A. Cumberland, 1870, New Orleans.

Emily Lobre, 1870, New Orleans.
Laura Ogilvie, 1870, New Orleans.
Mrs. Emma V. Summers, 1870, New Orleans.
Laura G. Whiddin, 1870, New Orleans.
Miss E.C. Williams, 1870, New Orleans.
Lucinda Wright, 1870, New Orleans.
Emily P. Dawse, 1870, New Orleans.
Ezekiel DeWolf (New Orleans), 1870, Moodyville.
L.A. Fuller (New Orleans), 1870, Port Hickey.
Nellie Dearth (New Orleans), 1870, St. James Parish.
James Hedgepath (New Orleans), 1870, St. James Parish.
Mary Carson (New Orleans), 1870, St. John Baptist Parish.
The Rev. S.W. Rogers (New Orleans), 1870-71, Terrebonne.
Daniel Clary (New Orleans), 1870, Terrebonne.
Robert J. Walker*, 1871, 1872, New Carthage.
Nathaniel B. James*, 1871-72, New Iberia; 1876, Carrollton.
Peter P. Proctor*, 1871-72, New Orleans.
Thomas E. Hillson*, 1871-72, New Orleans.
Charles G. Austin (Straight U. student), 1872, New Orleans.[30]
Thomas Brown (Straight student), 1872, New Orleans.
Hardy Mobley* (Brooklyn, New York), 1873, New Iberia.
Mrs. Hardy Mobley, 1873, New Iberia.
Miss M.C. Mobley, 1873, New Iberia.
Miss M.E. Mobley, 1873, New Iberia.
Miss S.J. Mobley, 1873, New Iberia.
Laura F. Mobley*, 1872, New Iberia; 1873 Lake Semminett.[31]
Evans Green, 1873, Carrollton.[32]
D.S. Baker, 1873, Carrollton.

MARYLAND

AMA work in Maryland was ended in 1870. Although Association efforts in the state were not very extensive, most of the workers were African Americans.

Edmonia G. Highgate* (Syracuse, N.Y.), 1865, Darlington.
Mrs. H. F. Highgate* (Edmonia's mother), 1865, Darlington.
Winella C. Highgate* (Edmonia's sister), 1865, Darlington.
Mrs. E. Garrison Jackson* (Concord, Mass.), 1865-68, Port Deposit.[33]

Miss J.V. Benjamin (assistant), 1866, Port Deposit.
Sallie L. Daffin* (Philadelphia), 1866, Mt. Pleasant.
Marie A. Magnos* (Norfolk, Va.), 1865-66, Worton (Lincoln
School). Mrs. Magnos had an enemy in African American lecturer,
William Davis*. She was 23 in 1866 and had been a slave for her
first 13 years, purchased by her father for $1775. She was a widow,
her husband having been lost in the sinking of a coastal steamer.
Her father was a Baptist preacher, the Rev. Mr. Taylor of Hampton, Virginia. She came with a good recommendation from J.M.
Brown, but William Davis claimed that both she and her father
were on the side of "the ruling class of Virginia." This seems hardly
credible in view of her past and the fact that she was president of
the Colored Ladies Soldiers' Aid Association during the war and
did much to help wounded soldiers. That Samuel Hunt took
Davis's word would seem, nevertheless, to have been the case. She
was not recommended after 1866. The writer feels that the AMA's
confidence in William Davis was misplaced, but understands their
sentimental attachment to one of the first freedmen to respond to
their work. Davis also lectured for them in the North.[34]
Mary E. Watson* (Newport, R.I.), 1866-69, Darlington. Watson
was a well-educated young woman. She had many talents and was
much esteemed by the people of Darlington. In addition to her
regular duties, she gave lectures for which she charged a small fee
and donated the money to the stone schoolhouse (the best, white or
black, in town), which she persuaded the people to build. She
started an Educational Association among the adults for their
general "elevation," in which each one took turns leading the
sessions. She also instituted debates among the adults. Watson also
taught an AMA school in Virginia.[35]
Miss M.L. Hoy* (Brooklyn, N.Y.), 1868-70, Prince Frederick
(Asbury School). Hoy was very energetic, and (like Mary Watson)
not shy of giving lectures to the people on topics like temperance.
She was an Episcopalian. Her letters fairly jump with energy and
joy in work.[36]

MISSISSIPPI

The following African Americans taught grade schools in
Mississippi.

Clara P. Freeman (Vermont), 1865-66, Natchez.[37]
Charles W. Fitzhugh, 1866, Woodville. Fitzhugh was of mixed blood and a member (and local preacher) of the AME Church.[38]
Nathan Tappan Condol*, (Elmira N.Y.), 1866-67, Aberdeen. Despite his name, Condol proved a great disappointment to the AMA. He was teaching school in Geneva, N.Y., and was twenty-three years old in 1864. He was sent to Oberlin College with a scholarship provided by Whipple and aid from Thomas K. Beecher's Congregational Church of Elmira, N.Y. Once commissioned on the field, however, he proved an extremely sectarian Methodist, working against other teachers.[39]
Scott Sykes, 1866-67, Aberdeen (assistant).
Mrs. Lily A. Granderson*, 1866-68, Natchez.
Blanche V. Harris* (Oberlin), 1866-67, Natchez. Harris had taught at Norfolk, Virginia, while the war was still in progress, but was forced to suspend work because of illness.[40]
Elizabeth E. Harris (Blanche's sister), 1866-67, Natchez.
J.H. Murray (Dover, Delaware), 1871-73, Lowndes County.
B.P. Luckey* (Chicago), 1871, West Point Colfax; (1872 see Texas); 1874 West Point Colfax.
Mrs. R.A. Leslie*, 1873, Osyka. Mrs. Leslie was Miss N.A. Ramsey, see section on Straight University, New Orleans.
Fannie M. Burwell*, 1872, Jackson. She also taught in Kentucky.
F. Marion*, 1874-75, Columbia. He was given a scholarship to Talladega College and planned to go to the Mendi Mission in Africa.[41]

MISSOURI

The following African Americans taught common schools in Missouri:

Sara G. Stanley* (Cleveland), 1865, St. Louis; (1866 see Kentucky); 1867, St. Louis.
James H. Washington* (Oberlin), 1870, Fulton. He was later a teacher in Texas. The author has been unable to determine why the AMA addressed him with the title "Hon."[42]
Hardy Mobley* (Brooklyn, N.Y.), 1870-72, Lebanon.

NORTH CAROLINA

The following African Americans taught common schools in North Carolina:

Sallie L. Daffin* (Philadelphia), 1865, Wilmington.

William Moore (freedman, Baptist preacher), 1865-66, Brunswick County.[43]

Sarah Williams, 1866, Fayetteville.

John S. Leary*' 1866, Fayetteville, in charge of night school. Leary was the brother of Lewis Sherrard Leary who was killed in John Brown's raid on Harper's Ferry. He became a member of the North Carolina legislature in 1868.

Julia Leary*, 1866-67, Fayetteville. She is mentioned in letters of Robert Harris.

Carolyn Bryant, 1866-67, Fayetteville. She is mentioned in letters of Robert Harris.

Mary Payne, 1866-67, Fayetteville. She is mentioned in letters of Robert Harris.

Michael Jerkins*, 1867-70, Morehead City.[44]

Rev. John W. More, 1868, Beaufort. More was a Methodist preacher desirous of obtaining a school. The author believes that John More and William John Moore (below) are the same person.[45]

Melinda Rue, 1868, New Bern.

Hannah Rue*, 1868, New Bern.

B.W. Morris*, 1868, New Bern.[46]

F.C. Sadgwar*, 1868-70, Whitesville.[47]

Mrs. F.C. Sadgwar, 1868-70, Whitesville.

Hattie Fulford, 1869-70, Morehead City.

Joseph P. Weaver (Hampton student), 1869, Winton.[48]

William John Moore* (Washington, N.C.), 1868, Hull Swamp. See also Rev. John W. More above.

Elisha McKellar, 1868-71, Wilmington.[49]

A. Golden Smith, 1869-70, Beaufort.[50]

Mary Green, 1869-70, Fayetteville.[51]

D.C. Granderson*, 1869-70, Dudley.[52]

Phillip T. Willis, Jr., 1870, Kinston.[53]

Patsy A. Willis (Mrs. Phillip), 1870, Kinston.

John A. Holt, 1871.[54]

Richard A. Tucker* (Howard graduate), 1874-76, Dudley. Tucker was minister of the Dudley church, but he also taught school there.
Mrs. George S. Smith, 1877, Raleigh, Washington School. We know of Mrs. Smith through the letters of another worker, Esther P. Hayes (white). Miss Hayes preferred the aid of Lovey Mayo, Sarah Dunstan, and Ida Ransom (see chapter on Normal Schools above) to that of Mrs. Smith.
___**Harris**, n.d. Raleigh, Washington School, assistant. He was probably Robert Harris, a student of Lydia P. Auld at Wilmington, N.C., in 1868, who was sent to Hampton for further education.[55]

In addition to the commissioned workers in North Carolina, there were others who affected the AMA's progress in the state in various ways. An African American named **Lowrey** boarded the AMA teachers at Wilmington for several months.[56] Several members of the state legislature (in addition to **John S. Leary**, mentioned above) had some associations with the AMA or affected its work to some degree.

James Edward O'Hara was born free, graduated from North Carolina State, and studied law at Howard University. He was engrossing clerk of the North Carolina Constitutional Convention in 1868, and a member of its House of Representatives, 1868-69. He was elected a member of the 48th and 49th Congresses of the United States. He was also a Roman Catholic, a fact that concerned the AMA representatives in North Carolina when he taught a school in New Bern in 1864. The AMA saw little reason to think that the rulers of the Roman Catholic Church had changed their goal of winning America, having stated publicly that once the Roman Catholic Church captured a majority of the population (as it expected to do by the year 1900), "religious liberty" would be limited to the dominant Church.[57]

After teaching a self-supporting school at New Bern, O'Hara evidently taught for the Society of Friends in his home town of Goldsboro. He denied, however exercising "any sectarian influence on the minds of his pupils." In any case, he was relieved of his position "for unfaithfulness to his work in accepting the post of engrossing clerk to the Constitutional Convention . . . without consulting [his patrons] till after he had entered on his duties" at Raleigh. When O'Hara became principal of the Miles School in

228 His Truth Is Marching On

Raleigh in 1868, AMA Fisk P. Brewer (a son of Josiah Brewer), thought it his duty to inform the people of "the nature of Catholicism."[58]

Henry C. Cherry, a member of the Constitutional Convention of 1868 and a member of the legislature from Tarboro, asked the AMA to send a "Lady school Teacher" to Tarboro, and the people there would pay her salary and care for her board. He did not care what her color was so long as she did not mind boarding with African Americans. Cherry was sustained in his request by Samuel S. Ashley, State Superintendent of Public Instruction in North Carolina, and former AMA Superintendent.[59]

Ashley described **John Hyman**, African American State Senator, as "a young man of good sense and reliable judgment." Hyman had written asking Ashley for two female teachers for Warrenton. The people there were able to pay them each $10 per month and would provide them a house and a school with between 80 and 90 scholars.[60]

SOUTH CAROLINA

In addition to those African Americans working in South Carolina mentioned in sections above, the following were teachers there.

Mary Still* (Philadelphia), 1865; 1866, Beaufort. Miss Still was a sister of William Still of underground railroad fame.[61]
Paul Gustavus Barnswell*, 1865, Beaufort.
James L. Hagerman*, 1868-69, Georgetown.
Sarah A. Crum, 1870-71, Charleston, Avery Institute.
Mrs. John W.A. Shaw*, 1875, Charleston, Avery Institute.

Jonathan Jasper Wright*, black teacher and law student of Wilkes Barre and Montrose, Pennsylvania, taught the black soldiers of the 128th Regiment in a school at Camp Stanton, situated about one half mile from Beaufort, 1865-1866. The school, taught in two large tents fastened together, was first limited to the non-commissioned officers of the 128th (Colonel Charles H. Howard's command). Later the enlisted men were also taught to read and write and an additional school was set up on Paris Island by Wright.

Wright's assistant, until he proved too weak to withstand the temptations of camp life and succumbed to drink, was African American **Paul Gustavus Barnswell** of Brooklyn, New York. Barnswell had offered to produce testimonials from most of the prominent black men in the nation and several white ones, when he applied for a commission. He protested his innocence when he resigned, saying that a bar "detached from the house" where he lived with his brother in town, was the probable reason that AMA Superintendent Richardson thought his brother's house was not a fit place to stay. Barnswell was an example of a black man who had had the advantages of a northern education but who proved a failure in the work at the South. Such failures could also be catalogued for the white teachers as well, of course.[62]

It was his work for the AMA that took Wright to Beaufort, where he would return to enter Republican politics and become the first African American to serve as an Associate Justice of a state supreme court. It was also as an AMA teacher and Sunday school teacher that he became intimately involved with the problems of the freedmen in South Carolina and practiced law for the first time in their behalf.

Wright's monthly report for December, 1865, showed an average attendance of 91 at the Camp Stanton school. The Paris Island school was also still in operation. In addition he taught a class of adults in his room three nights a week.[63] He was sent to the Colored Convention in Charleston as a delegate from his area and while there had the "pleasure" of seeing F.L. Cardozo's school in session. He recommended it to anyone desiring to see a black school "conducted as refined and educated white folks conduct theirs. Each teacher and scholar had a place in the school, and they were in it." Ten of the twenty teachers were "of African descent."

He heard a class of boys reciting from Clark's *Advanced Grammar*. The teacher told him that all the boys in the class aspired to the professions. He could not help thinking as he listened "that the time was not far distant when there would be more then one colored lawyer South of Mason's and Dixon's line to vindicate the cause of the downtrodden and oppressed of the race of Ham."[64]

Wright had promised when he began to work that he would not grow weary in it. As the new year began, he declared himself

well paid, for he felt "elevated" every day. At last the black man
was showing even his worst enemies that he was also a child of
God, a part of the human race. Surely, "Ethiopia" was "about
stretching forth her hands unto God." On one day he addressed
about five thousand people and failed to see one drunk man and
heard but a single oath and that from an Irishman.

During the month of December he was able to visit his
school on Paris Island only once a week because of the lack of boat
service, but it continued as well as his school at Camp Stanton. On
several occasions Wright tried to explain the special problems of a
teacher on a military post, subject to the peculiarities of camp life.
His men were drummed to class for two sessions (10 a.m. to 11.30
and 1.30 p.m. to 3). He did not call the roll in order to save precious
time; in any case, the make-up of the class varied from day to day
as army duties called groups away. He assured AMA Secretary
Hunt that all the men could read the New Testament, while several
could parse common sentences and had passed simple arithmetic.

Hunt had suggested that Wright was giving the AMA only
part of his time. Wright countered that if Hunt could tell him of a
more important missionary work to do when school was not in
session than giving legal advice, to tell him and he would do it
"with all his heart." Hunt said that he heard of Wright more as a
lawyer than as a teacher. Wright agreed; he had been a teacher for
three years and caused no stir at all, but after he became a lawyer in
the spring of 1865,[65] he was suddenly "a perfect show," and people
at "a great distance" knew of him.

> When a white man is admitted to the U.S. Court, there is not
> much said about it, but when John S. Rock was admitted, he
> was heard of. Had I been contented to settle down, and been
> what the masses of white persons desired me to be (a boot-
> blacker, a barber, or a hotel waiter) I would have been heard
> of less. But I always thought that God was the black man's
> as well as the white man's God. I think so still. I came here
> for the express purpose of working among this people, and
> while I am here if any body stops me from so doing they will
> have to put me in jail. . . . And there is one thing certain, that
> wherever ignorance, prejudice, oppression & the devil, come
> in contact with me there will be a fuss & people will hear
> from me. If my race were elevated, and stood as high in the
> estimation of the people as the Caucasian race, I might

perhaps pretend to work three or four hours a day and lie down the rest of the time contented.

He was willing to keep a strict account of any monies received for his legal advice, but that was very little. When he had left Pennsylvania for South Carolina, he had had a good suit of clothes and ninety-four dollars of his own savings. Now his suit was not so good, and he had less than ten dollars. Occasionally a client gave him a chicken or a peck of potatoes in payment. Of course, he would turn over all fees he received to the AMA, for his time belonged to them. When he was shot at by "some enemy of his race," Major Donelson said he would write to the Rooms and tell them what a good job Wright was doing. But he would leave off trying to defend himself. He realized that Hunt was doing his duty as he saw it in his "ardent desire for the progress of the work"; nevertheless, Hunt's letter had caused Wright's "heart to bleed," for he had done his best.[66]

At the end of February, the 128th went to Charleston to be mustered out. Having had good health during his stay in South Carolina, Wright spent his last two months in AMA service suffering from chronic diarrhea, and was advised by his doctor to go North for a while. He had kept close accounts of all monies received for legal work, and found that it amounted to $3.29 for the month of February. Twenty-nine cents he applied to costs of stationery and deducted $3 from his teacher's salary of $25, leaving $22 due him from the AMA.[67]

This ended his tour as a commissioned missionary of the AMA, but not his relationship with the men at the Rooms. He returned to South Carolina in 1866 with an appointment from General O.O. Howard as legal adviser to the freedmen.[68]

As a leader in the black community of Beaufort, he was elected to the school board, and soon actively engaged in trying to raise funds for a school building, since the buildings in which black schools had been held were to be turned over to their white owners by March 1, 1867. Wright was not then himself teaching day school, but was teaching in the evening. The freedmen had given as much as they were able, and he appealed to the AMA for aid.[69]

Agent Edward P. Smith replied that the AMA was unsure of its ability to help but would like to know more of Wright's plans.

Wright had held mass meetings among the African Americans at which $509 had been pledged toward the $1500 building they wished to purchase, but only $180.50 of actual money had been received. The people were in difficulties; many of the houses and lands they had purchased from the government were to be sold in a few days because they were unable to meet the payments.[70]

The Association did help, and in December, 1867, the board again asked the AMA for assistance in paying the remainder of the money due ($694). They were assured that the Bureau would pay $350 of that amount as rent for the building. But the cotton crop had failed during the year, and the freedmen were unable to pay the rest. In order to save the building for the black community, the board was willing either to mortgage it to the AMA, or turn it over to the AMA "to hold in trust for the people" as the board held it. They were willing to do "anything to save this property for the object for which it was purchased."[71]

The AMA complied and sent teachers to Beaufort through the school year of 1868-69. Work stopped at that point probably because of the insistence of the new School Commissioner L.S. Langley (an African American appointed under the new state constitution) that he choose any teachers the AMA intended to support in Beaufort. Probably Langley remembered with something less than charity, that the AMA had refused to commission him when, as a young man of twenty-two, living in Burlington, Vermont, he had applied to them for work as a teacher in 1863. He had not then met their requirement of church membership. For similar reasons (their desire to support only evangelical Christians), the AMA would not agree to let Mr. Langley choose their representatives in Beaufort.

Langley was very critical of the AMA teachers who worked in the city during 1868, except for Miss C.M. Keith (a white Baptist). The rest of the teachers, he said, were "very unpopular, because, forsooth, the schools taught by them were of a *demoralizing* character." Several AMA teachers, he charged vaguely, belonged "to that class of persons in whom the freedmen have no confidence. . . ." He, on the other hand, knew that he could find among the local black people those in whom the people would have confidence.[72]

Whatever the relationship of the AMA to the colored school board in Beaufort, Jonathan Jasper Wright remained a warm friend of the Association. As a member of the South Carolina Senate in 1869, and later, he was anxious that men like Robert Smalls, J.A. Green, and Hutson J. Lomax have subscriptions to the *American Missionary*, in order to know what the Association was doing among the black people of the South. He bought subscriptions for at least nineteen persons and single copies for many others.[73]

TENNESSEE

The following African Americans taught under the AMA in Tennessee in addition to those already mentioned above.

The Rev. E.H. Freeman* (Newark, N.J.), 1866-68, Franklin. The Rev. and Mrs. Freeman were members of the Plane Street Presbyterian Church in Newark, where the minister was the Rev. C.H. Thompson. After Thompson read a letter from the Freemans to his congregation, they sent four barrels of clothing for their work.

Mrs. E.H. (Sophia) Freeman (Newark, N.J.), 1866-68, Franklin.

E.H. Gurney*, 1868, Dover, Fort Donelson School

George W. Bates* (Fisk student), 1870, Cornersville.

Hattie F. Kimbro* (Fisk student), 1870, Maury County, Hampshire School.

Sarah L. Grant* (Fisk student), 1871, Cornersville.[74]

Mrs. M.J. Robinson, 1869-70, Fisk University.

TEXAS

William A. Jones* (Elmira, N.Y., and Oberlin), 1870-72, Brazoria.

Hon. James H. Washington* (Oberlin), 1870-73, Navasota.

B.P. Luckey* (Chicago), 1872, Houston.

Anna L. Burwell, 1870-71, Galveston.[75]

Mitchell Thompson*, 1873, Goliad.

Solomon M. Coles* (Yale Divinity School graduate), 1877-80, Corpus Christi.

VIRGINIA

The following were among the African Americans who taught under the AMA in Virginia during Reconstruction.

Mary E. Watson* (Newport, R.I.), 1865-66, Norfolk. Mary Watson was a graduate of the Rhode Island State Normal School and had taught for five years. Later she taught under the AMA in Maryland.

Charlotte Jackson, 1867, Norfolk Night School.
Mary Parker, 1867, Norfolk Night School.
Richard Tucker, 1867, Norfolk Night School.
William Watkins, 1867, Norfolk Night School.
John H. Collins, 1867, Norfolk Night School.
Samuel Humphreys, 1867, Norfolk Night School.
Sarah Greenbrier* (Cleveland, Ohio), 1867, Arlington.
Sallie L. Daffin* (Philadelphia), 1866-67, Arlington.
John Wesley Cromwell* (Philadelphia), 1866-67, Norfolk. Cromwell succeeded Robert W. Harris at Providence Church School, Norfolk County, Virginia, and served the school year. Although he attended the AME church and presented testimonials from J.M. Brown, W.D. Harris, and James Lynch, he was not a church member. He was born a slave in Portsmouth, September 5, 1846, redeemed by his father and taken to Philadelphia in 1851. He graduated from Ebenezer D. Bassett's Institute for Colored Youth in 1864. He taught schools in Columbia, Pa., Portsmouth, Va., and Baltimore, Md. In 1880, when he was a clerk in the Treasury Department at Washington and editor of *The People's Advocate*, he found time every Sunday afternoon to work with the children of the AMA's Lincoln Mission. The Rev. Simon Peter Smith (black) said of him, "Indeed, he manifests such zeal in our work that we cannot but believe him to be one of our warmest friends. He is our example for all colored young men."[76]
Julia Bailor (Hampton), 1868, Hick's Farm.
Lucinda A. Spivery* (Hampton), 1868, 1869, Pungoteague
Martha J. Smith* (Washington, D.C.), 1868, Chickahominy.[77]
Annie M. Wilson, 1868. Miss Wilson was the daughter of William Joseph Wilson and had taught with her parents under the AMA in Washington, D.C.

Matthew G. E. Fitch* (Watertown, Conn.), 1868, 1869, Matthew's Court House

Rufus Sibb Jones (Pittsburgh), 1868-69, Newport News. Jones became a member of the Virginia legislature.

James A. Fields* (Hampton student), 1869-71, Williamsburg Intermediate School.[78]

Merrit R. Wallace* (Hampton student), 1869-70, Fort Magruder

David P. Allen*, 1869, Drummondtown; (1872 Lumberton, N.C.). David P. Allen was introduced to the Executive Committee of the AMA by one of the AMA's illustrious members, Amasa Walker, whose son, Francis Amasa Walker had served as an officer in the Army of the Potomac, and was incarcerated in the notorious Libby Prison at Richmond. When the war was over, Francis took David Allen home with him to North Brookfield, Mass., where the latter obtained a good common school education. Allen taught at Drummondtown from November 1868, to July, 1869, where he was shocked at the immorality of the people. He thought the people less progressive than those in his home part of Virginia. Although intoxicated persons could be seen at all hours, little money was invested in schools for their children. After graduating from Westfield State Normal School, Allen took a school at Lumberton, N.C., another place of "ignorance, indifference, intemperance and every other vice," where he worked "10 or 11 hours a day" and did not expect to receive half the salary promised.[79]

Elias Fenwick Jefferson* (Charleston, S.C.), 1869, Gloucester Court House.

A.J. Montgomery*, 1869, Capeville.

Mrs. E. Garrison Jackson* (Concord, Mass.), 1868-69, Chickahominy, James City County. See above for her work in Maryland.

Phebe E. Henson* (New Bedford, Mass.), 1869, Onacock. Phebe was the daughter of Thomas Henson of Norfolk, Va. Her work was near that of David Allen. Like Allen she was surprised to find the people indifferent toward education and filled with excuses for keeping children from school. She realized that they were poor and that men worked from sunrise to sunset for $8 a month and women for $3. She acknowledged that there was no such thing as justice for the black people in the courts and hoped that she was not expecting too much from people so terribly conditioned by slavery.

The Rev. William A. Jackson*, 1869-71, Berryville. The Jacksons were Free Will Baptists. Jackson was born in slavery and had been Jefferson Davis's driver when he became a refugee in 1862. He was sent north with a letter to George Whipple, suggesting that he be given an education. He did learn to read and write and also made a triumphant speaking tour of England. Jackson was called to the pulpit of the Congregational Church at Savannah in 1873, but died that same year.
Sarah S. Jackson* (Mrs. William A., from S. Middleboro, Mass.), 1869-71, Berryville. Mrs. Jackson was a native of Massachusetts, with a better education than her husband. She was the teacher of the school; her husband assisted her.[80]
Jesse Robinson* (Hampton student), 1868, 1870, New Market. Robinson was supported at least in part by the Free Baptist Home Society, and hired a black assistant.[81]
Edward A. Bowman* (Hampton student), 1870 Drummondtown.
Peter Jacob Carter* (Hampton student), 1870, Chincoteague
Robert A. Fields, 1870, Berryville. Fields assisted Mrs. Jackson at Berryfield. He was a student at a normal school at Harper's Ferry.
Abraham Giddings* (Hampton student), 1870, Capeville.
Everett Williams* (Hampton student), 1870, Bridgetown.
Maria L. Fields* (Hampton student), 1870, Fort Magruder.
Anthony Williams* (Hampton student), 1870, Newport News.
Anna Eliza Pitts* (Hampton student), 1870, Franktown.
Bridget J. Booker* (Hampton student), 1869, Bridgetown.
John Holmes* (Lexington, Va.), 1869-70, Hillwood.
Mrs. Mary Harly (assistant), 1870, Alexandria Industrial School.[82]

WASHINGTON, D.C.
In addition to those African Americans who began work in Washington during the war and continued during Reconstruction (see above), and the Howard University students who taught in the Lincoln Mission (also listed above), were **Mary Ann Shadd Cary** (a teacher) and **George G. Collins** (superintendent) of the Lincoln Industrial Mission. Collins was one of the few black men during Reconstruction with both collegiate and seminary training. Because of his unique qualifications, Collins was both educator and pastor.
There is no direct line from the AMA's school begun in 1864 at the Lincoln Hospital in Washington and the official founding of

the Lincoln Industrial Mission in October, 1869, because the AMA withdrew its teachers from the District in 1867, to help induce the Public School Board there to adopt the colored schools into the system. "Vigorous efforts of the friends of the Freedmen and the Bureau officers in Washington" had brought about the desired result, and a free public school system was established. Many of the northern teachers at work there continued; so "the most improved" northern methods of teaching were a part of the system also. This was the "natural and happy result of the educational work" carried on in Washington by various benevolent organizations for five years.[83]

Lincoln Industrial Institute was a night school begun for those (mostly adults) unable to attend day schools. In addition to the regular common school curriculum, it offered classes in sewing for women. George G. Collins arrived in Washington to take charge of Lincoln on May 9, 1870. Collins and his wife **Clara Emma Collins** had served as AMA teachers in Danville, Kentucky, and made their home in Princeton, New Jersey, where George had graduated from the Theological Seminary.[84]

Collins was also a graduate of Oberlin College and had been recommended by Oberlin President James H. Fairchild for the position of instructor in the Theological Department of Straight University at New Orleans. Soon thereafter he was asked to undertake the work at Lincoln Institute, with a simultaneous tutorship at Howard University.[85]

As soon as he was settled in Washington, Collins sent a list of all those who had worked in the Lincoln Industrial Institute since its founding. There were forty-eight names altogether, and that was one of the problems at the school—the rapid turnover of teachers. It was an "unavoidable" situation because the teachers were drawn from the Howard University student body, who left when the pressure of work at the University became too great. There was also the fact that the students at the Institute slowly left school as the warm weather approached, in larger and larger numbers. Still, the school was a large one (96 males and 117 females) and the interest was high.

Amanda Wall, wife of Captain O.S.B. Wall, and personal friend of Collins, applied for a position at the Mission. The Walls had moved to Washington in the late 1860s, and Mrs. Wall had worked as a volunteer teacher in Washington until a trip to Oberlin in the summer of 1869. Captain Wall had attended Howard Law School under his brother-in-law John Mercer Langston, and was now a Justice at the Second Precinct Station in Washington. General Otis Howard added his personal recommendation to Mrs. Wall's application. The author has been unable to determine whether or not Mrs. Wall worked at Lincoln; Lincoln personnel was not published in the AMA Annual Reports. **Warren Brown**, a clerk in the Department of Internal Revenue, worked there in 1870.[86]

The Sunday school met on Sunday afternoon and church services were held immediately afterwards, at 4:30. Collins hoped eventually to gather a goodly congregation for the afternoon service, by gaining the good will of the black community, especially of their ministers. The prayer meetings held at 6:15 on Tuesday evenings were well attended. There had been some conversions, "but the old idea" that associated "conversion with great physical demonstration and almost miraculous experiences" died hard. Collins heard such remarks as "You folks don't believe in a change of heart. If you felt the work of the Holy Spirit you would do just like we do." Collins was convinced that education and religious training "must go hand in hand." He much feared that the younger generation would not have the respect for religion that their parents expressed.

The recent Democratic victory, Collins thought, would cause great suffering among the laboring class. The victorious party had announced its purpose of driving as many blacks from Washington as possible, thus reducing the Republican vote.[87]

When Chief Red Cloud and his "suite" visited Washington, they attended the Mission Sunday School and expressed the wish to have "similar schools for their children." The Sunday School connected with the Mission was enormous. On Sunday, June 15, 1870, it numbered 793.

Collins had formed a class for neighboring African American ministers. Eight or ten of them met at 6 o'clock each evening "for instruction in English studies" as well as courses in Church History, Gospel Harmony, and the Book of Romans.[88]

Collins had had ready "for some weeks" what he thought were a "sufficient number of members" with which to start a church. Finally in December a meeting was called with Dr. Jeremiah Eames Rankin (pastor of First Congregational Church) and a committee from the Lincoln Missionary Association. The latter was a society composed of sixty persons in the Washington area; and although Collins's salary was paid by the AMA, he had to answer also to the local society.[89]

Opposition arose to the formation of what would be virtually a black church. Deacon Danforth B. Nichols (white) of the First Congregational Church, John H. Cook (black Chief Clerk of the Freedmen's Bureau), and others took the position that it would be "inexpedient" to form a black Congregational church in Washington. After a consultation with General Howard and Dr. Rankin, it was agreed that Washington Congregationalists could not afford to have it said of them—after their long fight against caste that had resulted in the establishment of an integrated First Congregational Church—that they were now building up a colored Congregational church. Collins saw virtue on both sides of the issue. But he was for beginning the new church and letting its racial characteristics take care of themselves. If there was need for a Mission, there was need for a church also: "No one who has visited the homes of the Freedmen," he said, "and attended the religious services in their churches who takes into consideration the years of mental moral & pecuniary privation wh. have been theirs can reasonably say they do not need special care & training." Collins had been told to use the same "exertion" he would use to form a new church to persuade the people to join First Congregational Church. He thought that a good idea "if practicable, but when the mountain will not come to Mohammed he had better go to the mountain."[90]

The warm weather of spring in 1871 "sent forth into the streets many little ragged ones" who had "shivered at home" during the winter. "Soleless shoes and ribboned pants" could no longer keep them indoors. But their rags did keep them from attending Sabbath school, and Collins was grateful! for the gift from Central Congregational Church in Bangor, Maine. More clothing was needed, especially for boys.[91]

Mary Ann Shadd Cary, former AMA teacher in Canada, was one of the twenty-five teachers in the Lincoln Institute in 1871, of whom twenty-four were African Americans. The Carys had moved to Washington in 1865, and Mary Shadd Cary had entered the Law Department of Howard University.[92] There is a difference of opinion as to when Cary received her law degree. Rayford Logan says it was 1883; Hallie Q. Brown gives the date as 1884. The biographical sketch included in the Cary Papers at Howard University gives 1870 as the date. This seems borne out by a letter from D. Bethune Duffield in the same collection. It would seem unlikely that it would take the Cary the author has come to know from 1867 to 1883 to earn any degree. It also seems unlikely that Langston would have spoken of her graduation from the law department if that had occurred so long after his leaving that department.[93]

George Collins's Superintendent's Report for the month of June did not arrive at AMA headquarters in New York. John H. Cook wrote E.M. Cravath that "extreme illness" prevented Mr. Collins from communicating with the AMA. When Collins died in Washington on June 22, 1871, it was a tremendous loss to his race as well as the AMA. George C. Collins was "one of the few colored men of the country," wrote the editor of the *American Missionary,* "who have an education so thorough and liberal, and a character so stable and Christian, as to qualify them for the duties of instructors in the growing colleges and universities established to promote impartial Christian education in the South."

Resolutions passed by Howard University's Board of Trustees described Collins as "a young man in whose short service of one year were exhibited native ability, large acquirements, excellent character and a genial disposition, traits which in the future, as in the past, would have rendered him of great service to our university."[94]

James B. Johnson, Secretary and Treasurer of Howard University, was still volunteering his time in AMA Sunday schools in Washington in 1875—at that time in the Sabbath school at the Lincoln Mission. Johnson was convinced that eventually a church would grow there out of the services then conducted by Howard theologue Robert F. Wheeler, should he continue long enough and convince the people that regular preaching services would be held. Johnson felt "the formation of a church" depended on the minister.[95]

For twelve years the Lincoln Industrial Mission was maintained at the corner of Eleventh and R Streets, N.W., in the

Capital. Attendance in the evening school rose as high as five hundred students. By 1881 the educational portion of the work was absorbed by the city school system, the religious portion having become Lincoln Temple Congregational Church (now Lincoln Temple, United Church of Christ).[96]

* * * *

In the above lists of AMA teachers of common schools, Delaware and Arkansas are missing. The author has not identified any African Americans working in those states under the AMA.

NOTES

1. There are many examples in the Archives; see Carrie M. Blood, Chattanooga, Tennessee, July 8, 1874, to Cravath, AMAA, and *AM*, XVI (November, 1872), 255-256; XVII (January, 1873), 3-5.

2. Chadwick, [received January 13, 1866], to Whipple; see also February 21 to Hunt; Teacher's Monthly Report, Washburn Seminary, for December, 1869; January, 1870; May, 1870; Beals, May 30, 1868, to Whiting; Edward Bull, Beaufort, December 3, 1869, to Smith, AMAA; *Twenty-first Annual Report* (1867), 28; *AM*, XIV (June, 1870), 122.

3. Many marriages took place on the field. This was particularly true of the Mendi Mission in Africa. Mary Still was born August 31, 1808, see the PS Papers. Several African Americans were mothers of AMA personnel who also taught. They may have been almost as old as Still. Examples are Lily Granderson of Natchez, Mississippi, and Mrs. H.F. Highgate of Syracuse, New York.

4. *Twenty-second Annual Report* (1868), 43; *AM*, XIII (May, 1869), 98.

5. *Thirty-fifth Annual Report* (1881), 34.

6. *AM*, XVIII (January, 1874), 8; see also letters and Monthly Report of Celia E. Williams, AMAA.

7. See letters of Hiram Eddy, DeWitt C. Jencks and W.P. Russell, 1866, AMAA.

8. Frederick Ayer, Atlanta, February 15, 1866, to Whipple, AMAA.

9. See letters of R.N. Gladding, 1869, and of A.N. Niles, 1872, AMAA; *AM*, XII (November, 1868), 249.

10. John A. Rockwell, Teacher's Monthly Report, Macon, Lincoln Night School, for February, 1866; Rebecca M. Craighead, Missionary Report for March, 1866; Cravath, Report of AMA Work in Middle Tennessee and Georgia, for six months, to May 1, 1866; Sarah W. Stansbury, Superintendent's Monthly Report, Howard School, Cuthbert, Georgia, for May, 1871; statistics of illness and deaths from yellow fever, Savannah *Morning News*, October 30, 1876, AMAA. Also, see letters of G.L. Eberhart, Rebecca M. Craighead and Mrs. F. Ayer, 1866, AMAA.

11. W.H. Roberts, Macon, Georgia, September 29, 1865, to Prof. John Ogden, AMAA. Another teacher, Henry Watson, was accused of burglary and other crimes, and Roberts did not recommend paying him. Henry Owen, although accused of having "the French pox," was probably paid. See Owen, Macon, Georgia, October 5, 1865, to "Dear Sir," in which the author swears that the rash that kept him out of school was not syphilis.

12. Testimonials for McClellan from Watkins and Percy, AMAA.

13. See Monroe M. Work, "Some Negro Members of Reconstruction Conventions and Legislatures and of Congress," *JNH* V (January, 1920), 72.

14. See E.E. Rogers, Macon, Georgia, November 18, 1872, and M.E. Sands, Macon, Georgia, April 4, 1871, to Cravath, AMAA; *AM*, XV (May, 1871), 98; *Twenty-fifth Annual Report* (1871), 48.

15. See also letters of William A. Golding, Aaron Rowe, Albert P. Miller (Mendi), AMAA.

16. See also *Twenty-eighth Annual Report* (1874), 50.

17. *AM*, LVIII (November, 1904), 302; XX (April, 1876), 78.

18. See also letters of Cyrus W. Francis and R.F. Markham, AMAA.

19. See Julia Marshall, Savannah, May 31, 1866, to Hunt, AMAA.

20. See Thomas N. Chase, Macon, Georgia, September 6, 1877, to Strieby, AMAA.

21. See letters of Wilkes Flagg, John A. Rockwell, and Hiram Eddy, AMAA.

22. See letters of John G. Fee, AMAA. See also the many references to Berea in the *AM* (where graduation exercises and school examinations of all AMA colleges appeared in late summer issues) and in the Annual Reports of the Association.

23. See also letters of John G. Fee, Mary Colton, Mrs. A.E. Williams, J.G. Hamilton, AMAA.

24. See also *Twenty-second Annual Report*, (1868).

25. See (Simmons 1887, 723-728).

26. J.G. Hamilton, Lexington, Kentucky, April 23, 1874, to Cravath, AMAA

27. (Simmons 1887, 922-927).

28. *AM*, XIV (June 1870), 129.

29. Howard and Alvord, November 1, 1869, Testimonials for Emma V. Brown; Martin, November 2, 1869, AMAA. See also BRFAL Miscellaneous Records in Box 16, National Archives.

30. There was also a Charles A. Austin, Jr., AMA teacher at Monroe, Louisiana, 1869-70. The author does not know if these were two different men.

31. *AM*, XVII (June 1873), 128; XVIII (1874), 9, 10, 59, 153, 224.

32. J.A. Adams, New Orleans, August 29, 1874; J.A. Martling, May 5, 1874, to Cravath, AMAA.

33. See also letters of John W. Martin, AMAA. Miss J.V. Benjamin assisted Mrs. Jackson. In 1869, Mrs. Jackson taught for the AMA in James City, Va..

34. Her signature sometimes appears as Mary Magnos. J.M. Brown, Norfolk, Virginia, September 1, 1865; Thomas Henson, New Bedford, Mass., September 13, 1865, Testimonial for Marie Magnos, AMAA.

35. See letters of J.B. Armstrong in her behalf and Testimonials from the Darlington Colored School Committee, August 17, 1868 & July 10, 1869; letter from School Committee of Port Deposit, Maryland, August 18, 1868, to Whipple, AMAA; *Twenty-first Annual Report*,(1867), 22; *AM*, XI (September, 1867), 194; XII (May, 1868), 101.

36. See also petition of the School Board (black trustees) on her behalf; Report of Joseph Hall, n.d.; the letters of James Gross and Sutton Gross, AMAA; *AM*, XIII (November, 1869), 245.

37. See letters of Blanche V. Harris; Palmer Litts, December 16, 1865, to Whiting, AMAA.

38. See Teacher's Monthly Report, Union School, Woodville, Mississippi; J.P. Bardwell, Vicksburg, February 20, 1867, AMAA.

39. See letters of Thomas K. Beecher, Elmira, N.Y.; Hattie A. Lewis, Aberdeen, Miss.; J.P. Bardwell, Vicksburg, Miss., AMAA.

40. See letters of Bardwell, Palmer Little, and B.P. Luckey, AMAA.

41. *AM*, XVI (July, 1872), 147, contains an early letter from Tougaloo, Alabama.

42. *AM*, XVII (September, 1873), 201.

43. See William Moore, Teacher's Monthly Report Sown [?] Creek, Brunswick, N.C., November, 1865, AMAA.

44. See also letters of Elizabeth P. Worthington, AMAA.

45. See letters of E.L. Boing and H.S. Beals, AMAA.

46. See letters of Augusta A. Cook and A.A. Ellsworth,AMAA.

47. See also *AM*, XIII (May, 1869), 100; XIV (June, 1870), 122; (Sadgwar n.d. AMA publication).

48. See also Joseph P. Weaver's Teacher Monthly Reports; see also letter of S.C. Armstrong, AMAA.

49. See Elisha McKellar's Teacher's Monthly Reports for Williston School, Wilmington, and letter of H.S. Beals, AMAA; *AM*, XV (May, 1871), 97.

50. See also A. Golden Smith's Teacher's Monthly Reports for North River School, Beaufort; letters of S.S. Ashley and Edward Bull, AMAA.

51. See letters of Robert and Cicero Harris, AMAA.

52. See also letters of John Scott, AMAA.

53. See Willis's Teacher's Monthly Report, AMAA.

54. *AM*, XV (August, 1871), 171.

55. See letters of Lydia P. Auld, AMAA.

56. J.D.M. Lanlin, Wilmington, N.C., September 9, 1865, to Whipple, AMAA.

57. James Edward O'Hara, Teacher's Monthly Report, Queen Street School, New Bern, N.C., for March and April 1864; letters of Fisk P. Brewer, AMAA. For fears of the AMAA concerning expanding Roman Catholicism see *AM*, XI (December, 1867), 267-278; XIII (September, 1869), 205-206: Father Hecker said in a public lecture in New York that Roman Catholics made up one-third of the population of the United States, and if the church continued to grow in the next thirty years as it had in the previous thirty, "in 1900 Rome will have a majority, and be bound to take this country and keep it." Growth of the RC Church noted in the Boston *Pilot* (an RC paper) were cited. The AMA also cited figures published by the New York *Herald* giving the offices held in New York by Irish Roman Catholics: "Sheriff, Register, Comptroller, City Chamberlain, Corporation Counsel, Police Commissioner, President of the Croton Board, Acting Mayor and President of the Board of Alderman, President of the Board of Councilmen, Clerk of the Common Council, Clerk of the Board of Supervisors, five Justices of the Courts of Record, all the Civil Justices, all the Police Court Clerks, three out of four Coroners, two Members of Congress, three out of five State Senators, eighteen out of twenty-one Members of Assembly, fourteen-nineteenths of the Common Council, and eight-tenths of the Supervisors." The AMA also admitted elsewhere that only slightly over 100,000 New Yorkers were children of parents both of whom were born in the United States. Because it considered the Roman Church (in the words of the Rev. G.W. Perkins) "That huge conglomeration of error and superstition. . . .", another example of religion based on ritual and formulae of church-administered absolution rather than individual responsibility for ethical action, it seemed in many ways akin to the "impure Christianity" of the freedmen that put the magical power of baptism in the place of moral behavior as the key to immortality. Roman Catholics and Campbellites were accused of like emphases.

The Roman Catholic nuns and priests were also criticized by AMA teachers for refusing to allow their students to visit AMA Sunday schools. Instances were reported of persecutions of colored persons who disobeyed such rules. See *AM*, XII (January, 1868), 14-16; XIII (March, 1869), 60-61; XVI (February, 1873), 32; XVIII (February, 1874), 31; (June, 1874), 127-128; XIX (May, 1875), 113-114.

58. Brewer, Raleigh, February 27, 1868, to Whipple; June 7, 1868 to Smith, AMAA. For Josiah Brewer, see (DeBoer 1994,26).

59. Cherry, Tarboro, September 23, 1868; Ashley, Raleigh, August 10, 1868, to Smith, AMAA.

60. Hyman, Warrenton, September 22, 1868, to Ashley; Ashley, Raleigh, September 23, 1868, to Smith, AMAA.

61. *Nineteenth Annual Report* (1865), 24.

62. Barnswell, Woodbine Cottage, Beaufort, June 30, 1865, to Jocelyn; W.T. Richardson, Beaufort, June 8, 1865; June 17; June 24, 1865, to Whipple, AMAA.

63. See Wright's letters to the AMA from January, 1865 through September, 1865, and Monthly Teacher's Report for December, 1865; C.H. Howard, Beaufort, September 29, 1865, to Whipple; J.W. Raynor, Springfield, Pa., Testimonial for J.J. Wright, February 21, 1865, AMAA; R.H. Woody, "Jonathan Jasper Wright, Associate Justice of the Supreme Court of South Carolina, 1870-77," *JNH* (1933), 115.

64. Wright, Beaufort, December 4, 1865, to Hunt, AMAA.

65. Cf. Woody, "Jonathan Jasper Wright," *JNH* (1933), 115, who derives the date of August 13, 1866.

66. Wright, Beaufort, February 5, 1866, to Hunt; see also Wright's Teacher's Monthly Reports for December 1865, January 1866, February 1866, AMAA.

67. Wright, Beaufort, March 1, 1866, to Whiting, AMAA.

68. R.H. Woody, "Jonathan Jasper Wright," *JNH*, XVIII (1933), 115.

69. Wright, Beaufort, December 12, 1866, to Strieby, AMAA.

70. Wright, Beaufort, January 19, 1867, to Smith, AMAA.

71. Jonathan J. Wright, Robert Smalls, W.J. Whipper, L.S. Langley, S. Simons, and Israel J. Cohen, Officers of the Beaufort School Board, December 31, 1867, to the AMA. AMAA.

72. See the letters of Langley, AMAA.

73. Wright, Columbia, South Carolina, January 20, 1869; Abbeville, South Carolina, June 25, 1869, to Smith, AMAA.

74. Letterbook (Fisk University) of George L. White, Adam K. Spence, and Henry W. Hubbard, 1869-73, 197 (September 7, 1870); and 221 (October 1, 1870, for two examples of the friendly letters written to students by White; Letterbook (Fisk University) of Thomas C. Steward, 1872-74, 349 (February 17, 1874; and 374 (March 6, 1874), AMAA.

75. *American Missionary*, XV (May, 1871), 100-101.

76. Certificate stating that Cromwell "was a member of the 'Normal Class' of the Baltimore Assoc. for the Moral and Intellectual improvement of the Colored People," dated Baltimore, December 22, 1865, and signed by E.W. Sampson, Principal, AMAA; *American Missionary*, XXXIV (September, 1880), 273; (Simmons 1887, 898-907).

77. BFRAL, Records, District of Columbia, Superintendent of Education, Misc. Records in Box 16, No.4, National Archives; *American Missionary*, XII (April, 1868), 74.

78. (Gibson and Crogman 1902, 259-260).

79. *American Missionary*, VIII (April, 1864) for letter from Amasa Walker; XIV (July, 1870), 153.

80. *American Missionary*, XVII (September, 1873), 213-214; Benjamin Quarles, "Ministers without Portfolio," *JNH*, XXXIX (January, 1954), 40-41.

81. *American Missionary*, XII (April, 1868), 74.

82. Mrs. M.N. Parker, Alexandria, Va., May 2, 1870, to Smith, AMAA.

83. *Twenty-second Annual Report* (New York, 1868), 31.

84. George G. Collins, Washington, May 9, 1870, to Whipple, AMAA. See also *American Missionary* XV (May, 1871), 97, which gives Collins's home address as San Francisco, California.

85. See the letters of George Collins for 1869 and 1870, AMAA. The position of Dean of Theology at Straight went to Charles H. Thompson, black Presbyterian minister of Newark, N.J.

86. Amanda Wall, Oberlin, Ohio, July 18, 1869, to D.B. Nichols; Washington, May 31, 1870, to Smith; Oliver Otis Howard, June 2, 1870 (written on Wall letter), AMAA.

87. George Collins, Washington, June 18, 1870, to Smith, AMAA.

88. George Collins, Washington, June 18 and June 21, 1870, AMAA.

89. George Collins, Washington, December 12, 1870, to Cravath, AMAA.

90. George Collins, Washington, January 10, 1871, to Cravath, AMAA.

91. George Collins, Washington, March 29, 1871, to Cravath, AMAA.

92. Mary Ann Shadd Cary, Teacher's Monthly Reports, Lincoln Industrial Mission School, March, April and May, 1871; George Collins, Superintendent's Monthly Reports, Lincoln Industrial Mission, March and May, 1871; Collins letters of April 5 and May 8, 1871, to Cravath, AMAA.

93. (Logan 1969, 471); (Brown 1926, 95); Mary Ann Shadd Cary Papers, Moorland-Spingarn Collection, Howard University Library; D. Bethune Duffield, Detroit, Michigan, July 29, 1870, to

I.M. Howard and T. Chandler, Moorland-Spingarn Collection, Howard University Library; (Langston 1894, 306); (DeBoer 1994, 182-183).

94. *American Missionary*, XV (November, 1871), 263-264.

95. Johnson, Washington, June 22, 1875, to Cravath, AMAA.

96. (Dyson 1941, 425); *1972 Year Book of the United Church of Christ*, 58. Lincoln Temple dates its origins from 1869, when the Lincoln Industrial Mission was begun.

**Jubilee Hall, Fisk University,
built with funds raised by the Jubilee Singers**
Courtesy Amistad Research Center

X

THE JUBILEE SINGERS AND
OTHER AFRICAN AMERICANS

The son of a village blacksmith, who, from limited advantages of culture, became a successful country school teacher . . . and to no human agency, nor to all other human agencies combined, are the triumphs of this glad hour so much indebted as to George L. White. . . .

He gathered around him the children of the freedmen, and with them "Sung the old song."

He conceived the idea of coining the slave melodies of the old plantation and the camp-meeting into gold and silver wherewith to purchase this commanding site, and upon it erect Jubilee Hall.
　　　　　　　　　—General Clinton B. Fisk
　　　　　　　　　at the dedication of Jubilee Hall
　　　　　　　　　Fisk University, 1876

There was a small group of talented African Americans who worked for the AMA and added not only to its renown but made an ineradicable contribution to American culture. They made their mark neither as missionaries nor as teachers (although several of them taught school); yet, in a real sense, they were both. They were students of Fisk University, who brought to the notice of the public what has been called America's distinctive contribution to music, the Spiritual. Led by George L. White, white teacher, son of a blacksmith, whose musical genius was intrinsic and unschooled, they captivated audiences in the United States and Europe, sang before Queen Victoria, Prime Minister Gladstone, and the crowned heads of the Continent, earning thousands of dollars for their university and making the Spiritual a part of the world's music.

251

At first they were simply "a troupe of colored singers" at Fisk, who loved music and met during their lunch hour to practice the music of American and European composers. White had some difficulty in the beginning persuading them to sing the songs their parents had created in ignorance and slavery. They were ashamed of the over-emotional, nescient, and often ignoble religion of their parents and associated the Spirituals with all that was evil in the past, and therefore better forgotten. Little by little they began to appreciate the beauty of the music that had arisen from the horror of slavery, and their concerts changed from programs containing one or two Spirituals to those predominated by the contributions of African Americans. Ella Sheppard (black), singer, accompanist, and assistant director of the group, explained how their affection for Professor A.K. Spence and George White brought them to love the Spirituals. Spence, former professor at the University of Michigan and principal of Fisk, had been called the one white man in addition to White who could successfully lead in singing Spirituals. Filled with the love of music, the warm Scot used the slave songs during chapel exercises at Fisk. "It was only after many months that gradually our hearts were opened to the influence of these friends," Ella Sheppard said, "and we began to appreciate the wonderful beauty and power of our songs. . . ."[1]

None of the AMA Schools was financially comfortable, for as many students were allowed to enter as could possibly be accommodated, whether or not they had the money for tuition. Sometimes, faced with the question of turning away students who could get higher education no place else, some AMA personnel accepted even more students than could be housed. General Armstrong did, putting boys who volunteered in tents at Hampton Institute. Booker T. Washington tells the story of that winter in the tents at Hampton, and said of General Armstrong: "One might have removed from Hampton all the buildings, class-rooms, teachers, and industries, and given the men and women there the opportunity of coming into daily contact with General Armstrong, and that alone would have been a liberal education." Armstrong, the son of missionaries to Hawaii, spent two of the last six months of his life in Washington's home. Washington also said that Armstrong "was but a type of that Christlike body of men and women who went into the Negro schools at the close of the

Courtesy of Amistad Research Center

war. . . ." He also paid compliments to AMA teachers Mary F. Mackie and Nathalie Lord. It was Miss Mackie who introduced him to the satisfaction of a common job well done. She had given him an examination in cleanliness when he first arrived and when he passed, the job of janitor. Each year she helped prepare the school for the opening term: "Miss Mackie was a member of one of the oldest and most cultured families of the North, and yet for two weeks she worked by my side cleaning windows. . . ." Miss Lord from Portland, Maine, taught him to love the Bible. "The education that I received at Hampton out of the text-books was but a small part of what I learned there. One of the things that impressed itself upon me deeply . . . was the unselfishness of the teachers."[2]

Fisk was no exception to this practice of admitting more students than could properly be accommodated. No one knew better than George White how hard it was for the students to find the money or farm products to pay their tuition; for, in addition to his jobs of teaching music and penmanship, White was also treasurer of Fisk.[3] It was a position that weighed heavily upon him and was accommodated only uncomfortably with his artist's temperament.

White was certain that he could earn money for Fisk with concerts, if he could only persuade the AMA or individuals to give him enough money to launch a tour. The Association, however, felt it could not risk donor's money on such a venture. For a while White seemed to stand alone in his faith in the group of young African American singers. He wrote to General Fisk asking him to advance $300. Fisk's reply was that White should give up the idea, it would not only be a failure, but would "disgrace us all." Hurt and angry, White had wired Fisk: "Tis root, hog, or die; I'm depending on God, not you." Fisk, speaking at the dedication of Jubilee Hall on January 1, 1876, included the incident in his remarks: "How well do I remember when this good brother wrote me at my home in St. Louis and asked me to loan him $300 to take his singers north of the Ohio River. I wrote an answer and told him not to think of such a thing; that he would bring disgrace upon us all, and told him to stay at home and do his work. He wrote back that he trusted in God and not in Gen. Fisk." Field Secretary E.M. Cravath (later president of Fisk) gave a personal contribution of $100 to help launch the troupe.

White managed to raise forty-dollars locally which he invested in clothing for the male singers. The group was incredibly poorly dressed. Not even White owned an overcoat. All wore woolen scarves to protect their voices; the girls wore waterproof ponchos of a sort, and White "had an old gray shawl." The teachers at Fisk loaned what money they had and shared their clothes with the singers as well.

After some successful practice concerts in Congregational churches in the vicinity, the troupe left for a tour of the North, taking all available money from Fisk. Professor Spence did not know the full nature of the financial crisis until the bills started coming in and merchants began giving poor meat as they had in earlier bad times. "Old Ben" was the name the students gave the tough product, declaring "every time they met a cow they felt like apologizing." It was a hard time for Fisk and the AMA. Money was borrowed from teachers who had savings, and many and fervent were the prayers that ascended for the success of the tour in 1871.[4]

An article about the Jubilee Singers of Fisk is entitled "Sing in the Cause of Education."[5] But that is only part of the truth. The Jubilees sang for Fisk University, to repay the initial debt of money advanced for travelling expenses, and beyond that to help Fisk onto its feet financially and help provide buildings to replace the Civil War barracks in which it was housed. During the life of the original Jubilee Singers (1871-1878), they earned $150,000 which was translated into "frozen music" (as Michael E. Strieby called Jubilee Hall), into Livingstone Hall, and other buildings and furnishings for Fisk.[6] But their singing was a religious experience, an expression of the primitive faith of their enslaved parents, tempered, elevated, and glorified by their missionary teachers at Fisk. It was indeed "genuine soul music," as a contemporary termed it.[7]

Most of the American engagements of the troupe were in churches, usually Congregational ones, like Henry Ward Beecher's Plymouth Church in Brooklyn. Often they were refused lodging or service in hotels, but were welcomed in the homes of the leading people. In New York they were housed for six weeks in the homes of AMA Secretaries E.M. Cravath, E.P. Smith, and Gustavus D. Pike, who were neighbors in Brooklyn. A hotel proprietor in Newark, New Jersey, turned them out when he learned they were not "cork" minstrels, but the public reaction was so great "that the city council took advantage of the occasion to pass an ordinance opening the city public schools to colored children." President Grant received them at the White House, and Tennessee Senator Brownlow cried as he listened to their songs.

One important appearance was a concert for the National Council of Congregational Churches at Oberlin, Ohio. It was the year of the great Chicago fire, and their first earnings (almost $50) at Chillicothe, Ohio, were donated to the Chicago Relief Fund.

As Ella Sheppard said, it was the era of the Ku Klux Klan and the Civil Rights bill, and the girls could ride in a first class coach if they once got on. They were thrown out of railroad waiting rooms and threatened by bullies, but they sang to enthusiastic audiences and returned to Nashville with the money to pay Fisk's debts and $20,000 to purchase the twenty-five acres for a new school.[8]

On that first tour, the group was chaperoned by Miss M.F. Wells of Ann Arbor, Michigan, teacher of the AMA's Trinity School, Athens, Alabama. Miss Wells brought along George Wells, an eight-year-old black orphan she had adopted as her son. George gave readings during the performances until it was thought that all the applause and adulation was turning his young head, and his mother decided he should retire from the concert stage. His mother came in for her own share of publicity on that tour. She made a speech against the KKK which was reported in Athens. It was feared the Klan would take out their revenge on Trinity School, but a move was on against the KKK in the County and several were in jail in Athens.[9]

On a later tour of Europe, they were entertained by Prime Minister and Mrs. Gladstone, who dismissed their servants and waited on the singers themselves. Everywhere they were applauded and honored. The Irish, whom they thought of as their "natural enemies" because of their "experiences in both the North and the South," were "even more demonstrative than other peoples in expressing their appreciation." Irish American youth had accosted them on their tour, and in Nashville the city government was in the hands of Irish Americans, who opposed Fisk University and made arrangements for securing property and installing streets as difficult as possible.[10]

Their name was chosen by George White in 1871 after a prayer meeting at Columbus, Ohio, at a time of discouragement. The Jewish Year of Jubilee was a symbol in many of the Spirituals, expressing hope for emancipation. Although the original group of Jubilee Singers was disbanded in 1878, the Jubilee Singers were reinstated at Fisk University in 1899 under Professor John Wesley Work.

Another group, the Hampton Singers, was gathered at Hampton Institute and made several successful concert tours of the United States. Professor Work declared that Negro Folk Music probably "owes its life and much of its currency to Hampton Institute, which has been very consistent in collecting and singing it." After the success of the Jubilee and Hampton Singers, several imitative groups sprang up.[11]

The following Fisk students composed the first group of Jubilee Singers. An asterisk [*] indicates letters survive in the AMA Archives.

Ella Sheppard* (20 years old), born a slave, February, 1851,Nashville. Her father was torn between being allowed to purchase his daughter or lose both her and her mother. The latter was sold into the deep South, but at the end of her life was reunited with Ella and lived with her daughter and her husband Dr. Moore. Mrs. Moore's career as a member of the Fisk faculty and a leader in AMA work has been told in the chapter on colleges above. George White, whose relationship with the Jubilees was a warm and loving one, was nevertheless a perfectionist where music was concerned. Because they loved him, the group was willing to spend the long hours of rehearsal he required. But on the night of a concert, George White remained in the wings, and the on-stage direction of the Singers was in the hands of his assistant Ella Sheppard.

Eliza Walker, born a slave, 1857, Flatrock, Tennessee. She married a man named Crump. Together they pursued concert work and lived in Chicago.

Thomas Rutling*, born a slave, 1854, Wilson County, Tennessee. He remained in Europe after the disbanding of the group in 1878, singing and teaching music. He made his home in England. Rutling was a person of spirit from his boyhood up. At a concert in Steinway Hall, New York, General Fisk said that Tom Rutling "was a colored boy, about my headquarters, known as 'Rollicking

The Nine Original Jubilee Singers Who Left Fisk University October 6, 1871
From left: Minnie Tate, Green Evans, Isaac Dickerson, Jennie Jackson, Maggie Porter, Ella Sheppard, Thomas Rutledge, Benjamin Holmes, Eliza Walker. Courtesy Amistad Research Center.

Tom.' His last cash valuation was $450. (Laughter.) I think he would go quick now at $500, for continued service in Steinway Hall. (Applause.)"[12]

Benjamin M. Holmes*, born a slave, September 25, 1846 or 1848, Charleston, S.C. He had been apprenticed in 1853 to a black tailor. In 1868 he entered Fisk and became a deacon of the church at the university. In 1870, he wrote to George White, "we know that we can never remunerate you for your pains and benevolence towards us, but our grateful hearts will ever pray for your prosperity." He gave news of Fisk students teaching at summer jobs: James Burrus, in "his old school at Edgefield Junction," Taylor Ewing and John Burrus in the 13th district school on Jefferson Street. Roberts was teaching at Rogersville; Bonner "a flourishing school near Rogersville"; Green Evans (a Jubilee) was teaching at La Grange; Holmes himself was teaching "in the 15th C.D. of this County about 2 1\2 miles out on the 'Chicken Pike.'" He had not been paid and was concerned for his salary. In 1874 and 1875, he gave the AMA names of possible contributors in Scotland and England and suggested they be sent the *American Missionary.*[13]

Jennie Jackson, born free in 1852.

Minnie Tate, born free in 1857 in Nashville. She married a Mr. Hall. Although she was born of free parents, her mother had been born a slave. She spoke as the representative of the Jubilee Singers at the dedication of Livingstone Hall.[14]

Maggie L. Porter*, born a slave, February 24, 1853, Lebanon, Tenn. Her married name was Cole. She toured with her own troupes in the United States and Canada.

Isaac P. Dickerson*, born a slave, July 15, 1850, in Wytheville, Va. Dickerson was taught his letters by the son of his Jewish employer after the war. He was hired as a cook for the AMA Mission Home at Chattanooga. He also taught school at Wauhatchie, Tennessee, for six months, but left when he was not paid and had received several threats on his life. At Fisk, he was chosen for the role of Haman in the Cantata "Esther." Dickerson and Rutling (tenor) almost lost their chance to travel with the Singers by breaking some rules. But Dickerson's address at a church in London was the cause of the conversion of one "of our elder scholars."[15]

Green Evans, born a slave, September 19, 1848, Fayette Co., Tennessee. The *American Missionary* for March, 1871, contains an account of "A Hero Worker," which is the story of Evans's trials and triumphs as a teacher, although his name is not used.
Phoebe Anderson remained only a few days with the troupe because of the death of her father, A.E. Anderson, an AMEZ preacher and good friend of Fisk. Her name is often spelled Phebe.[16]

In 1872 the following were added:
Edmund Watkins
Mabel R. Lewis, probably born in New Orleans, the child of a slave and her master. She was raised in the North and married a man named Imes.
Julia Jackson*
Georgia Gordon, born free in Nashville. She married a man named Taylor.[17]

"From time to time new voices were added, as the original members rested or left the company."[18]
Hinton D. Alexander, after the disbanding of the troupe, Alexander became the chorister and active member of the Chattanooga Congregational Church.
Frederick J. Loudin was a magnificent bass, and had been music teacher, organist, and choir director of Avery Chapel, Memphis. At his death he bequeathed his library to Fisk.[19]
B.W. Thomas
America W. Robinson
Patti Malone
Maggie A. Carnes
Benjamin F. Ousley*, the *American Missionary* for November, 1904, has a life sketch of Ousley, who became principal of Normal Institute, Mound Bayou, Mississippi.
Lucinda Vance was from Washington, D.C.
Josephine Moore
Henry Morgan

History is preoccupied with important people and how they shaped the flow of time. Many African Americans influenced the work of the AMA: the great black abolitionists who were its officers, the black teachers, and the personnel of its colleges. But there was another group—the largest of all—whose impact was also the greatest. This was the nameless mass of millions of freedmen, for whose souls and welfare the AMA cared, sight unseen, and whose acquaintance at first hand only intensified that affection.

Some of the influence of the freedmen has been seen in the testimonies of the teachers, but volumes could be filled with such anecdotes. The men (and women) at the Rooms in New York and most of those who backed their work financially believed long before the Civil War in the brotherhood of man and the equal potential of the races. They proved their thesis, not only by educating the African Americans, but by doing the job with the same curriculum and the same methods employed among white children in the public schools of the North.

The freedmen's children proved as capable and as dull as white children in the North, and in like proportions. Not only could the black child learn, but he would. One teacher described her "own hard heart" as moved when 500 young people participated in what she called a riot, so anxious were they to be among the 250 for whom her AMA school had room. Many, many teachers were moved to strain their health by extra hours of work by the example of children who walked as many as six miles each way to attend school, often barefoot through freezing mud, and plagued by taunts and worse from white youths. Small wonder, in the face of such determination, that the teachers bought them food and clothing out of their small salaries, pleaded with friends to provide scholarships, sent some youngsters to foster homes in the North, and adopted other black orphans as their own.

Many teachers—black and white alike—declared that all the privations they suffered and the ostracism they experienced from white Southerners were more than balanced by the inspiration they received from their students and their students's parents. One such parent, Harriet Lynch Wright, walked almost two hundred miles from Cuthbert, Georgia, to Atlanta, with Richard Robert Wright and two other children, to put them in the AMA's Storrs School there.[20]

Richard Robert Wright himself caught the attention of General Howard, when the head of the Freedman's Bureau asked

the children in Atlanta what message they wanted to send north
with him. Richard's "Tell them we are rising!" became the basis for
a poem by John Greenleaf Whittier and a rallying cry for AMA
fund raisers. In the original version, the fifth stanza read

> And he said: "Who hears can never
> Fear for or doubt you;
> What shall I tell the children
> Up North about you?"
> Then ran round a whisper, a murmur,
> Some answer devising;
> And a little boy stood up: "Massa,
> Tell 'em we're rising!"

But the great abolition poet had made an error, and the student in
Atlanta, corrected him: "*Mr. John G. Whittier.* My Dear Sir: I have
heard your poem read, and like it very well. I go to school to Miss
Twitchell, from Connecticut. I study Third National Reader,
Davies' Intellectual Arithmetic, Walton's Written Arithmetic, and
Geography. I have a very good teacher. . . . You make a mistake in
thinking that I said 'massa,' for I have given up that word. I thank
you very much for your interest in our people. Very respectfully,
Richard R. Wright". "Massa" was changed to "General."[21]

Richard Wright turned down a chance to be educated in the
North because his mother needed his earnings as a miller. For such
a boy—who studied at odd hours and worked days—Jennie
Twitchell from Connecticut would give special attention and
tutoring at night after her day's work was done.

Perhaps Wright is a poor example to use, because he did
become an eminent African American, but Miss Twitchell did not
spend extra time with him because she knew he would someday be
a college president or represent his race at the establishment of the
United Nations. Many reasons prompted the Yankee school marms
(and the men) to go south to teach the freedmen. The most telling
of those reasons were humanitarian and religious. But the reason
they stayed and pleaded to be returned year after year was the
influence of the freedmen.[22]

NOTES

1. Ella Sheppard, "Historical Sketch of the Jubilee Singers," *Fisk University News*, II (October, 1911), 43.

2. (Washington 1970, 49, 50, 56, 60).

3. Letter Book (Fisk University) of George L. White, Adam K. Spence, and Henry Hubbard, 1869-73; also letters of White and Taylor C. Ewing, AMAA.

4. *Fisk University News*, II (October, 1911), 45. For the whole story of the Jubilee Singers, see (Marsh 1880).

5. (Dannett 1966, 179-185).

6. Strieby was paraphrasing Madam De Stael's statement that "Architecture is frozen music." For the dedication of Livingstone Hall and the Fisk students who participated, see the *Thirty-first Annual Report* (1877), 61-63.

7. Theodore L. Cuyler, January 17, 1872, cited in (Pike 1873, 118-119).

8. *Fisk University News*, II (October, 1911), 46-49.

9. *AM*, XV (December, 1871), 282-283; H.S. Bennett, Nashville, December 7, 1871, to Cravath, AMAA.

10. *Fisk University News*, II (October, 1911), 54; George White, Nashville, April 26, 1871, to Cravath, AMAA. The Hon. Horatius Gates Jones of Philadelphia was one American who proved to the troupe that not all those of Irish descent were bigots and haters of African Americans.

11. *Fisk University News*, II (October, 1911), 47.

12. Thomas Rutling, "My Life Since Leaving the Jubilee Singers," *Fisk University News*, II (October, 1911), 8, 36-37; H.W. Hubbard,

Nashville, June 1, 1872, to Cravath; Rutling, Bennett, et al, Nashville, March 5, 1870, AMAA.

13. Holmes, July 16, 1870; January 22, 1871, to White; Blackburn, England, January 12, 1874, to Cravath; June 18, 1875, to Whiting, AMAA.

14. *AM*, XVI (April, 1872), 89; *Thirty-first Annual Report* (1877) 63.

15. N.T. Robjohns, London, England, March 4, 1874; White, Nashville, December 2, 1874, to Cravath, AMAA.

16. Letters of A.E. Anderson; Letter Books of Fisk AMAA.

17. Mrs. Mercy Gordon, to White; Helen C. Morgan, October 29, 1871; White, July 27, 1871, to Cravath, AMAA.

18. *Fisk University News*, II (October, 1911), 7.

19. *AM*, XIX (September, 1875), 200-201.

20. (Lemon 1949, xi-xii).

21. The letter was printed in the New York *Tribune* and cited in *AM*, XIII (June, 1869), 134; see also (April, 1869), 90.

22. See the sketch of Richard Robert Wright in *Who's Who in America* (1947), cited in (Wright, Jr., 1965, 19-20); (Logan, 1969, 68); (Wright 1894); Circular for Howard Normal School, Cuthbert, Georgia, August, 1877, AMAA; *Minutes for the Southwestern Georgia Teachers Association, Held at Howard Normal School, December 1, 1877* (Cuthbert, Ga., 1878), AMAA. Wright named the school of which he was principal 1890-91 (Ware High School) after Edmund Ware, president of Atlanta University, Wright's alma mater, which he served as a trustee from 1889-98. Wright was president of Georgia State Industrial College from 1891-1921. He refused appointment as E.E. and M.P. to Liberia, offered by President McKinley.

XI

CATOS AND CONGREGATIONALISTS

The old-time [colored] preachers . . . who hold such a strong sway over the people, see in the coming change the waning of their power, and naturally resist its coming. The people themselves, reveling in the happy ecstasy of their enkindled emotions, and hugging their vices, which are undisturbed thereby, naturally also repel the light that chills their enjoyment and rebukes their sins. Their religion cherishes the old vices inherited from slavery, and welcomes the new ones that come in with freedom. There is always a danger to a people breaking away from the old moorings of their faith. When the cables are cut, the drifting is apt to be into the shoals of skepticism. Especially is this liable to happen when a people of ardent temperament are called to pass from a warm superstition into a colder faith and a more exacting morality.
—Michael E. Strieby for the AMA, 1885

Influence is not always positive and/or progressive. An influential man, a great wielder of power, may throw his weight against progress. A large and frustrating opposition to the work of the AMA was presented by the blacks themselves. This unhappy state of affairs was a hard one to face wherever it occurred for several reasons. One important consideration arose out of the very nature of the AMA. Dependent upon the freewill offerings of northern Christians, the Executive Committee naturally was anxious to show the uses to which those offerings were put in their most favorable light. But even more important was the AMA's raison d'etre: the conviction that the Christian brotherhood they espoused was a relationship, a fellowship among equals, and that—contrary to many of the charges of the day—the black person was no less able than any other representative of the human family.

265

It was therefore exceedingly difficult for missionaries who believed strongly in this principle to report instances of stupidity and immorality when they discovered them among the blacks who were professing Christians. But the reluctance of the missionaries to report such unsettling facts was minimal compared with that of the New York secretaries as dispensers of news about the workings of the missionary dollar.

Nevertheless, wherever one searches the records, there is an element among the leaders of the freedmen who opposed outside control by anyone, regardless of color. Their jealousy was motivated by a feeling of inferiority. They were fearful that their ignorance would be exposed if seen alongside the talents of educated experts imported into their environment from outside. Usually these men were preachers or exhorters—often as illiterate as the people they ruled, sometimes more so. "Ruled" is used advisedly, for their struggle was for power, influence, status, control. And "preachers" best describes them, for they neither ministered to nor were pastors of their people.

Yet despite the general reluctance on the part of missionaries, teachers, and officers of the AMA to air the facts of black opposition, intransigence, and seeming obscurantism, the facts were always there and were reported truthfully, if reluctantly. If the missionary letters were ofttimes censored of their most discouraging sentences—and they were—the careful reader of the *American Missionary* finds them.[1] Even more often appear editorial explanations of the problem—eloquent testimony to the soul-searching at the Rooms.

Much less care is needed in reading the letters from the workers in the field to reap an abundant harvest of thorns among the roses and tares in the wheat. One notorious example of editing for a purpose concerns Jamaica, in whose emancipation the AMA officers sanguinely sought to prove the ability of the black man to handle his freedom.[2] Such censorship wounded David Hotchkiss, AMA missionary to the refugees in Canada West. So persecuted and hounded was he by black opposition (buildings burned, his well poisoned, preached against and lied about by black "preachers"), that he blasted AMA editing with blistering irony after reading a report in the *American Missionary* of Lockwood's work among the contrabands at Fortress Monroe: "Again about those good and intelligent ones, now if slavery turns out such, it is not quite so bad a thing after all."[3] Hotchkiss believed the case was not so rosy as the *American Missionary* accounts would have the reader believe. That many of the blacks were untrustworthy and were not practicing Christians was his experience. But he attributed their depravity to slavery.[4]

Missionary life was hard, poorly paid, filled with privations, illness, and loneliness. Much that was unsanguine in their letters was attributed by the men at the Rooms to temporary bouts with the blues. Whipple once counselled Mrs. David Hotchkiss at a time of discouragement to follow the Latin motto *"Festina Lente"* (hasten slowly). Hotchkiss was to throw the suggestion back into the teeth of the Association regarding its optimism about Norfolk.[5]

It has been said by a modern southern historian that "most AMA workers never fathomed the slave's religion which emphasized joy and collective hope rather than personal guilt and self-denial."[6] The AMA workers, of course, were not present among slaves, only among freedmen. But the religion of the freedmen should not be characterized as though it were homogeneous. There was a wide variety of religious experience. In some instances it resembled African *gree-gree* worship with the Bible as the *gree-gree*. In some cases it was a faith that looked with hope to a better life beyond, as did the unknown authors of the spirituals. Often it exhibited itself in ecstatic, drunken performances led by ignorant African American preachers.

The "Uncle Catos"

It is difficult to find a designation for this phenomenon of the ignorant preacher in opposition to progress. A white AMA missionary in North Carolina provides the titles wanted: Uncle Catos and Aunt Janes—Uncle Cato, the ignorant preacher, and Aunt Jane, his "Termagant Disciple." Interestingly enough, both letters describing these living examples were published in the *American Missionary.*

The editorial note at the beginning of John Scott's letter about Uncle Cato, "A Marked Character," explains: "There is a gratifying skill in drawing the portrait, but there is sadness in the thought that such men are still left to exert a pernicious influence on the colored people." There was no desire on the part of the

Association or of Scott [who was not identified in the account] to "reflect upon" any denomination. Scott had indeed said that any "right-thinking Baptists would deplore such ignorance, if they knew it" as deeply as he did. "Uncle Cato is a fair example of the old preachers, who rule the colored people of the South with despotic tyranny," wrote Scott, "a class of ignorant bigots, now holding unbounded power, but whose sway must cease in the present generation." Scott knew one called Uncle Cato, an archetype of the breed, but no unique example—for "every teacher of the freedmen has seen his counterpart and been annoyed at his obstinate resistance to the progress of education and true religion." The particular Uncle Cato in John Scott's story was "an orthodox Hard Shell Baptist," a preacher who harangued the people from 5 to 8 hours every Sunday, "according to the patience of [his] hearers."[7]

Such men hated schools because they realized that educated persons would not listen to them. They were illiterate themselves and too proud to learn to read; they were as frightened of the Bible in the hands of the people as had been the English Crown in the days of the Lollards, or the Medieval Roman Church that wanted to preserve the privilege of interpretation for the clergy. If his audience was ignorant, Uncle Cato could fantasize that he could read, had in fact been taught miraculously by God in a vision or dream. After some study of the Uncle Cato phenomenon and the reasons for the inordinate control such men exercised over their people, the missionaries decided that the prime reason for their popularity was an alleged act of God whereby Uncle Cato was given the rank of "old prophet." The second reason was "his strong self-will & determination to rule."

While his religion seemed based on the Bible and was called Christian, its "orthodoxy" was like no western catechism "or the written formula of any known Christian Church, "but Georgia traditions are the higher law from which there is no appeal." The fundamental doctrine was a belief in dreams, visions, and "travels," which prepared the initiate for the most important article of faith, baptism by immersion. Another tenet of Uncle Cato's theology was a kind of Perfectionism, for baptism guaranteed salvation "without any reference whatever to holy living." The Uncle Catos and their disciples preached that anyone who had "been under the water" or had had a vision could live as he pleased and break any of the Ten Commandments without losing his promise of eternal life.

The missionaries did not suggest that the Catos were slow-witted; quite the reverse. Although ignorant of book learning, they were remarkably astute. John Scott had managed to best some of them in religious debates, but Uncle Cato could always call on Bible verses he had heard and memorized or his innate logic for unassailable answers. The use of intoxicating liquors was explained as Biblically sanctioned, for did not Jesus make wine and get drunk? (Probably Uncle Cato confused Jesus with Noah here). And since the Bible advised temperance in all things; how could one be temperate and *abstain* from liquor?

Scott's description pointed out that his particular Uncle Cato was a man who could drink large quantities without reeling, and that he had never seen him when there was not alcohol on his breath. The better members of his church thought it shameful that he fed his habit while allowing his family to suffer "from want of food and clothes." Scott had witnessed a baptism ritual in which both Uncle Cato and the man being baptized were the worse for liquor and one pulled the other under the water. The teachers "sometimes wish the Keeper of the Vinyard would remove this man from his place, and they grow impatient and weary that their own work is hindered and crippled by his powerful and pernicious influence...."

But there was hope. In Uncle Cato's church there were people who had learned to read and took their Bibles with them to church. The Uncle Catos preached against "Bible Christians" and wanted the Bibles left at home. "In vain! The desire to display knowledge, and examine texts is stronger than the fear of ecclesiastical authority, and the word of God appears every Sabbath in one or more hands. Thus has the 'irrepressible conflict' between truth and error begun," said Scott. "Uncle Cato with his leathery frame, powerful voice, unconquerable will, and the prestige of old traditions, is beating against the silent, unseen influence of an open Bible."[8]

Booker T. Washington, a product of the AMA's Hampton Institute, gives a noteworthy description of such "not only ignorant but in many cases immoral men" in his autobiography:

> At my home in West Virginia the process of being called to
> the ministry was a very interesting one. Usually the "call"
> came when the individual was sitting in church. Without
> warning the one called would fall upon the floor as if struck
> by a bullet, and would lie there for hours, speechless and
> motionless. Then the news would spread that this individual
> had received a "call."

Washington gives credit to the "many capable, earnest, godly men
and women" of his race who became teachers and preachers, but
confesses that in his youth he had a fear that when he learned to
read and write he would receive a "call" like those preachers whom
he denounced.[9]

Although the missionaries and teachers were appalled by the
irreligion and moral depravity of the freedmen—so much so that
many despaired of *any* hope for the adults and fairly cried out for
intensive work with the children—it was more often not the lack of
religion but a plethora of pseudo-Christianity that was their
greatest obstacle. This was true in Canada in the early days, a
decade or more before the war, as it was in the deep South a decade
after. At Mendi in Africa the religious problems seemed, at least, to
be different, for the African missionaries encountered a strongly
entrenched religious animism with its many gods and *gree-grees.*[10]

The Bible as *Gree-Gree*

For every enlightened black man working to free his brethren
from the darkness of ignorance in the South and in Canada there
was a battalion of Uncle Catos striving to remain in power and
resisting the change that education would make in the number of
Aunt Janes who stood in awe of them, hung on their "magic"
words, and sustained them with their gifts. "Magic" comes readily
to mind in this regard. One can, in fact, make a good case for
calling the Uncle Catos the United States replacement of the
African witch doctor. Both Uncle Cato and the African religious
leaders had great power of interpretation—each operating without
a written text (although ostensibly Uncle Cato used the Bible). In
both Africa and America, baptismal rites and visions were vital
forces interpreted as bestowing power on the participant. John
Brooks, AMA missionary at the Mendi Mission, saw the syn-
cretism of Africa's animism with Islam and feared that the same

thing would happen with Christianity. "If their heathen confidence in greegrees is transferred to our Bible, prayer and confession, we will have grounds to fear and tremble for the issue."[11] In a sense that is what happened among the freedmen for a time: the Bible seemed, like an African *gree-gree*, to be a powerful charm. Even the missionaries were amazed at the tremendous longing of the freedmen to have a copy of the Bible—some risking great hardships to obtain and keep such a prize even though they could not read. Uncle Cato's power would have been safe if illiterate freedmen possessed that American *gree-gree* but remained dependent on him to interpret its magic to them. Once the people learned to read for themselves, however, and to interpret the Bible individually in the fashion of New England theology, his power as intermediary priest was gone.

"We are told that these people are naturally very religious," John Scott said, "and they are, and that is the worst thing about them. They have got *too much religion*, but it is not the religion of Christ." It may not stand as anthropologically acceptable evidence, but at least to missionaries and teachers who had experienced both African rites and black religion in the United States and Canada, the similarities were astonishing. One missionary who had lived in Africa for fifteen years noted the similarities to African religious rites in some of the black churches in Washington. An AMA missionary who had served both in Canada and Africa saw the same parallels and denounced the more exaggerated methods of revivalism as being akin to African religious excitement. The missionaries at Mendi were almost totally preoccupied with the influence of African kings (chiefs) and made few references in their letters to witches or other religious leaders. Religious power seemed to be wielded by the chief, not unlike divine rule in the West. Fear of witches was demonstrated by children in the Mendi schools, who were frightened of spirits in the night.[12]

It was not immediately apparent to the uneducated African American leaders in the South that education was a threat to them. (John Scott's article was written in 1870.) Neither was the AMA quick to decide that the black churches of the freedmen were obstacles to its progress. That this was a grave mistake and cost much valuable time they later admitted.[13] But the very nature of the AMA was the basis of the error, if it was one, on their part.

Because they were an unsectarian, inclusive organization, they hired teachers without regard to denominational affiliation. Although the majority of their teachers were Congregationalists, many were not, and the original purpose of the work was education—albeit in the hands of evangelical teachers. There was no plan for the establishment of churches in the early days and no time for the teachers to do such work.

In general the city schools of the Association were held in black church buildings. This was necessitated by the fact that some cities like Atlanta and Hampton had suffered so much from fire as to have few buildings of any kind available. Others like Savannah had been saved from fire, but often in such cases few rebels had left their property, and the buildings confiscated by the army were few. The opposition of the whites who would not lease buildings for black schools was of course another factor. It was therefore a logical subsequence that black church buildings were often used (usually leased) by the AMA for schools. The teachers taught school in them during the week and helped with the Sabbath school on Sundays, where they also taught reading and writing.

At first the apparent natural aptitude of the southern Negro for religion seemed an unexpected blessing, and the teachers cooperated with the local black preachers in sustaining their churches. The teachers finally realized that much of what passed for religion was worse even than the diluted Christianity of the southern whites. It was entrenched and buttressed by southern sectarianism that induced each sect to proclaim itself "the only true faith" and to deny efficacy to any and all others.

The "Uncle Roberts"

Apart from the nonsectarianism of the AMA teachers, which prevented their being crusading denominationalists and church founders, there was a black element in the South that stood in strong contrast to the Uncle Catos. For example, there was an Uncle Robert, described in 1864 by a teacher in North Carolina as "a genuine negro preacher." Uncle Robert had been sixty years a slave and had seen his wife mistreated by her master and had been himself punished for his look of pity at the sight. His daughter had been taken from him and sold. Uncle Robert was an unlettered man also, but unlike the Uncle Catos had tried to learn at night by "the light of pitch-pine fires." His sermons often had "clearness of statement, and earnestness of address, a sublimity and splendor of imagery, together with a deep pathos," which imparted "great power" to his addresses.

Uncle Robert's power was different from Uncle Cato's. It was not the power of the intermediary priest interpreting magical rites. It lay rather in his living example of a life embodying the simple truths of the gospel he preached. "I wish the secret of his power was understood among educated men, said AMA teacher E.J. Comings. "It is not in the gift of natural genius, nor in the well-chosen words of 'man's wisdom,' for he speaks in the broken negro dialect. . . ." The story of Uncle Robert's life was an argument against the slave system, said Comings, and helped the observer "to form some just estimate of the capacity of the enslaved race."[14]

Appreciation of the Uncle Roberts of the South and their particular brand of uneducated emotional religion appears often in the correspondence of the AMA workers. Such men whose lives were consonant with their piety inspired real affection in the Northerners. Knowing and liking the Uncle Roberts made them more vulnerable to the feigned piety of the Uncle Catos. The eloquent oratory of an occasional untaught genius with "strong affections and sympathies, quick perceptions of truth, and a lively imagination" had given people at the North who heard such reports the idea that all the leaders of the freedmen were Uncle Roberts.

Needed: "An Educated, Intelligent and Pious Clergy"

John Mercer Langston was under no such delusion, as one of his Howard University faculty associates reported in 1872. After "an extended tour of inspection" Professor Langston declared that "the religious training of the freed people . . . in the main . . . is any other thing than desirable." He attended many church services among them and "in every single instance" when the preacher was a southern black man he found the people were neither instructed for life nor prepared for death. Langston also deplored "the prevalence of intemperance and licentiousness" which he blamed largely on the example of the ministers. At one Sunday meeting he "counted no less than twelve colored ministers very drunk." Langston's verdict was that "an educated, intelligent and pious clergy is greatly needed among these people."[15]

274 His Truth Is Marching On

To prepare such a ministry the AMA established theological departments at Howard, Atlanta, Straight, Fisk, and Talladega and encouraged AMA teachers to gather the local black pastors of whatever denomination into theological classes. These classes were not all taught by men. One of the most energetic of the AMA teachers, Miss J.A. Shearman, a native of England, had such a class. She totaled up the amount each of her students spent on tobacco each year, and pointed out how much better they could care for their families if they gave it up.

Perhaps the best statement of appreciation for Negro religion came from AMA teacher General Samuel Chapman Armstrong (founder of Hampton Institute), written six and one half years after the above material on Uncle Robert and in the midst of very great discouragement on the part of the AMA in so far as black religion was concerned. He said it was not easy "to make a fair statement of the Freedmen's illustration of Christian life. In the absolute it is imperfect, inconsistent, discouraging; but relatively all things considered, it is," Armstrong said, "the best that the light he has had, the opportunities he has not had, and the vices of slavery made possible." The freedmen's religion was "all expression, demonstration, ecstacy; but God made him with an acute religious sensibility. . . ." One should be careful in evaluating what has not been personally experienced. What to the Northerner was "a paroxysm" was to the freedman "normal and healthy action." Armstrong believed the freedmen had a capacity "to enjoy a vividness of spiritual insight, a genuine and pure religious delight" which those who had not their ability "should judge very carefully. I cannot but have a large respect for their worship, as genuine so far as it goes, so long as it lasts, a real elevation, as the logical development of their religious nature," Armstrong said. "It is religion—it has comforted the sick and those in prison, it has consoled and lifted up the sorrowing, it has transformed their lives from wretchedness to happiness."

But it was true of black religion in 1870—as the AMA would acknowledge in 1881 was true of its own original definition of evangelism—that "the condition that gave it its intensity" no longer existed. In the words of Samuel Chapman Armstrong:

For the slave to reason on life, was despair; for the Freedman not to do it, is ruin. Worship, was his only recourse;

now civilization makes demands of him, the result of which will be a frame of mind tending to evenness, steadiness of feeling and expression, and hence a higher morality; for alas, they were religious without being moral. But the danger is in a fondness for the old way; it was a sort of intoxication and is hard to give up; it *was* excellent, it is very fast becoming bad. Here is our work—to prevent his becoming worse than he was before—there is great danger of it. Latin and Greek are not the cure; we must build up character, habits of thinking; the work is mainly intellectual and moral now—to teach the Freedman to see; to get him in his right mind. . . . Kind, patient friends he needs unspeakably. . . . Give him plenty of *light*; let him pick his own way, but let floods of light be poured around him.[16]

Reluctance to Establish Churches

The reluctance of the AMA to enter the field of church-founding meant that it denied itself a source of African American leadership. After the Civil War the AMA was avowedly Congrega-tional (other co-operating bodies having withdrawn). This meant that the field from which the AMA could draw black men into its offices was somewhat circumscribed. There were very few African American Congregational churches in the North, partly because Congregtionalism was strongest in New England where the black population was small, partly because Congregationalism did not have the appeal to the black population that the more emotional Baptist and Methodist groups had, but partly, also, because it was against the nature of Congregtionalism to establish segregated churches. This was certainly true of the Congregationalists associated with the AMA.

The Congregational Association of New York and Brooklyn appointed a committee in 1867 to consider the question, "What ought we to do for the evangelization of the colored people in New York and Brooklyn." The report contained the information that there were between ten and twenty thousand colored persons in the city, among whom were three thousand servants, "but only thirty mechanics, ten editors and writers," a dozen wealthy men, and two merchants. The colored churches were crowded; the Congregation-al churches were not. "Our simplest and most obvious duty to our colored brethren, then, is to open our present churches to them."

The report urged the members of the Association to go out in search of those who did not come to church, and concluded:

> There is no negro quarter in the city of the Great King. There are no colored pews in the church of the First Born above. The ecclesiastical vehicle that carries the placard "No colored men allowed in this car," will run off the track before it gets to heaven. We accordingly discourage the organization of colored churches, as such by name, for the African race. We hope never to see an African Congregational church so entitled. In the true church of Christ there can be neither Jew nor Gentile, bond nor free, Scythian, Parthian, African or Anglo-Saxon.[17]

Within two years after the National Council of Congregational Churches officially designated the AMA as its channel for work among the freedmen, concern was voiced at the small number of churches established in the South. The officers of the AMA found it difficult to explain to those in the North who were unaware of the very real and very different problems in the South in church extension, problems not associated to the same degree with founding churches in the West. The American Home Missionary Society, it explained, would certainly not attempt to found a Puritan church in the West unless it found "a Puritan element of population, or at least a Puritan sentiment," in an area where the people would be willing to contribute to the costs. But the "Puritan element" was "rare" in the South among the whites, and as a result the AHMS was finding the establishment of churches even among them difficult. *"But how much greater these difficulties among the colored people* !" There were no Puritans among the blacks, and they had very little money with which to assist in founding churches. "Their New England or Yankee sentiment is abundant, but it pertains to civil liberty, and not at all to ecclesiastical affairs, for, in these, they are traditionally and heartily devoted to other denominations." The problems were so much greater than those involved in planting churches in the West and progress would be slow.[18]

Slow Growth

Those who grew impatient at the slow growth of the statistics were reminded of several facts by Secretary C.L. Woodworth: "Congregationalism was a name unknown and unheard of among the blacks. The other denominations had spread Southward, but Congregationalism, by its very instinct of liberty and equality, had stopped short at Mason and Dixon's line." It took time, therefore, to convince the black population that the denomination "was not some monster that might devour the churches for which they had a peculiar jealousy. And especially was time needed to educate a generation who could intelligently receive our polity." This had taken several years. "But at last, the blacks see that those who have labored with them so long and so unselfishly cannot be bad people." The fact of Congregationalism's history of opposition to slavery was a telling point among the young graduates of AMA schools, who "are turning away from their ignorant preachers, and demanding something more rational, and quiet, than they find in their churches." With such encouraging signs, Woodworth thought the time had indeed come "to propagate the faith of our Fathers in the Southern field . . . that the New England church is, henceforward, to keep company with the New England school." Woodworth's article went on to describe the churches already established among the black population by the AMA. "For experiment has shown that the time to carry our polity among whites is still in the future." In so far as integration was concerned, for the time being, white church members would be limited almost solely to white AMA teachers and missionaries.[19]

Because of the situation described above, of racial adjustment in the South and Congregational history, most of the churches established by the AMA became black churches. Generally, any church in the South bearing the name "First Congregational Church" and begun soon after the Civil War, is a black church: for example, First Congregational Church of Atlanta, Georgia; First Congregational Church of Chattanooga, Tennessee; First Congregational Church of Birmingham, Alabama; First Congregational Church of Louisville, Kentucky; First Congregational Church of Raleigh, North Carolina; First Congegational Church of Savannah, Georgia. The bulk of black Congregational leadership came eventually from the South, but this was a process of slow maturation.

Churches in the South

In 1868 Sella Martin suggested a Superintendent for the South, implying that he would himself like such an office. Nine years later, Professor Henry S. Bennett of Fisk presented a resolution at the Thirty-first Annual Meeting, "That the Secretaries of the American Missionary Association be invited to seriously consider the question of placing in the field at the South, as a general missionary agent, a suitable man, to be selected from among the graduates of the schools of the Association." The resolution was adopted. Although such a position was established within a few years, it was filled by white men until George W. Moore, graduate of Fisk University, became General Missionary for the South in 1892. In that office he was aided by George V. Clark, a graduate of Atlanta in 1897.[20] Dr. Henry Hugh Proctor, pastor of First Church, Atlanta, became a vice president of the AMA in 1906, and Dr. A.C. Garner, of Washington, D.C. was made a vice president at the Sixty-third Annual Meeting in 1909.[21]

The first church established by the AMA in the South was Plymouth Church at Charleston, South Carolina, from the remnants of the African American Membership of Circular Congregational Church (founded in 1681), one of the few churches of the denomination in the ante-bellum South. Although supplied with Presbyterian ministers for fifty years, the church had retained its original polity. Only when Sherman's army ravished the parsonage did the members elect to join the Southern Presbyterians. But the colored members did not. They remained Congregationalists; thus the continuity of the church that traced its roots back to seventeenth-century England would lie in its black members. Circular Church later rejoined the Congregational denomination.[22] Abolitionism and the war persuaded the white members of Circular Church to become Presbyterian temporarily, and the same reasons persuaded the white members of the old Midway Congregational Church in Liberty County, Georgia, to do so permanently.

The Dorchester Midway Church had been established in 1752, by a group who had emigrated with their pastor, first from

Dorchester, England, to Dorchester, Massachusetts; then to Dorchester, South Carolina; and finally to Midway, Georgia. The remnants of its former black constituents were discovered in Liberty County, by Hardy Mobley. Born a slave in Georgia, but educated in the North, Mobley had been an AMA missionary in Savannah until financial reverses had forced the Association to release some of its personnel. Mobley had discovered some three to four hundred African Americans who had been connected with Midway, and began to gather them into a church in 1867.[23]

At first the group at Midway, which voted to call Mobley as their pastor, were allowed to use the old Midway Church building by the white owners. Mobley organized a Sunday school with a superintendent and six teachers—all natives who could read. He also organized an educational board for the district and opened a school. It is unfortunate that Mobley did not persevere and that the AMA did not build on his beginnings, for he left to become their missionary in Lebanon, Missouri; and the AMA did not establish a church at Midway until 1874.

Mobley began a church in Lebanon in 1870, then took charge of the black Congregational Church at Topeka, Kansas, in February, 1872. The next year he started work at New Iberia, Louisiana, where his wife and four daughters taught in local schools. In 1875 his work for the AMA ended after an unfortunate series of events and personality clashes.[24]

Snelson and Golding

The AMA sent the first graduate of Atlanta University's Theological Department, Floyd Snelson, to Midway Church, where a power struggle developed between Snelson and William A. Golding, leading member of the church and member of the Georgia legislature. Snelson, as an early graduate, did not have collegiate training. There was some disagreement among AMA personnel about the value of giving theological training to men without a basic collegiate background. It was done in the emergency in order to have men of *some* training.[25] Golding was not an educated man. Some—if not all—of his letters were written to the AMA for him by others. He was critical and jealous of Snelson's leadership. Snelson tried to spread himself too thin, said Golding, and wanted to be top man among his people both in the church and in the school. As chairman of the church board of trustees and also one of the school trustees, Golding wanted both to prosper.

In the struggle, the AMA was in the middle, between the "old guard" Golding and the young man on the way up, Snelson. It had poured so much hope and aid into Floyd Snelson, and his weaknesses were discovered with pain. When he set himself up against Golding, he went against the man without whom there would have been no church there at all. When Golding saw that he was on the losing side of the battle, he sent a spirited, yet pitiable letter in his own defense, in which he said that he considered Snelson "only a child in experience" even if he did have education. Golding's life in the Congregational Church was eloquently described:

> I was raised a Congregationalist. I became a member of the Cong. Chh. Feb.1839. In 1843 I was elected as selectman unanimously by both white and colored, & was ordained as such. There are but two of us now living, one has turned Presbyterian, & I adhered to the Cong. My grandfather Parson Sharper Jones came over with the m [sic] from Carolina, as the first col'd Cong. Preacher, under the whites. . .& died in 1825, aged 85. Every child he had but one were Cong. & today must I be looked down upon, & considered as nobody by my own Chh.? I refer to the old citizens, white & colored, the Mallards, the Quartermans & the Cassels, and would be glad to know if ought can be brought against my character.

Golding declared that being a Congregationalist had worked against him politically and spiritually. He was not a Congregationalist for the name, but because he believed in the Pilgrim Way. The whites were against his efforts to build up the church because they said it was bringing Yankees into Savannah; and the AMA seemed not to back his program to get the best possible teachers for the school. This was especially hard for a man who had served in the state constitutional convention after the war and had been one of the members of the legislature, cast out, and then reinstated, serving five terms, and retiring in 1874 on the advice of Aaron Rowe in order to work for the church.[26]

Floyd Snelson's march to power was clearly seen by Richard F. Markham, AMA missionary who replaced Rowe at Savannah. Snelson had persuaded the people of the Midway Church that it was time for new leadership, that it was time "to take Golding down." Snelson had not only tried to replace Golding in the church, but also ran for his job in the legislature. He put only his own people in the school and reserved the principalship and all power for himself, declaring privately that trustees were a mere formality, and the only power the AMA had over the school was to pay the bills. Markham thought Snelson "a good man, but an overbearing, tyranical [sic], obstinate *man*, and *very severe on all* who do *not yield to his plans.*"[27]

For teachers he chose his brother, Seaborn Snelson, George B. Snowden (a follower), and his brother-in-law, Silas Daniels. Golding's charge that everyone in office in school or church must be a Snelson man seems fairly secure in the face of such nepotism. Markham was convinced that Snelson prevented the hiring of H.R. Pinckney for the school out of jealousy. Pinckney had a superior education, having lived ten years in the North, attended Lincoln University for one year and Howard University for four. He was a Congregationalist, a member of the First Church at Savannah, and was voted a license to preach by a duly elected council (from which Snelson tried to evict Golding as a representative of the Savannah church), despite Snelson's unsuccessful attempts to persuade the council not to license him.

The AMA backed Floyd Snelson, child of their schools, whose chirography they had watched smooth out and whose orthography they had seen improve through the years as he wrote them from Andersonville as a boy and later from Atlanta as a theologue. They marked his ordination in council in 1871 and compared it to the visit of Jefferson Davis to Atlanta a few days later. Snelson's first field of labor was to be Andersonville. Jefferson Davis spoke passionately to an admiring crowd, and "fanned to a burning heat the embers of cruelty and treason," telling the people to rally to a cause that was not lost, that they had "the duty of teaching their children the lesson of hate and pride and scorn." The old spirit of the South that reared itself in the stockade walls of Andersonville was still there, but there was a new spirit," a Christ-like spirit seeking only to build up and to bless, cultivating only good will and love, which manifests itself in the mission schools and the church by its side." This spirit they hoped to see exemplified in the new ordinand.[28]

Perhaps the Executive Committee made the correct decision in standing behind Floyd Snelson. In 1877 he headed the first all-black corps of missionaries to the Mendi Mission.[29] But by 1879 he had been replaced in Africa by Albert P. Miller (black) and was back at Midway church, having successfully appealed to the church in his favor over the incumbent, Joseph E. Smith.[30]

Church Development in Georgia

Georgia was a difficult field, particularly around Savannah. At first glance it would seem to be an easier place than most in which to establish Congregational churches—there at least the freedmen had heard the name Congregational, which in most parts of the South was unknown. The three to four hundred former members of the Dorchester Midway Congregational Church were scattered in the area, many having bought lands of their former owners. So the churches started by Rowe and others—Savannah, Midway, Ogeechee (ten miles east of Savannah), Belmont (five miles west), and Woodville (three miles west)—were colonies of black people who were formerly members of old Midway Church.

In their haste and great desire to establish Congregational churches in and around Savannah, AMA agents C.W. Sharp and Aaron Rowe used the men at hand. And they were often men of the Cato stamp, willing to give lip service to Congregationalism so long as they received their salary regularly, and ready to become the worst sort of insinuating enemy when crossed. They wanted power. They were willing and able to dissemble, promising fidelity to the AMA and pledging adherence to Congregational principles, in order to be ordained.

After receiving a call to a church, which they *ruled* not in the spirit of Jesus, but with a rod of iron, they threatened to leave and build up rival churches if they were removed or their salaries not raised. Once a man of the Cato mold was hired, Rowe and his successor Markham had a tiger by the tail. After months of working with such men, Markham expostulated: "But how to get rid of some of the rubbish in the shape of preachers I know not. I shall be cautious about making and receiving preachers. They are the curse of the colored people down here." Markham began an evening class in theology, to raise up his own ministers.[31]

Some of the Cato types with whom he had to contend were John S. Cuthburt, Harrison W. Watkins, James W. Fleming, and Robert Carter. Carter was probably the worst of the group. Most of these men, especially Carter, were poor examples for their people. Carter said that the large expenditures he made for liquor were necessary because there was much sickness in his family. When James Fleming was brought before the congregation of First Congregational Church in Savannah for drunkenness, he struck a woman at the meeting and was arrested, causing a great scandal and impairing the AMA's work.[32]

Richard Markham was a man sensitive of the feelings of others, and dedicated to the work of "elevating" the freedmen to the point of assuming for themselves their educational and spiritual work. But experience had given him reason for pessimism. Commenting on the work of John David Smith shortly after the latter's arrival to work in Georgia, Markham said, "Brother J.D. Smith is doing well, But I expect he will soon be above his business and want much attention and power to rule. But I will hope for the best and pray on. But the time when colored people will be able to wisely manage the work of the AMA in the south is far distant. I am sorry it is so."[33]

Central Church, New Orleans

One of the AMA churches whose establishment was largely the work of African Americans was Central Congregational Church, New Orleans. New Orleans was one place where AMA aid to an AME (African Methodist Episcopal) church redounded to the benefit of Congregationalism. The establishment there of Central Congregational Church was closely tied to the founding of Straight University; but when AME preacher Jacob Norager, who was receiving aid from the AMA, converted to Congregationalism, he led a sizable group from St. James Church into Central Church.[34]

Charles H. Thompson (black), former AMA missionary in Ohio, was appointed Professor of Biblical Theology and Literature at Straight University (AMA) in February, 1871. Thompson was a graduate of Oberlin's Theology Department who had followed Amos N. Freeman at Brooklyn's Siloam Presbyterian Church and had subsequently served the Plane Street Presbyterian Church in Newark, New Jersey.[35] Thompson assisted with the founding of

Central Church in June, 1872, and became its first pastor. Led by the Rev. Jacob A. Norager, six men and twenty-six women took their letters from St. James Church and joined with the members of the University Congregational Church (integrated) and a few members of Morris Brown Church to become the Central Church.[36]

Before the actual organization, of the church, plans were made to purchase the centrally located property of the Fourth Presbyterian Church (white), and pledges were solicited from interested persons.[37] Difficulty arose in collecting the money pledged because of the terribly unsettled state of political affairs in Louisiana in the 1870's. In August Thompson could report only $15 of the first $100 note as having actually been paid, it being hard to collect money for any cause but political ones.[38]

Governor Warmouth was impeached in December, 1872, and Pinckney Benton Stewart Pinchback (black) served as acting governor until January, 1873, when the Kellogg administration took office only to be itself overthrown in 1874.[39] Central Congregational was the church with which many African American Louisiana politicians affiliated. In May, 1873, the president of the board of trustees of Central was William G. Brown (black), State Superintendent of Education,[40] and Thompson referred the AMA to Brown for answers to financial questions. Four months later, Samuel S. Ashley, acting president of Straight University, announced that the active politicians who attended Central and had pledged money to its building program would soon be home, and he would "push the matter" of payment of their pledges. The problem lay in the fact that they were politicians and more willing to give "a thousand dollars for politics sooner than a hundred dollars for religion."

Actually, they were "peculiarly able" to take the "entire burden" of the cost of the building off the AMA. William G. Brown's annual salary was $5000; Lt. Gov. Antoine received the same; Barber, the harbor master, earned "not less than $3000;" Col. James Lewis, Administrator of Public Improvements, received $7000; James H. Ingraham, who had been surveyor of the port, was currently without a position, but was "not poor." Pinchback, having been elected a Representative at large as well as Senator, had "the pay of a member of Congress."[41]

These well-to-do African Americans had all been free before the war. They had promised to pay the interest on the $20,000 debt of the church. Ashley thought they should also pay Thompson's salary and the insurance and repairs on the building. Ingraham had promised to pay his pledge of $1000 in November, and Antoine his of $250 when it fell due.[42]

The first of the great industrial depressions spread over the United States in 1873, affecting benevolent organizations like the AMA even more severely than business firms. The failure of the Freedmen's Bank was another result affecting appreciably those African Americans who had practiced economy and trusted their savings to their bank. Of Louisiana, a state enmeshed in political contests, Ashley declared: "Politics swallows up everything here, money as well as morals."[43]

Thompson rationalized early in 1874 that only two of the communicant members were "worth anything": Deacon Adolph Zemar, who owned three houses in New Orleans, and widow Betsey Cole, who owned a house on Canal Street and had money in the bank. Only five holders of notes were communicant members of the church: Zemar ($500), Robert H. Isabelle ($100),[44] Isaac Wilson ($200), Jacob Norager ($400), and Daniel Sanders ($500). The remainder of the $5000 in notes was held by the politicians affiliated with, but not communicant members, of the church. Thompson expected Isabelle and Zemar to pay their notes when due. All the others had taken the notes in good faith but had had financial reverses resulting from the general depression in the country. Wilson was a Deacon of the church and in need. Thompson, in his capacity as a member of the City School Board, controlled the personnel of ten of the largest schools in the city, and gave Wilson a place as a porter in one of those schools. As for the others, Ingraham had lost his post as surveyor of the port and had also lost some $8000 in the failure of the bank in which he was a stockholder, but promised to pay when he could, pledging an installment of $100 in a month.[45] Col. Lewis was able and promised to pay his note ($500) if the title of the property would go to the people locally. The AMA had made a good investment in Central Church, "a success beyond peradventure," said Thompson. The present financial situation was caused by "circumstances beyond control." The Association must be patient.[46]

Col Lewis, however, paid only $50 of his note, blaming the flooding Mississippi, "This year's scape goat." Central Church had realized $2500 from a fair, but the trustees gave only $345 toward the $1666.66 due. Another $500 was allocated to pay Thompson's expenses on a money-raising tour of the North. Ashley felt that more could have been raised had Thompson cooperated with him in pushing for collections.[47]

New Orleans was within the area allotted to the Southwest Conference of Congregational Churches, established in 1870. That group chose Dr. Thompson and Rev. S.S. Ashley as delegates to the National Council of Congregational Churches in 1874. The list of Congregational Conferences in the South, with their dates of establishment is as follows:

Southwest Conference—churches of Louisiana (1870)
Southwest Texas Association—churches of Corpus Christi, Goliad, Helena, Paris, Schulenburg, Flatona (1871)
Central South Conference—churches of Tennessee, Mississippi, and the Alabama churches in Athens, Florence, Sand Mountain (1872)
Kentucky Conference—churches in Kentucky (1871)
Alabama Conference—churches not in Central South (1876)
Georgia Conference—(1878) Many of these churches formerly belonged to the Central South Conference and the former Southeast Georgia Conference
North Carolina Conference—(1879)[48]

Thompson was appointed president of Alcorn College in November by Mississippi Governor Ames, and resigned his position in New Orleans as of December 1st of 1874. He was especially concerned about his successor for Central Church, whose special people demanded a special pastor. He said that his successor in either post must be a black man and must be secured at once, but the only person he could recommend was Dr. John B. Reeve, Dean of the Theological Department at Howard University.[49]

In the same month (December, 1874) that he became president of Alcorn, Thompson's name was placed in nomination on the slate for president of Howard.[50] The position at Alcorn was of short duration; six months later Thompson was back in New

Orleans.[51] His new work in New Orleans was to establish a Presbyterian church, but that would not give him a good living. He suggested to Secretary Whipple that a job teaching at Straight (he "could work for less than another male teacher") would help both him and the AMA, for he would then be able to pay them a debt of seven years' standing.[52]

Thompson was lecturing on Church History at New Orleans University (Methodist) in 1877, but his wife was anxious to leave New Orleans because of the unsettled state of affairs there.[53] He asked the Association for a position elsewhere. Perhaps he was refused, for he wrote an anonymous article criticizing the AMA that was printed in Pinchback's newspaper, the *Louisianian*, in March. Seymour Straight (white Baptist), a vice president of the AMA and benefactor of Straight University, wrote Thompson that his only "honorable course" was to decline reelection to the Straight board of Trustees. "No honorable man can remain in the Board of trustees longer than he is friendly to the American Missionary Association and its supporters, —who are making great pecuniary and other sacrifices for the education and elevation of a people *some* of whose leaders," said Straight, who were "too utterly selfish to make any sacrifices for their own race, find pleasure in denouncing those whose *works* are philanthropic." Because he had "heretofore" held in high esteem Thompson's "learning, piety & philanthropy," he wished to remain on friendly terms, and that was possible only if they were not associated in any way.[54]

No black man was found, and Thompson's replacement at Straight and Central Church was Walter S. Alexander. Alexander reported that occasionally white Congregationalists attended his services, but concluded that "the spirit of caste is about as strong in New Orleans as it is in India. . . ." He said not to worry about Thompson "causing friction," for he had "absolutely no following in the Central Church. His administration of affairs here was thoroughly and in every sense bad. . . . He could not, even if disposed, do us the slightest possible harm."[55]

Political and Racist Turmoil
The late 1870's continued to be a time of great need in New Orleans, and a time of great political turmoil. Governor Antoine told Alexander at a church meeting that 11 black men had been

killed at Laurel Hill, and that "200 rebels were on the rampage," the black population fearing "extermination in that quarter." The order of the White Camelia was active in a campaign of intimidation and terror. Alexander was insulted twice in Iberia for walking on the streets with the Rev. Peter P. Proctor (black). "Shot guns and 'Regulators'" were "too plenty" before the election of 1876 "for a white man to be too prominently identified with the colored people in the country parishes." He expected the approaching political campaign to "be one of unexampled ferocity & bloodshed," and one which the Republicans would lose.[56]

Straight University was burned by incendiaries in February, 1877, missed one day of classes, and was temporarily housed in Central Church. Straight was described by Alexander as "the only Institution for Colored students in Louisiana" that offered "equal advantages"; not even the rebel sympathies of James A. Adams could keep black students away. At a general meeting after the fire, Pinchback and Antoine were among the black men who spoke. Antoine, president of the Central Church board of trustees, and Senator Pierre Landry were on the committee to draft resolutions of friendship to the AMA and their desire to rebuild.[57]

A group of Congregational churches was started in the vicinity of New Orleans, manned in part by the early theologues of Straight's Theological Department. Since most of the pastors were poorly educated, "half-trained," or illiterate, few of the churches thus begun were sustained long. Most of the people in the area were Baptists. They had never heard of Congregationalism before, and their pastors often were not informed enough to explain. Central Church, however, celebrated its 100th year in 1972, and St. Paul's Church at New Iberia its 103rd.

Roster of New Churches

The chart below includes the AMA churches receiving aid in 1877, with their dates of establishment and current pastor. An asterisk (*) denotes men identified as African American.

Location	Year	Pastor	Members
Hampton, Va., Bethesda	1869	Richard Tolman	121
Beaufort, N.C., Christ	1870	——	20
Dudley, N.C.	1870	David Peebles	64

McLeansville, N.C.	1871	John Ingle	92
Raleigh, N.C.	1874	George S. Smith*	44
Wilmington, N.C.	1870	D.D. Dodge	17
Charleston, S.C.	1867	W.G. Marts	229
Orangeburg, S.C.	1875	William L. Johnson*	29
Atlanta, University Ch.	1874	Cyrus W. Francis	54
Atlanta, First Congr.	1867	Samuel S. Ashley	159
Byron Sta., Ga.	1873	Harrison Watkins*	18
Golding's Grove, Ga., Midway Church	1874	Floyd Snelson*	239
Macon, Ga.	1868	G.J. Webster	57
Marietta, Ga.	1877	Thomas N. Stewart*	21
Savannah, Ga.	1869	Richard F. Markham	53
Belmont, Ga.	1873	——	46
Louisville, Ga.	1874	Leonadus Rutherford*	24
Ogeechee, Ga.	1872	——	22
Woodville, Ga.	1871	John H.H. Sengstacke*	28
Berea, Ky.	1853	John G. Fee	151
Big Hill, Ky., Waln. Ch.	1871	A. Crawford	13
Cabin Creek, Ky.	1850	——	20
Hillsdale, Ky., Bethesda	1850	——	23
Camp Nelson, Ky.	1864	Gabriel Burdett*	146
Chattanooga, Tenn.	1867	Temple Cutler	77
Nashville, Tenn.	1868	Henry S. Bennett	141
Nashville, Howard Ch.	1876	George W. Moore*	17
Memphis, Tenn., 2d	1868	William Mallery*	113
Florence, Ala.	1876	Laurine C. Anderson*	24
Talladega, Ala.	1868	G. Stanley Pope	146
Alabama Furnace, Ala.	1874	Noah Lowry*	34
Anniston, Ala.	1875	Peter McIntosh*	51
Childersburg, Ala.	1874	Alfred Jones*	26
The Cove, Ala.	1873	Barbour Grant*	8
Kymulga, Ala.	1874	Preston Young*	35
Athens, Ala.	1871	Lindsey A. Roberts*	47
Marion, Ala.	1870	Joseph E. Smith*	65
Montgomery, Ala.	1872	E.C. Stickel	87
Selma, Ala.	1872	H.W. Carter	86
Mobile, Ala.	1876	A.B. Irwin	42
Gretna, La.	1869	W. Putney Ward*	210

Lockport, La.	1869	Nelson Taylor*	130
New Iberia, La.	1871	William M. Butler*	85
Terrebonne Sta., La.	1872	Benjamin Fields*	62
New Orleans, Central	1860	W.S. Alexander	105
New Orleans, Greenville	1869	C.W. Lewis*	30
New Orleans, Howard	1869	Henry Ruffin*	22
New Orleans, Morris B.	1870	Isaac Hall*	60
Carrolton, La.	1873	Nathaniel B. James*	16
La Fouche Crossg, La.	1873	Henry Armstead*	30
Abberville, La.	1877	Charles E. Smith*	18
Tougaloo, Miss.	1871	L.A. Darling	82
Lawrence, Kan., 2d	1862	——	48
Leavenworth, Kan., 3rd	1869	——	22
Helena, Tex.	1874	Mitchell Thompson*	32
Corpus Christi, Tex.	1866	Samuel M. Coles*	20
Goliad, Tex.	1872	B.C. Church	19
Paris, Tex. w/missions	1868	Albert Gray*	173

NOTES

1. XII (August, 1868), 182-183; XIII (February, 1869), 31; (June, 1869), 127; (July, 1869), 147; XIV (May, 1870), 99; (July, 1870),146-147, 160-161; XV (March, 1871), 55; XV (April, 1872), 73, are examples.

2. (Johnson 1959, 321).

3. Hotchkiss, Canada West, January 6, 1862, to Whipple, AMAA.

4. Hotchkiss, January 3, to Whipple, AMAA.

5. Mrs. Hotchkiss, December 17, 1861; Hotchkiss, January 6, 1862, to Whipple, AMAA.

6. (Richardson 1986, 143).

7. Scott, August 26, 1870, in *AM*, XIV (October, 1870), 221; (September, 1870), 193-195; (Washington 1970, 66-67).

8. *AM*, XIV (September, 1870), 195; XVI (July, 1872), 154.

9. (Washington 1970, 66-67).

10. (DeBoer 1994, 156-159; 106-110).

11. (DeBoer 1994, 109).

12. *AM*, XIV (October, 1870), 221; XIX (July, 1875), 159; see also (Herskovits 1968,74).

13. *AM*, XIV (July, 1870), 74.

14. Comings, in *AM*, VIII (April, 1864), 100-101.

15. Prof. E. Whittlesey, April 1872, in *AM*, XV (April, 1872), 154.

16. Armstrong, "Negro Worship, What Is Its Essential Character?" *AM*, XIV (October, 1870), 229-230.

17. *AM*, XI (May, 1867), 110-111.

18. *Twenty-first Annual Report* (1867), 19.

19. Woodworth, "Congregationalism in the South," *AM*, XII (June, 1868), 136-137.

20. Martin, Glasgow, Scotland, April 14, 1868, AMAA; *Thirty-first Annual Report*, II (1877), 12.

21. (Ferris 1913, 897). Muriel Proctor Holcomb, daughter of Henry Hugh Proctor and a former AMA teacher who had saved one of her lower school pupils from a lynch mob, told the author that when her African American acquaintances asked her why she did not join a black church, instead of the predominantly white First Congregational Church in Montclair, New Jersey, she told them: "If colored people knew anything about American history, they would all be Congregationalists."

22. *AM*, XII (July, 1868), 161-162; C.L. Woodworth, "The Church of the Pilgrims—South: Lost but Found," *AM*, XIX (September, 1875), 202-207.

23. Mobley, June 6, 1867, to Whipple; *History of church and school at McIntosh, Georgia* (New York, n.d.), AMAA.

24. Mobley, July 25; August 15, 1867, to Whipple, AMAA; *Twenty-fourth Annual Report* (1870), 45-46; *Twenty-fifth Annual Report* (1871), 27; *Twenty-sixth Annual Report* (1872), 64; *Twenty-ninth Annual Report* (1875), 35. For a picture of a white slaveholding family who were members of Midway Church, see (Myers 1972, *passim*).

25. See the explanation in the chapter below dealing with the theological schools; also the letters of Golding and Snelson, AMAA.

26. Golding, December 3, 1875, to Strieby, AMAA.

27. Markham, December 1, 1875, to Strieby, AMAA.

28. *AM*, XV (August, 1871), 172-173.

29. *Thirty-first Annual Report* (1877), 24-25; *Thirty-second Annual Report* (1878), 89.

30. *Thirty-third Annual Report* (1879), 64.

31. Markham, December 11, 1876, to Strieby, AMAA.

32. J.T. Ford, June 4, 1873, to E.M. Cravath; Savannah *Morning News*, August 5; August 7, 1875, AMAA.

33. Markham, July 12, 1878, to Strieby, AMAA.

34. Letters of Jacob A. Norager, AMAA. Thompson consistently spelled his name Norago.

35. Thompson, Newark, N.J., February 27, 1865, Testimonial for
H.H. Hunter; *AM*, XV (January, 1871), 13; (October, 1871), 230-
231. In 1930, Straight united with New Orleans University
(Methodist Church, North) to form Dillard University.

36. Records of the Central Congregational Church, New Orleans;
see "Resolution of a Meeting of the Board of Incorporators of St.
James Chapel," to the AMA, n.d., signed by A. Zemar, president
and J.A. Norager, secretary, AMAA.

37. Thompson, October 23; December 11, 1871, to Cravath; *AM*,
XVI (March, 1872), 51-52.

38. Thompson, August 7; September 30, 1872, to Cravath, AMAA.

39. Lt. Gov. C.C. Antoine remained in office under Governor
Packard, serving right years.

40. Thompson, May 15, 1873, to Cravath; Ashley, May 16, 1873, to
Cravath, AMAA.

41. Ashley, September 24, 1873, to E.M. Cravath, AMAA. Ashley's
salary was $2000 per year; Thompson's was $1000 for the post at
Straight, plus a salary from the church. See also Alice Dunbar,
"The People of Color in Louisiana, Part II," *JNH*, II (January,
1917), 51-78.

42. *Annual Report of Central Church*, September 30, 1873,
AMAA; benevolent contributions were given as $80; raised for
church purposes, $1500.

43. Ashley, December 13, 1873, to Cravath, AMAA.

44. Isabelle had been temporary chairman of the lower house of the
Louisiana legislature; in 1875 he was head of the New Orleans
agency for the U.S. Pension office; Isabelle, February 13, 1875, to
Cravath, AMAA.

45. Ingraham's note was for $1000. He became a communicant member of the church in April, 1874, Thompson, April 16, 1874, to Cravath, AMAA.

46. Thompson, January 28, 1874, to Cravath, AMAA.

47. Ashley, April 2; April 7; May 6; May 15, 1874; Thompson's financial report, April 16, 1874, to Cravath, AMAA.

48. *Thirty-third Annual Report* (1879), 71-72.

49. See 1874 letters of Thompson to Cravath, AMAA.

50. Thompson left December 15 for Alcorn; James Hartling, December 16, 1874, to Cravath. Hartling added this word about Thompson: "Even had he remained he is not a man who takes kindly to such work as is needed in this field. A man 'naturally inclined to the work' of evangelism, of broad views . . . wholly laborious and trained to self-denial, is the man for this general church work." For the Howard nomination, see James B. Johnson, Washington, D.C., December 26, 1874, to Whipple, AMAA.

51. Ex-Senator Hiram Rhoads Revels (he had taken the seat formerly held by Jefferson Davis) resumed his old job as president of Alcorn, see M.C. Cole, July 14; October 26, 1875, to Strieby, AMAA. Cole suggested recalling Thompson to Central Church, where Cole (a Methodist) was interim pulpit supply. Cole was secretary to W.C. Brown (black) State Supt. of Public Education.

52. Thompson, Alcorn, Mississippi, June 26, 1875, to Whiting; New Orleans, December 28, 1871, to Cravath; July 28, 1876, to Whipple, AMAA. Thompson had gone to New Orleans in 1871 from Newark, New Jersey, leaving a debt of some $300, which the AMA assumed for him, receiving in return his promise of payment. His new salary at Alcorn ($2500) seemed adequate, but Thompson said that the "unsettled state of matters" at Alcorn kept him from being able to repay the AMA. The writer found no record that Thompson ever repaid the debt.

53. Thompson, July 28, 1876, to Whipple, AMAA.

54. Letter book copy, Seymour Straight, April 13, 1877, to Thompson; Straight, April 14, 1877, to Strieby, AMAA. Straight admitted to Strieby that he had "*perhaps* too little patience with internal enemies." Thompson was still a Straight trustee through 1878; *Thirty-second Annual Report* (1878), 64.

55. Alexander, March 3, 1876, to Strieby, AMAA.

56. For evidence of the great need in New Orleans, see Martling, New Orleans, December 16, 1874, to Cravath; also the letters of Ingraham and Zemar, who served on a committee that distributed money given by the AMA for the aged sick and helpless. Ingraham was secretary of Central Church Board of Trustees in 1875.

For the political situation, see Alexander, May 15; June 23, 1876, to Strieby. Unique among AMA people, Adams, acting president of Straight, was a Democrat, although he had been anti-Democratic in 1874, and told of people being murdered on the Red River and the Democratic papers with their "most incendiary articles," and the need of President Grant to send in the troops to prevent bloodshed in the coming election. (Adams, September 2, 1874, to Cravath). Something happened to Adams in the month of September, for by the 30th, he was writing to Cravath in a very friendly vein in re New Orleans whites and saying that there would be no violence. As his attitude toward Democrats changed, so did his attitude toward black students. He admitted thinking that black students were not equal to whites in the higher branches of learning, and objected to teaching Latin and Greek before they had a sound basis in English. (December 31, 1874, to Cravath). C.C. Antoine said that some of the tricks Adams pulled to get things his way in Central Church were "beneath the dignity of a common ward politician." Both Antoine and Alexander asked that Adams be removed for the good of both Straight and Central Church. The AMA sent James Powell, District Secretary at Chicago, to investigate. Powell did a masterly job, discovering in the process that Adams saw in Alexander a threat and feared that the more charismatic Alexander would replace him. Adam's removal was definitely advised for the good of the school, but in a manner not to cause Adams, who was a fine satiric writer with influence with the

Nation and other sources, to harm the AMA. See Antoine, February 6, 1877; Alexander February 2, 1877; James Powell, February 19; February 22, 1877, to Strieby, AMAA.

57. Alexander, February 1, 1877, to G.D. Pike, AMAA; *AM*, I (New Series) (April, 1877), 2; *Thirty-first Annual Report* (1877), 68-70.

XII

RELIGIOUS EDUCATION
OF THE FREEDMEN

Knowledge, merely acquired, has no saving grace: Only as it is digested, assimilated, worked into daily life, forming habits, sustaining principle, creating sentiment, is it power for good. Till then it may be "a dangerous thing."
—Editorial
American Missionary, 1877

  The religion of the freedmen, as the AMA encountered it in the South, prompted the establishment of theological departments at several chartered institutions and gave the Association its second major emphasis; the education of ministers was added to the education of teachers and the people in general.

  At first it was only coincidental that many of the men sent to the field from the North were ministers. They were educators whose primary business was the establishment of schools, or they were scouts (like the Rev. L.C. Lockwood) sent to see what the freedmen needed and to enlighten the benevolent in the North in the ways they could help.

  The need for ministers as such from the North was first recognized in a request from the teachers themselves. Thomas W. Cardozo (African American superintendent at Charleston, South Carolina) voiced their feelings when he pleaded with the Association to send a northern minister (color unspecified) to supply the spiritual needs of the teachers, who did not object to working in the local colored Sunday schools but found the typical noisy, emotional church service inconducive to worship on their part. Cardozo suggested that the AMA make it a regular policy to send a

297

clergyman with each group of teachers to serve as their minister and to be the pastor for any others in the community who would prefer an educated ministry.[1]

As the freedmen learned to read, they began to realize that their unlettered preachers were often frauds who pretended to be able to read hymns and scripture they had memorized. As they lost respect for their religious leaders, and stopped following them, the educated African American children often discarded religion as well. The AMA and its teachers were fearful of the result if such a situation should continue whereby the schools would be producing intelligent, amoral—even immoral—graduates.

Spirited Debate

It was a discouraging prospect and one that prompted a spirited debate with the Unitarians and others who argued that it was enough to give the freedmen an education and that religion, in fact, should play no part in the work. Congregationalists, Presbyterians, and like-minded denominations replied that education was an adjunct of their brand of Protestantism, and that the public school was an imperative of their religious inheritance; therefore, to give the freedmen only a secular education was to deny them the basis without which the public school would not exist.[2]

There was an even more telling argument, perhaps, in view of the fears North and South of the impact on American society that would result from the release of four million slaves. If a man were evil, it was argued, education alone would not make him good; it would simply enable him to operate more cleverly. The Association's work in Africa had shown the results of providing only the material and educational aspects of western culture. Along the coast many native Africans had learned a kind of broken English, but they had also acquired a fondness for rum and other less desirable traits from the sailors who had been their teachers. (This was the testimony of Elymas P. Rogers when he visited Africa for the AMA and the African Civilization Society.) Even at Mendi the sons of native chiefs who simply learned to read and cipher without accepting the ethical claims of Christianity, returned to their families better able to keep accounts of their business in the slave trade.

The slaves in America had been allowed a religion of sorts—one without morality. To prepare themselves properly for full citizenship in American society, reasoned the AMA, they needed not only an education in order to make a living; they needed also the education for life that religion promised. For these reasons the AMA began theological departments, and AMA teachers and missionaries gathered local preachers to teach them to read and to realize that, in addition to its well-known teachings about immortality and salvation, the Bible proclaimed an ethical religion. But the situation was critical and it would be years before the new schools produced an educated ministry for the South. Added to the tremendous job of teaching the freedmen—a program requiring thousands of persons that was never adequately staffed because of lack of funds—there was added the burden of training African American leaders, also requiring thousands of persons.

Just as the AMA did its best to hire black teachers for the freedmen, it did its best to hire black ministers for them. They found, however that they were limited to three sources: educated African American ministers from the North; poorly educated or ignorant southern preachers; and the products of their new theological schools in the South.

There were very few of the first sort, especially after 1865 when Congregationalism was often a requisite. Yet it was only this first source that came near providing the caliber of men required. Because the AMA was at work educating the freedmen for professional careers as well as non-professional occupations, their ministers needed to be professionally qualified. And, as Erastus Milo Cravath (Secretary of the AMA's Middle West Department) put it, "Such men as are required are scarce."[3]

Educated in the North

There were about a dozen and a half black men educated in the North who were employed by the AMA to work with the freedmen primarily in the religious arena. Their preparation varied from the equivalent of a common school education to full collegiate and seminary training. An asterisk [*] indicates that letters survive for these individuals in the AMA Archives.

John N. Mars* (AMEZ minister), served 1864-65 at Portsmouth, Va., he also helped William Harris in the Portsmouth school.

Huston Reedy* (AME minister),1865, Baton Rouge, La., vicinity

Hardy Mobley*, born a slave in Georgia, educated in the North, a resident of Brooklyn, N.Y., common school education, served 1865-67 in Savannah, Ga.; 1869-72 in Lebanon, Mo.; 1872, Topeka, Ks.; 1873-75, New Iberia, La. In addition to church work, Mobley, his wife and four daughters all taught schools.

Ennals J. Adams* (Presbyterian minister), former minister of Plane Street Church, Newark, N.J., educated at Gerrit Smith's school, Peterboro, N.Y. From 1863-65 served the Mendi Mission, Africa; 1865-66 in Charleston, S.C.

Francis Frederic* (Congregational city missioner among blacks) 1866-67, Baltimore, Md. His name was spelled variously from Fedric to Frederick, since he did not write his own letters, it is difficult to determine the correct spelling. He was born a slave in Kentucky. After escaping, he spent several years in England lecturing on abolition and temperance. He was employed on the recommendation of the pastor and members of the First Congregational Church (mostly white) of Baltimore. This church had some black members (Thomas Cardozo was one).

William W. Mallery* (Congregationalist), Massachusetts native; had supplied churches in Springfield, Mass., and Windsor, Vt. From 1867-79 he served the 2nd Congregational Church of Memphis.

Theophilus Guild Steward* (AME preacher), 1865 in Beaufort, S.C. He came under the AMA through the Plan of Cooperation worked out by Daniel A. Payne and discussed later in this book. His brother William served the AMA as a teacher. Steward showed his literary ability in the letters he wrote to the AMA, one of which was published in the *American Missionary.* He was born in Cumberland County, New Jersey, in 1843.[4]

James A. Handy, 1865, North Carolina. Handy also came under the cooperative work of the AMA with the AME Church.[5]

George G. Collins (graduate of Oberlin and Princeton Theological Seminary), 1870-71, Lincoln Mission, Washington, D.C.

Mr. and Mrs. Collins also served the AMA as teachers in Kentucky, and George Collins taught at Howard University.

John Bunyan Reeve, D.D.* (Educated at N.Y. Central College, McGrawville. D.D. from Lincoln University), 1871-76, Dean Theological Department, Howard University, Washington, D.C. He also filled pulpits in Washington and helped in the founding of the Congregational church associated with Howard. In April of 1867 he was the unanimous choice of the session of the Fifteenth Street Church (Presbyterian) to replace H.H. Garnet as pastor. He declined.[6]

Charles H. Thompson*, 1872-74, Central Congregational Church, New Orleans, La. Thompson also served the AMA as a home missionary.[7]

Daniel R. Miller (Oberlin student), 1872, Selma, Alabama. He also worked at Marion, Alabama.[8]

Edward B. Sellers* (from Andover, Mass.), 1874-76, First Congregational Church, Chattanooga, Tenn. He was educated in Massachusetts.[9]

Solomon M. Coles* (graduate of Lincoln University and Yale Divinity School), 1874, 3rd Congregational Church, Leavenworth, Kansas; 1876, Charleston, South Carolina; 1877-80, Corpus Christi Texas. He was one of the best educated of all AMA ministers and the first African American graduate of Yale Divinity School. He was more interested in teaching than in the ministry, however.

John H.H. Sengstacke* (born free in the South, educated in Europe), 1875, Pilgrim Congregational Church, Woodville, Ga. He also edited *The Gospel Trumpet* (Savannah), a monthly publication containing national African American news as well as local church news.[10]

John W.A. Shaw* (from First Congregational Church, Washington, D.C.), 1875, Savannah, Ga.[11]

William L. Johnson* (graduate of Lincoln University and Theological School), 1876 (summer), Central Congregational Church, New Orleans, Louisiana; 1876, Orangeburg, South Carolina. Johnson was a Northerner with full college and theological school training. He had the distinction of being the only African American minister of the Reformed Dutch Church in America. He was plagued in his work for the

AMA by an African American woman who falsely accused
him of fathering her child.
William H. Ash* (graduate of Lincoln University and Boston
Theological Seminary), 1877, Mobile, Alabama. Ash also
served the church at Florence, Alabama. He had been a
member of Central Congregational Church, Providence, R.I.
Thomas N. Stewart* (from Columbus, Ohio; a teacher there),
1877-78, Marietta, Ga. Stewart was a convinced Congregationalist, but was not successful in raising congregations. He
had been an AME.[12]

Aided, Uneducated, Black Southern Ministers
    The AMA also employed poorly educated African American
southern preachers. The fact that it believed in an educated ministry
as the ideal did not prevent the Association from respecting and
using the talents of such men. Time was important, and it would
take several years before men could be properly trained as
ministers, especially since most candidates also lacked a college
education, which was a prerequisite for seminary training. In the
interim the measure followed was the least desirable alternative but
one forced on the AMA by the situation. The Association employed these preachers to found Congregational churches. The area
superintendents or theological professors had first to acquaint the
men they chose with Congregational polity—no easy feat when
even the name of the denomination was unknown among most
freedmen. There were very few Congregational churches in the
South, and those few became Presbyterian before and during the
war because of the abolitionist character of the Congregational
churches of the North. (Southern Presbyterian churches also split
with northern Presbyterians for the same reason.)
    The following is a list of AMA-connected southern preachers
identified as being African Americans. Some of these men were very
disappointing to the AMA. They were men of the "Uncle Cato
stripe" (see preceding chapter) and are identified in the table as
such. An asterisk (*) identifies those for whom letters survive in the
Archives.

James Tynes*, 1864-67, Norfolk, Va.[13]

Robert Carter* (Cato style), 1868-73, Savannah, Ga. (founded 1868); 1871-73, Savannah on the Canal (founded 1872); 1871-73, Ogeechee, Ga. (founded 1872). Carter was once the slave of Howell Cobb of Macon, Georgia. He also assisted George A. Hood for a time in the night school at Beach Institute, Savannah. Carter was one of the greatest disappointments in the Georgia work and a most accomplished "Uncle Cato."[14]

Joseph Dutch, 1868, Zion Church, New Orleans (founded 1868).[15]

Isaac Williams (Baptist, aged, illiterate), 1869, Howard Church, New Orleans (founded 1869).[16]

Isaac Tongue, 1870, Jefferson City Church, New Orleans (founded 1870).[17]

W.J. Brown, 1870-1873, Morris Brown Church, New Orleans (founded 1869).[18]

David Johnson, 1870, Fauce Point, La., Church (founded 1870).[19]

Israel Cummings, 1870, Ile Piquant, La., Church (founded 1870).[20]

Daniel Clay*, 1870- , Terrebonne, La., Church (founded 1870). Clay, probably the son of Henry Clay, was an uneducated man much appreciated by the AMA workers who knew him. Unable to read, he left the portions of the service that required such ability to an assistant. He acted as an unofficial "bishop," establishing churches for colored people. He was the father of eleven children, one of whom, Reason Clay, became a theologue at Straight. A slave until emancipation, he was a leader of colored people in Louisiana.[21]

W. Putney Ward*, 1869- , New Hope Congregational Church, Gretna, La. (founded 1869).[22]

John E. Weir* (Originally Cumberland Presbyterian; became Congregational 1869), 1869- , Leavenworth, Kansas Church (founded 1869). He came to AMA work from Liberia. He could barely read and write, but worked in the Leavenworth Congregational Church until the depression of the 70's forced him to leave. He described the Leavenworth African Americans as the most degraded and least able of the race. Unable to care for themselves, they had followed the Union troops to Fort Leavenworth, he said. His brother, Moses T. Weir, was educated and would not recommend John to the AMA for its work after John left Kansas.[23]

William W. Weir, 1871-72, Lawrence, Kansas Church (founded 1863). An AMA document says that William was also John Weir's brother.[24]

Benjamin Fields (aged, former slave), 1872- , Terrebone Station, La. (founded 1872). Fields, a former slave, was 70 years old in 1877. He was given his post by Daniel Clay, 5 years his junior.[25]

Mitchell Thompson*, 1873, Goliad, Texas, Church (founded 1872); 1874- , Helena, Texas, Church (founded 1874). Thompson had a long tenure under the AMA and was still at work in Texas in 1881.[26]

Albert Gray*, 1873-77, Paris, Texas, Church (founded 1868).[27]

James Porter* (Assistant Pastor at churches listed. Cato style), 1874, Belmont, Ga., Church; 1874, Louisville, Ga., Church; 1874, Ogeechee, Ga., Church; 1874, Woodville, Ga., Church. Porter also assisted at Savannah. He was a lay preacher in the Episcopal Church in 1865, teaching school in Savannah. Porter was educated and actually belongs in the section of educated clergy with S.W. Rogers and Gabriel Burdett. He is included here because of his Cato characteristics. AMA Superintendent Aaron Rowe employed Porter because he was the best educated man in Savannah, but soon became convinced that Porter's denominational shifts (from Episcopal to AME to Congregational) were based on a desire to obtain as much money as possible. Rowe was willing to forgive him that weakness as a relic from past prejudice, but was upset when Porter's promise to give up his Justice of the Peace position was not kept. He was receiving full salary as assistant minister of Savannah Congregational Church ($60 per month) but was still on full salary as a teacher ($75 per month). His wife did an excellent business as a seamstress, and a daughter was a teacher. Rowe said that if he had Porter's income, he would give his services to the AMA free![28]

Harrison Watkins* (Cato style), 1870-77, Byron Station, Ga. (founded 1872); Andersonville, Ga. (founded 1868).[29]

Evans Green*, 1873-74, Carrollton, La., Church (founded 1873). Green died of tuberculosis on August 27, 1874, and the AMA lost a willing leader.[30]

Henry Armsted, 1873-76, La Fouche Crossing, La. (founded 1873).[31]

James W. Fleming* (Cato style), 1875-76, Belmont & Louisville, Ga., churches.[32]

George W. Swan* (AME, Cato style), 1875-76, Corpus Christi, Texas. There was a dispute involving Swan which was adjudicated in a special meeting in 1876. Some members of the church and the Church clerk protested the results.[33]

Charles E. Smith, 1877, Abbeville, La., Church (founded 1877). Smith had been a student at New Orleans University (Methodist).[34]

Anthony Copy, 1877, Petteance, La. (founded 1877).[35]

Wilson Callen, 1877, Belmont, Ga., Church (founded 1873); 1877, Louisville, Ga., Church (founded 1874). Wilson was licensed to preach (by official action of the Conference at Talladega, 1873) and worked at Selma before going to Savannah.[36]

John H. Stephens* (AME preacher), 1878, Lawsonville, Alabama (founded 1877).[37]

T.B.W. Evans, 1876, Mt. Horeb Congregational Church, Greenville, La. (founded 1869).[38]

William Reed, 1876, La Fouche Crossing, La.[39]

Black Southern Ministers with Some Education

The following men were not included above because they had some education:

S.W. Rogers (also an AMA agent; Indian & Negro blood), 1870-72, LePeigneur, La. (founded 1870). For three years before his death Rogers was commissioned as a school teacher and minister by the AMA. He taught a school at New Iberia, Louisiana, and gathered four churches in interior Louisiana. His death in July, 1872, was a loss to the AMA and the African Americans of Louisiana. In recognition of his service, the Annual Report of 1872 declared the need of educated black men like Rogers in Louisiana: "None of those now acting as pastors are educationally fit for the places."[40]

William Andrew Jackson*, 1873, Savannah, Ga. The Jacksons had taught a school at Berryville, Virginia, before his call to the Savannah church. Unfortunately, he died shortly after going to Savannah.[41]

Gabriel Burdett*, 1865-77, Camp Nelson, Ky (1864). Burdett is dealt with at some length above in the chapter concerned with the violence of the reaction of Southern whites to emancipation.

Leonadus A. Rutherford*, 1877, Louisville, Ga. Rutherford took a kind of medical course and called himself a doctor. The letterhead of the school reads, "College of American Medicine and Surgery, A Thoroughly Organized School of Eclectic Medicine, with a Faculty of Able and Experienced Teachers, Annual Sessions open on the first Monday in November, and close on the first Monday of March following. For particulars address A.L. Clinkscales, M.D., P.O. Box 236, Macon, Ga." Rutherford also worked at Byron, Georgia, in 1878. Although he had some education, Rutherford probably should be classified with the "Catos." Although his wife was white, Rutherford worked against the white ministers.[42]

Ministers from AMA Schools

The third source of African American ministers was the AMA's own schools. In 1870 the Association declared its intention of establishing theological schools not separated from the higher institutions of learning, but "a part and an outgrowth" of the latter. Such schools would not immediately equal seminaries in the North, just as the AMA colleges and universities in the South did not measure up at once to their northern counterparts. Many of the ministers, old and young, could give only part of their time to theological education while they carried on manual and pastoral duties. Many would attend undergraduate classes in the daytime and theological courses at night and require scholarship assistance. But the AMA was convinced of the need for an educated clergy: "The foundation on which the colored people must be built-up is intelligent piety." Many would not be able to complete their education, yet it was "far better that some should be helped to preach as well as they can by the aid of a little education rather than not preach at all, or preach as they are, or wait for a nine years' course of study." The AMA designed its theological departments "to meet the present want, and to grow as the demand enlarges."[43]

Atlanta University

In 1870 a theological class was begun at Atlanta University, and a Theological Department established at Straight University, money being given for this purpose by Deacon Josiah Reed of South Weymouth, Massachusetts. The Annual Report of 1870 stated that "no class [needed] a Christian education more than the ministers and missionaries of Freedmen. As is the minister, so will be the church." It was altogether fitting that such work should begin on the 250th anniversary of the founding of the Plymouth Colony, for the spiritual descendents of the Pilgrims "have ever encouraged an educated ministry." Fisk had four students of theology in 1871. In 1872 there were 34 students enrolled in theology in AMA schools, 5 at Fisk under Henry S. Bennett, Professor of Rhetoric and Theology. In 1873 there were 47 theological students: 3 at Fisk, 4 at Atlanta, 6 at Talladega. In 1874 there were 6 at Fisk, 4 at Atlanta under Cyrus W. Francis, 10 at Talladega, 24 at Straight. In 1875 there were 70 theological students in AMA schools.[44]

The work at Atlanta was under the general direction of the Rev. C.W. Francis (white), and some of the important graduates in the period under study are listed below. An asterisk (*) indicates letters survive in the Archives.

Floyd Snelson*, 1871-74, Andersonville, Ga.; 1872, Byron Station, Ga.; 1874-77, Goldings Grove, Ga., Midway Church (founded 1874). From 1877-79 Snelson headed the Mendi Mission in West Africa. He was the first graduate of an AMA theology course. On his return from Africa, Snelson was again called to the pastorate of Midway Church.[45]

Joseph E. Smith*, 1874 at Andersonville, Ga.; 1876 at Marion, Ala. Church (founded 1870); 1877-79 at Goldings Grove, Ga., Midway Church; 1879- at Chattanooga, Tenn. Smith was licensed in 1874 and ordained in 1876. In 1880 he went to Africa to evaluate the Mendi Mission for the AMA. He

had a long and fruitful pastorate in Chattanooga where he was a civic leader.[46]
George S. Smith*, 1876- at Raleigh, N.C. church (founded 1874). Smith had a long pastorate at Raleigh.

Fisk University
Fisk University in Nashville had a theological department headed by Henry S. Bennett (white) of Wakeman, Ohio. He was professor of Rhetoric and Theology, pastor of the Union Church at Fisk, and secretary of the University![47] The following have been identified as black theologues at Fisk during Reconstruction.

Moses T. Weir*, 1871-72 at Lawrence, Kansas, church (founded 1867); 1873-75 at Athens, Ala., church (founded 1871). Weir attended Chicago Theological Seminary for one year prior to Fisk. Formerly a Cumberland Presbyterian.[48]

Lindsey A. Roberts*, 1872 and 1876-78 at Athens, Ala., church; 1876 at Florence, Ala. Roberts was the first graduate of Fisk's Theological Department. He was ordained in 1872. Athens was his home town. Roberts had lost his right arm as a soldier on the Union side in the battle of Nashville.[49]

G.A.P. Brown was a Baptist aided by AMA funds.
Horace Loving was aided by AMA funds.
J.W. Turner
I. Ducket
William Nichol was a member of the AME Church.
_____ **Husky**
Quinton B. Neale*, 1876 he taught at Florence, Ala. He was a Cumberland Presbyterian from Fayetteville, N.C. Neale became a convinced Congregationalist and was instrumental in the founding of the Florence, Alabama, Congregational Church. Neale wanted very much to be a minister and help correct the perverted idea of Christianity held by so many freedmen. But he had difficulty with the study of Greek and in raising enough money from teaching school to continue his work at Fisk. It required far less education to teach school than to be a Congregational minister.[50]

Laurine C. Anderson*, worked the summers 1876-78 at the Florence, Alabama, church. In 1878, the emigration to Kansas took most of the Congregationalists of Florence, "the best people in town." Anderson was licensed to preach in 1877, and was a speaker at the groundbreaking of Livingstone Hall at Fisk. He graduated from Fisk in 1880 and in 1881 was teaching school in Chapel Hill, Texas.[51]

George W. Moore* (later became General Field Secretary for the South for the AMA), 1877- , In charge of Howard Chapel at Fisk. Moore was born a slave, the son of a famous general. He was licensed to preach in 1877 and served Howard Chapel at Fisk. He later served Lincoln Memorial Congregational Church, Washington, D.C., and was Lecturer on Pastoral Theology at Howard University. He was a member of the Fisk Board of Trustees, and served the AMA as General Field Missionary for the South from 1902 until his retirement in 1917. He was married to Ella Sheppard, one of the original Jubilee Singers and member of the Fisk faculty.[52]

Straight University

When the AMA established a theological department at its Straight University in New Orleans in 1870, it looked for an African American man to head it and appointed Charles H. Thompson in 1871 with the title of Professor of Biblical Theology and Literature.

Although there were white theologues at Howard University, most of the theology students at the other AMA schools were African Americans. In contrast to its Theology Department, Straight's Law Department had several white students. The following have been identified as African American theologues at Straight during Reconstruction:

Henry A. Lewis, 1869-75, served the church at Greenville, La. (founded 1869). A letter from a contemporary reveals Lewis's feeling about this place of service: "Lewis, has lost his wife, gives up his field, and gone to North Carolina. He thinks that Greenville stands upon the old site of Sodom and Gomorrah or somewhere there about."[53]

Nelson Taylor, 1870-74, LaFourche, La., Lockport Congregational Church (founded 1869); 1874- , went to Jamaica. Taylor was ordained in 1870.[54]

Nathaniel B. James*, 1871-73, New Iberia, La., Church (founded 1870); 1873-75, Howard Church, New Orleans (founded 1869); 1875- , Carrollton, La., Church.[55]

S.W. Otts, 1870, Algiers, La., Church[56]

Thomas E. Hillson*, 1869, Greenville Church, New Orleans; 1878- , Carrollton, La., Church.[57]

Peter P. Proctor*, 1872, Howard Church, New Orleans; 1873, Morris Brown Church, New Orleans; 1875-77, New Iberia, La., Church.[58]

Henry A. Ruffin, 1875, Howard Church, New Orleans.[59]

Isaac Hall* (Baptist), 1875-77, Morris Brown Church, New Orleans. Hall was from Shreveport and was ordained in 1877.[60]

William Butler*, 1877, St. Peters Church, Lake Peigneur, La., and New Iberia, La., churches.

William Hamilton, 1877- , Paris, Texas, Church (founded 1868).[61]

Robert A. Anderson (Methodist, received AMA scholarship help)

William H. Bolding. He was licensed to preach in 1877.

____ **Carter**

Reason Clay (son of Daniel Clay)

Henry Green (Baptist, received AMA scholarship help)

____ **Huston**

____ **Marshall** (Methodist). This was probably J.F. Marshall, Straight student, who taught school at Lockport, Louisiana, in 1876.

Charles McPherson (from Scotland, a scholarship student). When S.S. Ashley went abroad in the interests of Straight University, one result was that McPherson was given a scholarship to study theology there. Mrs. McPherson was white and had been a chamber maid in a hotel in Scotland. The McPhersons had three children. The AMA workers in New Orleans were of the opinion that his marriage to a white woman kept him from being hired in Louisiana. For whatever reason, the people in the Greenville church would not accept him as their pastor. He left Straight for Maryville College in 1874.[62]

Howard University

The Theological Department was officially organized at Howard University in 1870, and the AMA engaged John Bunyan Reeve, African American Presbyterian minister from Philadelphia in 1871 to be its Dean. The following have been identified as black theologues (there were also some white students) at Howard during Reconstruction:

W.A.L. Campbell* (West Indian), 1873 (summer), Dudley, N.C., Congregational Church (founded 1870).[63]

Richard A. Tucker* (one of Howard's most promising students), 1874-76, Dudley, N.C., Congregational Church (founded 1870).

Michael Jerkins* (previously teacher of freedmen, N.C.; ordained 1879), 1879- , Beaufort, N.C., Congregational Church

Green Musgrave (member of Dudley, N.C., Congregational Church; scholarship student)

L.C. Jowell (promising student)

Robert F. Wheeler*, 1875-76, In charge of preaching services, Lincoln Mission, Washington, D.C.

Edward W. Turner* (attended Lincoln University; had been for 9 years a Presbyterian missionary among freedmen)

John B. Graham (Baptist scholarship student)

____ **Robinson** (Baptist scholarship student)

Talladega College

At Talladega College, Alabama, the Theological Seminary (established ion 1873) was under the direction of H.E. Brown (white), who taught Biblical Literature, and J.N. Brown (white), Systematic Theology and Homiletics. There were also additional lecturers.[64] Later George W. Andrews (white) headed the school.

The following have been identified as African American theologues at Talladega. (Much information about these men was found in *The Graduates of Talladega College and What They Are Doing*, published by the college in 1900.)

Noah Lowry (from Marion, Alabama), 1874-77, Alabama Furnace Congregational Church (founded 1874).[65]

Thornton T. Benson (from Marion, Alabama), 1874, Kingston Church, Kymulga, Ala. (founded 1874). In 1878 Benson moved to the church at Alabama Furnace, Alabama.[66]

Wyatt Fuller (from Marion, Alabama; graduated 1876), 1874-75, The Cove, Ala., Congregational Church (founded 1874).[67]

Peter J. McIntosh (Montgomery, Ala.; graduated 1880), 1875-81, Anniston, Ala., Congregational Church (founded 1875).[68]

John Rufus McLean * (Greensboro, N.C.; post-Reconstruction pastorate at Macon, Ga.), 1877, Ogeechee, Ga., Congregational Church (founded 1872). McLean was a scholarship student at Talladega and served Congregational churches until his death in 1919.[69]

Alfred Jones (Marion, Alabama; graduated 1876), 1876-77, The Cove, Ala.; 1877, Childersburg, Ala.[70]

John Barbour Grant (graduated 1880), 1877-78, The Cove, Ala.[71]

Preston W. Young (Montgomery, Ala.; graduated Theological and Normal Departments, 1879), 1877-78, Kymulga, Ala.[72]

Yancy Benjamin Sims * (Talladega; Attended Oberlin a year; graduated from the Normal Department at Talladega 1879, from the Theological Department 1880), 1878, Marietta, Ga.; 1882-1914, Little Rock, Ark., Congregational Church. A minister of great influence, Sims was one of the original 17 members of the Talladega Congregational Church when it was organized in 1868.[73]

John Wesley Strong (graduated 1880), 1877, Started Lawsonville, Ala., Congregational Church. In 1890 Strong was teaching a school at Corpus Christi, Texas, where he had been pastor of the Congregational Church from 1881-1890.[74]

Andrew Jackson Headen (from Talladega; graduated from the Normal Department 1878, from the Theological Department 1879), 1878, Selma, Ala., Congregational Church. He worked at Selma during the summer of 1878. In 1900 he was listed as a farmer living in Talladega.

Henry S. Williams (graduated from the Theological Department 1879), 1878, Montgomery, Ala., Congregational Church. He worked at Montgomery in the summer of 1878. He died in Athens, Alabama, January 8, 1892.

John David Smith (graduated from the Theological and Normal Departments 1878), 1878, Savannah, Ga. Smith took

Markham's place at Savannah during the summer of 1878 after graduating from Talladega. He was ordained at Shelby, Alabama, in 1879 and served the church there until 1881. In 1900 he was listed in alumni records as an engineer living in Chicago, Illinois.[75]

Spencer Snell (received the school's first B.D. 1884; Born Monroe County, Ala., ca. 1852. Attended AMA school in Mobile, Ala.). The first day school attended by Snell was the AMA's Emerson Institute at Mobile. He served post-Reconstruction pastorates at Louisville, Ky., Birmingham, Ala., and Talladega.[76]

Edward Hunter (Eufala, Ala.)[77]

* * * * *

These, then, were the African Americans the AMA chose to help carry on its religious-sector work among the freedmen. In each group there were successes and failures. Education was no guarantee of an effective pastorate. The best leaders were among those who were native products of AMA schools and several of the best of these came from the most disadvantaged sections of the South.

No impersonal listing as above can show the impact of a man's life for good or ill on the work of the AMA. Some of the men above were not at all suited to the task of establishing Congregational churches, which required serving them as guides and fellow members rather than as dominating "rulers." Some were unsuccessful for other reasons. In 1873, A.M. Niles made a tour and reported to the men at the Rooms in New York. If the work at Charleston had a fault, it was the minister. "I should judge it must not be easy to get colored men admirably adapted to your work. The feeling is I am sure gaining ground among the colored people of the South," Niles said, "that they have no longer any use for the white people of the North—that it is time to establish a colored mental and moral republic. I need not give you my views touching that question or tell you how thoroughly in line with the ex-slaveholders wishes it is."[78]

Although the freedmen were beginning to side with the southern Democracy in opposing white Northerners in their schools and churches, they had been conditioned to admire power in slavery and accepted the arbitrary use of it in the hands of black men. They had no experience of the democratic polity of a free church. In a very real sense, the AMA ministers were going into foreign territory where most of the African Americans were either Baptists or Methodists, where the very name "Congregationalist" was so tarred with the abolitionist taint as to be anathema to the whites and almost unknown to the blacks.

Hardy Mobley, with perhaps the least education of those in the list of educated men above, seemed fairly successful in his labors, or else did not allow himself to become so easily discouraged as some of his fellow missionaries. His work with the AMA ended, however, when he clashed with a leading layman, who was also a member of the state legislature, and the unresolved conflict resulted in a split congregation.[79]

John W.A. Shaw would seem at first glance to fit in with the arising ethnocentrism of the southern black. Overly sensitive and contentious, determined that no white man would tell him what to do, he could not work harmoniously with any AMA superintendent. But neither could he work with the freedmen. Not only was he prejudiced against white men, he also disliked those freedmen unfortunate enough (in his view) to have some white blood. And like some other educated African Americans, he had little patience with the failings of the freedmen, and was more demanding of them than a white man would be in the same position.

Shaw and his wife decided to start a pay school of their own at a town called Thunderbolt about four miles from Savannah, with a Sunday school and preaching services as well. Richard Markham helped them to get settled there. Shaw declared he would be "firm and loyal to Congregationalism." For reasons of health and finance, Shaw was back in Washington, D.C. in 1877 and hopeful of again serving the AMA. Shaw was a member of Jeremiah Rankin's First Congregational Church in Washington.[80]

W.A.L. Campbell's two years at the church in Macon were not an unqualified success despite his superior education. Several problems arose because his wife was a Roman Catholic and thus not interested in the work of the church. She also taught some pupils in competition with the AMA school.[81]

John H.H. Sengstacke was born in Savannah, Georgia, of a German father and a Negro mother. The mother died before the Civil War, and the father, fearful that his children might be enslaved, took them (a daughter and John) to Germany, where the daughter remained. Sengstacke was confirmed in the Lutheran Church and well educated, learning to speak four languages and broadening his experience by world travel. After his father's death, he returned to the United States in the almost futile attempt to claim his inheritance. He became a teacher in Savannah and was acquainted with the AMA through its Beach Institute there.

He was a dedicated and hard working man. Since the Lutheran Church was not at work among the freedmen, he had tried the Episcopal Church but found he could not work freely under its hierarchical and theological strictures. He therefore drew up a church form of his own and gathered a group of people with like feelings together. When he heard of Congregationalism through the AMA, he sent for a Congregational manual and discovered that he was at heart a Congregationalist. Happy to find a congenial denominational home, he made his church the Plymouth Congregational Church of Woodville, Georgia, and served it for thirty years until his death.[82]

The African American with perhaps the best education of any of those of his race who served in the churches of the AMA during Reconstruction was **Samuel M. Coles**, born in slavery in Virginia where he somehow managed to acquire the rudiments of education, and was thus—as he put it—"mentally free." After the Civil War, he made his way to Guilford, Connecticut, where he joined the Third Congregational Church. Thanks to that church and the American College and University Society, he completed the collegiate course at Lincoln University and entered the Yale Divinity School in 1873 to prepare for the Congregational ministry. He graduated in 1875, the first African American to complete the full course of theology at Yale.[83]

During his seminary course he spent his summer working for the AMA, the institution he felt was doing the most for the freedmen. In 1874 he served the "black" Congregational Church in Leavenworth, Kansas, a town whose African American community, he said, contained not one educated leader, either among the laity or clergy. While "the majority of the older people" would "not bear real instruction," their educated youngsters were leaving the churches of the ignorant preachers.[84]

The summer of 1875 was spent at his old home of Petersburg, Virginia; and after graduating from Yale, he spent a year working in the Charleston, South Carolina, Congregational Church. Although Coles declared himself to be a Congregationalist, he did not sound like one when he argued that the best course in Charleston would be one in which the AMA ran the church through the office of its pastor. After all, the Charleston people were accepting aid, and that fact might be bluntly brought home to them. This was the only way, Coles felt, that progress could be made among that contentious group. It was "to their discredit," he said, "and yet not more so than any other people having like experiences. They will work better by being forced than they will if left to act in perfect freedom." This was one of the effects of slavery, and would not be easily overcome. "There must be force used until the people learn or are educated to know, that arbitrary force is not a virtue. . . ."[85]

In February of 1877 he began work in the Congregational Church of Corpus Christi, Texas, which had been founded by Aaron Rowe (white) in 1871. On the way there he looked over Florence, Alabama for the AMA, and said the place looked promising, that the small church recently gathered there should be aided, and that a school should be established there also to augment it. Coles served the small church at Corpus Christi until 1880, and was, in the opinion of white AMA missionary B.C. Church, too big a man for the post. The public school Coles taught there was given his name.

Church described Coles as a worker, and said he was "greatly beloved by his people." It may be that Coles's dicta about Charleston was limited to that particulr congregation. Certainly Francis Cardozo had found the African Americans there a contentious people. He declared that when he filled their pulpit (which he did often), he preached on love and Christian forgiveness, for he saw so little of either in that people. He declared flatly that he did not think they were material from which to build a viable Congregational church. Perhaps if the people at Charleston had been a more tractable group, Cardozo might have entered the Congregational ministry to stay.[86]

Implicit in Coles's stance was the idea held by many that Congregationalism was not suited to the freedmen, a theory the men at the Rooms refused to accept. Unfortunately, in some cases, the good of a church was prostituted to the principle of local autonomy. Although the Association made suggestions to its aided fields as to personnel, the final choice was left to the congregation. When **Floyd Snelson** returned from Africa and pressed the people of Midway Church in Georgia to return him to its pulpit, all the men at the Rooms as well as the local AMA agents thought that Joseph E. Smith (who had followed Snelson at Midway) would be better for the church. The congregation, however, preferred Snelson's overbearing bluster to Smith's humble quietness. The AMA did, however, make sure that Snelson would not reimpose his authority over the school (which became Dorchester Academy) by placing the authority for the school in the hands of John McIntosh.

Snelson was an example of a freedman who seemed unable to temper power with humility in the proper proportions when he achieved a position of influence. He found it easier to act like a bishop than like a Congregational pastor. Unfortunately his congregation preferred it that way, although their short experience under Smith had begun a different kind of pastor-and-people relationship that might have matured in time.

Mature Theological Graduates

It was not until there were mature, indigenous graduates who had completed both collegiate and advanced theological training (in contrast to the stopgap intitial AMA programs), that the Association had men of the proper qualifications for black Congregationalism in the South. The AMA African American ministers were individuals, of course, and any discussion of their impact on the work must not lose sight of that fact; but there are some general classifications. As often as not the educated African Americans of the North were as far removed culturally and spiritually from the freedmen of the South as were the white AMA northern ministers. Some educated African Americans like **John W.A. Shaw** and **W.A.L. Campbell** (who was educated in the West Indies and at Howard) seemed even farther removed from the freedmen than the white men were. It was almost as if the educated African Americans could not forgive their own race for its weaknesses, even if those weaknesses were the results of slavery. Black and white missionaries alike deplored the sexual promiscuity, the abuses of tobacco and alcohol; but the white missionaries seemed more willing to forgive what they characterized as the evil fruits of slavery on the one hand and to extend the blessings of democratic church polity on the other, while some black men insisted on the need for paternal oversight.

The Congregationalists of New England glorified in their autonomy—and still do, to the consternation of some state conference executives of the United Church of Christ. One active worker in Massachusetts confided in the author, "We're so autonomous, it's obscene!" But the Congregationalists of the nineteenth century came to see the value in fellowship one with another, for the sharing of ideas and help. For these reasons the regional Associations of churches developed. They operated in a different manner than synods or conferences of other church bodies. The Associations, and later the state Conferences, had no control over a local congregation, but a majority vote of the delegates (both clergy and laity, even from the early days) could register disapproval of a church's course. Associations were also entrusted with the responsibility of examining ministers for ordination and maintaining the standards whereby any clergyperson would have recognized ministerial standing in the denomination. These practices of mutual help and counsel were instituted very early among the churches of the AMA in the South. Often gatherings of clergy heard papers on topics of current interest, which were discussed by those present.

Joseph E. Smith was an example of one of the early graduates of Atlanta's Theology Department who would warrant all the faith and time and money invested in his education. He was sent to fill the pulpit of the Savannah church during Richard Markham's absence in the summer of 1876. He reported to Markham about the "Catos" he met that summer. He had been told that Markham's heart was "wrapped up" in the men. That was fine if indeed they were "*true* men and *worthy* of your love and trust." But Smith did not think so. He mentioned no names in his letter, but the Catos had named names, saying unkind things about each other to Smith. Like the original twelve disciples, each seemed anxious to be greatest. "I do not think they are heart and soul in our work. They do not seem stabled in Congregationalism." They were too ready to say that they would leave for another church if not treated well. Smith thought that they were disappointed in what they had managed to get out of the AMA—that they were "wolves in sheep's clothing."[87]

Smith was born a slave in Smithfield, Virginia, in 1853. During the second year of the Civil War, in territory under the control of federal troops, he was kidnapped, forever separated from his mother and siblings, and taken to Richmond, where he "had the distinction of being sold five times within one day." After the war he went to Atlanta University and was one of its first students and graduates. For thirty-eight years he served his alma mater as a trustee. In 1880 the AMA sent him with Thomas N. Chase to Africa to survey the field there. Something of his character is shown in the fact that "a well known white clergyman of Southern birth" volunteered to take care of his church in his absence, even asking for the church roll in order to make calls.

Smith's last pastorate for the AMA was as minister of the First Congregational Church of Chattanooga, Tennessee, which post began in 1879 and ended in 1917 at his death. He brought that church "from infancy to self-support." He was a leading figure in Chattanooga public life, serving on the school board for many years. This was the same man who stepped aside when Floyd Snelson returned from Africa and wanted to return to Midway Church.[88]

The experience of the AMA showed that it took a very special man indeed—even of those with seven years of higher education—to prosecute the work successfully. He must not only be black, he must not only be willing to work with people almost all of whom were his cultural inferiors, but he must labor for little pay and with great tolerance and affection. He must not only be black, he must have grown up in America's prejudiced climate without having his own sensitivities blunted or his innate compassion poisoned by hate. Francis Lewis Cardozo was such a man, but he preferred to teach and that expertise led him into politics. Joseph E. Smith, George W. Moore, Yancy B. Sims, George C. Collins, and Henry H. Proctor were others who could forgive the sins of white and black alike, and help both races to grow toward the Christian ideal of a society without caste.

NOTES

1. Cardozo, Charleston, June 23, 1865, to Strieby, AMAA.

2. *AM*, X (September, 1866), 193-195, 202-204; XII (June, 1868), 132-133; (July, 1868), 160; XIV (June, 1870), 130-132.

3. Cravath, Cincinnati, Ohio, October 2, 1866, to Jocelyn, AMAA.

4. *AM*, IX (September, 1865), 199-200. (Steward 1904, Arno Press reproduction 1969), has a biographical sketch by William Loren Katz. See also *Nineteenth Annual Report* (1865), 23.

5. *Nineteenth Annual Report* (1865), 21. See also Daniel A. Payne, Proposed Plan, New York, May 8, 1865, and letters of William Harris, Richmond, Virginia, AMAA.

6. See Records of the Session of the Fifteenth Street Presbyterian Church, MSC, Howard University Library.

7. (DeBoer 1994, 223-225).

8. *AM*, XVI (May, 1872), 98.

9. *American Missionary*, XIX (July, 1875), 156, 158.

10. Letters of Markham, AMAA; *The Gospel Trumpet*, I (April, 1877), AMAA; *AM*, XX (April, 1876), 78; LVIII (November, 1904), 302; *Thirtieth Annual Report* (1876), 46.

11. See also letters of Aaron Rowe, R.F. Markham, and Henry Smith, AMAA.

12. See also letters of Henry S. Bennett, AMAA.

13. *AM*, VIII (August, 1864), 189.

14. See also letters of Niles, Aaron Rowe, and Markham, AMAA; *AM*, XVI (October, 1872), 220.

15. *AM*, XV (May, 1871), 100.

16. *AM*, XV (May, 1871, 100; *Twenty-sixth Annual Report* (1872), 61.

17. *Twenty-fourth Annual Report* (1870), 48.

18. *Twenty-fourth Annual Report* (1870), 47; *AM*, XVII (May, 1873), 105.

19. *Twenty-fifth Annual Report* (1871), 27.

20. *Twenty-fifth Annual Report* (1871), 27.

21. Annual Report, St. Marks Congregational Church, Terrebonne, Louisiana, 1873, AMAA; *Thirty-first Annual Report* (1877), 38; *Thirty-second Annual Report* (1878), 48.

22. Annual Report of Gretna Congregational Church, 1873; *AM*, XV (May, 1871), 100; *Twenty-seventh Annual Report* (1873), 77.

23. See letters of both brothers, AMAA; *Twenty-seventh Annual Report* (1873), 81.

24. *Twenty-fourth Annual Report* (1870), 45.

25. Annual Report of Morning Star Congregational Church, Terrebonne, Louisiana, 1873, AMAA.

26. See also letters of B.C. Church, AMAA; *Twenty-seventh Annual Report* (1873), 35; *Thirty-fifth Annual Report* (1881), 79; Annual Report of the Goliad Congregational Church, Goliad, Texas, 1873, AMAA; *AM*, XVI (February, 1872), 33; (October, 1872), 223.

27. See also Annual Report of the African Congregational Church, Paris, Texas, 1873, AMAA; also in the Archives, see letters of Mahlon Willett and W.J. Evans; also *Twenty-seventh Annual Report* (1873), 79.

28. See also letters of Aaron Rowe, AMAA.

29. See also letters of E.E. Rogers, AMAA.

30. See also letters of J.A. Martling, James A. Adams, C.H. Thompson, AMAA; *Twenty-seventh Annual Report* (1873), 76; *Twenty-eighth Annual Report* (1874), 24-25.

31. Annual Report of the Equal Rights Congregational Church, Terrebonne, Louisiana, 1873, AMAA.

32. See also letters from J.W.A. Shaw and R.F. Markham, AMAA; *AM*, XX (April, 1876), 78.

33. See also letters of Henry Reed, George Guilmenott and B.C. Church, AMAA; also, Minutes of a Special Meeting January 18, 1876, Corpus Christi, Texas; protest against the actions of the January 18 meeting, signed by members of the church and J.K. Polk, Clerk, AMAA.

34. *Thirty-first Annual Report* (1877), 55.

35. *Thirty-first Annual Meeting* (1877), 43, 55.

36. *Thirty-second Annual Report* (1878), 54.

37. See also letter of J.E. Roy, AMAA; *AM*, XX (April, 1876), 78.

38. *Thirty-second Annual Report* (1878), 54.

39. *Thirty-second Annual Report* (1878), 55.

40. *Twenty-sixth Annual Report* (1872), 71; *AM*, XV (May, 1871), 61.

41. See also letters of Sarah S. Jackson, AMAA.

42. See also J.E. Roy, Atlanta, Georgia, December 21, 1878, to Strieby; R.F. Markham, Savannah, Georgia, September 21, 1877, to Strieby, AMAA.

43. *Twenty-fourth Annual Report* (1870), 18.

44. *Twenty-fourth Annual Report* (1870), 49; *Twenty-fifth Annual Report* (1871), 38; *Twenty-sixth Annual Report*, 79; *Twenty-seventh Annual Report*, 47, 59, 61-62; *Twenty-eighth Annual Report*, 36, 38, 39, 40; *Twenty-ninth Annual Report*, 55.

45. See the letters of Seaborn Snelson, George Snowden, William A. Golding, AMAA.

46. See the letters of C.W. Francis, AMAA; see also *The Negro—A Congregational Opportunity* (New York, 1920), 16, 66, AMAA; *AM*, LIX (1905), 244, 322.

47. See the letters of Bennett; 9488, undated Fisk University Circular; A.H. Burr, Nashville, October 18, 1871, to Cravath, AMAA; *Forty-ninth Annual Report* (1895), 22.

48. See his letters and also those of Henry S. Bennett, AMAA; *Twenty-seventh Annual Report* (1873), 76, 81.

49. *AM*, XV (August, 1871), 186; XVII (January, 1873), 6, 15; XX (October, 1876); *Thirtieth Annual Report* (1876), 38.

50. See Neale and Bennett letters, AMAA; *AM* (July, 1873), 148.

51. See the letters of Anderson and Bennett, AMAA; *Thirty-first Annual Report* (1877), 44, 62.

52. *AM*, XX (January, 1876), 3; LXXIV (May, 1920), 84; *Thirty-first, Fifty-first, Fifty-third Annual Reports of the AMA.*

53. See James A. Adams, New Orleans, Louisiana, October 31, 1874, to Cravath; February 1, 1875, AMAA.

54. See Annual Report of Lockport Church, LaFourche, La., 1873, AMAA.

55. See also letters of Adams and Martling, AMAA.

56. *AM*, XV (May, 1871), 100; *Twenty-seventh Annual Report* (1873), 77.

57. See also Report of Mt. Horeb Congregational Church, Greenville, Louisiana, 1873, AMAA; letters of S.S. Ashley, James A. Adams, James A. Bartling, AMAA. *Thirty-first Annual Report* (1877), 43.

58. See also letters of S.S. Ashley, James A. Martling, Walter S. Alexander, AMAA; *AM*, XVI (May, 1872), 100.

59. See letter of James A. Hartling, January 26, 1875, to Cravath, AMAA; *Thirty-first Annual Report* (1877), 43.

60. See also letters of James A. Martling, Mrs. James A. Adams, AMAA; *Thirty-first Annual Report* (1877), 43; *AM*, XX (February, 1876), 31.

61. See James A. Martling, New Orleans, January 26, 1875, to Cravath, AMAA.

62. See letters of Mary A. Ashley and S.S. Ashley, AMAA.

63. See also letters of J.B. Reeve, Willis Epps, Frank Haley, Mr. and Mrs. G.J. Webster, AMAA; *AM*, XIX (June, 1875), 129, 159.

64. Circular: Talladega Theological Seminary connected with Talladega College, Talladega, Alabama, July, 1875, AMAA.

65. *Thirty-first Annual Report* (1877), 55.

66. *Twenty-eighth Annual Report* (1874), 29.

67. *Twenty-eighth Annual Report* (1874), 29.

68. *Thirty-second Annual Report* (1878), 49.

69. See also *Thirtieth Annual Report* (1876), 46; *AM*, LXXIII (May, 1919), 103.

70. *Thirty-first Annual Report* (1877), 55.

71. *Ibid.*, 55.

72. *Ibid.*, 55.

73. See also Sims's obituary, *AM*, LXVIII (May, 1914), 102.

74. *Thirty-second Annual Report* (1878), 55.

75. *Thirty-third Annual Report* (1879), 73.

76. See Spencer Snell, *Broken Chains—A Life Sketch* (n.p., n.d.) probably published by the AMA, AMAA.

77. Circular: *Talladega Theological Seminary connected with Talladega College, Talladega, Alabama*, July, 1875, AMAA.

78. A.N Niles, Charleston, South Carolina, June 4, 1873, to Cravath, AMAA.

79. See the letters of Hardy Mobley and Samuel Wakefield, AMAA, Wakefield was a member of the New Iberia, Louisiana, church and, in 1877, a trustee of Straight University.

80. See letters of Shaw, Aaron Rowe, R.F. Markham, and Henry Smith, AMAA.

81. See letters of Campbell, Frank Haley and Deacon Willis Epps, AMAA.

82. See the letters of Sengstacke, Aaron Rowe and R.F. Markham., AMAA; *Thirtieth Annual Report* (1876), 46; *AM*, XX (April, 1876), 78; LVIII (November, 1904), 302.

83. See letters of Coles in 1874 to Cravath and Patton, AMAA.

84. Samuel M. Coles, September 21, 1874, New Haven, to Cravath, AMAA.

85. See letters of Coles from Petersburg, Virginia, and Charleston, especially May n.d., 1876, to Stieby, AMAA.

86. See the letter of Coles from Corpus Christi; also the letters of B.C. Church from Goliad, Texas, and of Francis Cardozo, AMAA.

87. Joseph E. Smith, Savannah, Georgia, October 10, 1876, to Markham, AMAA.

88. *AM*, LIX (December, 1905), 322; LXXI April, 1917), 37. See also Smith letters, AMAA.

XIII

THE AMA AND BLACK RELIGIOUS GROUPS

Proposed Plan of the Executive Committee of the Parent M. Society of the A.M.E. Church, for co-operation with the Executive Committee of the A.M. Association.

a. We propose to furnish an indefinite number of laborers as missionaries to the Freedmen of the South, whose testimonials shall be satisfactory to the Executive Committee of both the A.M.E.M. Society and the American Missionary Association.

b. We propose to furnish one half of the support needed for said missionaries, provided the Executive Committee of the A.M. Association will furnish the other half. . . .

—Daniel A. Payne [AME bishop],
New York, May 8, 1865,
AMA Archives

The American Missionary Association had both a co-operative and a competitive relationship with the African Methodist Episcopal Church, although the two organizations were far apart in many respects. Polity is an obvious example. While the AMA promoted democratic local autonomy, the AME Church operated under the episcopal system, an approach defended by the presiding bishop at the AME Conference (bishops and ministers) in 1852: "To those who would have the Church of the Living God reduced to a form corresponding to the American republic, let me say, stop and consider well what you are about." He then drew a

327

contrast between a monarchy and the government of the United States and concluded: "The form of a government is nothing; its just laws, impartial administration and equal freedom, everything." How there could be "equal freedom" in a church ruled by bishops, all of whose decisions were made without lay participation, the AME prelate did not explain.[1]

The AMA also had some co-operative arrangements with representatives of the African Methodist Episcopal Zion Church. Although the AMA did not specifically establish and support churches in Virginia headed by black men during the period under study, it did support James B. Tynes (AME) and John N. Mars (AMEZ) in the Portsmouth area while the Civil War was still in progress. Huston Reedy (AME) was employed in Louisiana.

Mars preached on Sunday either in Norfolk or Portsmouth and assisted William D. Harris in the Gosport School during the week. Harris and Mars also started a Sunday school at Whitehead Farm near Portsmouth, with 125 in attendance. Mars had had difficulties with James F. Sisson (white), a competing AME minister. A noteworthy situation arose in the South as the slaves were freed. Many of them—as slaves— had been associate "back gallery" members of the churches to which their masters belonged. With the coming of the Civil War, the former slaves were cast adrift, and the two black branches of Methodism in the North sent representatives down, each Church anxious to add the southern black Methodists to its membership.

At Portsmouth the AMA had commissioned John N. Mars (AMEZ) as its missionary. At Norfolk James F. Sisson (AMA missionary) decided to become a minister in the AME Church. Although Sisson resigned as AMA missionary, under the plan of co-operation between the AMA and his new denomination, a part of his support probably still came from the AMA. Sisson claimed Gosport Methodist Church as his by the authority of Bishop Daniel Payne; so Mars did not preach there (to the people whose children he taught), but went only to help Harris in his Sunday school. The Sunday school continued to prosper despite the fact that the church was in a sad state. Harris was sure that things would be otherwise there if Brother Mars had been allowed to take charge of both church and Sabbath school.[2]

Other notable AMEZ personalities aided at various times by the AMA include Jermain Wesley Loguen, William Henry Hillery, and Cicero R. Harris (all later bishops of the denomination). Robert Harris, afterward an active member of the AMEZ Church, was an AMA teacher in Fayetteville, North Carolina. J.W. Hood, later bishop, advised the AMA about the disposition of its normal schools in the area, when he was an agent of the board of education in the Office of Public Instruction in North Carolina.[3]

Daniel Alexander Payne, free-born in Charleston, South Carolina, and educated in the North, did much to move his denomination from an obscurantist stance to a sustainer of Wilberforce University and, if not dedicated to an educated ministry, at least not thoroughly opposed to one. His job was not easy. His illiterate fellow churchmen did not take it lightly when he referred to "heathenish," "disgraceful," and "disrespecting modes of worship" of AMA preachers. He was often unpopular with the leaders of his denomination, and his own educated ministry was not acceptable to many of the AME churches. Many of the illiterate clergy might be proud of being unable to read the Bible, but to Payne the fact that the denomination's first four bishops did not have even a primary school education was a cause to mourn.[4]

Payne received his theological training at a Lutheran seminary and became a Methodist. After six years in the ministry (two in Washington and four in Baltimore), he decided to spend the rest of his life in the North and asked the AMA to appoint him a missionary in Philadelphia.[5] The proposed job did not materialize, and that was doubtless a loss to the Association but a blessing to the AME Church, for it retained as a leader an idealist devoted to uplifting the educational and spiritual standards of the black ministry.

In 1864 the AMA presented a two-fold proposition to the Baltimore Annual Conference of the AME Church asking that denomination to furnish buildings for the education of the freedmen, and to furnish "wherever possible" board for the AMA teachers. That the proposition was accepted unanimously by the Conference, was probably due in large measure to Daniel Payne. That same year the AME Church released a commissioned missionary, Gorham Greely (white) into the care of the AMA, and the latter commissioned Mrs. Greely as well (as the AME had been unable to do).[6]

As the President of Wilberforce University, Payne was involved in raising money and seemed, as he told George Whipple in 1864, to be "struggling almost single handed to build a great Educational institution. . . ." He asked the AMA to supply $500 or $1000 for the support of teachers at Wilberforce. Whipple's reply was an apology for not being able to contribute. There was the serious consideration of being constitutionally prevented from contributing funds given to the AMA for a purely racial institution in a free state. Although the funds of the AMA could not conscientiously be donated to Wilberforce, individual members of the Association did make contributions, and at least two commissioned teachers of the AMA served on the faculty of the school at Xenia, Ohio. Esther T. Maltbie (AMA teacher at Portsmouth) became the Female Principal at Wilberforce, and in a reverse exchange, Mrs. B.Y. Messenger (who had later held that same office at Wilberforce), joined the staff of the AMA's Washburn Academy at Beaufort, North Carolina. There were eight students at Wilberforce in January, 1865, some of whom had just escaped through rebel lines, and there was an oppressive debt on the property. [7]

As early as 1859, the AMA requested information from Payne about AME ministers for the Mendi Mission in Africa and received his hearty cooperation. Payne said he had "a strong desire to do all in my power to aid you in your glorious undertaking to Christianize benighted Africa."[8]

In 1864 Payne enlisted the aid of the AMA "to open a model school for girls in Baltimore." He was in favor of the teaching methods of the AMA and hoped that "New England ideas and ideals" would "ultimately" prevail in "the entire South."[9]

In the spring of 1865, Payne proposed that the AME supply missionaries and the AMA pay half the salaries of such men. By this plan the Association would really be supporting the AME Church in planting denominational churches among the freedmen. This was truly an anomalous situation: unsectarian Congregationalism helping to sustain a Methodist group that was not only sectarian, but whose polity was almost diametrically opposed to the Congregational Way. It was only possible in the first place because of the unsectarian, unecclesiastical nature of the AMA, and in the second place because of the nature of Bishop Payne—a member of the free missions organization during its beginnings in the Union Missionary Society, who sustained a warm relationship with Lewis Tappan.[10]

Thus the AMA found itself in the same situation it had endured in Canada with Lewis C. Chambers, aiding African Methodist ministers who were under the paramount and ecclesiastical control of a bishop. Such was its relationship with Gorham Greely at Portsmouth in 1864, and would have been the case with James Sisson at the same place had he not resigned his AMA commission when he joined the AME Church.[11]

Having secured the cooperation of the AMA, Payne proceeded to organize the South Carolina Conference within a week of the meeting in New York, with six missionaries stationed there. In addition three were assigned to Georgia and two to North Carolina. Payne apologized for the fact that most of the men were uneducated, and asked for aid, stating the salaries he thought each would need. Of the eleven men recommended by Payne, there is evidence that James Anderson Handy (Wilmington, N.C.) and Theophilus Gould Steward (Beaufort, S.C., River Circuit) were supported by the AMA.[12]

South Carolina

Charleston City	Richard H. Cain
Charleston Circuit	Richard Vanderhorst
Georgetown Circuit	John Graham
Beaufort River Circuit	Theophilus Gould Steward
Hilton Head Circuit	James H.A. Johnson
Edisto Island	William Bradwell

Georgia

Savannah	Anthony L. Stanford
Ogeechee River Circuit	William Bentley
Georgia State Mission	William Gaines

North Carolina

Wilmington	James A. Handy
Raleigh	George W. Broudie

Payne recommended $700 yearly salaries for Charleston, Savannah, Beaufort, Hilton Head, Wilmington, and Raleigh, and $500 for those on circuits. No doubt the AMA considered those rather high salaries for uneducated men, particularly since some aid would be expected from the congregations gathered. At that time, the salary of Thomas Cardozo, AMA Superintendent in Charleston, S.C., was $41 per month, plus board.

William D. Harris

Ironically, the move of William D. Harris from the Wesleyan Connection to the AME Church was helped along by the AMA. Harris, a Wesleyan Methodist from Cleveland, Ohio, and one of the truly fine African American minister-teachers in AMA service, had been an AMA teacher in Portsmouth, Virginia, before the end of the Civil War. He was more than happy to do all that he could "for the elevation and salvation of my people in this auspicious and momentous hour as they have just begun to struggle up from chattelism, to manhood, from bruised and mangled slaves, to good citizens. . . ." But after adding up his accounts for the year, he found that expenses exceeded salary in the amount of $64.48; so he had to have a raise or be allowed to take an additional position. In offering to go anywhere in the cause of suffering humanity, Harris reminded the AMA officers that no work was possible unless there was military protection or a preponderance of blacks.[13]

A cooperative arrangement among John Mifflin Brown (corresponding secretary of the AME Baltimore Conference), Bishop Payne, and the AMA resulted in Harris becoming pastor of the alleged five-hundred member Third Street AME Church of Richmond, Virginia. Brown had said that it would be an excellent arrangement, for Harris could give some of his time to the AMA school held in the same building; thus the AMA could share in his support. Unfortunately, communications broke down in the AME camp, and the building was leased to the Boston Freedmen's Society.[14]

Elizabeth P. Worthington (white), a Presbyterian minister's daughter from Vineland, New Jersey, was anxious that she had not received a commission for the 1865-66 school year, and expressed a strong desire to be sent to Richmond. She had begun her teaching with William Harris, "whose fervent piety did much towards making the School a pleasant one." When her request was refused on the ground that she was a poor disciplinarian, she defended herself stoutly, quoting Harris who had written urging her to return to the work to which he felt God had called her. He had written that the organ that she had played in the North Street Methodist Church at Portsmouth had "emitted no sound" since she left and the people were asking when she would return. She declared that her critic was certainly not so well qualified to judge her teaching ability as Harris, with whom she had spent seven of her eight months of work.[15]

Harris was ordained an elder (minister) at the Central Ohio Yearly Conference of the Wesleyan Connection, a group that considered the AME Church extremely illiberal in requiring a minister to join their denomination before serving one of their churches. H.B. Knight, secretary of the Central Conference of the WMC, wrote AMA Secretary Strieby: "I hope the Assoc. will oblige these denominations it helps, to occupy the liberal basis the Asso. is planted on. To *force* men to join them, or not serve their churches, is not right."[16]

Evidently AMA Secretary Samuel Hunt had been thinking of organizing an all-colored staff at Portsmouth under the leadership of William Harris. But Harris had joined the AME Church (after receiving, he thought, permission from the AMA), in order to work for both organizations, and thus make enough money to support his family. And the AME bishop sent him to Richmond.[17]

Despite the fact that his church building was used by another society during the day, Harris opened a night school there on the plan of the AMA school at Norfolk. By December it looked as if he could expect no aid from the AME Society and but little from the alleged six-hundred member church. (He expressed doubt about the number of members, since they were scattered and he had been unable to find many of them.) There was such great need in the city that he thought many would starve unless supplies came from the North. The situation was equally bad in North Carolina, his home state. There many had been turned off their newly acquired lands, or allowed to remain by the preempting owners until the crops were in and then "driven off without pay and threatened with death" if they reported it to the Bureau: "and then these former owners raise the Cry that they won't work without compulsion." It seemed the whites were determined to reduce the blacks to a condition worse than slavery, and Harris hoped "Congress and the Capitalists of the North" would "counteract" that spirit.

Harris conducted two Sunday schools in addition to the one in his church: at the orphan asylum at Camp Lee, one and a half miles from the city, and another at Howard Grove Hospital. The ladies of his church formed a sewing circle to help the poor, and Harris asked the AMA to send goods and clothing for them to distribute. His was a very strenuous week that began with a sunrise prayer service on Sunday at 7 a.m. and ended on Friday night at 9 p.m. with the close of the night school[18]

Harris did not find at Richmond the naked prejudice against African Americans that whites exhibited at Portsmouth. There was a spirit of caste at Richmond, to be sure, and hatred against blacks, Yankees, and especially against Harris who was both and also "the yankee nigger teacher," stirred up and abetted by "2 or 3 Secesh Editors" Harris called the "most bitter enemies of the colored people." Most of Richmond's racial problems, he said, were incited by the *Examiner* and *The Times.*

Harris expressed the belief to W.S. Bell, AMA Superintendent at Norfolk, that the AMA could establish and sustain schools in Richmond "with as little expense as in Norfolk." He believed that the AMA was "more needed and can do more than any other Society. Sectarianism is already, almost overwhelming, and is mistaken by some for Christianity, ought this to be strengthened? God forbid."

He was more than a little happy that the excesses of black religion were absent from his church. He told Bell that he could worship with the Richmond congregation without embarrassment. "I mean you will find very little of that wild excitement—shrieks, and boisterous demonstrations, rolling on the floor, and a kind of dancing around the altar which you, and I, will always remember with a shudder." In Richmond proper he established four mission churches and three others in the surrounding area (Staunton, Wytheville, and Fredericksburg), supplying them with teachers and exhorters from his own congregation whom he trained for the work.[19]

In order to deflate the spirit of sectarianism, interest the people in the cause of education, and demonstrate to the friends in the North that the freedmen were "anxious" to do all they could "for *their own* elevation and education," he organized a Union Educational Association in his church and invited others to join. By November, 1866, three black churches in Richmond and one in Manchester had done so, and $30 had been given to the treasury, a small sum, but Harris did "Not despise the day of small things."

The people were in great distress and many had left for the North to hunt for work. The previous winter had been a hard one, the people forced to pay "exorbitant rents for cellars, stables & smoke houses." Rents were as high as $25 a month for one room. The church was unable to meet its commitment for its share of his salary. But Harris had never in his life experienced the kind of desperation and want of the winter of 1866-67 in Richmond. He used what money he received from friends in the North to keep emergency supplies for the starving and freezing people. Some families had burned all their possessions, even their bedsteads, in order to try to keep their children warm.

In mid-January Captain Bates, Assistant Superintendent of the Freedmen's Bureau, asked Harris to screen applicants for relief and to write recommendations for fuel and rations for those he found in need. He asked the AMA if it approved of his accepting the work, for it did interrupt his studies. But it also enabled him to reach "a large class of persons that never attend church." He did not neglect the work of the church, but the extra time came from that allotted to his own personal education.

When the AMA determined on the course of planting Congregational churches among the freedmen and William Harris realized that his association with the AMA would be ended, he was depressed. His three years in the South had taught him that the South needed "preachers as much as teachers from the North, Northern Theology, as well as Yankee Literature." He believed "that the teacher & the preacher must go together or the Education of the Freedmen and the Evangelization of the South will be incomplete, if not a failure." He did not hold the argument valid that the freedmen were religious enough: "There is much dross in the gold—slavery has corrupted their religion as well as their intellects." Impoverished as they and the South were, they would be "very little better prepared to support their ministers than their schools." What Harris implied but was too modest to say, was that the freedmen needed educated men like himself to bring the enlightening force of the whole gospel to the colored men of the South.[20]

Harris was moved by his Church from Richmond to Georgetown, D.C., in 1867, much to his and the AMA's surprise, and the next year was moved again, this time to Charleston. Late in 1868 he was married to Elizabeth P. Worthington, the white AMA teacher who had assisted him in Virginia. In 1869 his bishop assigned him to Columbia, South Carolina, and he appears still to have been there in 1871, when Mrs. Dr. Harris sent the AMA a down payment on a life membership for her husband. Twice—once in Charleston and again in Columbia—Harris appealed successfully to the AMA on the part of his daughter Charlotte, asking that she be commissioned. Charlotte had attended Wilberforce for a year, all that her father could afford.

It was unfortunate for the AMA that it did not begin soon enough planting Congregational churches in the South to secure William Harris for that denomination. By the time they did, Harris admitted that there was much to deplore in the AME Church, but decided that it therefore needed his help and he would not desert it. As it was, he worked against sectarianism within the AME Church and was proud of the resolutions passed against prejudice by the Baltimore Annual Conference in April, 1867. And it is no great surprise that William Harris was secretary of the Report on Church Union presented and adopted by the first delegated General Conference of the AME Church in 1872.[21]

John Mifflin Brown

John Mifflin Brown, who had been George Whipple's student at Oberlin and who would become an AME bishop, was probably the prime mover in obtaining William Harris for his denomination, having declared that he wished there were "a dozen" William Harrises in Virginia.[22] Brown and his wife were in charge of the AMA Mission Home No. 3 in the Portsmouth-Norfolk area (48 Bermuda Street, Norfolk). During the war years Brown was the corresponding secretary of the Parent Home and Foreign Missionary Society of the AME Church (of which Society Bishop Payne was president).

In the 1870s, after Brown had become a bishop and was serving as a trustee of Howard University, his affectionate correspondence with the AMA changed, a change arising from the conviction that the AMA was a serious competitor in the South—and not just a source of funds for AME use. Bishop Brown led an official meeting of the officers of his Church at Memphis, Tennessee, in 1876, where copies of John Mercer Langston's Chillicothe speech denouncing white benevolence were distributed; and the AMA Southern Workers Conference, held at Atlanta, Georgia, in the spring of 1875, was much discussed.[23] Henry S. Bennett of Fisk's Theology Department "was pretty thoroughly canvassed and denounced, and the AMA work in general quite heartily sneered at." Andrew J. Steele, AMA principal of LeMoyne Institute at Memphis, was asked by fellow workers to attend the AME meeting in order to explain the AMA's position, but "deemed silence the better plan." The AME Conference "complained bitterly" of the practice of the AMA of erecting buildings in the South and retaining the deeds instead of turning them over to the local colored community. Such a practice as the AME officers advised would mean that in many cases the AMA schools would then be in AME hands.

Steele advised the men at the Rooms not to be concerned with the AME opposition. Such meetings as Brown's started the people thinking, Steele said, and in any comparison of AMA personnel and AME preachers and their use of funds, the AME would be the one to suffer. Bennett, as head of the Theology Department at Fisk, was active in founding Congregational churches and staffing them with theologues from Fisk. Steele said that the AME meeting "had an indirect effect in calling attention to the well known fact that most of the money raised by their churches, no small amount, is squandered by their dishonest ministers and agents."

In 1876 Bishop Brown wrote to Professor A.K. Spence of Fisk asking if Moses R. Johnston, AME minister of Nashville, would be a good choice for president of Howard University. This would indicate that Brown at least was one black member of Howard's trustees not completely settled on John Mercer Langston for that post and interested in securing an AME for it. Bennett did not think that Johnson had the business qualifications for the position, although he was better educated than most AME ministers. In addition, if Johnston were elected president, Howard "would become AME a consummation which you will not, probably, desire."[24]

Henry McNeal Turner

An element of opposition to AMA work in Savannah, Georgia, appeared in the formidable person of Henry McNeal Turner, AME minister and eventual bishop. In 1866 he had felt friendly enough toward the AMA, and, as elder in charge of Northern Georgia and School Agent of the Georgia Equal Rights Association (under Bishop Payne), he sent a long letter to AMA Secretary Whipple, listing Sabbath schools of the AME Church that needed books and Bibles and asked for aid in each case.[25]

In 1874 Turner, called by AMA Superintendent Rowe "the leading spirit among the colored people" of Savannah, was making plans to start a free colored school and bring in the best possible colored educators. They—like the city school board—would also want the AMA's Beach building. Aaron Rowe begged the AMA to find him some black teachers to quiet the opposition. Instead, the AMA rented its building to the local board, with disastrous results to their work in Savannah.

When the cornerstone of the Congregational Church of Savannah was laid in 1875, Turner delivered an hour-long address for the occasion. But in 1876 Dr. Turner did open a private school in his church in the city. His son had recently been ejected from Atlanta University, and Turner vowed to do all he could against the AMA.[26]

Interdenominational Friction

In the tug of war between the South and the benevolent institutions that gained in force toward the end of Reconstruction, it sometimes seemed to AMA personnel that the black Baptists and Methodists were actually on the side of the South in its efforts to rid the country of northern teachers. Charges were made by AME ministers like Francis Peek of Atlanta that the AMA "had declared the intention of destroying the AME Church in the South."[27] And while it was understandable when the church leaders of the black communities counselled their people to accept the free schools of the southern white establishment and remove their children from the AMA schools, it was most often a case of replacing good schools with inadequate ones.

In 1848, the great African American abolitionist, Henry Highland Garnet, had castigated the blacks of the North for their "monster meetings" which were but "sham and parade" while education and cultural affairs went unfunded. In 1877, John D. Smith, black Congregational minister in Mobile, deplored the excursions held by the AME churches there. He estimated that African Americans spent "over two hundred thousand dollars annually to keep up their pernicious excursions in the State of Alabama. As Superintendent Ashley explained, black pastors arranged such excursions always "under a religious pretext." In the process they made a great deal of money, the railroads giving the arranging preacher "a certain sum per passenger." Criticisms like those of Smith did not rest lightly with the AME establishment.

Another cause of black indignation against the AMA was an article written by Washington Gladden (member of the AMA Executive Committee 1871-1875), "The Southern Question," published in the New York *Independent.* In the article Gladden told some of the problems that the freedmen faced, particularly the violence they risked when attempting to vote. But he also said that uneducated black politicians were sometimes "rascals who have robbed the state" and added to the "bitter and wicked race prejudice" of the whites. The answer, as Gladden saw it, could not be left to politics, agreeing with a previous editorial in the *Independent* that the only hope for the South lay in "the education and Christianization of the Negro."[28]

Several AMA teachers were members of the AME Church, among them Mary Still is noteworthy. In general the AME's association with the AMA was a profitable one for the AME Church. AME ministers were sustained while building up congregations for the denomination. William Harris attributed the success of James A. Handy's North Street AME Church, Portsmouth, mainly to the missionary labors of AMA teachers and missionaries there, "for this is the church in which a day and Sabbath-school have flourished for at least a year and a half."[29]

Several of their leading ministers received their collegiate and/or theological education at AMA schools. Several AME

bishops were educated in AMA schools: Joseph Simeon Flipper,
H.B. Parks, William Henry Heard, all attended Atlanta University,
and Heard taught there a year. Abraham Lincoln Gaines attended
Knox Institute at Athens, Georgia, and Atlanta University.
Decatur Ward Nichols went to Avery Institute and Howard;
Cornelius Thaddeus Shaffer went to Berea College.[30]

Many preachers in the South were taught to read and given
the basis of a theological education by AMA teachers and ministers
who gathered the local black clergy into evening classes. And the
example of educated ministers forced the AME Church to provide
educated ministers also or lose all its young people.[31]

It was this last reason—the raising of the general level of
black religion in the South by example—that encouraged the AMA
in the belief that its planting of Congregational churches was not
just the compounding of sectarianism, nor the giving of more
religion to people who had too much already. AMA churches
presented a different kind of religion, one which when properly
followed imposed New Testament ethics on everyday life. For it
was not the emotionalism of black religion that was at fault—here
in fact it could teach something perhaps to its white brethren—but
the fact that it was religion without morality, a magical system of
salvation divorced from ethical imperatives. The freedmen did not
need "more preaching or worship or enthusiasm, but *an entirely
new ideal of Christian character.* . . ."

Bishop Payne asked the AMA for the address of Sella
Martin, and evidently tried to persuade Martin to enter the ministry
of the AME Church by pointing out the rapid growth of that
denomination in the South. Martin's reaction was not quite what
Payne had hoped, for he used the information to persuade
Presbyterians to contribute to the work of the AMA: "Bishop
Payne had just sent me . . . a private letter showing the enormous
increase of his denomination among the freedmen; and after
explaining what I believed to be the reasons of it—namely the love
of animal excitement among all ignorant people, and their regard
for high-sounding titles, as well as the seductiveness of social class
meetings, when they enjoyed at once the pleasure of boasting about
their spiritual strength and enjoyments and gratified the gregarious-
ness of their natural disposition, I asked him if he thought an
attempt to make Presbyterians of them while in this moral and

intellectual state would be attended with success. His reply was characteristic 'It might be so attended' he said 'but it would be a very bad thing for Presbyterianism if it were.'"[32]

AFRICAN CIVILIZATION SOCIETY

The African Civilization Society (ACS) was another religious organization with which the AMA cooperated. The ACS, like the AMA, was unsectarian. It began in 1858 in New York City (offices at 26 Bible House) with the purpose of promoting "the Evangelization and Civilization of Africa, as well as the welfare of her children in all lands." Concomitant with that aim was the destruction of the African slave trade, "the promotion of the growth of cotton and other products there . . . and generally, the elevation of the condition of the colored population of our country, and of other lands." Like the AMA with which it hoped to cooperate, the ACS was a missionary organization requiring "only those doctrines known as evangelic" of its missionaries. Two members of its charter Board of Directors were also members of the Executive Committee of the AMA: the president of the Society, Henry Highland Garnet, and Dr. Alonzo S. Ball (white). Joseph Parrish Thompson (white), pastor of Broadway Tabernacle, who was one of its vice presidents in 1861, was a vice president of the AMA from 1864 to 1867.[33]

Elymas Payson Rogers

A cooperative venture was worked out in 1860 whereby Elymas Payson Rogers, a member of the Board of Directors of the ACS and since 1846 pastor of the Plane Street Presbyterian Church, Newark, New Jersey, would represent both the ACS and the AMA on an exploratory mission to Africa. His purpose was to look for suitable locations for the establishment of mission stations. Information communicated by missionaries at Mendi had persuaded the men at the Rooms in New York that the interior of Africa was far more healthy than the coastal region where the Mendi Mission stood. Rogers, accompanied by Stephen V. Douglass (also African American), was "to visit Lagos, and other places on the West Coast of Africa, and the Yoruba country interior from Lagos." He was expected to spend a year there.

Rogers was a product of the Talcott Street Congregational Church (black) of Hartford, Connecticut. He and Amos G. Beman were "ministers raised up" by this church served by J.W.C. Pennington, Amos N. Freeman, James A. Prince, Reading B. Johns, William W. Mallery (all members of the AMA) during its history. The church lives today as Faith Congregational Church, Hartford.[34]

They sailed November 1, 1860, on the *Daylight* for Freetown; Dr. and Mrs. Hinman of the Mendi Mission were on the same vessel. Rogers thought that Dr. Hinman had some rather "radical" ideas, but perhaps not too radical for a missionary. Both Hinmans seemed to be "persons of ardent piety," filled with "the right spirit for the missionary work" which demanded "men and women of more than ordinary salvation."

Rogers's heart "leaped" when he stood upon African soil for the first time and saw its beauty. He asked himself as he had done so often before seeing his fatherland, why it was plagued with the slave trade. The answer he once again decided lay in the inscrutable mind of God. Yet he believed that Africa had a "bright future," that "Ethiopia shall stretch forth her hand unto God." That golden promise he thought would soon come to pass. Certainly the awakened interest in Africa on the part of people everywhere meant that God would soon "redeem his people." Rogers was impressed with the results he saw of Christian philanthropy in Sierra Leone. He was especially glad to see black men—almost all of them native Africans—serving as public officers, guards, and military men. It was gratifying to attend worship services led by black ministers. He was encouraged; missionaries should be sent, for the field was "white all ready to harvest."[35]

Rogers wrote again after he had visited Monrovia, Bassa, Sinou, and Cape Palmas. He talked of the many Africans who were "idolatrous and superstitious," who could be turned "from darkness to light" only by "civilization and the gospel of Christ." It would take both education and religion, working side by side to "raise their moral condition." Livingstone had been right when he said that a missionary must be more than a man with a Bible under his arm. "And missionary societies should so establish and arrange their missions, that the arts of civilized life may be taught in connection with the gospel." He sincerely hoped such a policy would be pursued "by our society."

The need for the gospel to accompany the trappings of civilization to Africa was made apparent in his conversations with the Kroomen along the coast. Their relations with the Western World consisted in meeting its representatives among the sailors arriving at their ports. Rogers learned that the Kroomen kept the Sabbath by buying a bottle of rum and drinking it. Sailors taught them to cheat, to blaspheme, and to drink; yet Rogers was told these same Kroomen might be "among the first" who would be civilized and Christianized in Africa.[36]

Rogers had always shown an interest in the work of the AMA in Africa, and for several years prior to his journey had apprised the Association of his wish to be commissioned as a missionary. Some obstacle had always prevented the fulfillment of his desire until 1860. Having looked for qualified African Americans to serve as their agents on such a mission to Africa, the officers of the AMA were pleased to have acquired the services of a man of such ability as Elyman P. Rogers. His final message from Africa was a call to mission and sacrifice:

> Oh! that some of the hundreds of our people, who can well be spared from America, could feel it their duty to come here and labor in the missionary work; and in the end God will plentifully reward them. True they may fall at their post, as hundreds of Christian men and women have already done, but they may derive consolation from the thought that, if they lose their lives, they shall find them again.

It was his farewell. Elymas Payson Rogers died in Africa and was buried at Cape Palmas. His wife, whose protests had kept him from going to Africa sooner, gave his estate through the AMA to educate an African boy for the Presbyterian ministry.[37]

NOTES

1. (Payne 1891, 291-292). It was not until 1872 that the General Conference of the AME Church permitted lay delegates, see (Smith 1922, 98).

2. See the letters of Harris and Mars for 1864, AMAA.

3. See Hood's letters from 1866-70; see also Henry B. Blake, Wilmington, N.C., December 4, 1868, to Smith, AMAA. In 1869-70, Samuel S. Ashley, former area superintendent for the AMA, was Superintendent of Public Instruction for North Carolina.

4. (Wright 1963, 266-279); (Smith 1922, 376); (Payne 1891, 419).

5. Payne, September 25, 1848, to William Harned, AMAA.

6. Payne, Washington, April 29, 1864, to Jocelyn; Xenia, Ohio, September 14, 1864, to Whipple, AMAA.

7. Letters of Payne, Maltbie, AMAA; (Payne 1888, 155); (Smith 1922, 76); *Twenty-sixth Annual Report* (1872), 47; circular, "Wilberforce University," No. 111955, AMAA.

8. Payne, June 13, 1859, to "Rev. & Dear Brother," AMAA.

9. (Payne 1888, 159, 163); see also letters of John A. Payne, John M. Brown, S.L. Hammond and N. Noyes, AMAA.

10. Manuscript: "Proposed Plan of the Executive Committee of the Parent M. Society of the A.M.E. Church, for Co-operation with the Executive Committee of the A.M. Association," New York, May 8, 1865, signed by Daniel A. Payne.

11. David Hotchkiss, Canada West, July 13; July 22; August 8, 1857; March 16; March 22, 1858, to Whipple, AMAA; these are all letters that deal with the difficulties Hotchkiss had with the AME Church and its representatives in Canada. For Chambers, see (DeBoer 1994, 184-188); see also letters of Gorham Greely in which he explains the necessity of submission to the power of the bishop.

12. Payne, Xenia, Ohio, July 6, 1865, to Whipple, AMAA.

13. Harris, Delaware, Ohio, July 26, 1865, to Strieby, AMAA.

14. See letters of Harris and Payne in 1865, AMAA.

15. Letters of Elizabeth P. Worthington, AMAA.

16. Knight, Cleveland, September 5, 1865, to Strieby, AMAA.

17. Letters of William D. Harris, 1865-66, AMAA.

18. William D. Harris letters, 1865-66, AMAA.

19. Harris, May 3, 1867, to Whipple, AMAA. Harris sent out altogether 3 local preachers, 4 exhorters, 5 day school teachers, and 13 Sunday school teachers.

20. Letters of William D. Harris, 1866-67; undated clipping from Richmond *New Nation* (a rebel paper) [December, 1866], AMAA.

21. See letters of William D. Harris and E.P. Worthington Harris, 1867-71, AMAA; "Preamble and Resolutions Passed at Baltimore Annual Conference, A.M.E. Church, April, 1867."

22. Brown, October 27, 1864, to Whipple, AMAA.

23. A.J. Steele, Memphis, Tennessee, October 19, 1875, to Strieby, AMAA; *AM,* XIX (June, 1875), 122-134.

24. Henry S. Bennett, Nashville, December 8, 1876, AMAA.

25. Turner to Whipple, No.20056; R.F. Markham, Savannah, February 23, 1876, to Strieby, AMAA.

26. Markham, February 23, 1876, to Strieby, AMAA; *AM,* XIX (August, 1875), 186.

27. Ashley, Atlanta, August 11, 1877, to Strieby, AMAA.

28. (DeBoer 1994, 49); Smith, September 18, 1877, to Strieby, AMAA. *AM,* XX (November, 1876), 253-255.

29. *AM,* VIII (October, 1864), 234-235.

30. (Wright 1963, *passim*).

31. *AM*, XX (October, 1876), 225.

32. Payne, August 5, 1868; Martin, London, England, July 10, 1868, AMAA; *AM*, XIX (June, 1875), 124.

33. Constitution of the African Civilization Society, 1858, AMAA; *AM*, III (June, 1859), 129.

34. See *Contributions to the Ecclesiastical History of Connecticut* (Hartford, 1861), 406; *Contributions to the Ecclesiastical History of Connecticut, II* (Hartford, 1967), 278-279. The church was called African Congregational until 1837 when it was changed to Colored Congregational. *AM*, IV (December, 1860), 274; see also Memo No. 78397 regarding Elymas P. Rogers, 1861; S.V. Douglass, Cape Palmas, Liberia, West Africa [1861], to Whipple, AMAA; *Fourteenth Annual Report* (1860), 18.

35. Rogers, Sierra Leone, West Africa, December 2, 1860, to Whipple, AMAA; *AM*, V (March, 1861), 49-50.

36. Rogers, Cape Palmas, Liberia, January, n.d., 1861, to Whipple, AMAA; *AM*, V (April, 1861), 73-74.

37. Henry B. Stewart, Greenville, Liberia, February 7, 1861, to Whipple; see also the letters of Rogers and Mrs. Rogers, AMAA; *AM*, V (May, 1861), 112; *Fifteenth Annual Report* (1861), 11, 17-18.

XIV

PREJUDICE AND PATERNALISM: WHITE AND BLACK IN THE AMA

The Association has never been foolish enough to believe that any race could be educated by the missionaries of an outside race. Every race must educate itself; must provide its own leadership. That is true of China, of Japan, and of the South. The Association is not only convinced that the Negro is capable of the higher education, but that we are under democratic and Christian obligation to give it to him, and that only thus can we educate the educators, teach the teachers and lead the leaders, which an aspiring race demands. This has become especially imperative on account of the new race consciousness and faith in themselves which is the inevitable product of the education afforded during the last fifty years. It is always dangerous to the supremacy of a ruling race to bring education to the exploited—it is only more dangerous not to.

—*Our Goodly Heritage,* 1925

It is understandable that many of the difficulties arising between black and white employees of the American Missionary Association were perceived solely as racial problems by the blacks involved. Not all the instances where African Americans failed either to obtain a desired position or to perform adequately in positions actually achieved, however, can be blamed on prejudiced whites. This is especially true of AMA relationships with African Americans. The men at the Rooms in New York realized that most often the first reaction of an African American to a canceled commission or a word of advice would be that he was being discriminated against because of his color. It was a favored ploy of

347

white Southerners and also of black men, who wished to discredit
the work of the AMA or of white teachers generally for sectarian
and selfish reasons, to spread the word that AMA personnel were
prejudiced.

This scheme was used to estrange Mrs. Elizabeth Keckley
and Mrs. William Slade, socially conscious African American
women in Washington, D.C., from AMA workers Rachel Patten
and Mary Doxey.[1] One black AMA teacher, Nathan Tappan
Condol, spread such rumors to discredit white AMA workers Selig
G. Wright and John D. Backenstose in the interests of Methodism
and his own reputation among the freedmen in Aberdeen,
Mississippi.[2]

The Mississippi case so upset Lewis Tappan, who was
dismayed that any AMA employee could harbor the spirit of caste,
that he suggested a resolution for the impending annual meeting of
the Association to the effect that any substantiation of such charges
would mean immediate dismissal:

> Last evening I conversed with a minister from the
> West on the subject of *Caste*. He said that it was believed by
> many that the brethren at *these Rooms* were not up to the
> mark on the subject; and he said furthermore that Rev. S.G.
> Wright openly inculcated that our teachers ought not to eat
> with colored personnel! Can this be true?
>
> I write (hoping you will get it in season) to say that a
> strong Resolution ought, in my judgment, to be passed at
> the meeting on the subject of Caste: Let it be known that any
> agent, teacher or officer who allows Caste to influence him
> there will be cause of dismission.[3]

The following resolution was adopted as a result:

> **Resolved,** That, believing the feeling of prejudice, extensive-
> ly existing in this country against the people of color, to be
> both wicked in itself and a great barrier in the way of their
> elevation, we renew the expression of the principle that has
> underlain the operations of this Association from the
> beginning, that no person who yields to that prejudice, or
> suffers himself to be influenced thereby, ought to be appoint-
> ed or sustained among its officers, teachers or agents.[4]

When Mrs. L. Williams at Camp Nelson, Kentucky, was shown to have suggested that Belle Mitchell (a teacher with a tinge of Negro blood, hired by John G. Fee) eat with some of the colored people in the camp instead of at the Refugee Home where the other teachers and army personnel messed, her dismissal by the AMA was prompt indeed.[5]

Prejudice is a two-way street, of course. Deacon Henry Smith (mulatto) of Savannah's Congregational Church wrote the AMA about J. Shaw (black), successor of Aaron Rowe (white); Smith said that Shaw "hates whites & mulattoes," and pleaded: "when you send us another man, please send one with charity for all men, (like Bro Rowe) and dont send us another, who goes in for color, for we are not responsible that God has seen fit to make some white some yellow and others black, in a word send us a Christian who is blind to the question of color, but loves all in the Lord Jesus Christ."[6]

William W. Mallery

Another situation, one in which the AMA sided with a black man, was the case of the Rev. William W. Mallery at Memphis, Tennessee. There, when a conflict of personalities arose between Mallery, pastor of the largely black Second Congregational Church, and Joseph H. Barnum, white principal of LeMoyne Institute, the AMA did not renew the white man's commission. Despite Barnum's protests that he worked in the First Congregational Church (white) rather than in Mallery's only because Mallery did not want his help and because he thought Mallery was not reaching the young people who were the best recruits for Congregationalism, the AMA preferred not to hurt Mallery's feelings.

Another principal of LeMoyne confirmed Barnum's opinion and inferred that while there was too much emotionalism in most black churches, he wished that Mallery could excite enough in his to keep the congregation awake. In 1877 A.J. Steele finally convinced the men at the Rooms that "the relations existing between the church and school work were not what they should be." Steele admitted that Secretary Strieby was correct in saying that many of the people were "attached" to Mallery, "his uprightness and sincerity could not fail of securing personal friends." But

Steele was equally sure that "a great majority" of the people were
not satisfied with him as a pastor.

In answer to Strieby's "painful" question as to what the
effect on Mallery would be were he removed, Steele said that more
often than not Mallery was pessimistic and dispirited about his
work at Memphis and might very well be glad to be rid of it since
the results were so "indifferent." Still, Mallery was a man "of
peculiar persistence," and Steele recommended another post for
him.[7] Mallery's next charge after Memphis was the Talcott Street
Church, Hartford, Connecticut, where he remained until 1883.

Thus it came about that Mallery's aid was withdrawn after
he had worked in Tennessee for the AMA for a decade, and he was
replaced by a white man—not because he was white, but because he
was a better minister for the post than Mallery. In fact, the AMA
discriminated against white men in its quest to fill the pulpits of its
southern churches. A white man was a last resort, acquiesced in
only when no educated black ministers could be found willing to
work in the South. At the time Mallery was first employed, the men
at the Rooms could only think of Mallery and Amos G. Beman as
having the necessary qualifications.[8]

The Association tried unsuccessfully to persuade Francis
Cardozo to accept the pulpit of Plymouth Church, Charleston,
South Carolina, and remain titular head of Avery Institute. But
Cardozo, despite his seven years of theological training and the fact
that the church wanted him above all others, said his heart was in
education.[9] The AMA tried to persuade Sella Martin to take the
same pulpit on his return from Europe, but was unsuccessful. Only
when all black men of stature failed them did they send James T.
Ford (white) to candidate at Charleston.

William Joseph Wilson

The most striking case in which an AMA employee cried
"caste" when the real problems were his deficiencies as a disciplinarian and administrator coupled with the AMA's perennial
shortage of funds, concerned William Joseph Wilson. In 1865
(except for private schools run by people like John F. Cook,
George Cook, and Lizzie Smith) the only schools for black children
run entirely by black teachers were: the AMA's school at Camp
Barker under the direction of Wilson; and the African Civilization

Society's schools, one taught by Mr. Arnett and Miss Garnet, and one by Martha Smith. The New England Freedmen's Aid Society (Boston) had three colored assistants; and the New England Freedman's Aid Commission (Boston) had two.[10]

A comparison of Wilson's work week with that of any other AMA teacher in a similar position (Superintendent of a large school or several small ones) points up the glaring fact that Wilson simply did not expend anything like the same amount of effort in the cause.[11] Unlike other AMA personnel, Wilson and his staff preferred to attend Henry Highland Garnet's Fifteenth Street Presbyterian Church rather than work in the Sunday school which their pupils attended. Wilson was elected a ruling elder in his church, while the Sunday school work in his school was carried on gratuitously by Howard University Treasurer James B. Johnson in the black Baptist Church on Third Street.[12]

From the beginning Wilson had complained that the salary paid him and his wife was too low, yet he declined to spend the summer of 1865 as AMA collecting agent and lecturer in the North. Instead he kept his school in session and received payment for the summer work from the AMA, as well as salary from the Freedmen's Bank, where he served as a cashier.[13]

The job at the bank kept him busy during the evenings during the school year and made it impossible for him to teach an evening school for adults, as almost all AMA teachers did. When he did teach evening school, it was for another society for extra money and decidedly against AMA policy. Other employees were dismissed for less.

In the fall of 1865, the AMA's new Washington Superintendent, William S. Tilden, called Wilson's "past success ... a sufficient guarantee for the future." But that was when he first arrived at Washington.[14]

Although his school at Camp Barker had been ungraded, Wilson agreed to grade the Third Street School and included plans for a grammar Department he hoped to make "equal to any *Grammar School* of the *kind in Washington.*"[15] Tilden heard daily reports that the Third Street School was very poorly run: that Wilson spent most of his time at the bank, leaving the school to his assistants. Wilson did not recognize Tilden as his superintendent and would take no assistance or advice from that aggressive young

man. Tilden hoped that Wilson would go into the bank permanently so that good teachers might be placed in his school "and greater
good accomplished.[16]

George Whipple visited the schools in Washington in the fall
of 1865, and Tilden visited Wilson's school several times afterwards, reporting it "in about the same state of confusion." Yet
Wilson did not seem "to have the slightest idea" that he was not
doing the best that could be done for his students. Wilson's idea of
a successful school was to have "a great mass of children together."
Tilden "sincerely" hoped a way could be found to remove the most
advanced pupils from Wilson's school and place them where they
might receive "some instruction . . . of real advantage to them."[17]

Wilson insisted that the lack of order that Whipple had
observed on his visit was inherited from the former teachers of the
school, and that he had made progress in so far as "stone throwing
and window breaking" in the neighborhood were concerned. Police
seldom had to be called and the neighbors were more content to
have the school there. He also insisted that he gave as much time to
his school as any other teacher and only gave his evenings to the
bank, which was patently untrue.[18]

Wilson did not comply with Tilden's suggestion to allow his
most advanced pupils to be placed in another school (although he
had received a letter from New York explaining that Tilden had
charge of all AMA schools in the District), but asked Tilden to call
at his school. Tilden found him "in great turmoil of mind,"
protesting "with a good deal of pathos and personal feeling" the
loss of his best students. "He had brought over his diploma, given
by some N.Y. society or school, in a gilt frame, and showed . . .
that, as his warrant as to qualifications," declaring his corps of
teachers— especially his daughter Annie—were as well qualified as
any teachers in the city. Tilden explained that his qualifications
were not in question; it was simply a matter of better grading of
schools. But Wilson said he was thereby being degraded in the eyes
of the colored community and insisted that he was being persecuted
"on account of his color, and that by those who styled themselves
Christian people." He had wanted to show that a school run by
colored teachers could be as good as any, but now he was not
allowed to prove his point. If he were back in slavery under his old
master, he would not change for the "tyranny" he labored under in

Washington. Tilden said that Wilson "managed the pathetic very adroitly," and he "felt moved for him. But yet, there was the stern fact right before my very eyes, while he was yet talking, the school was in such an uproar that I could scarcely hear his words, or he mine." There the matter stood. Tilden could do nothing, "any interference in his arrangements will be construed as the result of cruel prejudice against him because he is a black man." Tilden was sure that Wilson would not work "with much heart" unless he were entirely independent. But if allowed that independence, there would be one school in Washington with the name but not the approval of the AMA.[19]

Both the AMA and Wilson had a great deal of trouble with the black Baptist church whose building was rented for the Third Street School, from the time a Rev. Gaines became its pastor. At one point Wilson was sued for janitor service he neither hired nor wanted. The storeroom needed for supplies and which Wilson had planned to use for his Grammar Department, was rented out to a black family. Tilden thought that many of the "pranks" carried out against Wilson would not be tried against white teachers and that Wilson was "too good-natured a man to suspect them of just the mean kind of sharpness they possess."[20]

Tilden did not press the subject of the advanced students, not wanting to give Wilson the excuse to "complain of any personal unkindness" in Tilden's relationship with him. Tilden did, however, suggest that the huge school be divided into four classes, with each teacher in charge of the entire class. Since that would require Wilson's daily attendance, he did not agree, but preferred to divide into three classes. Tilden expressed himself uncharitable enough to think that Wilson had his salary from the bank in mind. Yet Tilden was sorry for Wilson "especially" because he was a black man, and because he disliked finding fault with any teacher.[21]

Wilson received thirty dollars a month from the bank. He admitted that it had been necessary to be absent on bank business for eight days, but had hired a young man to take his place. Wilson wrote a very emotional letter about the persecution of poor colored teachers in response to Whipple's statement that Wilson's time at the bank "caused dissatisfaction."[22]

The response from New York to Tilden's questions about Wilson were interpreted by Tilden to mean letting Wilson "gang his gait" and not interfere. The reaction of the men at the Rooms can only be seen as an attempt on their part not to hurt an African American who had been hurt enough already by caste. This is the only explanation for their extremely gentle treatment of a man who had broken several rules as their commissioned agent, and who did far less work than the average AMA teacher.[23]

In late December, 1865, Wilson asked for Whipple's "kind advice." He described his "relations" to those of his race in Washington as "a little peculiar—I may say novel." He was trying to find the place of greatest usefulness among them. If he decided to give up teaching and take another position, would the interests of the AMA suffer, and would his resignation jeopardize his wife's and daughter's jobs? Whipple replied that each case was judged on its own merits.[24]

Tilden left the Third Street School in the hands of Mrs. Wilson, Annie Wilson, and Julia Landre, but he suggested that the AMA send a strong disciplinarian soon. He thought, in fact, that the ladies had better be replaced by a new staff of teachers as soon as possible because the students there did not show them the proper respect. He suggested that the two young ladies might take one of the fort classes when they opened.[25]

The AMA's gentle handling of Wilson came back to haunt them when Bureau Agent Kimball used the disorder he saw at the Third Street School to deny the Association better additional facilities (he had earlier promised), saying that they had not improved the quarters they already had. Tilden wished General Howard would replace Kimball with someone with "executive ability" and a "Northern" point of view.[26]

From 1869 to 1874 Howard University offered evening courses held in the First Congregational Church. There were no academic requirements for these courses, students needing only to be at least fifteen years old. During the first year there was a total of thirty-three students, three instructors, and several additional lecturers. One of the latter was William J. Wilson, at the same time cashier of the Freedmen's Savings and Trust Company. Courses offered were "arithmetic, grammar, penmanship, bookkeeping, and 'simple law.'"

From 1868 to 1879 Wilson was a trustee of Howard University, and in that position rubbed shoulders with some of the

AMA secretaries he had known as a teacher. In 1869 in his capacity as trustee, he passed on the "fitness" of F.L. Cordozo for a professorship in Latin. He asked Whipple for information "in the strictest confidence" about both Francis and his brother Thomas, "whose career seems to cast a shadow" on Francis Cardozo, "being as near akin." It was important, Wilson asserted, to obtain the best black person available for the post.[27]

After the demise of the Freedmen's Bank, Wilson again applied for employment under the AMA. He said he had "the fullest confidence of thousands" of his people "the country over."[28]

John Mercer Langston

An example of an African American charging prejudice when the real culprit was the shortage of funds is the case of John Mercer Langston and the presidency of Howard University. Although Howard was not an AMA school (except for the Theological Department), most of the people involved in its founding were AMA members. And although Langston's differences would seem to have been aimed principally at some members of Washington's First Congregational Church, the AMA came in for its share of criticism.

Langston's association with the AMA was one of cordiality and long standing. In his days at Oberlin he had lived with George Whipple (then a mathematics professor), and after the Civil War had almost become an AMA officer himself. In the fall of 1866 the AMA sought the services of Langston as a lecturer and fund raiser for "the Educational & moral & religious Elevation of the Freedmen in the Southern States." Langston was approached by Erastus Milo Cravath, Secretary of the Cincinnati office. He was offered $1500 a year, and Edward P. Smith suggested that he preface his agency with a tour of the South in order to see the work first hand. Langston was favorably inclined toward the position.[29]

Probably Langston did not become an AMA officer because his appointment as Inspector of Schools for the Freedmen's Bureau was offered shortly afterward. He served in the latter office until 1869 and had many opportunities to observe and report on AMA schools. He addressed the Association at its New York Anniversary Meeting in 1868, describing some of the AMA schools as "the best

he had ever seen." Langston, who had graduated from Oberlin
Seminary and had once considered becoming a minister, testified to
the saving power of the gospel in the lives of the freedmen. He said
the education of the freedmen needed to be threefold: in letters; "to
value and acquire property"; and "in personal, Christian, and
moral character."[30]

Langston's general opinion of AMA schools continued to be
that they were among the best anywhere. Fisk University, he said in
1869, "commends itself in the highest terms to every lover of
learning and to every philanthropist." He "cordially" commended
the university to parents: "The interest that its teachers have
manifested in the education of the colored race, their Christian zeal,
their long experience, their well known abilities are the best
guarantees" black parents could have, "that your children at this
institution will be well cared for, properly trained and qualified for
the duties and responsibilities of life."[31]

He spoke at the laying of the corner-stone of Atlanta
University, June 1, 1869. The reporter of the Cincinnati *Gazette*
wrote that it was fitting that Langston speak on such an occasion,
as living proof of "what it was possible to become" through
education. Langston said that day what would become themes in
his public addresses. He praised Oberlin and spoke of the value of
integrated education, that destroyed "the spirit of servility and
fear" in one race "and arrogance in the other." Black Americans
were on trial. Some said they were dying as a race; he prayed "that
fifty years would elapse before they lost one curl of hair, one shade
less of their duskiness." Once they had produced "a Beecher, a
Chapin, a Sumner, a Harriet Beecher Stowe, then might they lose
their peculiarities as soon as they wished." Black Americans must
help themselves. They must stop defiling their bodies with alcohol
and tobacco and use the money to educate their children. Money
was moral power. The government had helped; the AMA had
contributed "individuals colored and white." Like the black man of
Macon who had given twenty dollars for the corner-stone, it was
their university and their duty to aid it.[32]

Money Raising

It was general practice in the nineteenth century to add
prominent white men to predominantly black committees and

organizations for their superior money-raising potential. The AMA declared it as common knowledge that even many philanthropic individuals did not like to contribute to black organizations. Given the imprimatur of wealthy white men, black groups were more likely to receive contributions from other white men of substance. When the black St. Louis Board of Education for Free Colored Schools was organized in 1864, for example, four white men (including AMA missionary Rev. George Candee) were added to the ten black men on the board, "that the whites who are expected to contribute largely, might be represented in the Board."[33]

There were some wealthy African Americans in the nineteenth century, of course, but the overwhelming majority were poor. Institutions like black northern Presbyterian and Congregational churches tended to remain mission churches sustained by denominational aid until the end of the century or well into the twentieth. Black newspapers like the *Colored American, Frederick Douglass' Paper*, and the *Provincial Freeman* were aided by white dollars. Much of the money to operate Wilberforce University came from whites; and, as has been seen, the AME Church was helped by the AMA in its work among the freedmen and its rapid expansion in the South during Reconstruction.

In the nineteenth century as in the twentieth, a man's money-raising ability was one of the most important criteria considered by a college board when seeking a new president. The success of a president's administration was judged on the fiscal soundness of the school during his tenure and his ability to secure appropriations for buildings, salaries, etc. The nineteenth-century African American who aspired to such office was at a considerable disadvantage. There were few with the educational requirements and perhaps none of those few had the Midas touch. No matter how much white liberals of the Reconstruction era were sentimentally attached to the African American's "elevation", they realized that it would take an unusual black man indeed to administer an infant black institution in the best of situations. It was John Mercer Langston's misfortune to campaign for the presidency of Howard University in the midst of the great depression of the 1870s.

The formal schooling of even educated African American abolitionists like J.W.C. Pennington and Henry Highland Garnet (although they received honorary doctorates) was seldom more than a high school education. Of course, high school curricula in the nineteenth century included Greek and Latin, and the best educated of the famous African Americans of that century were men whose education was not limited to the school room, of course. Very few had business training or the experience that would aid them in the financial world. Lewis Tappan's reputation as color-blind has been questioned because he once said (at a moment when David Ruggles of the New York Vigilance Committee was under fire about the way he used the Committee's funds) that he had known few colored men who knew anything about keeping financial records. Ovid Miner, concerned about Samuel R. Ward's bankrupt newspaper enterprises, declared Ward a better orator than business man. Of course, there were few white men with the business acumen of a Lewis Tappan or a James B. Johnson, but American social structure had allowed their genius to flourish.

Langston, Vice President at Howard

When the Freedmen's Bureau was abolished in 1873, General O.O. Howard resigned the presidency of Howard to re-enter the army. The trustees, however, gave him a leave of absence and elected John M. Langston, Dean of the Howard Law School, vice president. It was hoped that placing a colored man in that "high position would stimulate his own race and the white philanthropists to sustain the institution in its perilous struggles." But the depression continued and so did the lack of funds.[34] Langston's appointment was not the first time an African American was considered for the presidency of Howard in the nineteenth century, nor was it the last. As has been seen above, J.M. Brown, AME bishop and member of Howard's Board of Trustees, evidently wanted the presidency to go to a member of his denomination, and suggested Moses R. Johnston of Nashville as a possibility. In 1877 Francis L. Cardozo and Peter H. Clark, principal of Gaines High School in Cincinnati, were proposed for that office.[35]

Langston evidently believed that there was a strong possibility that he would not be nominated for the office when the slate was drawn by the trustees on December 25, 1874; a petition from twenty of his law students dated the day before the meeting "expressed the hope that 'Langston's color will not operate as an invidious bar to his election.'"[36] At that meeting on Christmas

Day, five men were nominated, including three African Americans: Langston, Douglass, and Charles H. Thompson (of Straight University); and two white men: President Erastus Milo Cravath of Fisk University, and Professor George W. Atherton, a professor at Rutgers and a member of the Board of Visitors of the United States Naval Academy. At that same meeting, it was voted to ask Langston to withdraw his resignation as vice president.[37]

Details are at best unclear, but the trustees decided not to elect a new president until the next year, and Langston continued to serve as acting president. When the vote for president took place on June 16, 1875, the nominees were Secretary George Whipple of the AMA and John Mercer Langston. How ironic that the field should have narrowed down to the man who fought so strenuously to prove that he was black (even if he did have blue eyes and was white in the sight of ante-bellum Ohio law) and the professor who had befriended him at Oberlin in his student days by taking him into his own home.

Langston's statement that all the black trustees voted for him and all the white ones voted for Whipple cannot be proven from the minutes of the meeting. There were four black and eleven white members of the board, ten votes were cast for Whipple, three for Langston, and one for Douglass. Douglass and Langston carried the fight to the public via the New York *Evening Post*, describing the problem as they saw it in racial and sectarian terms. For the two men to ascribe the vote to racial prejudice and an attempt of the AMA and the Congregationalists to gain control of the University "for their own selfish interests," was irresponsible.[38] The *Evening Post* described the black trustees of the University as determined that it "should not pass into the hands of any denomination without a determined fight." These are strange words indeed about Congregationalists, who exerted no ecclesiastical control over any schools, and indeed had not the theological propensity nor the institutional machinery to do so. Had such control been desired, it could have been easily exercised from the beginning by simply not opening the Board positions to any but Congregationalists. Had the African Methodist Episcopal Church of which Trustee J.M. Brown was a bishop gained control, the situation would have been quite different.

It is also interesting to note that at the same time (June, 1875) that Langston joined forces with Douglass to condemn the AMA and Congregationalists at Howard, he saw fit to accept the invitation from those same villains to address the first collegiate graduating class of Fisk University, where he shared the platform with George Whipple. On that occasion Langston "paid an eloquent tribute to the American Missionary Association—the foster mother of Fisk University—as represented by Rev. George Whipple, in such cordial words as called forth hearty applause."[39]

One can ask why the AMA was, in Langston's words, so admirable at Nashville and so untrustworthy at Washington—especially when some of the same men were involved, notably George Whipple, E.M. Cravath, and M.E. Strieby. Perhaps the fault lies with the fourth estate for the "garbled reports" that were published.[40]

Answering the Charges

The Langston-Douglass charges were answered in the same newspaper by an African American member of Howard's Medical Department, Charles B. Purvis. Dr. Purvis, although himself a Unitarian, discounted the charges against First Congregational Church, describing it as the only "orthodox" church in Washington where the black man was treated on an equal basis with the white. As for the AMA, Dr. Purvis praised it as the organization that had done more for the black man than all others combined. He was convinced that Langston's attack had come out of pique at his defeat in the election. That defeat was not a unilateral white against black arrangement, said Purvis, for one of the black trustees had been pleading with the white trustees for some time not to elect Langston to the post of president.[41]

Langston could not have it both ways. If he argued that, because board members were predominantly Congregationalists and backers of the AMA, and that, because the AMA did not believe black persons capable of professional training, funds were not forthcoming for the professional departments at Howard, he would have to explain how the professional departments at Fisk and Atlanta and Straight (as well as the Theological Department at Howard) received AMA funding. Langston's problems were two, one personal and one the dispensation of fate. He was sometimes a difficult man with whom to work, and the other obstacle was simply the depression of 1873. Funds were not available to spend on Langston's schemes of enlargement for the Law Department (or any other division, of Howard) funds he as Law Dean had made no successful effort to raise personally.

John Bunyan Reeve had to leave the University Theological Department and return to the parish ministry for the sake of his own financial welfare, because it was becoming more and more difficult for the AMA to find the $150 to pay his salary every month. On January 1, 1875, Reeve wrote to E.M. Cravath, AMA Field Secretary, to say that he was sorry to have to ask for his salary for December, and if he could "borrow any or ask credit for daily bread with hope of success I would not ask you for salery [sic] until after the 15th inst. Mr Whipple having intimated that your treasury might be under great pressure until that time."[42]

James B. Johnson, treasurer of Howard through all the controversy, and the one given the credit for saving the institution "from complete financial collapse," was greatly concerned about the future of Howard in the fall of 1874. In writing to Cravath about the coming Board meeting in December, he emphasized its importance, saying that it sometimes happened that the policies established at the annual meeting were reversed at the Board meetings. He feared it would be so again, "if some of those who most favor retrenchment & economy remain away." Despite Langston's pride in the economics of his administration, it is fairly obvious that Johnson is criticizing Langston's leadership in that regard.[43]

Those members of the AMA who were also trustees of Howard, were longtime abolitionists and workers for equal rights for African Americans. They were also realists who knew first hand that benevolent giving was tied to the country's prosperity, that hard times were felt first in eleemosynary institutions. As friends of Howard—yes, and as those who had helped to establish it in the first place—they did not want to see it go the way of other schools that had done so much to educate black persons. Oneida Institute and New York Central College were two examples that had gone under financially.

John Mercer Langston had had two years to show what he could do as acting president in the way of establishing a favorable image of the institution in the mind of the public and its necessary concomitant, the raising of funds. Evidently the majority of the Board felt that George Whipple, the man who was offered the presidency when Howard was being born, who was given the first Doctor of Divinity by its fledgling Theological Department, who had shown his friendship for African Americans since the days when he was a Lane Seminary rebel, who had proven his ability to elicit funds from churchmen, and who, perhaps most important of all, had friends in high places in Washington, could do a better job of raising money than Langston. It is notable that when Whipple declined (perhaps because of Langston's newspaper tirade), the Board elected Edward Parmelee Smith, AMA Secretary and former head of the Bureau of Indian Affairs, who also knew his way around Washington and had the friendship of influential men in Congress.[44]

Langston, in a revealing moment during the controversy, declared that he was certainly not a Congregationalist. Perhaps he changed his mind later, because he was identified as a Congrega-tionalist by an African American writer in 1920, or perhaps that writer made a justifiable error. After all, Langston had attended a Congregational college (Oberlin) where he had boarded with a Congregational mathematics professor (George Whipple); His daughter was married in the Congregational Church whose members he criticized so severely (First Church, Washington), and she and her husband John Carrol Napier were active members of the Nashville Congregational Church; Langston chose the minister of Washington's First Congregational Church to write the biographical portion of his *Freedom and Citizenship* (and at the time, Jeremiah Eames Rankin was a vice president of the AMA!); and he worked at Howard University, the idea for which was born in a Congregational prayer meeting and whose Board, according to Langston, was a hotbed of Congregationalists!

The interracial nature of First Congregational Church, Washington, and Langston's attachment thereto was described by Rankin in 1884:

> At no time, indeed, were not black people, yellow people, and red people welcome to the Sunday School of this church or to its communion. And probably there was no period during the 15 years with which this discourse has to do,

> when there were not from 30 to 50 colored members of this congregation; and there was a time, under General Howard's administration of the University, when many of the students regularly worshipped here. . . . These people were not here as colored people, but as belonging to the one family, which God has made of one blood, to dwell on all the face of the earth! They were here because they had been brought up Congregationalists or felt drawn to Congregationalism, that Mother of some of the noblest children, not a few from Oberlin, where they had been educated. *Frederick Douglass was often here; B.K. Bruce and John Langston, Professors Mitchell and Gregory with their families, were regular attendants.*[45]

Perhaps the most significant fact of all associating Langston with Congregationalism was that he had discussed with Samuel S. Ashley in 1870 the establishment of a "Congregational University" for the South—"an Institution that shall be to the South what Harvard or Yale is to the North—or Oberlin to the West." And Langston had favored such a plan.[46]

Langston and Douglass

On July 5, 1875, Langston and Frederick Douglass spoke on black self-reliance in Washington, Douglass framing a "Declaration of Independence, of the swarm of white beggars that sweep the country in the name of the colored race." Douglass declared, "We have been more injured than benefitted by the efforts of the so-called benevolent societies." He accused the leaders of such societies with having "selfish motives," and concluded: "Hence we now and here denounce and repudiate all such shams, and call upon the American people to do the same." Although he did not mention the AMA in his denunciation, and in the same year joined with Washington Gladden and others to produce a plea for funds for the AMA, and denied in a letter that he had meant to include the Association, his speech did not help increase contributions to the AMA's treasury.[47]

Secretary Strieby replied to Douglass that the officers of the AMA had always admired Douglass's talents and rejoiced in his successful struggle in reaching his high eminence as one of America's most eloquent speakers. More, he had considered

Douglass one of his personal friends, and did "not intend to erase his name from the list," despite their differences.

The men at the Rooms declared that Douglass was wrong about African Americans. As a group they were "*not* prepared to proclaim a 'declaration of Independence' of their former friends." Certainly self-reliance was their goal, but there was a difference between paternalism and friendship. The fledgling United States had declared its independence but had nevertheless accepted "thankfully the aid of Lafayette and the French." The great West was occupied by liberty-loving people, but it was still a mission field, needing aid from the East in the building of schools and churches. "Can the colored people—so very few of whom can read and write and own a home of their own—cut loose from all the ties of sympathy and charity that have befriended them thus far?" Certainly, some of the African Americans were wealthy and educated, but the AMA appealed "to the generous, patriotic and Christian sympathies of the American people" for the masses who were culturally deprived. "They have suffered much, the struggle before them is great, their resources are meagre, their destiny and the nation's are linked together."[48]

The themes of paternalism and ethnocentricity arise in any consideration of white and black relationships. Twentieth-century Americans, feeling the sting of the plank obscuring their own racial vision, are prone to discover motes spoiling the alleged color-blindness of nineteenth-century reformers.

There was certainly paternalism present in the attitudes of AMA teachers—black and white alike—toward the freedmen *as moral beings.* The masses of freedmen were seen like corrupt children, having been taught by their masters and the slave system that lying and stealing were only wrong if the perpetrator were caught, that power over others was the supreme achievement, that those without power who wished to escape punishment must appear to be submissive, that they were mentally inferior to white men. The AMA teachers, black and white, were determined to "elevate" those oppressed ones, to prove to them and to the whites that they were morally and intellectually prepared to enter the mainstream of American life. In that sense, the AMA can be seen as paternalistic, providing fatherly care for those raised without benefit of families, the educationally superior teacher imparting the joy of books to those long-deprived ones. But the paternalism of governors toward the governed, or any idea that whites would continue to dominate the schools once their initial purpose was realized, was not a part of AMA planning.

Fear of the Return of the Democratic Party to Power

It did not take much experience in the South to realize that as soon as the Democratic party was reinstated and the federal troops removed, what schools that were provided for blacks would be segregated. Since southern school boards would be unlikely to hire Yankees, and few white Southerners would care to work in black schools, black teachers must be found. Since also the South showed little interest in educating black teachers, unless benevolent Northerners like those backing the AMA carried out that office in a dedicated and thorough manner, there would be no competent black teachers in the South. Since the Southerners held the black's ignorance against him in the battle for jobs, without education the blacks of the South would be forever in a kind of economic servitude and unable to "rise."

AMA Hiring Standards for Teachers

The AMA's percentage of African American teachers was lower than that of the Freedmen's Bureau, but the Bureau hired many African Americans as "teachers" who could scarcely read themselves. Booker T. Washington described an ignorant teacher:

> Many became teachers who could do little more than write their names. I remember there came into our neighbourhood one of this class, who was in search of a school to teach, and the question arose while he was there as to the shape of the earth and how he would teach the children concerning this subject. He explained his position in the matter by saying that he was prepared to teach that the earth was either flat or round, according to the preference of a majority of his patrons.[49]

There is a tremendous hiatus between learning to read and learning to write and reproduce a language. While experience in reading affords an eventual proficiency in spelling, it is not necessary to be able to spell well in order to read. The AMA could have found many such "teachers" among the freedmen, but the AMA was interested in more than simply teaching black persons the alphabet. They saw education for the black man as the answer to caste. As one AMA officer put it, if the black man were superior to the white man, then it was safe to give him inferior schools; if he were equal, then equal schools would be fine; and if he were inferior, then he must have better schools than the whites. The AMA believed that the black man was equal, and if provided with schools like those of New England, he would become an integral part of American life.[50]

Of course, the men at the Rooms would have been pleased if all the students in all the schools elected also to accept New England's Congregationalism as their religious path. But no religious restrictions were imposed. Congregationalism by its very nature was unpaternalistic. Unlike less democratically organized communions, it could not dictate either to pastors or to people. It was sometimes very painful to the men at the Rooms when a church chose its minister unwisely, or a man refused to candidate in a church that needed his kind of leadership.

In the educational field, many of the common schools supported by the AMA were headed by African American men and women. But even in those cases where the teacher was white, the work of the school was overseen by a black committee or board of trustees, organized by the teacher among the people of the community if not produced by the people on their own. Although some teachers despaired of the adult freedmen becoming morally upright citizens because of the seemingly indelible stain of slavery, they did not cease trying to interest parents in the work of education.[51]

The AMA teachers instilled pride in their pupils, giving them an appreciation of their African heritage, asking friends in the North for books on and by Africans to fill their libraries. The recorded oration subjects given at graduation and examination exercises point up these facts. And the remarks of critical southern reporters about the "uppity" attitudes of AMA students complement the facts and compliment the teachers and their pupils. At his graduation from Fisk University's Collegiate Department in 1875, James Dallas Burrus spoke on "Elements of True Manhood," Amanda Malbania Perkins spoke on "Crispus Attucks," on her graduation from the Normal Department of Straight University in 1873; H. Kealing's oration at Straight in 1877 was "The Ancient Glory and Future Hope of the African Race," and A.H. Colwell spoke on "We can Make Our Lives Sublime," J.R. Hollowell on "The Power of Resolution and Effort," A.S. Barnes on "What is Power?" The program ended with the singing of "Hold Your Head Up Like a Man."[52]

As educated young people graduated from AMA schools, they joined the faculties of their alma mater or other schools. Eventually there would also be African American presidents of the colleges, but the principal of admission without regard to race, creed, sex, or color would inveigh against all-black faculties.

Paternalism and prejudice would seem to be inextricably bound up one with the other. It requires a kind of condescension to decide that a whole group of people needs eternal care and oversight. The goal of the AMA was to help the freedman through his introduction to education and a religion steeped in morality, and then, with the schools and churches in his own hands, he would be in charge of his own culture.[53] Of course, the AMA would have preferred that the schools of the whole country would be integrated ones, but since that was certainly out of the realm of possibility in the South for some time to come, at least the colored institutions where children were taught the basic morality that would prepare them to achieve their full potential as citizens and children of God, would be under black control.

When Edmund Ware, president of Atlanta University, was asked how he could stand working with blacks, he said there was no problem at all because he was color blind. Testimony from African Americans that the Association's record generally was estimable in that regard is readily available. One African American, not a Congregationalist, in giving credit to the record of the first missionaries and teachers who worked with the freedmen and to their successors still at work in the South, wrote:

> All the great religious denominations of the country have had a hand in this work of development, *but of them all the contribution made by the American Missionary Association ... has been of greatest value.* More than any other organization you have recognized the manhood of the negro; and in all your dealings with him you have more largely than

any other organization ... treated him as a man and a
brother; and so you have been swayed less than any other
organization ... by colorphobia; and I believe of all
organizations that have been working among us as a race,
your great Association has shown most of the spirit of what
I call true, genuine christianity.[54]

Reconstruction, A Failed Issue

Washington Gladden was one member of the AMA who
fairly shouted out at those who accepted politics as the panacea for
the country's ills. The Fifteenth Amendment, he said, would protect
the freedmen's right to vote only so long as the majority of those in
power in any area wished it to be so. The Constitution was what a
local power elite said it was.[55] Reconstruction was a failure
because the freedman was abandoned to the meager mercies of the
southern Democrats by the liberals of the North who salved their
consciences with three amendments and a handful of civil rights
acts—none of which were enforced.

The pressures on Congressmen to remove government
restrictions from the secession states were great from North and
South alike. Northern business men were anxious after the war to
resume relations with the South on a greater than ante-bellum
basis, and were, therefore, impatient at the restrictions of Reconstruction. Southern business men were perhaps even more anxious
to "get things moving" again.

Those in power, therefore, North and South, seemed willing
to forget the freedman in so far as possible. Even former abolitionists like William Lloyd Garrison and the so-called "radicals" who
had managed to persuade the world that they stood in the forefront
of the movement for racial equality, were willing to turn to more
"timely" issues like women's rights. After all, the country was tired
of hearing about the freedmen, and had not the southern states
established—or promised to establish—school systems that would
include blacks and poor whites?[56]

So American business and its glorified office manager, the
American Congress, abandoned the freedman after five years of
rations, enforced labor contracts, and five million dollars spent for
education. The AMA deplored the country's short memory and the
fact that even former abolitionists had given up the battle. Many of
the old abolitionists were dead, but the Association "feared that

some of these old abolitionists are so busy in recounting their battles and victories, that they forget, or remit to their children, the great problem of the fate of the emancipated slaves." To the AMA this was wrong: "It is not enough to tear down. It is even more important to rebuild something better."[57]

In 1867 William Lloyd Garrison told the British people not to contribute any longer to the work among the freedmen; two years earlier he had said that the work of the American Anti-Slavery Society was completed and called for its dissolution.[58] True, long before this the American and Foreign Anti-Slavery Society of the Tappanites had ceased as an active organization, but its thrust had been rechanneled into the AMA. There was therefore no need to reorganize at the time of the Civil War. More important, emancipation did not dictate its logical end as it did that of the American Anti-Slavery Society; for the AMA was not only an abolition society, it was a Christian abolition society—dedicated to the principle of the brotherhood of man. Its end could not be logically arrived at until caste was eliminated from American society, and the "despised" races of America—among whom the members of the AMA included African Americans, Indian Americans, Spanish Americans, Chinese Americans and other immigrants, and the poor whites of Appalachia—were accorded equal citizenship and opportunity.

Those goals could be reached, they felt, through the proper institutions: the public school, the church, colleges and universities, impartial courts and law enforcement, and a free press. The spiritual descendants of the Pilgrims had always believed in the freedom of the individual, but had also always believed strongly in the free church and the free school as channels of liberty and reform. For that reason, the men who founded the AMA chose to work through the churches in the abolition crusade. For that same reason, they chose the same avenue in the fight against caste, the evil that survived the war.

The AMA: Determined to Continue

It would not be enough, the AMA announced in 1869, for liberals in the North to send teachers to the South for a few years to teach a few thousand or even hundreds of thousands of black men the fundamentals of reading. Much of the "effort in the South," it said, was "as barren of result as rain upon the sand. Institutions are the only permanent forces in society." This early-day Elkinsianism continued:

> And yet many think that itinerant rushing through the South, scattering books here and there, can save it. There could not be a more idle dream. When the men are out of sight, and the books are thrown aside, their influence is ended. Only institutions carry on the thoughts of men, and the lessons of books, and repeat them from generation to generation.
>
> It is vain, therefore, to think of correcting the public sentiment of the South by any process that does not flower into institutions. The trouble with most Southerners now, is that their institutions are leading them astray.

Immoral institutions ("the church, the school, and the press") had wrongly instructed the South. "The pulpit brought the sanctions of religion to human chattlehood, and is responsible for the madness of the Southern people on that subject." The South's "political, social and religious life" had followed from "the assumption of the divine right of slavery. . . ." As long as such an erroneous idea was "sheltered and nourished in the leading institutions of the South," it could not be eradicated.

> Hence the first duty for the statesmanship and the christian patriotism of the country is to carry southward institutions that do not embody a wrong and teach the people a lie. Churches, schools, presses, courts must be established there, a vital part of whose central force shall be humanity. . . .
> The people of the South do not yet see their blindness, nor do they confess their guilt. They so believe in their old errors that they are determined to propagate them.

The people of the South claim to understand the Negro as the North does not, and demand that his education be left in their hands:

> But as a matter of fact they do not understand him at all, because they deny his manhood, the only key by which they can interpret him. . . .

> Hence it is clear, that only institutions which embody the oneness of man in the common fatherhood of God, can reconstruct the reason and conscience of the South on a true and lasting basis.[59]

In 1875, one of the white members of Straight's faculty wrote a report for the *American Missionary* in an attempt to explain why, even if Louisiana's legislators were all "disposed to secure wholesome instruction to all the youth of the South," it was not possible. The teachers simply did not exist in the South.

But even if there were teachers there

> in abundance, under such influences that prevail here, no such instruction could be given as would satisfy a New England community. You in the North have your churches, your Sunday schools, your pious parentage, your inherited leanings toward right doing, your social restraints, your enforced wholesome legislation, your checks on the corruption of the public press. The Southern Freedmen have not one of these things. Burn your school houses, shut up your churches, destroy all your accumulated apparatus of intelligence, forget all that you know, and you have left still, more than the poor Freedmen possesses when you give them all to him.[60]

The inculcation of free institutions in the South would not be easy, for the South had known neither an emancipated church nor a public school system. In 1871 the AMA found "the bulk of the whites in the South" were "as rebellious as ever at heart." Neither would the situation be changed by emigrants from the North. There were too few, and those who did go and stay in the South, purchased their security only "by surrendering their manhood." Neither was there hope that the next generation of white Southerners would be an improvement. The women of the South were "more intense in their feelings than the men," and would "see to it that the children shall be taught as a part of their sacred duty to hate the Yankees."

The "hope for the South" lay in the education of the colored people. Educated black men could combine with "the better class of whites" and exercise "the balance of power." It would be a slow process, but it was the only way to save the South. A public school system (sustained by the federal government where the South would not do so), normal schools to staff such a system, and "intelligent and pure churches" were the institutions that would give the freedmen "the intelligence and the moral stamina to meet the emergency" and help reform the rest of the South's institutions.[61]

Illustrious Graduates

One way to evaluate the importance of the AMA's work at the South is to name the illustrious graduates of its schools and enumerate their contributions to American and world culture. Both the controversial great African American educators were AMA graduates. Booker T. Washington went to Hampton a penniless student, remained to become a member of its faculty, and left with his heart filled with admiration for General Armstrong—to found Tuskegee, the foster child of Hampton. William Edward Burghardt DuBois, graduate of Fisk and American historian of note, was a professor at Atlanta and chairman of an annual series of conferences on the Urban Negro, beginning in 1897, and paralleling a series on the Rural Negro begun at Tuskegee in 1891.[62]

Frederick Leslie Brownlee, white general secretary of the AMA, and Charles S. Johnson (African American) established the Race Relations Department at Fisk University in 1943. Its first full-time chairman was Herman H. Long, an African American graduate of the college and later its president. The Department conducted annual institutes until 1969, providing a place where people of all races working for a desegregated America could meet. In addition, it served as "a continuous research agency gathering accurate information and analysis of the institution of segregation." It was under Herman Long at Fisk that the legal barriers to desegregation were challenged. He headed the data compilations upon which most of the legal briefs were based in the cases against restrictive covenants. The decisions of those cases, in turn, undergirded the brief in the momentous Supreme Court case, *Brown v. the Board of Education of Topeka, Kansas*, in 1954.[63]

Then there are the thousands of graduates of AMA schools who have not received special eclat, who became the teachers of hundreds of thousands of African Americans. Had the AMA and other church groups left the South when the first wave of enthusiastic giving for the freedmen ended, there would not have been a Hampton nor an Atlanta nor a Fisk. Would there then have been a Tuskegee or the sociological contributions of Dubois or a 1954 Supreme Court decision?

* * * *

Henry Hugh Proctor, graduate of Fisk and Yale Divinity School, and esteemed pastor of First Congregational Church, Atlanta, likened the AMA to the fountain of clear water that sprang—like an answer to a Union soldier's prayer—in the midst of the foulness of Andersonville prison. The AMA was such a fountain "opened in the spirit of charity to all and malice toward none. Without exception." Proctor said, "this was the very finest thing in American history."[64]

NOTES

1. Patten, February 12, 1863, to Jocelyn, AMAA.

2. Hattie A. Lewis, November 8, 1866, to Wright; J.P. Bardwell, Vicksburg, Miss., February 20, 1867, to Smith, AMAA.

3. Lewis Tappan, New York, October 16, 1867, to Whipple or Jocelyn, AMAA. The letter is on AMA stationery.

4. *Twenty-first Annual Report* (1867), 4.

5. The Rev. L. Williams, October 18, 1865; Mrs. A.E. Williams, September 28, 1865 to Whipple; see also letters of Carrie Damon, Mary Colton, John G. Fee, and Bell Mitchell, AMAA.

6. Smith, August 1, 1875, to Cravath, AMAA.

7. The First Congregational Church was a white aided field of the AHMS. Barnum, Memphis, May 10, 1873, to Cravath; Steele, April 28; May 22, 1877, to Strieby AMAA; *Contributions to the Ecclesiastical History of Connecticut*, II (Hartford, 1967), 279.

8. For Beman, see (DeBoer 1994, 225-233).

9. Cardozo eventually became principal of the Colored High School in Washington. His name was proposed for president of Howard in 1877. William W. Patton received 12 votes and Cardozo 2. Since there were 4 black members of the board, that could be interpreted to mean that at least 2 did not vote for him. The writer thinks that W.J. Wilson and J.M. Brown might very well have voted against Cardozo, and it is quite possible that Cardozo's 2 votes came from white trustees. (Logan 1969, 83).

10. BFRAL, District of Columbia, Superintendent of Education, Misc. Records, Box 16, Nos. 3, 4, National Archives.

11. For the strenuous life of the more nearly typical AMA male teacher, see Henry C. Percy, Norfolk, February, 1865, AMAA.

12. William S. Tilden, October 22, 1865, to Hunt, AMAA.

13. Wilson, September 16, 1865, to Whipple; October 14, to Hunt; Julia B. Landre, September 20, 1865, to Whiting, AMAA.

14. Tilden, October 14, 1865, to Hunt; October 12, 1865, to Editor of *AM*, AMAA; *AM*, IX (December, 1865), 279.

15. Tilden, October 25, 1865, to Whipple, AMAA.

16. Tilden, November 3 and 8, 1865; Wilson, November 8, AMAA.

17. Tilden, Washington, November 16, 1865, to Whipple, AMAA.

18. Tilden, November 10; November 16, 1865, AMAA.

19. Tilden, December 19, 1865, to Hunt; Wilson, December 14, 1865, to Whiting; Teacher's Monthly Report, Third Street School, December, 1865; Superintendent's Monthly Report, December, 1865, AMAA.

20. Tilden, December 20; 26; 28, 1865, to Whipple, AMAA.

21. Tilden, December 23, 1865, to Whipple, AMAA.

22. Wilson, December 23, 1865, to Whipple, AMAA.

23. Tilden, December 30, 1865, to Hunt, AMAA.

24. Wilson, December 27, 1865, to Whipple, with Whipple's notes on letter, AMAA.

25. See letters and Monthly Reports of Wilson, Annie M. Wilson, Mary Wilson, Landre, Tilden, January, 1866, AMAA.

26. Tilden, February 3, 1866, to Whipple, AMAA.

27. Wilson, August 13, 1869, to Whipple, AMAA; (Dyson 1941, 418); (Logan 1969, 53).

28. Wilson, November 27, 1874, to Whipple, AMAA.

29. Langston, Oberlin, Ohio, October 17, 1866, to Smith, AMAA.

30. *AM*, XII (June, 1868), 130-131.

31. Report of John M. Langston, General Inspector of Schools, BFRAL, to the Trustees of Fisk University [June, 1869], AMAA. See also letters of A.A. Ellsworth, H.S. Beals, Hannah Goodman, and E.L. Boing, AMAA.

32. *AM*, XIII (July, 1869), 160-162.

33. Constitution of the St. Louis Board of Education for Free Colored Schools, April 12, 1864, AMAA.

34. Dwight Holmes, JNH, III (October, 1918), 368-369.

35. (Logan 1869, 83).

36. *Ibid.*, 75.

37. Cf. (Logan 1869, 75), who states that the fifth nominee was "also white," omitting the name of Charles H. Thompson.

38. New York *Evening Post*, June 24; June 26, 1875; see also (Dyson 1941, 57-60).

39. *Twenty-ninth Annual Report* (1875), 39-40; *AM*, XIX, (August, 1875), 182.

40. (Dyson 1941, 57).

41. New York *Evening Post*, June 24, 1875. AMA officers declined to squabble in public, a stance taken long before as the best reaction to attacks in the *Liberator*. George Whipple did, however, persuade the Trustees of Howard to pass a resolution in 1874, thanking Langston for the way he had carried out his duties as Acting President: (Langston 1894, 314).

42. Reeve, January 1, 1875, to Cravath, AMAA.

43. Johnson, December 7, 1874, to Cravath, AMAA.

44. For the life of Edward Parmelee Smith see (Armstrong 1993).

45. (Alldredge 1965, italics added); (Langston 1894, *passim*)

46. Ashley, Wilmington, North Carolina, November 24, 1867, to Smith and Whipple, AMAA.

47. *AM*, XX (September, 1876), 208; *The Nation Still in Danger: or, Ten Years after the War, a Plea by the American Missionary Association, with Confirmatory Articles by Rev. T.D. Woolsey, D.D., LLD., Hon. Frederick Douglass, Rev. Washington Gladden, Gov. D.H. Chamberlain, and Hon. J.P. Hawley* (New York, 1875), 12-13. Governor Chamberlain wrote a testimonial for Francis L. Cardozo in 1877 when the latter candidated for the presidency of Howard.

48. *AM*, XIX (September, 1875), 197-198.

49. (Washington 1970, 66).

50. The men at the Rooms felt it was important "that the pupils who are to be the teachers ultimately of their own race should never become acquainted with any save first class schools." *AM*, XI (March, 1867), 62.

51. See, for example, *AM*, XIII (April, 1869), 86.

52. *Twenty-ninth Annual Report* (1875), 40; *AM*, XVII (August, 1873), 177; Straight University, Annual Exhibition at Central Church, May 18, 1877, AMAA. For African libraries, see Samuel S. Ashley, Atlanta, September 1, 1877, to Strieby, AMAA.

53. *AM*, XII (September, 1868), 202.

54. (Beard 1909, 321-322).

55. Gladden, "The Southern Question," from the New York *Independent*, reprinted in *AM*, XX (November, 1876), 253-255.

56. The latter was a reason given by the American Freedmen's Union Commission and the New York Society when they disbanded in 1869: *United* States Department of the Interior, Bureau of Education, Bulletin, 1916, No. 38 (Washington, D.C., 1917), 274-275.

57. *AM*, XX (June, 1876), 123.

58. (DeBoer 1994, xiii); *The Scotsman*, (Edinburgh, July 13, 1867), 7.

59. *AM*, XIII (July, 1869), 155-156.

60. *AM*, XIX (March, 1875), 58-59.

61. *AM*, XV (February, 1871), 37-38.

62. The studies at Atlanta for which DuBois was editor and corresponding secretary, were reprinted in 1969 by Arno Press (New York) as The Atlanta University Publications. Other AMA personnel took part, see, for example, H.H. Proctor, "The Church As an Institution for Social Betterment," in *Some Efforts of American Negroes for Their Own Social Betterment*, Third Conference for the Study of Negro Problems (Atlanta, 1898), 46, 49, 50-51.

63. Personal notes from Wesley A. Hotchkiss to John C. DeBoer, October 31, 1972; [Clifton H. Johnson], "The Amistad Research Center Presents An Exhibition of Selected Items. . . .," mimeographed pamphlet (New Orleans, 1870), 9-10.

64. H.H. Proctor, *A Living Fountain* (New York, n.d.), 1-3.

BIBLIOGRAPHY

For expanded bibliography see: (DeBoer 1994) and (DeBoer 1973). Some papers and printed addresses are completely identified in the text and not listed here.

Alldredge, Everett O. 1965. *Centennial History of First Congregational United Church of Christ, Washington, D.C.: 1865-1965.* Washington.

American Home Missionary Society Archives, Amistad Research Center, Tulane University.

American Missionary Association Archives, Amistad Research Center, Tulane University.

———, *American Missionary.* New York.

———, *Annual Reports.* New York.

Armstrong, William H. 1993. *A Friend to God's Poor: Edward Parmelee Smith.* Athens, Georgia: University of Georgia Press.

Anglo-African Magazine. New York.

Beard, Agustus Field. 1909. *A Crusade of Brotherhood: A History of the American Missionary Association.* Boston.

Beman (Amos Gerry) Papers. Beinecke Library, Yale University.

Bentley, George R. 1955. *A History of the Freedmen's Bureau.* Philadelphia.

Bergman, Peter M. & Bergman, Mort N. 1969. *The Chronological History of the Negro in America.* New York.

British and Foreign Anti-Slavery and Aborigines Protection Society Papers. Rhodes House, Bodleian Library, Oxford University.

Brown, Hallie Q. 1926. *Homespun Heroine.* Xenia, Ohio.

Brown, William Wells. 1874. *The Rising Son.* Boston.

———. 1865. *The Black Man.* Boston

Brownlee, Frederick L. 1946. *New Day Ascending.* Boston

———. 1963. *Heritage of Freedom.* Boston.

Cary, Mary Ann Shadd. Papers, Moorland-Spingarn Collection, Howard University Library.

Colored American. New York.

Congregational Yearbook. Boston.

Congregationalist. New York.

379

Contributions to the Ecclesiastical History of Connecticut. 1861. Hartford: Congregational Churches of Connecticut.

Contributions to the Ecclesiastical History of Connecticut, II. 1967. Hartford: Connecticut Conference of the United Church of Christ.

Crummell, Alexander. 1891. *Africa and America, Addresses and Discourses.* Springfield, Mass.

Dabney, Lillian G. 1949. *The History of Schools for Negroes in the District of Columbia, 1807-1947.* Washington.

Dann, Martin E., ed. 1971. *The Black Press, 1827-1890: The Quest for National Identity.* New York.

Dannett, Sylvia, ed. 1966. *Negro Heritage, II, Women of the Nineteenth Century.* New York.

Daily News. London.

DeBoer, Clara Merritt. 1994. *Be Jubilant My Feet: African American Abolitionists in the American Missionary Association 1839-1861.* New York: Garland.

———. 1973. Bibliographical Essay, in "The Role of Afro-Americans in the Origin and Work of the American Missionary Association: 1839-1877." Ph.D. dissertation, Rutgers University. 767-828.

———, "Blacks and the American Missionary Association" in Barbara Brown Zikmund, Ed., 1984. *Hidden Histories in the United Church of Christ.* New York: United Church Press.

Dictionary of American Biography. 1936.

Drake, Richard Bryant. 1957. "The American Missionary Association and the Southern Negro, 1861-1888." Ph.D. dissertation, Emory University.

DuBois, W.E.B. 1969. *Souls of Black Folks.* New York: Fawcett Premier.

———. 1971. *Autobiography of W.E.B. DuBois.* Milwood, N.Y.: International Publishers.

Dyson, Walter. 1941. *Howard University.* Washington.

Ferris, William H. 1913. *The African Abroad, or, His Evolution in Western Civilization, Tracing His Development under Caucasian Milieu, II.* New Haven, Conn.

Fifield, L. Wendell. n.d. *What It Means To Be a Member of the Congregational Church.* New York.

Fifteenth Street Presbyterian Church, Washington. Records of the Session and the Church Register. 1841-1868. Moorland-Spingarn Collection, Howard University Library.

Fisk University News. Nashville.

Garnet, Henry Highland. 1841. "Shall Africa Have the Gospel?" in *Colored American.*

———. 1865. *A Memorial Discourse.* New York.

Herskovits, Melville J. 1968. *The Myth of the Negro Past.* Boston.

Howard, Oliver Otis. 1907. *Autobiography of Oliver Otis Howard,* 2 Vols. New York.

Independent, New York.

Johnson, Clifton H. 1959. "The American Missionary Association, 1846-1861." Ph.D. dissertation, University of North Carolina.

Journal of Negro History. New York.

Karp, Abraham J., ed. 1969. *The Jewish Experience in America: Selected Studies from the Publications of the American Jewish Historical Society, III, The Emerging Community.* New York.

Langston, John Mercer. 1894. *From the Virginia Plantation to the National Capitol.* Hartford.

Lemon, Harriet Beecher Stowe Wright, ed. 1949. *Radio Speeches of Major R.R. Wright, Sr..* Philadelphia.

Lockwood, Lewis C. [1863]. *Mary S. Peake: The Colored Teacher at Fortress Monroe.* Boston.

Logan, Rayford W. 1969. *Howard University.* New York.

Long, Herman H. 1958. *Fellowship for Whom? A Study of Race Inclusiveness in Congregational Christian Churches.* New York.

Mackelvie, William. 1873. *Annals and Statistics of the United Presbyterian Church* [of Scotland]. Edinburgh.

Marsh, J.B.T. 1880. *The Story of the Jubilee Singers; With Their Songs.* Boston.

Maurer, Oscar E. & Atkins, Gaius Glenn & Rogers, John R. 1925. *Our Goodly Heritage: A Short Sketch of the History of the American Missionary Association.* New York.

McFeely, William S. 1970. *Yankee Stepfather: General O.O. Howard and the Freedmen.* New York.

Moore, Ella Sheppard. 1912. *Before Emancipation.* New York.

Morning Star. London.

Myers, Robert Manson, ed. 1972. *The Children of Pride: A True Story of Georgia and the Civil War.* New Haven: Yale University Press.

Negro Heritage Library, Profiles of Negro Womanhood, I (1619-1900).

Ottley, Roi & Weatherby, William J. 1967. *The Negro in New York: an Informal Social History.* New York.

Payne, Daniel Alexander. 1891. *History of the African Methodist Episcopal Church.* Nashville.

————. 1888. *Recollections of Seventy Years.* Nashville.

Pike, Gustavus D. 1873. *The Jubilee Singers: And Their Campaign for Twenty Thousand Dollars.* Boston.

Presbyterian Church in the United States, NS, *Minutes of the General Assembly.* New York. Presbyterian Historical Society, Philadelphia.

Proctor, Henry Hugh. n.d. *A Living Fountain.* New York.

————. n.d. *New England, The New South and the New Negro.* New York.

Quarles, Benjamin. 1969. *Black Abolitionists.* New York.

[Ray, Charles Bennett]. [1874]. *Origin and Future of the American Missionary Association.* [New York].

Ray, Florence. 1887. *Sketch of the Life of Rev. Charles B. Ray.* New York.

Richardson, Joe Martin. 1986. *Christian Reconstruction: the American Missionary Association and Southern Blacks, 1861-1890.* Athens, Georgia: University of Georgia Press.

Robson, John. 1900. *Our Last Synod and the Last of Our Theological Hall.* Edinburgh. Public Reference Library.

Scotsman, Edinburgh.

Shiloh Church, Philadelphia. Minutes of the Session. Presbyterian Historical Society, Philadelphia.

Simmons, William J. 1887. *Men of Mark.* Cleveland, Ohio.

Simonhoff, Harry. 1956. *Jewish Notables in America, 1776-1865: Links of an Endless Chain.* New York.

Small, Robert. 1904. *History of the Congregations of the United Presbyterian Church [of Scotland]: From 1733 to 1900.* Edinburgh.

Smith, Charles Spencer. 1922. *A History of the African Methodist Episcopal Church.* Philadelphia.

Smith, James McCune. 1865. "Sketch of the Life and Labors of Rev. Henry Highland Garnet" in (Garnet 1865).

Steward, T.G. 1904. *The Colored Regulars in the United States Army.* Philadelphia.

Still, Peter. Papers, Rutgers University Library.

Tribune, New York.

Theological Hall Calendar of the United Presbyterian Church [of Scotland]. 1878. Edinburgh & Glasgow, National Library of Scotland, Edinburgh.

United Church of Christ. *1972 Year Book.*

United States Government Documents, 41st Congress, 2nd Session, House of Representatives, Report No. 121. National Archives.

———, *39th Congress, 1st Session, House of Representatives, Report No. 101, Memphis Riots and Massacres.*

———, *Department of the Interior, Bureau of Education, Bulletin 1916, No. 38.*

———, *Bureau of Refugees, Freedmen and Abandoned Lands, Miscellaneous Records,* in Box 16. National Archives.

Ward, Samuel Ringgold. 1855. *Autobiography of a Fugitive Negro: His Anti-Slavery Labours in the United States, Canada, and England.* London.

Washington, Booker T. 1970. *Up from Slavery.* New York: Dell.

Williams, Edward F. Papers, Amistad Research Center, Tulane University.

Woodson, Carter Godwin. 1925. *Negro Orators and Their Orations.* Washington.

Woodworth, Charles L. 1878. *Historical Summary of the American Missionary Association.* Boston.

Woodworth, Frank G. n.d. *Tougaloo University, Tougaloo, Mississippi.*

Wright, Richard Robert. 1894. *A Brief Historical Sketch of Negro Education in Georgia.* Savannah.

Wright, Richard Robert, Jr. 1965. *87 Years Behind the Black Curtain.* Philadelphia.

Wright, Richard R. 1963. *The Bishops of the African Methodist Episcopal Church.* Philadelphia.

INDEX

The names of persons identified as African Americans appear in bold face type.

Printed in the United States
by Baker & Taylor Publisher Services